Energy Optimization and Security in Federated Learning for IoT Environments

Other related titles:

You may also like

- PBPC066 | Srivastava (eds) | Federated Learning for Multimedia Data Processing and Security in Industry 5.0 | in press Jan 2025
- PBPC068 | Abdel-Basset | Explainable Artificial Intelligence for Trustworthy Internet of Things | published Nov 2024
- PBPC057 | Al Turjman (eds) | AIoT Technologies and Applications for Smart Environments | published Feb 2023
- PBSE014 | Crabtree (eds) | Privacy by Design for the Internet of Things: Building accountability and security | published Nov 2021

We also publish a wide range of books on the following topics:
Computing and Networks
Control, Robotics and Sensors
Electrical Regulations
Electromagnetics and Radar
Energy Engineering
Healthcare Technologies
History and Management of Technology
IET Codes and Guidance
Materials, Circuits and Devices
Model Forms
Nanomaterials and Nanotechnologies
Optics, Photonics and Lasers
Production, Design and Manufacturing
Security
Telecommunications
Transportation

All books are available in print via https://shop.theiet.org or as eBooks via our Digital Library https://digital-library.theiet.org.

IET COMPUTING SERIES 72

Energy Optimization and Security in Federated Learning for IoT Environments

Edited by
Balamurugan Balusamy, Daniel Arockiam and Pethuru Raj

The Institution of Engineering and Technology

About the IET

This book is published by the Institution of Engineering and Technology (The IET).

We inspire, inform, and influence the global engineering community to engineer a better world. As a diverse home across engineering and technology, we share knowledge that helps make better sense of the world, accelerate innovation, and solve the global challenges that matter.

The IET is a not-for-profit organisation. The surplus we make from our books is used to support activities and products for the engineering community and promote the positive role of science, engineering, and technology in the world. This includes education resources and outreach, scholarships and awards, events and courses, publications, professional development and mentoring, and advocacy for governments.

To discover more about the IET, please visit https://www.theiet.org/

About IET books

The IET publishes books across many engineering and technology disciplines. Our authors and editors offer fresh perspectives from universities and industry. Within our subject areas, we have several book series steered by editorial boards made up of leading subject experts.

We peer review each book at the proposal stage to ensure the quality and relevance of our publications.

Get involved

If you are interested in becoming an author, editor, series advisor, or peer reviewer please visit https://www.theiet.org/publishing/publishing-with-iet-books/ or contact author_support@theiet.org.

Discovering our electronic content

All of our books are available online via the IET's Digital Library. Our Digital Library is the home of technical documents, eBooks, conference publications, real-life case studies, and journal articles. To find out more, please visit https://digital-library.theiet.org.

In collaboration with the United Nations and the International Publishers Association, the IET is a Signatory member of the Sustainable Development Goal (SDG) Publishers Compact. The Compact aims to accelerate progress to achieve the SDGs by 2030. Signatories aspire to develop sustainable practices and act as champions of the SDGs during the Decade of Action (2020–30), publishing books and journals that will help inform, develop, and inspire action in that direction.

In line with our sustainable goals, our UK printing partner has FSC accreditation, which is reducing our environmental impact on the planet. We use a print-on-demand model to further reduce our carbon footprint.

Published by The Institution of Engineering and Technology, London, United Kingdom

The Institution of Engineering and Technology (the "**Publisher**") is registered as a Charity in England & Wales (no. 211014) and Scotland (no. SC038698).

First published 2024

The Institution of Engineering and Technology
Futures Place,
Kings Way, Stevenage,
Herts, SG1 2UA
United Kingdom

www.theiet.org

British Library Cataloguing in Publication Data
A catalogue record for this product is available from the British Library

ISBN 978-1-83953-962-6 (hardback)
ISBN 978-1-83953-963-3 (PDF)

Typeset in India by MPS Limited

Cover image: Issarawat Tattong/Moment via Getty Images

Contents

Preface

The Internet of Things (IoT) has revolutionised industries by enabling real-time data collecting, processing, and decision-making through a network of smart devices in an era of rising connectivity. This shift has been particularly important for industries including manufacturing, transportation, smart cities, and healthcare. But as the number of connected devices soars, a host of pressing issues surface, including cybersecurity dangers, energy usage, data privacy, and effective communication. These needs are difficult for centralised ways to manage IoT data to achieve, especially in settings where data security, scalability, and latency are critical requirements. Federated learning (FL) shows itself to be a viable remedy in this situation.

Federated learning offers a decentralised framework for training machine learning models across distributed devices without transferring sensitive data to a central server. This decentralised intelligence has revolutionised how we think about data privacy, energy efficiency, and security in IoT environments. By allowing edge devices to collaboratively learn from shared models whilst keeping data local, FL helps to address the challenges of data privacy, communication overhead, and cybersecurity threats, making it an ideal solution for IoT ecosystems.

This book, *Energy Optimization and Security in Federated Learning for IoT Environments*, was written with the goal of addressing two of the most critical concerns in the adoption of FL for IoT environments: energy efficiency and security. As IoT devices are often battery-powered or rely on limited energy sources, ensuring that FL operations are energy-efficient is essential for scalable deployment. Equally important is the need to secure FL models from cyberattacks, as these distributed systems are vulnerable to a range of security breaches.

The chapters in this book are organised to provide both theoretical insights and practical solutions for overcoming these challenges. We begin with an Overview of federated learning, exploring its foundational concepts, architecture, and the unique advantages it offers for empowering decentralised intelligence. Readers unfamiliar with the basics of FL will find this chapter to be a helpful introduction to the key components and design principles of FL in the context of IoT.

The book then delves into Energy-efficient federated learning algorithms and frameworks for energy-efficient IoT, providing readers with a deep understanding of how FL can be optimised for resource-constrained environments. Given the need to minimise energy consumption, these chapters examine techniques for reducing the computational and communication burdens typically associated with FL. By exploring real-world algorithms and frameworks, we hope to inspire the development of more energy-conscious federated systems in IoT applications.

As communication is a major bottleneck in federated learning, the book also covers Communication efficiency in federated learning in IoT environments, which focuses on optimising the transmission of model updates between devices. This section introduces protocols and methods to reduce the amount of data that needs to be exchanged between IoT nodes, thus improving overall efficiency and reducing energy usage.

In the chapters on Energy harvesting and energy optimisation in IoT communication, we discuss how IoT devices can utilise renewable energy sources or energy-harvesting techniques to extend their operational lifetime. These insights are crucial for ensuring long-term sustainability in federated learning implementations, particularly in smart cities and remote IoT deployments.

No discussion of IoT would be complete without addressing security, which is why we dedicate a significant portion of the book to exploring Adapting federated learning models to dynamic cyber threats, Hybrid security for IoT networks, and Secure data protection in federated learning. These chapters emphasise the importance of building robust FL models that can not only learn from decentralised data but also defend against attacks such as adversarial data poisoning, man-in-the-middle attacks, and data breaches. We also touch on AI-driven security mechanisms that enhance traditional security solutions for more resilient IoT networks.

Finally, the book concludes with practical case studies in Energy-efficient federated learning for IoT, where readers can explore real-world applications of the concepts covered throughout the book. By presenting case studies from healthcare, smart cities, and industrial IoT, we aim to bridge the gap between theory and practice, demonstrating how energy-efficient and secure FL models are being implemented today.

In addition to covering the current state of federated learning, we also explore Future trends and research directions, shedding light on the ongoing research that will shape the future of FL and its applications in IoT.

This book is written for a diverse audience, including researchers, engineers, and industry professionals working in IoT, AI, and cybersecurity. We hope it serves as a valuable resource for those looking to understand the potential of federated learning to address the energy efficiency and security challenges of the IoT era. Through the insights and frameworks provided in this book, we hope to inspire further innovation and research in this exciting and rapidly evolving field.

About the editors

Balamurugan Balusamy is the associate dean of student engagement at Shiv Nadar University, Delhi-NCR, India. His research focuses on cybersecurity, blockchain, data science, cloud environments, IoT, and engineering education. He has published over 200 papers, contributed to 80 edited and authored books, and given 200 talks at international events and symposiums. He serves in the advisory committee for several start-ups and forums and does consultancy work for the industry on Industrial IoT. He holds a PhD degree in 'Investigations of Cloud Computing Access Control Techniques' from VIT University, Vellore, India.

Daniel Arockiam is an associate professor in the Department of Computer Science and Engineering at Amity University, Gwalior, Madhya Pradesh, India. His research areas include neural networks, AI, ML, DL, FL, and cloud computing. He has published 45 papers in international journals and conferences. He is a member of CSTA, IFERP, and IAEng. He was a member of the organising committee for GuCon 2019 and 2020 conferences. He holds a PhD degree in 'Hybrid Approaches to Optimise the Performance of Load Balancing and Task Scheduling in Cloud Environment' from Shri Venkateshwara University, India.

Pethuru Raj is a chief architect and the vice president of Reliance Jio Platforms Ltd. Bangalore, India. He focuses on the Internet of Things (IoT); artificial intelligence; big data analytics, blockchain, digital twins; edge, fog, and cloud computing; reliability engineering; microservices architecture (MSA), 5G and 6G, and event-driven architecture (EDA). He previously worked at IBM global Cloud Center of Excellence (CoE), Wipro Consulting Services (WCS), and Robert Bosch Corporate Research (CR). He has authored and edited 35+ books and contributed to 35 book chapters. He is a member of ACM. He holds a PhD degree on 'Formal Language Theory and Finite Automata' from Anna University, Chennai, India.

Chapter 1

An overview of federated learning: empowering decentralized intelligence

Ghanshyam Prasad Dubey[1], Ayush Giri[1], Daniel Arockiam[1] and V. Sathya Priya[2]

Abstract

Federated learning has emerged as a transformative example in machine learning, allowing collaborative model training across decentralized devices while preserving data privacy. Federated learning (FL) has emerged as a ground-breaking paradigm in machine learning, allowing for collaborative model training across a network of decentralized devices while maintaining data privacy and security. Unlike typical centralized systems, FL keeps data localized on the clients' devices, meeting important privacy issues and legal constraints. We begin by explaining the fundamental principles of FL, such as the roles of clients and servers, the process of local training and model updates, and methods for aggregating these updates to enhance a global model. A strong emphasis is made on the numerous federated optimization algorithms that enable effective model training in a distributed environment. We also look at advanced privacy-preserving technologies like differential privacy and secure multi-party computing (SMPC), which are critical to FL's operation. This chapter provides a comprehensive exploration of federated learning, encompassing its foundational principles, methodologies, applications, and challenges by delving into the intricacies of federated learning techniques, like federated optimization algorithms, privacy-preserving mechanisms, and communication protocols. Through case studies and real-world examples, we highlight the diverse applications of federated learning across domains such as healthcare, finance, Internet of Things, and mobile devices. Moreover, we discuss the inherent challenges of federated learning, including communication overhead, privacy concerns, and heterogeneity of data distributions. By surveying recent advancements and research trends, we identify future directions for federated learning, emphasizing its potential to revolutionize distributed machine learning. This chapter serves as a comprehensive resource for researchers, practitioners, and

[1]Department of Computer Science and Engineering, Amity University Madhya Pradesh, India
[2]Department of Computer Science and Engineering, B V Raju Institute of Technology, India

enthusiasts seeking to understand and leverage the power of federated learning in decentralized intelligence.

Keywords: Federated learning; Federated learning techniques; Privacy concerns; Challenges; Federated transfer learning

1.1 Introduction

In recent years, federated learning (FL) has emerged as a promising approach to address the challenges of training machine learning models across decentralized data sources while preserving user privacy. Unlike traditional centralized approaches, where data is aggregated in a single location for model training, federated learning enables collaborative training directly on distributed devices. This decentralized paradigm offers several advantages, including improved data privacy, reduced communication overhead, and scalability to large-scale and heterogeneous datasets.

Federated learning is a decentralized machine learning strategy in which different clients (e.g., mobile devices, edge devices, or enterprises) collaborate to train a common model while keeping their data local. Instead of sending raw data to a central server, each client trains the model on its own dataset and only transmits computed model updates, such as gradients or weights, to the central server. The central server consolidates these updates to refine a global model, which is subsequently redistributed to the clients for additional training. This method iterates until the model converges or meets the necessary performance metrics.

The concept of federated learning was first introduced by Google in 2017 as a solution for training predictive models across numerous mobile devices while keeping user data on-device. This innovation addressed the growing concerns about data privacy and security, especially with the increasing use of mobile and Internet of Things (IoT) devices that continuously generate vast amounts of personal data. By training models locally and sharing only the model updates, federated learning minimizes the risk of data breaches and ensures compliance with stringent data protection regulations [1].

Since its inception, federated learning has garnered significant attention from both academia and industry. Numerous research efforts have been dedicated to advancing the field, focusing on enhancing the efficiency, scalability, and privacy-preserving aspects of federated learning. These efforts have led to the development of sophisticated optimization algorithms, secure aggregation protocols, and adaptive learning strategies that cater to the dynamic and heterogeneous nature of decentralized data environments.

Federated learning represents a significant advancement in the field of machine learning, offering a decentralized approach to model training that prioritizes data privacy and scalability. By enabling collaborative learning across distributed devices, federated learning has the potential to revolutionize various industries, from healthcare to finance, and beyond. As research and development in this area continue to evolve, federated learning is poised to become a cornerstone of future AI and machine learning applications, driving innovation while safeguarding user privacy.

This chapter provides a comprehensive overview of federated learning, covering its foundational principles, methodologies, applications, and challenges. Drawing from a wide range of literature, we delve into the technical underpinnings of federated learning, exploring optimization algorithms, privacy-preserving mechanisms, and communication protocols. Furthermore, we discuss the diverse applications of federated learning across various domains, including healthcare, finance, IoT, and mobile devices. By examining real-world case studies and recent advancements, we highlight the potential of federated learning to revolutionize distributed machine learning in practice. The rest of the chapter contains the following sections; Section 1.2 focuses on the fundamentals of federated learning, Section 1.3 describes about federated learning workflow, federated learning techniques, and privacy discussed in Section 1.4 followed by conclusion in Section 1.5.

1.2 Fundamentals of federated learning

Federated learning, a decentralized machine learning approach, revolutionizes model training by enabling collaboration across multiple devices while maintaining data privacy. Its fundamental principles encompass privacy preservation, scalability, and collaborative model training. At its core, federated learning operates on a client–server architecture, where a central server coordinates the training process and aggregates model updates from multiple client devices. Unlike traditional centralized approaches, federated learning allows each client to train a machine learning model locally using its own data, ensuring data privacy and confidentiality. This local model training process generates model updates or gradients, which are then sent to the central server for aggregation. The central server aggregates these updates to produce a global model, employing techniques such as federated averaging or secure aggregation while preserving privacy. This iterative learning process continues until convergence or a predefined stopping criterion is met. To safeguard privacy during model aggregation, federated learning relies on various privacy-preserving mechanisms, including differential privacy, secure aggregation, and encryption-based methods. These techniques prevent the leakage of sensitive information from individual client datasets. Federated learning finds applications in various domains such as mobile predictive keyboards, healthcare analytics, and federated analytics in telecom networks. However, it also presents challenges such as communication overhead, non-IID data distributions, and heterogeneity among client devices. The core principles of federated learning include privacy preservation, scalability, and collaborative model training [2].

1.2.1 Client–server architecture

The client–server architecture in federated learning is a fascinating approach that brings together the strengths of both centralized and decentralized systems.

Imagine a bunch of smartphones, each with its own little stash of data, like photos or text messages. Instead of sending all this data to a big server somewhere (which could be risky for privacy and overwhelming for the network), these phones do something smart: they train a part of the machine learning model right there on the device. Once they are done, they send just the "lessons learned" back to a central server—think of it like sending the gist of a book rather than the whole book.

The server collects all these "lessons" from the phones, blends them together, and updates the overall model. This refined model is then sent back to the phones, and the cycle continues. This way, each phone benefits from the collective intelligence of all the other devices without ever sharing its personal data [3].

This setup has some cool advantages. For one, it keeps personal data private since nothing leaves the device. It also reduces the amount of data that needs to be sent over the network, which means less strain on bandwidth and faster updates. Plus, it can handle lots of devices at once, making it great for things like apps that run on millions of phones.

However, it is not without its challenges. Getting all these devices to communicate efficiently can be tricky, and the data they have can vary a lot, which complicates things. However, with ongoing improvements in technology, federated learning is becoming better at addressing these issues, making it a promising tool for the future of smart, privacy-conscious applications (Figure 1.1) [4].

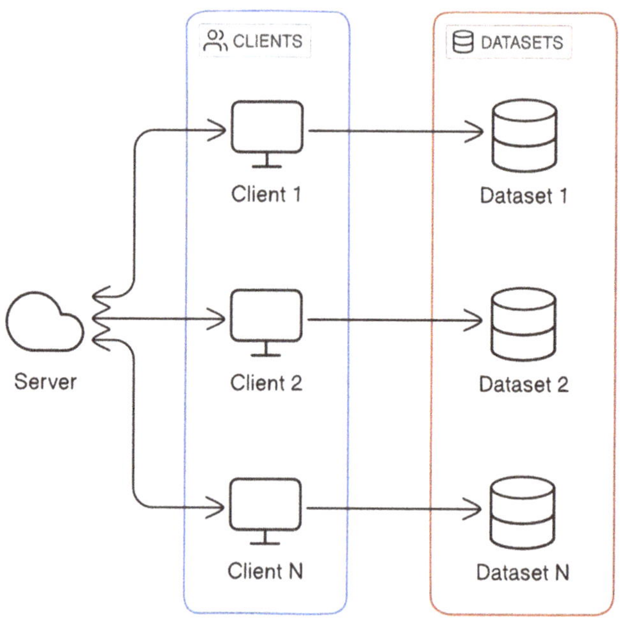

Figure 1.1 Client–server architecture

1.2.2 Local model training

Local model training is a fundamental aspect of federated learning, wherein each client device independently trains a machine learning model using its own local dataset. This decentralized approach ensures that raw data remains on the client device, addressing significant privacy and security concerns associated with traditional centralized machine learning methods.

The local model training process begins with the central server initializing a global model, which is then distributed to all participating client devices. This initial model acts as a starting point for the local training conducted on each device. Upon receiving the global model, the client device preprocesses its local dataset to ensure it is in a suitable format for training. This preprocessing may include steps such as data normalization, augmentation, and cleaning, which are essential for maintaining data consistency and improving model accuracy [5].

Once the data is preprocessed, the client device proceeds with training the model. This involves several iterations, where the model parameters are updated using optimization techniques such as stochastic gradient descent (SGD). During each iteration, the model learns from the local data by adjusting its parameters to minimize the loss function. This process is akin to refining a rough draft into a polished version through iterative improvements. The training phase is computationally intensive and leverages the device's processing power, thereby distributing the computational load across multiple devices.

After completing the local training phase, the client device computes the model updates. These updates, often represented as gradients or weight adjustments, encapsulate the insights gained from the local data without exposing the raw data itself. The computed model updates are then transmitted back to the central server. It is important to note that only the model updates are shared, not the underlying data, thus preserving the privacy of the client's data [6].

The central server collects the model updates from all participating devices and aggregates them to refine the global model. This aggregation process typically involves averaging the updates, a method known as federated averaging (FedAvg). By incorporating the updates from diverse data sources, the global model becomes more robust and generalizable. The refined global model is subsequently redistributed to the client devices, and the process of local training and global aggregation is repeated iteratively until the model converges to a satisfactory level of performance.

Local model training in federated learning offers several significant advantages. Foremost, it enhances data privacy by ensuring that sensitive data never leaves the client's device. This approach aligns well with stringent data protection regulations such as GDPR and CCPA. Additionally, local model training reduces communication overhead, as only model updates, rather than raw data, are transmitted between clients and the server. This reduction in data transfer not only conserves bandwidth but also accelerates the overall training process. Furthermore, the decentralized nature of local training allows federated learning to scale efficiently, accommodating large and heterogeneous datasets distributed across numerous devices [7].

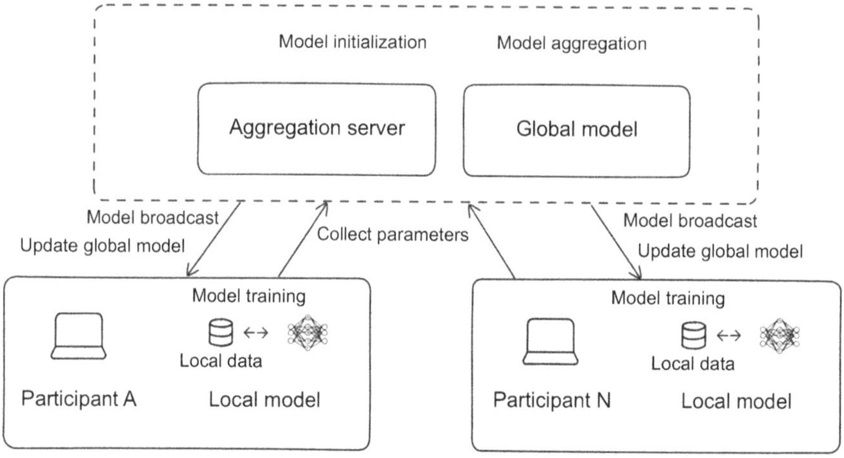

Figure 1.2 Model training

Despite its benefits, local model training presents several challenges. One of the primary challenges is ensuring the effective aggregation of model updates from clients with non-identically distributed data. Variability in data distribution can lead to model divergence and suboptimal performance. Techniques such as personalized federated learning and federated transfer learning are being explored to address these issues by allowing models to adapt to local data characteristics. Additionally, the computational capabilities and connectivity of client devices can vary widely, impacting the consistency and timing of model updates. Addressing these disparities requires robust algorithms and protocols that can handle asynchronous and intermittent communications.

In conclusion, local model training is a pivotal process in federated learning that leverages the computational power of client devices to collaboratively train machine learning models while preserving data privacy. By distributing the training load and maintaining data locality, federated learning offers a scalable and privacy-conscious solution for modern machine learning applications. Ongoing research and development efforts continue to refine local model training techniques, enhancing their efficiency, robustness, and adaptability to diverse real-world scenarios (Figure 1.2).

1.2.3 Model aggregation

Model aggregation is a critical phase in the federated learning process, where the central server combines the model updates from multiple client devices to form an improved global model. This step is essential for ensuring that the collaboratively trained model benefits from the diverse data distributed across various clients, without compromising the privacy of the individual datasets.

The process of model aggregation begins once client devices have completed their local training and sent their model updates to the central server. These updates typically include changes to the model parameters, such as gradients or weights, which reflect the learning acquired from the local datasets. The central server then aggregates these updates to create a unified global model. One of the most commonly used aggregation techniques is federated averaging (FedAvg), where the server computes a weighted average of the model updates received from the clients.

In federated averaging, the updates are weighted based on the size of the local datasets used for training. For example, if one client has significantly more data than another, its updates will have a greater influence on the global model. This weighting ensures that the aggregated model reflects the contributions of clients proportionally to the amount of data they possess, thereby improving the generalization and robustness of the global model [8].

Model aggregation in federated learning offers several advantages. First and foremost, it enhances the privacy of client data. Since only model updates, rather than raw data, are sent to the central server, the risk of data breaches is significantly reduced. This privacy-preserving feature is crucial for applications in sensitive domains such as healthcare and finance, where data confidentiality is paramount.

Another advantage is the reduction in communication overhead. Transmitting model updates is typically less bandwidth-intensive than sending raw data, making the process more efficient and scalable. This efficiency is particularly important in scenarios involving numerous client devices, such as mobile applications with millions of users.

Furthermore, model aggregation allows the global model to benefit from the diversity of data distributed across different clients. By combining updates from various sources, the aggregated model can capture a wide range of patterns and variations, leading to improved performance and generalizability. This is especially beneficial in applications where data is inherently heterogeneous, such as personalized services and recommendations [9].

Despite its benefits, model aggregation in federated learning also presents several challenges. One of the primary challenges is handling the heterogeneity of data across clients. Non-identically distributed data can lead to updates that vary significantly, potentially causing instability and slower convergence of the global model. To address this issue, advanced aggregation techniques such as adaptive weighting, cluster-based aggregation, and personalized federated learning are being explored. These methods aim to account for data heterogeneity by dynamically adjusting the influence of individual updates or by creating personalized models that better align with local data characteristics.

Another challenge is ensuring the security and integrity of the aggregation process. Malicious clients could potentially send corrupted updates to disrupt the training process or bias the global model. To mitigate this risk, secure aggregation protocols, such as homomorphic encryption and differential privacy, are employed. These protocols ensure that model updates are securely transmitted and aggregated without revealing sensitive information, thereby enhancing the robustness and trustworthiness of the federated learning system.

Moreover, the computational and communication capabilities of client devices can vary widely, affecting the consistency and timing of updates. Some devices

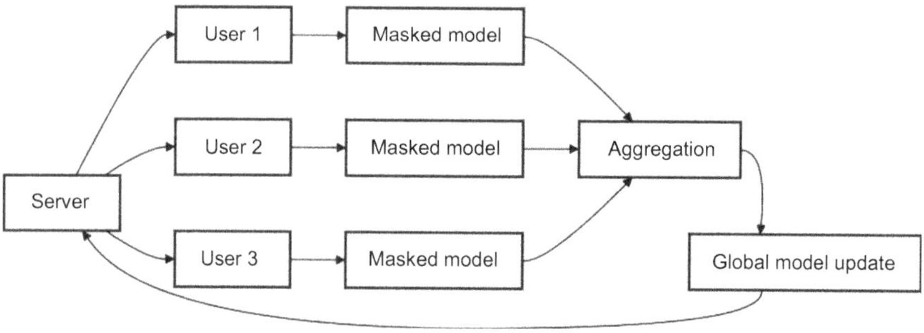

Figure 1.3 Federated learning model aggregation

may have limited processing power or intermittent connectivity, leading to delays in receiving updates. Asynchronous aggregation techniques and federated learning algorithms that accommodate such variability are being developed to ensure efficient and reliable model aggregation.

Model aggregation is a vital component of federated learning that enables the creation of a robust and generalizable global model by combining updates from multiple clients. By leveraging techniques such as federated averaging and incorporating advanced methods to handle data heterogeneity and security concerns, model aggregation ensures that federated learning systems can effectively utilize distributed data while preserving privacy and efficiency. Ongoing research and innovations in this area continue to enhance the effectiveness and scalability of federated learning, making it a promising approach for privacy-conscious and large-scale machine learning applications (Figure 1.3).

1.2.4 Iterative learning process

The iterative learning process is a fundamental characteristic of federated learning, involving repeated cycles of communication between the central server and the client devices to progressively refine the global model. This process starts with the central server initializing a global model, which is typically either pre-trained on a public dataset or initialized with random weights. This initial model is then distributed to all participating client devices.

Once the clients receive the global model, they engage in local training using their individual datasets. Each client device processes its local data to update the model parameters in an effort to minimize a local loss function. This local training is conducted over multiple epochs, allowing the model to learn from the unique data patterns present on each device. The outcome is a locally trained model that incorporates the knowledge gained from the client's data, without the raw data ever leaving the device.

After completing the local training phase, each client computes model updates, typically in the form of gradients or weight adjustments. These updates encapsulate the learning achieved during the local training and are crucial for improving the global model. The clients then transmit these updates to the central server, ensuring that only the updates, and not the raw data, are shared, thereby preserving privacy.

Upon receiving the updates from all participating clients, the central server aggregates them to refine the global model. This aggregation often uses methods like federated averaging (FedAvg), where the server computes a weighted average of the updates, giving more influence to clients with larger datasets. This ensures that the aggregated model is representative of the diverse data sources contributing to it. The updated global model is then redistributed to the clients, and the next iteration of local training begins. This cyclical process repeats, continuously improving the global model with each round of updates until it converges to a satisfactory level of performance.

The iterative learning process in federated learning offers several notable advantages. It enhances privacy by keeping raw data on the client devices and only sharing model updates, significantly reducing the risk of data breaches. The continuous integration of updates from various data sources also improves the accuracy and generalization capabilities of the global model, as it learns from a wide range of patterns and variations. Moreover, the iterative process is scalable and capable of accommodating large numbers of client devices and vast distributed datasets. By transmitting only model updates, the communication overhead is reduced, making the process more efficient, especially in environments with limited bandwidth.

However, the iterative learning process also presents challenges. One significant challenge is the heterogeneity of data across clients, which can result in updates that vary widely and cause instability or slower convergence. To address this, researchers are developing techniques such as personalized federated learning and adaptive aggregation that account for these variations. Additionally, the asynchronous nature of communication due to differences in client device capabilities and connectivity can complicate the process. Asynchronous aggregation methods and protocols are being explored to manage these disparities [10].

Ensuring the security and integrity of model updates is another critical challenge. Techniques like secure aggregation protocols, differential privacy, and homomorphic encryption are employed to protect the updates from tampering and ensure robust model training. Furthermore, client devices often have limited computational power and energy resources. Methods like model compression and efficient optimization algorithms help mitigate these constraints by reducing the computational load on the devices.

In conclusion, the iterative learning process is a cornerstone of federated learning, enabling the collaborative training of machine learning models across distributed and diverse data sources. Through iterative refinement involving local training and global aggregation, federated learning ensures enhanced privacy, scalability, and model accuracy. Despite the challenges associated with data heterogeneity, communication, and security, ongoing research and technological advancements continue to improve the efficiency and robustness of this process,

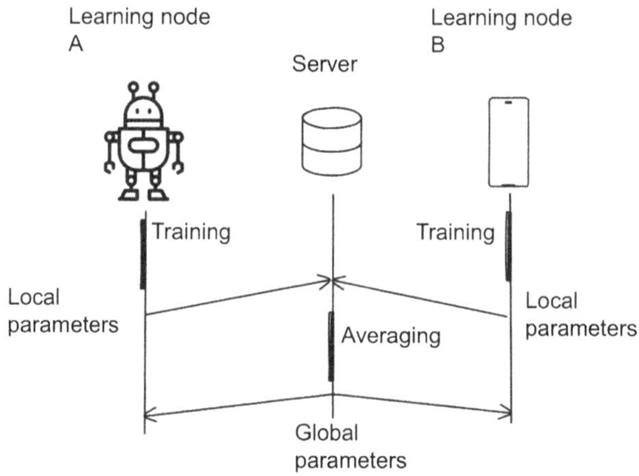

Figure 1.4 Iterative learning process

making federated learning a promising approach for decentralized and privacy-preserving machine learning applications (Figure 1.4).

1.2.5 Privacy-preserving mechanisms

Privacy-preserving mechanisms are crucial in federated learning, where the primary goal is to train machine learning models collaboratively across multiple clients without compromising the privacy of individual data. These mechanisms ensure that sensitive information remains protected throughout the training process. Several techniques and protocols have been developed to achieve this, including differential privacy, SMPC, and homomorphic encryption.

Differential privacy is a mathematical framework that provides strong privacy guarantees by ensuring that the output of a computation is statistically indistinguishable whether or not any single individual's data is included in the input. In the context of federated learning, differential privacy can be applied to the model updates sent from clients to the central server. By adding carefully calibrated noise to these updates, it becomes difficult for an adversary to infer any specific data point's presence or absence in the training set.

The noise addition process in differential privacy must balance privacy and utility; too much noise can degrade the model's performance, while too little may not provide sufficient privacy. Techniques such as the Laplace mechanism and the Gaussian mechanism are commonly used to introduce this noise. Differential privacy ensures that the aggregated model updates protect individual data points, providing a robust defense against data reconstruction attacks [11].

SMPC is another powerful technique for preserving privacy in federated learning. SMPC allows multiple parties to jointly compute a function over their inputs while keeping those inputs private. In federated learning, SMPC can be used to perform secure aggregation of model updates. Each client encrypts its model updates before sending them to the central server. The server, using SMPC protocols, can then aggregate these encrypted updates without learning the individual updates themselves.

SMPC protocols, such as Shamir's secret sharing and the Paillier cryptosystem, facilitate this secure aggregation. These protocols ensure that the aggregated result can be decrypted and used to update the global model, but individual client updates remain confidential. This mechanism provides a high level of privacy, making it suitable for scenarios where data confidentiality is paramount.

Homomorphic encryption is a form of encryption that allows computations to be performed on encrypted data without needing to decrypt it first. This property is particularly useful in federated learning, where model updates can be encrypted before being sent to the central server. The server can then perform the necessary aggregations on the encrypted updates and return the aggregated encrypted result to the clients. Clients can decrypt this result and continue with the next round of local training.

Fully homomorphic encryption (FHE) supports arbitrary computations on encrypted data but is computationally intensive and currently impractical for large-scale federated learning. Partially homomorphic encryption (PHE) schemes, which support a limited set of operations (e.g., addition or multiplication), offer a more practical balance between security and computational efficiency. These schemes enable secure aggregation of model updates while preserving the confidentiality of individual updates.

Trusted execution environments (TEE) provide a hardware-based solution for privacy-preserving federated learning. TEEs create a secure enclave within the client device, ensuring that data and computations within the enclave are protected from external access, even from the device's operating system. In federated learning, TEEs can securely perform local training and generate encrypted model updates that are safe to transmit to the central server.

Using TEEs, federated learning systems can achieve high levels of data security and integrity. However, the adoption of TEEs requires hardware support, which may not be available on all client devices. Despite this limitation, TEEs offer a promising approach to enhancing privacy in federated learning.

Privacy-preserving mechanisms are essential for the success and adoption of federated learning. Techniques such as differential privacy, SMPC, homomorphic encryption, and TEE provide robust defenses against privacy breaches while enabling collaborative model training. Each method offers a different balance of security, efficiency, and practicality, allowing federated learning systems to be tailored to specific application requirements and threat models. As federated learning continues to evolve, these privacy-preserving mechanisms will play a crucial role in ensuring that data privacy is maintained without compromising the utility of the trained models (Figure 1.5) [12].

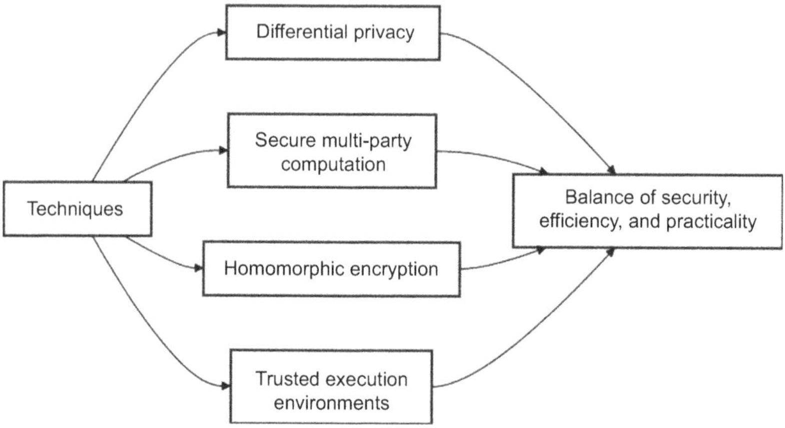

Figure 1.5 Privacy-preserving mechanism

Aspect	Client–server architecture	Local model training	Model aggregation	Iterative learning process	Privacy-preserving mechanisms
Description	Central server coordinates training with multiple clients	Clients train models on local data	Central server combines updates from clients	Repeated cycles of local training and aggregation	Techniques to ensure data privacy during federated learning
Role	Central coordination and global model maintenance	Learning from local data without sharing raw data	Combining client updates to refine the global model	Continuous improvement of the global model via iterations	Protecting client data while enabling collaborative training
Advantages	Efficient central control, scalable	Preserves data privacy, leverages local data	Enhances model generalization, benefits from diverse data	Progressive refinement, scalable	Strong privacy guarantees, protects against data breaches
Challenges	Single point of failure, potential bottleneck	Limited by local data quality, requires client resources	Handling heterogeneous updates, ensuring fairness	Communication overhead, varying client capabilities	Computational overhead, balancing privacy and utility
Communication	Central server and clients exchange model updates	Clients process data locally and send updates to server	Server aggregates updates, sends global model to clients	Iterative communication between server and clients	Encrypted or obfuscated data transmission, secure protocols

(Continues)

(*Continued*)

Aspect	Client–server architecture	Local model training	Model aggregation	Iterative learning process	Privacy-preserving mechanisms
Data handling	Data remains on clients, only updates are shared	Local data used for training, raw data stays on device	Aggregates parameter updates, not raw data	Data never leaves client devices, updates are iteratively shared	Data privacy ensured via various mechanisms
Security	Requires secure communication channels	Local data stays private, minimal risk of data leakage	Secure aggregation needed to prevent tampering	Secure communication and aggregation protocols necessary	Strong focus on data privacy, advanced encryption techniques
Scalability	Scalable with central coordination	Scalable as clients operate independently	Scalable, but aggregation complexity increases with clients	Highly scalable with iterative processes	Scalable, but may add computational complexity
Performance	Impact can handle large numbers of clients, potential bottlenecks	Performance dependent on client device capabilities	Aggregation efficiency affects global model improvement	Incremental model improvement, dependent on client participation	May impact model performance due to noise or encryption overhead

1.3 Federated learning workflow

Federated learning presents a unique workflow that enables collaborative model training across decentralized devices while preserving data privacy. The typical federated learning workflow can be outlined as follows:

Initialization: Initially, a global model is initialized either randomly or based on a pre-trained model.

Client training: Participating client devices, such as mobile phones or edge devices, perform local model training using their respective datasets. This training is typically done using SGD or variants thereof.

Model update: After local training iterations, client devices compute model updates based on the changes made to the local model parameters.

Model aggregation: The model updates from client devices are sent to a central server or aggregator, where they are aggregated to update the global model. This aggregation step is crucial for combining the diverse knowledge learned from different devices while mitigating communication overhead and preserving privacy.

Evaluation: The updated global model may be evaluated on a validation set to assess its performance and convergence. If convergence criteria are not met, the process iterates, with model updates sent back to client devices for further training.

1.3.1 Challenges and opportunities

1.3.1.1 Challenges

Communication overhead

The communication overhead involved in federated learning poses a significant challenge, especially in scenarios with a large number of participating devices or limited bandwidth communication overhead challenges in federated learning.

Communication overhead is a significant challenge in federated learning, where the process involves frequent exchanges of model updates between a central server and numerous distributed client devices. Unlike traditional centralized machine learning, federated learning aims to preserve data privacy by keeping raw data on the client devices and only sharing model updates. This decentralized approach introduces several communication-related challenges that can impact the efficiency and scalability of the federated learning system.

One of the primary challenges is the sheer volume of data that needs to be transmitted during the federated learning process. Each client periodically sends model updates, which typically consist of large matrices of weights or gradients, to the central server. The server then aggregates these updates and sends the updated global model back to the clients. This bidirectional exchange of large data payloads can lead to significant communication overhead, especially when dealing with a large number of clients and complex models with millions of parameters. Frequent communication can saturate network bandwidth, leading to delays and increased latency.

Moreover, the heterogeneous nature of client devices and their network connections exacerbates the communication overhead problem. In a federated learning system, clients can range from high-performance servers to low-power IoT devices, each with varying computational capabilities and network bandwidth. Clients with slower connections or limited bandwidth can become bottlenecks, delaying the overall training process. This heterogeneity necessitates adaptive communication strategies that can accommodate the diverse capabilities of clients without compromising the efficiency of the learning process.

Another challenge is the asynchronous nature of client participation. In real-world scenarios, not all clients may be available or willing to participate in every round of training. Clients may go offline, become idle, or face interruptions, leading to irregular and unpredictable communication patterns. This asynchrony can cause issues in coordinating updates and ensuring consistent global model updates. Managing asynchronous updates requires sophisticated algorithms that can handle partial updates and still converge to an accurate global model without excessive communication overhead.

To mitigate these challenges, several strategies have been proposed and implemented in federated learning systems. One approach is to reduce the frequency of communication by increasing the amount of local computation. Instead of sending updates after every local epoch, clients can perform multiple local training epochs before communicating updates to the server. This reduces the number of communication rounds but requires careful tuning to balance local computation and model convergence [13].

Model compression techniques, such as quantization and sparsification, are also employed to address communication overhead. By compressing model updates before transmission, the amount of data exchanged can be significantly reduced. Quantization reduces the precision of the model parameters, while sparsification removes less significant parameters, both leading to smaller updates. These techniques, however, must be applied cautiously to avoid adversely affecting model accuracy.

Another promising approach is the use of federated averaging (FedAvg), where model updates are averaged across clients before sending them to the server. This reduces the variance in updates and can lead to more stable and efficient communication. Additionally, hierarchical federated learning architectures, where clients are organized into clusters with local aggregators, can help reduce the communication burden on the central server by performing intermediate aggregations within clusters.

Communication overhead presents a significant challenge in federated learning, driven by the large volume of data exchanged, heterogeneous client capabilities, and asynchronous participation. Addressing these challenges requires a combination of strategies, including reducing communication frequency, employing model compression, and utilizing efficient aggregation techniques. By mitigating communication overhead, federated learning can become more scalable and efficient, enabling the widespread adoption of privacy-preserving machine learning across diverse and distributed environments.

Privacy concerns

Privacy concerns are at the forefront of federated learning, a paradigm designed to allow collaborative model training across multiple clients without requiring them to share their raw data. While federated learning inherently aims to enhance privacy by keeping data local to the devices where it is generated, several privacy challenges still arise. Addressing these concerns is crucial for the adoption and success of federated learning systems in sensitive domains like healthcare, finance, and personal data applications.

One major privacy concern is the potential for indirect leakage of information through model updates. Even though raw data never leaves the client devices, the model updates (such as gradients or weights) sent to the central server can still inadvertently reveal sensitive information. Sophisticated attackers could analyze these updates to infer properties of the underlying data, potentially compromising individual privacy. For instance, gradients can carry information about the specific features of the data that influenced the model's learning process, which could be exploited to reconstruct the original data.

To mitigate this risk, differential privacy techniques are commonly employed. Differential privacy introduces noise to the model updates in a controlled manner, ensuring that the contribution of any single data point is masked. This statistical approach provides strong privacy guarantees, making it difficult for an attacker to discern whether a particular data point was part of the training set. However, balancing the amount of noise added with the utility of the model is challenging; too much noise can degrade the model's performance, while too little may not provide sufficient privacy.

SMPC is another technique used to address privacy concerns. SMPC allows multiple parties to collaboratively compute a function over their inputs while keeping those inputs private. In federated learning, SMPC can be utilized to perform secure aggregation of model updates, ensuring that the server only receives the aggregated result without seeing individual updates. This approach enhances privacy but comes with significant computational and communication overhead, which can be a barrier to scalability.

Homomorphic encryption offers a different approach by enabling computations on encrypted data. With homomorphic encryption, model updates are encrypted before being sent to the server, which can then perform aggregation directly on the encrypted updates. The aggregated result is then sent back to the clients, who decrypt it to obtain the updated model. This method ensures that data remains encrypted during the entire process, providing strong privacy protection. However, the computational cost of homomorphic encryption is currently high, making it less practical for large-scale federated learning tasks [14].

TEEs provide a hardware-based solution to privacy concerns. TEEs create a secure enclave on client devices, protecting both data and computations from external access, even by the device's own operating system. In federated learning, TEEs can securely execute local training and generate encrypted model updates, which are safe to transmit to the central server. While TEEs offer robust security, they require specific hardware support, limiting their applicability to devices that include this technology.

Despite these advanced techniques, several open questions and challenges remain in ensuring privacy in federated learning. One significant issue is the trade-off between privacy and model performance. Techniques like differential privacy and homomorphic encryption introduce noise or computational overhead, which can impact the accuracy and efficiency of the learning process. Developing methods that provide strong privacy guarantees without significantly degrading model performance is an ongoing area of research.

Another challenge is the robustness of privacy-preserving techniques against sophisticated adversaries. As attacks on machine learning models become more advanced, it is essential to continually update and improve privacy-preserving mechanisms to counteract new threats. Additionally, the heterogeneity of client devices and data distributions adds complexity to implementing consistent privacy protections across all participants in a federated learning system.

Privacy concerns in federated learning are multifaceted and require a combination of techniques to address effectively. Differential privacy, SMPC, homomorphic encryption, and TEE each offer unique advantages and trade-offs. Ensuring robust privacy while maintaining model performance and scalability is critical for the widespread adoption of federated learning, particularly in domains where data sensitivity is paramount. Ongoing research and innovation in privacy-preserving technologies will be essential to overcoming these challenges and realizing the full potential of federated learning [15].

Heterogeneity of data

The heterogeneity of data in federated learning presents significant challenges and opportunities, impacting the performance, accuracy, and fairness of the models being trained. Federated learning involves multiple clients, such as mobile devices, edge devices, or organizations, each generating and storing their own data. Unlike traditional centralized learning, where data is pooled and homogenized, federated learning must contend with the intrinsic diversity of data distributed across clients. This heterogeneity can arise from differences in data distribution, feature spaces, labeling, and client capabilities.

One of the primary forms of heterogeneity in federated learning is the variability in data distribution across clients. This non-IID (non-independent and identically distributed) nature of data means that each client may have data that follows different statistical patterns. For instance, in a federated learning system involving multiple hospitals, each hospital might have patient data that varies significantly based on demographics, local disease prevalence, and healthcare practices. Such diversity can cause the global model to underperform if it fails to adequately capture the variations in data distribution. The model may become biased toward the data from the clients with the most prevalent patterns, ignoring the less frequent but equally important variations.

Another aspect of data heterogeneity is the difference in feature spaces among clients. Not all clients may have data with the same features, and some features might be missing or irrelevant in certain datasets. For example, in a federated learning scenario involving different IoT devices, the sensors on each device might capture different types of data, leading to inconsistencies in the feature sets. Addressing these discrepancies requires sophisticated techniques to align and integrate disparate feature spaces into a cohesive global model. Ensuring that the global model can effectively interpret and utilize varying feature sets is a complex but essential task for achieving accurate and generalizable predictions [16].

Labeling inconsistencies can also pose significant challenges in federated learning. Different clients might use varying criteria for labeling data, leading to noise and discrepancies in the labels. For instance, different medical institutions might have slightly different protocols for diagnosing and labeling medical conditions, which can result in inconsistent training data. Ensuring label consistency or developing models that are robust to such inconsistencies is crucial for the effectiveness of federated learning. Models need to be capable of handling noisy labels and learning underlying patterns despite the variations in labeling practices across different clients.

The heterogeneity of client capabilities adds another layer of complexity. Clients in a federated learning system can range from high-powered servers to low-resource devices like smartphones and IoT sensors. These clients have varying computational power, memory, and energy resources, which can affect their ability to participate in the training process. Some clients might be able to perform extensive local training, while others might be limited to minimal computation. Balancing the workload and ensuring fair participation from all clients without overburdening the less capable ones is a significant challenge. Effective federated learning systems must be designed to accommodate this variability, potentially through adaptive methods that dynamically adjust the learning process based on client capabilities.

To address the challenges posed by data heterogeneity in federated learning, several strategies have been proposed. Personalized federated learning aims to tailor the global model to individual clients by creating personalized models that incorporate local data characteristics. Techniques such as multi-task learning and meta-learning can be used to achieve personalization while maintaining a shared global model structure. Federated transfer learning leverages the knowledge from clients with abundant data to improve the models of clients with sparse or heterogeneous data. By transferring learned representations, federated transfer learning can enhance the performance and robustness of models across diverse clients.

Advanced aggregation methods like federated averaging, weighted averaging, or clustering-based aggregation can help mitigate the impact of data heterogeneity. These methods consider the variability in data distribution and client reliability to produce a more accurate global model. Additionally, data augmentation and synthesis techniques can help bridge the gaps in feature spaces and labeling inconsistencies. Data augmentation can create diverse training samples, while synthetic data generation can standardize feature sets across clients. Adaptive federated learning methods dynamically adjust the learning process based on client capabilities and data characteristics, ensuring a balanced and efficient training process.

The heterogeneity of data in federated learning presents unique challenges that require innovative solutions to ensure the effective and equitable training of global models. By addressing variability in data distribution, feature spaces, labeling, and client capabilities, federated learning can harness the power of distributed data while preserving privacy and efficiency. Ongoing research and development in this field will continue to refine these strategies, making federated learning more robust and widely applicable across diverse domains [17].

1.3.1.2 Opportunities

Scalability

Federated learning offers promising scalability opportunities, making it an attractive approach for training machine learning models on a large, diverse set of data sources. Unlike traditional centralized learning, federated learning leverages the computational resources of numerous distributed client devices, enabling the processing of vast amounts of data without the need for data centralization. This decentralized approach brings several advantages that can enhance scalability and efficiency in various applications.

One of the key scalability opportunities in federated learning is its ability to handle large-scale data distributed across numerous devices. Traditional centralized machine learning requires transferring vast amounts of data to a central server, which can be impractical due to bandwidth limitations and privacy concerns. Federated learning, by contrast, allows data to remain on local devices, reducing the need for massive data transfers. This approach not only preserves user privacy but also significantly lowers the communication overhead, making it feasible to scale up to millions of devices. This capability is particularly beneficial in scenarios like mobile applications, IoT networks, and edge computing, where data is naturally distributed across many devices.

Another significant scalability benefit comes from the inherent parallelism in federated learning. Since the training process is distributed across multiple clients, each performing computations on their local data, federated learning can leverage the aggregate computational power of all participating devices. This parallelism can lead to faster model training times, especially when compared to the bottlenecks often encountered in centralized systems where a single server processes all data. By distributing the computational load, federated learning can efficiently utilize the available resources, enabling the training of complex models on large datasets.

Federated learning also offers opportunities to scale across heterogeneous environments. In many real-world applications, client devices vary widely in terms of computational power, memory, and network connectivity. Federated learning's flexibility allows it to adapt to this heterogeneity by employing strategies like federated averaging, where model updates from all clients are aggregated, and adaptive training, where the frequency and volume of updates are adjusted based on each client's capabilities. This adaptability ensures that even devices with limited resources can contribute to the model training process, broadening the scope of scalable applications [18].

Moreover, federated learning can enhance scalability through its robustness to asynchronous updates. In traditional centralized training, all data must be synchronized and processed together, which can lead to inefficiencies and delays. Federated learning, however, allows clients to train and send updates asynchronously, accommodating the natural variability in client availability and connectivity. This asynchronous communication model ensures that the learning process continues smoothly even if some clients are temporarily offline or have intermittent connections, thereby supporting continuous and scalable model training.

The scalability of federated learning can also be boosted through advanced aggregation techniques. Methods such as hierarchical aggregation, where intermediate aggregations are performed within clusters of clients before sending the results to the central server, can reduce communication overhead and enhance scalability. This hierarchical approach can efficiently manage large numbers of clients by breaking down the aggregation process into manageable steps, allowing for more efficient and scalable training.

Furthermore, federated learning can be scaled by employing efficient compression techniques to reduce the size of the model updates exchanged between clients and the server. Techniques such as quantization, sparsification, and delta encoding can significantly compress the model updates, reducing the communication cost and enabling the system to scale to a larger number of clients. These techniques ensure that the communication bandwidth is used efficiently, which is crucial for scaling federated learning in bandwidth-constrained environments.

Federated learning presents substantial scalability opportunities by leveraging the computational power of distributed devices, handling large-scale and heterogeneous data environments, and employing efficient communication and aggregation strategies. Its decentralized nature reduces the need for data centralization, preserving privacy while enabling the processing of vast amounts of data. By adapting to the capabilities of diverse clients and supporting asynchronous updates, federated learning can maintain efficient and continuous training across large, distributed networks. As research and development in federated learning continue to advance, its scalability benefits will become increasingly critical in a wide range of applications, from mobile and IoT devices to edge computing and beyond.

Privacy preservation

Privacy preservation is a cornerstone of federated learning, designed to enable collaborative model training without exposing sensitive data. In federated learning, data remains on the client devices, and only model updates are shared with the central server. This decentralized approach significantly mitigates the risk of data breaches and enhances user privacy. However, preserving privacy in federated learning involves addressing several challenges and implementing advanced techniques to ensure that sensitive information is not inadvertently leaked through the shared model updates.

One of the primary privacy-preserving techniques used in federated learning is differential privacy. Differential privacy provides a formal framework for quantifying and controlling the risk of privacy breaches. It works by adding controlled noise to the model updates before they are sent to the central server. This noise masks the contribution of individual data points, making it difficult for an attacker to infer specific details about any single data point from the aggregated updates. The level of noise is carefully calibrated to balance privacy protection and model accuracy, ensuring that the model remains useful while providing robust privacy guarantees.

Another critical technique for privacy preservation in federated learning is SMPC. SMPC enables multiple parties to jointly compute a function over their inputs while keeping those inputs private. In the context of federated learning, SMPC can be used to securely aggregate model updates from multiple clients. Each client encrypts its model updates before sending them to the server, which can then perform the aggregation without decrypting the individual updates. This ensures that the server never has access to the raw updates, thereby preserving the privacy of the clients' data. However, SMPC introduces computational and communication overhead, which can be a barrier to scalability.

Homomorphic encryption is another advanced method for privacy preservation. Homomorphic encryption allows computations to be performed directly on encrypted data. In federated learning, clients can encrypt their model updates before sending them to the central server. The server can then perform the aggregation on the encrypted updates and send the result back to the clients, who decrypt the aggregated model. This method ensures that data remains encrypted throughout the entire process, providing strong privacy guarantees. The primary challenge with homomorphic encryption is its high computational cost, which can limit its practical application in large-scale federated learning scenarios.

TEEs offer a hardware-based solution for privacy preservation. TEEs create secure enclaves on client devices, protecting both data and computations from unauthorized access. In federated learning, TEEs can be used to securely perform local training and generate encrypted model updates. These updates can then be transmitted to the central server with the assurance that they have not been tampered with or exposed. While TEEs provide robust security, they require specific hardware support, which may not be available on all devices participating in the federated learning process.

Despite these advanced techniques, several challenges remain in ensuring effective privacy preservation in federated learning. One significant issue is the trade-off between privacy and model performance. Techniques like differential privacy and homomorphic encryption introduce noise or computational overhead, which can impact the accuracy and efficiency of the learning process. Developing methods that provide strong privacy guarantees without significantly degrading model performance is an ongoing area of research [19].

Another challenge is the robustness of privacy-preserving techniques against sophisticated adversaries. As attacks on machine learning models become more advanced, it is essential to continually update and improve privacy-preserving mechanisms to counteract new threats. Federated learning systems must be designed to anticipate and mitigate potential attacks, such as model inversion and membership inference, which aim to extract sensitive information from model updates.

Furthermore, ensuring privacy in heterogeneous environments with diverse client capabilities and data distributions adds complexity to the implementation of privacy-preserving techniques. Clients with limited computational resources may struggle to implement computationally intensive methods like homomorphic encryption or SMPC. Balancing the need for strong privacy protection with the practical constraints of diverse clients requires adaptive and scalable solutions.

Privacy preservation in federated learning is a multifaceted challenge that requires a combination of advanced techniques to ensure that sensitive information remains secure. Differential privacy, SMPC, homomorphic encryption, and TEE each offer unique advantages and trade-offs. Ensuring robust privacy while maintaining model performance and scalability is critical for the widespread adoption of federated learning, particularly in sensitive domains like healthcare, finance, and personal data applications. Ongoing research and innovation in privacy-preserving technologies will be essential to overcoming these challenges and realizing the full potential of federated learning.

Decentralized intelligence

Decentralized intelligence, a core concept in federated learning, refers to the ability to harness the collective power and knowledge of multiple distributed devices or entities to create intelligent systems. Unlike traditional centralized machine learning, where data and computations are aggregated in a central server, federated learning distributes the model training process across various client devices. This approach not only enhances privacy but also capitalizes on the computational resources and local insights of each participating device, leading to more robust and adaptive models.

The primary advantage of decentralized intelligence lies in its ability to preserve data privacy. In traditional centralized models, raw data from individual devices or sources is collected and processed at a central location, posing significant risks to data security and user privacy. Federated learning addresses this concern by keeping data on the local devices where it is generated. Only model updates, such as gradients or weights, are shared with a central server for aggregation. This method significantly reduces the risk of exposing sensitive information, as raw data never leaves the clients' control.

Another significant benefit of decentralized intelligence is the efficient utilization of distributed computational resources. Modern devices, including smartphones, IoT sensors, and edge computing nodes, possess considerable processing power. Federated learning leverages this distributed computational capacity, allowing each device to perform local model training on its own data. This parallel processing capability accelerates the overall training process and reduces the computational burden on a single central server. By distributing the workload, federated learning can scale more effectively and handle larger datasets and more complex models.

Decentralized intelligence also enhances the adaptability and robustness of machine learning models. In a federated learning setup, models are trained on data that reflects the diverse environments and conditions experienced by individual devices. For example, in a federated learning system for mobile devices, each device contributes updates based on its unique user interactions and local context. This diversity enriches the training data and helps the global model generalize better to varied scenarios. The resulting model is more robust and capable of performing well across different environments and user conditions.

Furthermore, decentralized intelligence fosters innovation and collaboration across multiple stakeholders. In industries like healthcare, finance, and smart cities, data is often siloed across different organizations and entities due to privacy regulations and competitive interests. Federated learning enables these stakeholders to collaborate on building powerful machine learning models without sharing their raw data. For instance, hospitals can collectively train a predictive model for disease diagnosis by contributing their local data insights while maintaining patient confidentiality. This collaborative approach can lead to significant advancements in various fields, driving innovation and improving outcomes.

However, implementing decentralized intelligence through federated learning comes with its own set of challenges. One of the primary concerns is the heterogeneity of data and computational resources across clients. Each client may have different data distributions, feature sets, and hardware capabilities, making it challenging to create a unified and effective global model. Techniques like personalized federated learning, where models are tailored to individual clients, and federated transfer learning, which leverages knowledge transfer between clients, can help address these issues.

Communication overhead is another critical challenge. Although federated learning reduces the need to transfer raw data, it still requires frequent communication of model updates between clients and the central server. This can be bandwidth-intensive and may slow down the training process, especially in environments with limited connectivity. Compression techniques, efficient update protocols, and asynchronous communication models are being explored to mitigate this overhead and improve scalability.

Privacy and security concerns also persist, despite the inherent privacy advantages of federated learning. Adversaries could potentially infer sensitive information from the shared model updates through sophisticated attacks. Techniques like differential privacy, SMPC, and homomorphic encryption are crucial for enhancing the privacy and security of federated learning systems. These methods add layers of protection, ensuring that individual data points remain confidential even in the presence of malicious actors [20].

Decentralized intelligence in federated learning offers a transformative approach to machine learning by leveraging the collective power of distributed devices while preserving data privacy. By enabling parallel processing, fostering collaboration, and enhancing model robustness, federated learning addresses some of the key limitations of traditional centralized models. However, realizing the full potential of decentralized intelligence requires addressing challenges related to data heterogeneity, communication overhead, and security. Ongoing research and development in this field will continue to refine federated learning techniques, making them more efficient, scalable, and secure, and paving the way for broader adoption across various domains.

1.4 Federated learning techniques and privacy

FL represents a ground-breaking approach to decentralized machine learning, allowing multiple clients—such as mobile devices, edge nodes, or organizations—to collaboratively train a global model without the need to share their raw data. This paradigm shift addresses significant concerns around data privacy and security, which are increasingly critical in the modern digital landscape. In federated learning, data remains on the local devices where it is generated, and only model updates, such as gradients or weights, are shared with a central server for aggregation. This decentralized process not only preserves privacy but also leverages the computational resources distributed across many clients, making FL a robust and scalable solution for a variety of applications.

One of the foundational techniques in federated learning is federated averaging (FedAvg). In this approach, each client trains the model locally on its dataset and then sends the updated model parameters (typically weights) to a central server.

The server aggregates these updates, typically by computing their average, to produce a new global model, which is then redistributed to all clients. This process is repeated iteratively until the model converges. FedAvg is efficient and straightforward, making it the most commonly used method in federated learning. However, it assumes that all clients' data distributions are relatively similar, which may not be the case in many real-world scenarios, leading to challenges in handling non-IID (non-independent and identically distributed) data.

To enhance privacy, federated learning incorporates several advanced techniques. SMPC is a cryptographic method that allows multiple parties to jointly compute a function over their inputs while keeping those inputs private. In the context of federated learning, SMPC can be used to aggregate model updates in such a way that the server can compute the global model without ever seeing the individual updates. This ensures that even if the central server is compromised, the individual client data remains confidential. SMPC is particularly useful in environments where data privacy is of utmost importance, such as in financial institutions or healthcare systems.

Homomorphic Encryption offers another layer of security by allowing computations to be performed directly on encrypted data. In federated learning, clients can encrypt their model updates before sending them to the central server. The server aggregates these encrypted updates, and the resulting encrypted global model is sent back to the clients, who then decrypt it. This approach ensures that the data remains encrypted throughout the entire process, providing robust privacy protection. However, homomorphic encryption is computationally intensive, which can slow down the training process, particularly in large-scale federated learning systems.

Despite these techniques, several challenges remain in federated learning related to privacy and security. For instance, the effectiveness of differential privacy depends on the amount of noise added, which can impact the accuracy of the model. Similarly, while SMPC and homomorphic encryption offer strong privacy guarantees, they introduce significant computational and communication overhead, which can hinder scalability and efficiency. Moreover, adversaries may attempt to infer sensitive information from the shared updates using advanced attacks, such as model inversion or membership inference attacks. As such, ongoing research in federated learning focuses on improving these privacy-preserving techniques to make them more efficient, scalable, and secure.

Federated learning offers a promising solution to the challenges of data privacy and security in distributed machine learning. By keeping data on local devices and employing techniques like federated averaging, SMPC, homomorphic encryption, and differential privacy, federated learning ensures that sensitive information remains protected while still allowing the collaborative training of powerful machine learning models. As these techniques continue to evolve, federated learning will become increasingly essential in domains where data privacy is paramount, paving the way for broader adoption across industries.

1.4.1 Privacy in federated learning

Federated learning presents unique challenges and opportunities regarding privacy, as it involves training models across decentralized devices while preserving the confidentiality of sensitive data. Several privacy-preserving mechanisms have been proposed to address these challenges.

1.4.1.1 Differential privacy

Differential privacy has emerged as a critical technique in federated learning, providing a rigorous framework for protecting individual data privacy while allowing collaborative model training across distributed devices. Federated learning involves training a machine learning model on decentralized data sources, where raw data remains on the local devices, and only model updates are shared with a central server. However, even these updates can inadvertently leak sensitive information about the underlying data. Differential privacy addresses this concern by introducing controlled noise into the model updates, ensuring that the contribution of any single data point is obscured, thereby safeguarding individual privacy.

The core principle of differential privacy is to make it mathematically challenging for an adversary to distinguish whether any individual's data was included in the dataset based on the output of a computation. In the context of federated learning, this means adding noise to the model parameters or gradients before they are sent from the clients to the central server. The noise is typically drawn from a probability distribution, such as the Gaussian or Laplace distribution, and its magnitude is carefully calibrated to balance privacy protection with model accuracy. The idea is that even with access to noisy updates, it should be difficult for an attacker to infer specific details about any individual data point used in the training process.

In practice, implementing differential privacy in federated learning involves determining an appropriate privacy budget, often denoted by the parameter ε (epsilon). This budget quantifies the trade-off between privacy and utility: a smaller ε indicates stronger privacy protection, but at the cost of reduced model accuracy due to higher levels of noise. Conversely, a larger ε allows for more accurate model updates but provides weaker privacy guarantees. The choice of ε is crucial and depends on the specific application and its privacy requirements. In many cases, differential privacy is combined with techniques like SMPC or homomorphic encryption to further enhance the security of the federated learning process [21].

One of the challenges of applying differential privacy in federated learning is managing the cumulative effect of noise over multiple training rounds. As federated learning is an iterative process, noise is added in each round, which can degrade the model's performance over time. To mitigate this, researchers explore adaptive noise mechanisms, where the level of noise is adjusted dynamically based on the progress of the model training. Additionally, strategies like privacy amplification through sampling—where only a subset of clients participate in each training round—can help reduce the overall noise required to maintain a given level of privacy.

Despite its advantages, differential privacy in federated learning is not without limitations. The added noise can make the model less accurate, particularly in cases where the data is already sparse or highly variable. Moreover, the privacy guarantees provided by differential privacy are inherently statistical, meaning that there is still a small probability that some information could be leaked. These challenges highlight the need for ongoing research to refine differential privacy techniques and make them more adaptable to the specific needs of federated learning applications.

In summary, differential privacy plays a crucial role in enhancing the privacy of federated learning systems by ensuring that the model updates shared among clients and the central server do not compromise individual data security. By carefully introducing noise into the training process, differential privacy helps to protect sensitive information while enabling collaborative machine learning across distributed datasets. As federated learning continues to evolve and be applied in sensitive domains such as healthcare and finance, the development and optimization of differential privacy techniques will remain a key focus for researchers and practitioners alike.

1.4.1.2 Secure aggregation

Secure aggregation is a fundamental technique in federated learning that addresses the challenge of combining model updates from multiple clients in a way that ensures both security and privacy. In federated learning, each client trains a machine learning model on its local data and then sends updates, such as gradients or model weights, to a central server. The server aggregates these updates to improve a global model. However, directly aggregating raw updates poses significant privacy risks, as it could potentially reveal sensitive information about individual clients' data. Secure aggregation provides a solution by enabling the central server to perform the aggregation securely, without accessing the raw updates.

The primary goal of secure aggregation is to ensure that the central server receives only the aggregated result of the model updates, without being able to view or infer the individual updates from each client. This is achieved through cryptographic techniques that protect the confidentiality of the updates during the aggregation process. One common method is the use of homomorphic encryption, which allows computations to be performed on encrypted data. In this approach, clients encrypt their model updates before sending them to the server. The server performs the aggregation on the encrypted updates and sends the result back to the clients, who then decrypt the aggregated model. This method ensures that the server never sees the raw updates, thus preserving client privacy. However, homomorphic encryption can be computationally intensive and may introduce latency, which can impact the scalability of the federated learning system [22].

Another widely used technique is SMPC. SMPC allows multiple parties to jointly compute a function over their private inputs while keeping those inputs secret. In federated learning, SMPC can be employed to securely aggregate model updates from multiple clients. Each client computes partial results and shares them with other parties in a way that allows the central server to compute the aggregate without having access to the individual updates. SMPC protocols often rely on techniques such as secret sharing, where each update is divided into shares that are distributed among multiple parties. Only by combining these shares can the aggregate result be reconstructed. While SMPC provides strong security guarantees, it can also introduce significant communication and computational overhead, which can affect performance and scalability.

Privacy-preserving aggregation techniques further enhance secure aggregation by combining encryption with other privacy-preserving mechanisms. For example, homomorphic encryption can be combined with secure aggregation protocols to ensure that the updates are both encrypted and aggregated in a privacy-preserving manner. This hybrid approach leverages the strengths of different techniques to provide robust security while minimizing performance impacts.

Despite the advantages of secure aggregation, several challenges remain. One challenge is the computational and communication overhead associated with encryption and secure computation. Techniques like homomorphic encryption and SMPC can be resource-intensive, which can limit their applicability in environments with constrained computational power or bandwidth. Additionally, robustness to adversarial attacks is a concern, as sophisticated attackers might attempt to exploit vulnerabilities in the secure aggregation protocols. Researchers are continuously working on optimizing these techniques to reduce their overhead and improve their resilience against potential attacks.

Another consideration is the scalability of secure aggregation methods. As the number of clients in a federated learning system grows, the complexity of secure aggregation increases. Efficient algorithms and protocols are needed to handle large-scale systems without compromising security or performance.

Secure aggregation is a critical component of federated learning that ensures the privacy and security of model updates shared among clients and the central server. By employing cryptographic techniques such as homomorphic encryption and SMPC, secure aggregation enables the central server to perform model update aggregation without accessing raw data from individual clients. While there are challenges related to computational overhead, robustness, and scalability, ongoing research and advancements in secure aggregation techniques are crucial for the continued success and adoption of federated learning in privacy-sensitive applications.

1.4.1.3 Federated learning with encrypted models

Federated learning with encrypted models represents a sophisticated approach to maintaining data privacy while leveraging the collective intelligence of multiple distributed clients. In traditional federated learning, clients train models on their local datasets and share model updates with a central server, which aggregates these updates to improve a global model. However, to enhance privacy and security further, the concept of encrypting models during this process has been developed. This ensures that even the model updates exchanged between clients and the server are protected from potential eavesdropping and tampering.

Homomorphic encryption is a primary technique used in federated learning with encrypted models. This encryption scheme allows computations to be performed directly on encrypted data without needing to decrypt it first. In the context of federated learning, clients encrypt their model updates before sending them to the central server. The server then aggregates these encrypted updates and sends the aggregated result back to the clients, who decrypt the final model. This method ensures that the server never sees the raw updates, maintaining the confidentiality of each client's data. Homomorphic encryption provides strong security guarantees but is computationally intensive. The encryption and decryption processes can introduce significant latency and overhead, which may impact the efficiency of the federated learning system.

Another key approach is SMPC, which enables multiple parties to jointly compute a function over their private inputs without revealing their individual inputs to each other. In federated learning, SMPC can be used to securely aggregate encrypted model updates. Each client encrypts their updates using a secure scheme and distributes these encrypted updates among multiple servers or parties. The parties then collaboratively compute the aggregate result without ever seeing the individual encrypted updates. The final aggregated result is then sent back to the clients, who decrypt it. While SMPC provides robust security, it involves complex cryptographic protocols and can be resource-intensive, leading to increased communication and computational costs [23].

Secure aggregation protocols often combine encryption with other privacy-preserving techniques to enhance security. For example, techniques like differential privacy can be applied alongside encryption methods to add an additional layer of protection. Differential privacy introduces noise to the encrypted updates to obscure individual data points further, providing a quantitative measure of privacy while ensuring the aggregated result remains useful for model training.

The integration of encrypted models into federated learning systems poses several challenges. One significant challenge is the computational overhead associated with encryption and decryption. Homomorphic encryption and SMPC require substantial computational resources, which can be a bottleneck, especially in systems with a large number of clients or limited hardware capabilities. Researchers are actively working on optimizing these techniques to make them more efficient and scalable.

Another challenge is data consistency and synchronization. Encrypting model updates can complicate the process of ensuring that all clients and the central server are synchronized. Ensuring that encrypted updates are consistently aggregated and accurately reflect the global model is crucial for the effectiveness of federated learning. Techniques to handle synchronization issues and maintain the consistency of encrypted updates are areas of ongoing research [24].

Robustness against attacks is also a key concern. Encrypted models and updates must be protected against sophisticated adversarial attacks that might attempt to infer sensitive information through side-channel attacks or other vulnerabilities. Strengthening the security protocols and continually updating them to address emerging threats is essential for maintaining the integrity of the federated learning system.

In summary, federated learning with encrypted models offers a powerful way to enhance privacy and security by ensuring that model updates exchanged between clients and servers are protected through advanced cryptographic techniques. Homomorphic encryption, SMPC, and secure aggregation protocols each play a role in safeguarding sensitive information while allowing collaborative model training. Despite challenges related to computational overhead, data consistency, and attack robustness, ongoing advancements in encryption and cryptographic techniques are crucial for enabling secure and efficient federated learning systems in privacy-sensitive applications.

1.4.1.4 Privacy-preserving deep learning

Privacy-preserving deep learning represents an advanced domain within machine learning that seeks to balance the power of deep learning models with the imperative of protecting sensitive data. Traditional deep learning involves training complex neural networks on large datasets, often requiring centralization of data which can expose sensitive information to privacy risks. Privacy-preserving techniques aim to address these risks by enabling the development and deployment of deep learning models while safeguarding individual data privacy.

Differential privacy is a cornerstone technique in privacy-preserving deep learning. It provides strong privacy guarantees by introducing noise into the data or model parameters, making it difficult for an attacker to infer the presence or characteristics of any individual data point. In the context of deep learning, differential privacy can be implemented by adding noise to gradients or model updates during training. This noise ensures that the contribution of any single data point to the model is obscured, thus protecting individual privacy. Differential privacy provides a formal measure of privacy, quantified by parameters such as ε (epsilon) and δ (delta), which represent the privacy loss. While it ensures robust protection, differential privacy often requires a trade-off between privacy and model accuracy, as excessive noise can degrade model performance.

Homomorphic encryption is another critical technique that allows computations to be performed on encrypted data without decrypting it. In deep learning, homomorphic encryption can be applied to encrypted model parameters or gradients. Clients encrypt their data or model updates before sending them to a central server, which performs operations on the encrypted data and then returns the results. This approach ensures that sensitive information remains confidential throughout the computation process. However, homomorphic encryption is computationally demanding and can introduce significant latency, which may impact the practicality of its use in large-scale deep learning applications.

SMPC enables multiple parties to jointly compute a function over their private inputs without revealing the inputs themselves. In deep learning, SMPC can be used to securely aggregate model updates from multiple parties. Each party (or client) computes partial results and shares them with others in a way that maintains the confidentiality of the individual inputs. SMPC protocols often use techniques such as secret sharing, where each input is divided into shares distributed among multiple parties. The aggregate result can be reconstructed without any single party knowing the entire input. SMPC is robust but can be complex and computationally intensive, which may affect its scalability and efficiency in deep learning systems [25].

Federated learning is a distributed approach that enhances privacy by keeping data on local devices and only sharing model updates. In federated learning, clients train models on their local data and send updates (like gradients or weights) to a central server, which aggregates these updates to improve the global model. Techniques like differential privacy and secure aggregation can be integrated into federated learning to enhance privacy further. By keeping data decentralized and only sharing encrypted or noisy updates, federated learning mitigates the risk of exposing sensitive information.

Private information retrieval (PIR) is another technique that can be applied to privacy-preserving deep learning. PIR allows a client to retrieve data from a database without revealing which data was accessed. While not directly a deep learning technique, PIR can be combined with deep learning to enable private querying of data used in training or inference, ensuring that sensitive information is not disclosed during data retrieval.

Despite the advances in privacy-preserving techniques, several challenges remain. Implementing these methods often involves trade-offs between privacy, accuracy, and computational efficiency. Ensuring that privacy-preserving techniques do not overly compromise model performance or introduce prohibitive computational overhead is a key focus of ongoing research. Additionally, maintaining the robustness of privacy guarantees against sophisticated attacks and adversarial scenarios is crucial for the effective deployment of privacy-preserving deep learning systems.

In conclusion, privacy-preserving deep learning is a vital area of research that aims to protect sensitive data while harnessing the power of deep learning models. Techniques such as differential privacy, homomorphic encryption, SMPC, and federated learning play crucial roles in safeguarding data privacy. As the field continues to evolve, ongoing research will be essential to address challenges related to privacy, efficiency, and model performance, paving the way for secure and effective deep learning applications across various domains.

1.4.2 Applications of federated learning

FL has emerged as a transformative approach to machine learning, particularly in scenarios where data privacy, security, and regulatory constraints are critical. By enabling collaborative model training across distributed devices while keeping data localized, federated learning addresses several challenges associated with centralized data collection. Its unique architecture has led to significant advancements and applications across diverse domains, including healthcare, finance, mobile devices, and the IoT.

In healthcare, federated learning offers a powerful solution for training models on sensitive medical data while adhering to privacy regulations such as HIPAA (Health Insurance Portability and Accountability Act) in the United States or GDPR (General Data Protection Regulation) in Europe. Hospitals and medical institutions often have vast amounts of patient data that are crucial for developing predictive models for disease diagnosis, treatment recommendations, and patient monitoring. By using federated learning, institutions can collaboratively train models on their data without sharing raw patient information. For instance, federated learning has been employed to enhance medical imaging technologies, such as improving the accuracy of cancer detection from MRI scans or X-rays. Additionally, federated learning can support the development of personalized treatment plans by aggregating insights from various medical datasets, leading to more accurate and individualized patient care.

The financial industry benefits greatly from federated learning, particularly in areas like fraud detection, credit scoring, and personalized financial services. Financial institutions manage vast amounts of sensitive data, including transaction records, credit histories, and personal financial information. Federated learning enables banks and financial services companies to build robust models for detecting fraudulent activities and assessing creditworthiness while ensuring that sensitive customer data remains secure and localized. For example, federated learning can be used to train fraud detection models across different banks without sharing transaction data, allowing for the identification of suspicious patterns and the prevention of fraudulent transactions in real time. Similarly, federated learning can facilitate personalized financial recommendations by aggregating data from various institutions, improving the accuracy of investment advice and financial planning.

Federated learning has significant applications in the realm of mobile devices, where it enhances user experience and personalization while preserving privacy. Mobile devices, such as smartphones and tablets, generate extensive data related to user behavior, preferences, and interactions. Federated learning enables models to be trained directly on users' devices, allowing for personalized features and services without transmitting sensitive data to central servers. For instance, federated learning can improve predictive text input and voice recognition systems by learning from user interactions on individual devices. Additionally, it can enhance recommendation systems for apps and content by analyzing user preferences locally, resulting in more relevant and personalized suggestions.

The IoT landscape, characterized by a vast network of interconnected devices, presents unique challenges for data privacy and security. Federated learning is well-suited for IoT applications, where data is generated by various sensors and devices deployed in diverse environments. By using federated learning, IoT systems can collaboratively train models on data generated by edge devices without centralizing it. This approach supports a range of applications, including smart cities, autonomous vehicles, and industrial automation. For example, in autonomous vehicles, federated learning can aggregate data from multiple vehicles to improve self-driving algorithms while keeping vehicle-specific data private. In smart cities, federated learning can optimize traffic management and energy consumption by analyzing data from various sensors distributed across the city without compromising individual privacy [26].

In the retail and e-commerce sectors, federated learning enables companies to enhance customer experiences and optimize operations while maintaining data privacy. Retailers can use federated learning to improve recommendation engines, personalize shopping experiences, and optimize inventory management. For instance, federated learning can be applied to analyze customer purchasing patterns and preferences across different stores without aggregating sensitive transactional data. This allows retailers to offer personalized product recommendations and promotions based on local customer behavior. Additionally, federated learning can help in demand forecasting and inventory management by leveraging data from multiple retail locations while ensuring that proprietary sales information remains confidential.

The rise of smart healthcare devices, such as wearable fitness trackers and health monitors, has created opportunities for federated learning to improve health monitoring and predictive analytics. These devices generate continuous streams of health-related data, including physical activity, heart rate, and sleep patterns. Federated learning enables these devices to collaboratively train models on user data to detect health anomalies and predict potential health issues while keeping individual health data secure. For example, federated learning can be used to develop models for early detection of conditions like diabetes or heart disease by analyzing aggregated data from various wearable devices without compromising user privacy.

Federated learning represents a significant advancement in the field of machine learning, offering a powerful framework for collaborative model training while addressing privacy and security concerns. Its applications span across various domains, including healthcare, finance, mobile devices, IoT, retail, and smart healthcare devices. By enabling models to be trained on decentralized data sources without sharing raw data, federated learning facilitates the development of sophisticated, privacy-preserving solutions that can drive innovation and improve user experiences. As federated learning technology continues to evolve, its potential for transforming industries and enabling secure, privacy-preserving machine learning will likely expand, leading to new opportunities and applications across diverse fields.

1.4.3 Current research trends

FL is a rapidly evolving field that addresses the challenges of decentralized data and privacy while enabling collaborative machine learning. As the technology matures, several key research trends are emerging, reflecting the ongoing efforts to enhance the efficiency, scalability, and applicability of federated learning systems. These trends include advancements in communication efficiency, privacy-preserving techniques, model robustness, and practical implementations.

1.4.3.1 Efficient communication protocols

One of the primary challenges in federated learning is minimizing the communication overhead between clients and the central server. Current research is focused on developing efficient communication protocols to reduce the volume of data exchanged and improve the speed of model updates. Techniques such as model compression and quantization are being explored to minimize the size of model updates transmitted over the network. Researchers are also investigating sparse updates, where only a subset of model parameters or gradients are communicated, and adaptive communication strategies, which adjust the frequency of updates based on network conditions and client availability. These advancements aim to make federated learning more feasible for large-scale deployments and resource-constrained environments.

1.4.3.2 Enhanced privacy-preserving mechanisms

Privacy remains a critical concern in federated learning, and ongoing research is focused on strengthening privacy-preserving techniques. Differential privacy continues to be a major area of exploration, with efforts directed at improving the balance between privacy guarantees and model accuracy. Researchers are investigating more effective noise addition strategies and privacy amplification techniques to ensure robust privacy protections without significantly degrading model performance. Additionally, there is growing interest in SMPC and homomorphic encryption, with research aimed at optimizing these methods for federated learning applications. Innovations in combining these techniques with federated learning frameworks are also being explored to enhance overall privacy.

1.4.3.3 Robustness and fault tolerance

Federated learning systems must be robust and fault-tolerant, especially in environments with heterogeneous and unreliable clients. Current research is addressing these challenges by developing methods to handle client heterogeneity, including variations in data quality, computational resources, and network conditions. Researchers are working on robust aggregation algorithms that can tolerate and mitigate the impact of malicious or faulty clients. Techniques such as secure aggregation and robust optimization methods are being refined to ensure that the federated learning process remains stable and reliable even in the presence of adversarial or unreliable participants.

1.4.3.4 Scalability and large-scale deployment

Scalability is a critical consideration for federated learning, especially as the number of clients and the volume of data grow. Research is focusing on scaling federated learning systems to handle large numbers of clients and extensive datasets. This includes optimizing the communication infrastructure, data synchronization, and model aggregation processes. Techniques such as federated averaging and meta-learning are being explored to improve scalability. Additionally, researchers are investigating distributed federated learning approaches that leverage edge computing and cloud resources to enhance scalability and efficiency.

1.4.3.5 Application-specific adaptations

Federated learning is being adapted for various application domains, each with its own unique requirements and constraints. Research trends include domain-specific adaptations of federated learning techniques to address challenges in fields such as healthcare, finance, and autonomous systems. For example, in healthcare, federated learning models are being tailored to handle medical data with strict privacy requirements and diverse data formats. In autonomous systems, federated learning is being adapted to support real-time decision-making and collaboration among vehicles. These adaptations aim to make federated learning more effective and applicable to a wide range of industries and use cases.

1.4.3.6 Integration with other technologies

The integration of federated learning with other emerging technologies is an area of active research. For instance, there is growing interest in combining federated learning with blockchain technology to enhance security and accountability. Blockchain can provide a decentralized ledger for tracking model updates and ensuring the integrity of the federated learning process. Additionally, researchers are exploring the integration of federated learning with edge computing, where computation is performed closer to the data source to reduce latency and improve efficiency. These integrations aim to leverage the strengths of multiple technologies to enhance the capabilities of federated learning systems.

1.4.3.7 Regulatory and ethical considerations

As federated learning becomes more widespread, addressing regulatory and ethical considerations is becoming increasingly important. Research focuses on understanding the legal and ethical implications of federated learning, including compliance with data protection regulations and addressing issues related to fairness and transparency. Efforts are being made to develop frameworks and guidelines for the ethical deployment of federated learning systems, ensuring that they align with regulatory requirements and promote responsible use of technology.

Current research trends in federated learning reflect a dynamic and rapidly advancing field. Researchers are addressing key challenges related to communication efficiency, privacy preservation, robustness, scalability, and application-specific adaptations. Innovations in these areas are driving the development of more effective and practical federated learning systems, making them suitable for a wide range of applications. As federated learning continues to evolve, ongoing research and development will be crucial in overcoming existing limitations and unlocking new opportunities for collaborative and privacy-preserving machine learning.

1.4.4 Future directions

FL has demonstrated significant potential in advancing collaborative machine learning while preserving data privacy. As the technology evolves, several future directions are emerging that could shape the trajectory of federated learning. These future directions include addressing scalability challenges, enhancing privacy measures, integrating with emerging technologies, optimizing model performance, and tackling regulatory and ethical issues. The following exploration outlines these areas in detail, highlighting how they might influence the development and application of federated learning in the coming years.

1.4.4.1 Scalability and efficiency improvements

Scalability remains one of the most critical challenges for federated learning, especially as the number of participating clients and the volume of data increase. Future research is likely to focus on enhancing the scalability of federated learning systems to support large-scale deployments. One promising direction is the development of hierarchical federated learning, where clients are organized into clusters, and local aggregations occur within clusters before a global aggregation. This approach can reduce communication overhead and improve efficiency by managing data and updates in a more structured manner.

Another key area of focus is efficient communication protocols. Future research may explore advanced techniques such as asynchronous updates, where clients send updates to the server at different times, and incremental learning, where only changes in the model are communicated. Additionally, innovations in model compression and quantization techniques could further reduce the size of updates transmitted across networks, making federated learning more practical for resource-constrained environments.

1.4.4.2 Enhanced privacy and security measures

While federated learning provides inherent privacy benefits by keeping data localized, there is a continuous need to enhance privacy and security measures. Advanced differential privacy techniques are likely to play a significant role in this regard. Researchers may develop more sophisticated methods for adding noise to model updates, optimizing the trade-off between privacy and model accuracy. Additionally, privacy-preserving aggregation methods such as SMPC and homomorphic encryption will continue to evolve, with efforts aimed at reducing computational overhead and improving efficiency [27].

Federated learning with secure hardware is another promising area. Future directions may involve leveraging secure enclaves and TEEs to protect sensitive data and computations. These secure hardware solutions can offer an additional layer of protection by ensuring that data and model updates are processed in a secure environment, mitigating risks associated with data breaches and malicious attacks.

1.4.4.3 Integration with emerging technologies

Federated learning is increasingly being integrated with other emerging technologies to enhance its capabilities. Blockchain technology is one such integration that could provide decentralized and tamper-proof records of model updates and transactions. Blockchain can ensure the integrity of federated learning processes by creating an immutable ledger of contributions from clients, thus enhancing transparency and trust.

Edge computing is another technology that complements federated learning. By performing computations closer to the data source, edge computing can reduce latency and bandwidth usage, making federated learning more efficient. Future research may focus on optimizing the integration of federated learning with edge computing environments, enabling real-time data processing and decision-making.

Furthermore, artificial intelligence (AI) and machine learning (ML) operations (MLOps) practices are likely to become more integrated with federated learning. MLOps involves the end-to-end lifecycle management of AI and ML models, including deployment, monitoring, and updating. By incorporating MLOps practices, federated learning systems can achieve better model management, version control, and automated monitoring, improving overall performance and reliability.

1.4.4.4 Model performance and personalization

Improving model performance and personalization is a critical focus for the future of federated learning. Personalized federated learning aims to tailor models to individual clients' needs while benefiting from collective knowledge. Future research may explore personalized federated averaging techniques, where clients' local models are adapted to their specific contexts, and meta-learning approaches that enable models to learn from a diverse set of clients and adapt quickly to new environments [28].

Model robustness is another important area of research. Future directions may involve developing methods to enhance the resilience of federated learning models against adversarial attacks and ensuring robustness in the face of noisy or incomplete data. Techniques such as robust optimization algorithms and anomaly detection within federated learning systems could play a key role in addressing these challenges.

1.4.4.5 Regulatory and ethical considerations

As federated learning continues to gain traction, addressing regulatory and ethical considerations will become increasingly important. Future research will likely focus on developing frameworks and guidelines for the ethical deployment of federated learning systems, ensuring compliance with data protection regulations, and promoting responsible use of technology.

Researchers may work on creating regulatory compliance tools that help organizations adhere to legal requirements while leveraging federated learning. These tools could assist in managing data sovereignty, consent, and auditing processes, ensuring that federated learning systems operate within legal and ethical boundaries.

Additionally, fairness and transparency will be critical areas of focus. Future research may explore methods to ensure that federated learning models do not perpetuate biases or unfairness. Techniques such as explainable AI and bias mitigation could be integrated into federated learning frameworks to enhance the transparency of model decisions and promote fairness across diverse client populations.

1.4.4.6 Application-specific innovations

The continued evolution of federated learning will drive innovations tailored to specific application domains. For example, in healthcare, federated learning could enable the development of personalized treatment plans and early detection systems while ensuring compliance with stringent privacy regulations. In autonomous systems, federated learning can support collaborative learning among vehicles, improving safety and performance while preserving data privacy.

Retail and e-commerce could see advancements in personalized shopping experiences and optimized inventory management through federated learning, while smart cities could benefit from improved traffic management and energy optimization. Research into domain-specific adaptations will ensure that federated learning meets the unique needs and challenges of various industries [29].

The future of federated learning is poised to bring significant advancements that address current challenges and unlock new opportunities. Research trends in scalability, privacy, integration with emerging technologies, model performance, and regulatory considerations will shape the trajectory of federated learning systems. As these areas continue to evolve, federated learning has the potential to transform a wide range of industries, enabling collaborative, privacy-preserving machine learning on a global scale. Continued innovation and exploration will be crucial in realizing the full potential of federated learning and driving its adoption in diverse applications.

1.5 Conclusion

Federated learning has emerged as a transformative approach in the realm of machine learning, offering a paradigm shift from traditional centralized methods to a decentralized, privacy-preserving model. This innovative framework addresses critical challenges related to data privacy, security, and scalability, making it particularly suitable for applications where sensitive data is involved and privacy is paramount.

The core principles of federated learning revolve around collaborative model training across multiple clients while keeping data localized. By enabling local model training and aggregating updates to refine a global model, federated learning ensures that individual data points remain secure and confidential. This decentralized approach mitigates the risks associated with data breaches and unauthorized access, as raw data never leaves the client's device. Instead, only aggregated model updates are shared, which enhances both privacy and security.

In practice, federated learning has demonstrated significant benefits across various domains. In healthcare, it allows for the development of predictive models and personalized treatment plans without compromising patient privacy. By training models on medical data stored within hospitals and clinics, federated learning supports advancements in disease diagnosis and patient monitoring while adhering to stringent regulatory requirements. Similarly, in the financial sector, federated learning aids in fraud detection, credit scoring, and personalized financial services, enabling financial institutions to protect sensitive customer data while improving model performance.

The applications extend beyond healthcare and finance to include mobile devices and the IoT. Federated learning enhances user experiences in mobile applications by personalizing features such as predictive text input and voice recognition without transmitting sensitive user data. In the IoT realm, federated learning supports real-time data processing and decision-making by enabling collaboration among a network of interconnected devices while preserving data privacy.

Looking ahead, several key areas of future research and development will shape the evolution of federated learning. Scalability remains a major challenge, with ongoing efforts focused on developing hierarchical federated learning frameworks and efficient communication protocols to handle large-scale deployments. Innovations such as model compression, quantization, and asynchronous updates are anticipated to reduce communication overhead and improve system efficiency.

Privacy-preserving techniques will continue to be a critical focus. Advances in differential privacy, SMPC, and homomorphic encryption are expected to enhance the robustness of federated learning systems, ensuring that data remains secure throughout the training process. The integration of secure hardware solutions, such as TEEs, may also provide additional layers of protection against data breaches and malicious attacks.

The integration of federated learning with emerging technologies will further expand its capabilities. Combining federated learning with edge computing can optimize real-time data processing, while blockchain technology can offer decentralized and tamper-proof records of model updates. These integrations will enhance the efficiency, transparency, and security of federated learning systems.

Addressing regulatory and ethical considerations will be crucial for the responsible deployment of federated learning. Developing frameworks for compliance with data protection regulations and ensuring fairness in model outcomes will be essential for maintaining public trust and promoting ethical practices. Future research will need to focus on creating tools for managing data sovereignty, consent, and auditing, as well as mitigating biases and ensuring equitable outcomes.

In conclusion, federated learning stands as a significant advancement in machine learning, offering a robust framework for decentralized and privacy-preserving model training. Its applications across healthcare, finance, mobile devices, and IoT highlight its versatility and potential impact. As the technology continues to evolve, ongoing research will be vital in addressing scalability, privacy, and integration challenges, ensuring that federated learning can meet the demands of a rapidly changing technological landscape. By leveraging its strengths and addressing emerging challenges, federated learning is poised to play a pivotal role in shaping the future of secure, collaborative machine learning.

References

[1] McMahan, H. B., Moore, E., Ramage, D., Hampson, S., and Arcas, B. A. (2017). "Communication-Efficient Learning of Deep Networks from Decentralized Data." *Proceedings of the 20th International Conference on Artificial Intelligence and Statistics (AISTATS)*, PMLR, pp. 1273–1282.

[2] McMahan, H. B., Yu, F. X., Richtarik, P., Suresh, A. T., and Bacon, D. (2016). "Federated Learning: Strategies for Improving Communication Efficiency." arXiv preprint arXiv:1610.05492.

[3] Bonawitz, K., Eichner, H., Grieskamp, W., *et al.* (2019). "Towards Federated Learning at Scale: System Design." *Proceedings of the 2nd SysML Conference*. https://mlsys.org/Conferences/2019/doc/2019/193.pdf.

[4] Geyer, R. C., Klein, T., and Nabi, M. (2017). "Differentially Private Federated Learning: A Client Level Perspective." arXiv preprint arXiv:1712.07557.

[5] Shokri, R. and Shmatikov, V. (2015). "Privacy-Preserving Deep Learning." *Proceedings of the 2015 ACM SIGSAC Conference on Computer and Communications Security (CCS)*, pp. 1310–1321.

[6] Li, T., Sahu, A. K., Talwalkar, A., and Smith, V. (2020). Federated learning: Challenges, methods, and future directions. *IEEE signal processing magazine*, *37*(3), 50–60.

[7] Mohialden, Y. M., Hussien, N. M., Salman, S. A., and Aljanabi, M. (2023). Secure Federated Learning with a Homomorphic Encryption Model. *International Journal Papier Advance and Scientific Review*, *4*(3), 1–7.

[8] Li, Q., Wen, Z., Wu, Z., *et al.* (2021). A survey on federated learning systems: Vision, hype and reality for data privacy and protection. *IEEE Transactions on Knowledge and Data Engineering*, *35*(4), 3347–3366.

[9] Yang, Q., Liu, Y., Chen, T., and Tong, Y. (2019). Federated machine learning: Concept and applications. *ACM Transactions on Intelligent Systems and Technology (TIST)*, *10*(2), 1–19.

[10] Yin, X., Zhu, Y., and Hu, J. (2021). A comprehensive survey of privacy-preserving federated learning: A taxonomy, review, and future directions. *ACM Computing Surveys (CSUR)*, *54*(6), 1–36.

[11] Chen, Y., Sun, X., and Jin, Y. (2019). Communication-efficient federated deep learning with layerwise asynchronous model update and temporally weighted aggregation. *IEEE transactions on neural networks and learning systems*, *31*(10), 4229–4238.

[12] Levy, D., Sun, Z., Amin, K., *et al.* (2021). Learning with user-level privacy. *Advances in Neural Information Processing Systems*, *34*, 12466–12479.

[13] Sattler, F., Wiedemann, S., Müller, K. R., and Samek, W. (2019). Robust and communication-efficient federated learning from non-iid data. *IEEE transactions on neural networks and learning systems*, *31*(9), 3400–3413.

[14] Zhao, Y., Li, M., Lai, L., Suda, N., Civin, D., and Chandra, V. (2018). Federated learning with non-iid data. arXiv preprint arXiv:1806.00582.

[15] Zhao, C., Gao, Z., Wang, Q., Xiao, K., and Mo, Z. (2021). AFL: An adaptively federated multitask learning for model sharing in industrial IoT. *IEEE Internet of Things Journal*, *9*(18), 17080–17088.

[16] Majeed, A., and Hwang, S. O. (2024). A multifaceted survey on federated learning: Fundamentals, paradigm shifts, practical issues, recent developments, partnerships, trade-offs, trustworthiness, and ways forward. *IEEE Access*, *12*, 84643–84679.

[17] Yang, Q., Huang, A., Fan, L., *et al.* (2023). Federated Learning with Privacy-preserving and Model IP-right-protection. *Machine Intelligence Research*, *20* (1), 19–37.

[18] Kairouz, P., McMahan, H. B., Avent, B., *et al.* (2021). Advances and open problems in federated learning. *Foundations and trends® in machine learning*, *14*(1–2), 1–210.

[19] Wang, W., Li, X., Qiu, X., Zhang, X., Brusic, V., and Zhao, J. (2023). A privacy preserving framework for federated learning in smart healthcare systems. *Information Processing and Management*, *60*(1), 103167.

[20] Abreha, H. G., Hayajneh, M., and Serhani, M. A. (2022). Federated learning in edge computing: a systematic survey. *Sensors*, *22*(2), 450.

[21] Zhou, I., Tofigh, F., Piccardi, M., Abolhasan, M., Franklin, D., and Lipman, J. (2024). Secure Multi-Party Computation for Machine Learning: A Survey. *IEEE Access*, *12*, 53881–53899.

[22] Wei, X., Li, Q., Liu, Y., Yu, H., Chen, T., and Yang, Q. (2019). Multi-agent visualization for explaining federated learning. In *Proceedings of the Twenty-Eighth International Joint Conference on Artificial Intelligence (IJCAI)*, pp. 6572–6574.

[23] Tan, A. Z., Yu, H., Cui, L., and Yang, Q. (2022). Towards personalized federated learning. *IEEE transactions on neural networks and learning systems*, *34*(12), 9587–9603.

[24] Ma, C., Li, J., Ding, M., *et al.* (2020). On safeguarding privacy and security in the framework of federated learning. *IEEE Network*, *34*(4), 242–248.

[25] Yin, L., Feng, J., Xun, H., Sun, Z., and Cheng, X. (2021). A privacy-preserving federated learning for multiparty data sharing in social IoTs. *IEEE Transactions on Network Science and Engineering*, *8*(3), 2706–2718.

[26] R. Yu and P. Li, (2021). Toward resource-efficient federated learning in mobile edge computing. *IEEE Network*, *35*(1), 148–155.

[27] Al-Huthaifi, R., Li, T., Huang, W., Gu, J., and Li, C. (2023). Federated learning in smart cities: Privacy and security survey. *Information Sciences*, *632*, 833–857.

[28] Maurya, J., and Prakash, S. (2023). Privacy preservation in federated learning, its attacks and defenses using SMC-GAN. In *2023 Third International Conference on Secure Cyber Computing and Communication (ICSCCC)*, pp. 55–60. IEEE.

[29] Nguyen, D. C., Ding, M., Pathirana, P. N., Seneviratne, A., Li, J., and Poor, H. V. (2021). Federated learning for internet of things: A comprehensive survey. *IEEE Communications Surveys and Tutorials*, *23*(3), 1622–1658.

Chapter 2
Energy-efficient federated learning algorithms

Amutha Prabakar Muniyandi[1], *Daniel Arockiam*[2], *Feslin Anish Mon*[3] *and N. Deepa*[4]

Abstract

Federated Learning (FL) has emerged as a transformative approach for decentralized machine learning techniques, enabling collaborative model training while preserving data privacy. However, the distributed nature of FL imposes significant energy demands, particularly in resource-constrained environments. This chapter provides cutting-edge advancements in energy-efficient FL algorithms, focusing on methods that minimize computational and communication overhead without compromising model performance. It discusses key energy-intensive components in FL, including data transmission, local computation, and global aggregation, and investigates strategies such as model compression, sparse updates, adaptive aggregation, and client selection based on energy profiles. Additionally, it explores emerging techniques like quantized updates and knowledge distillation to optimize energy consumption. The chapter also highlights real-world applications and presents case studies that showcase trade-offs between energy efficiency, accuracy, and latency. Overall, it serves as a valuable resource for researchers aiming to enhance the sustainability of decentralized AI systems through a comprehensive overview of energy-efficient FL techniques.

Keywords: Federated learning; Energy efficiency; Decentralized AI; Model compression; Sustainable machine learning

2.1 Introduction to federated learning in IoT

The Internet of Things (IoT) connects various electronic devices for collecting information and automates across various applications. Federated learning (FL) provides an excellent solution to leverage this decentralized information while

[1]Department of Computer Engineering, Government Polytechnic College, Madurai, India
[2]Department of Computer Science and Engineering, Amity School of Engineering and Technology, Amity University Madhya Pradesh, India
[3]Department of Information Technology, University of Technology and Applied Sciences, Sultanate of Oman
[4]Department of Networking and Communications School of Computing, SRM Institute of Science and Technology, India

preserving privacy. Federate learning trains the models locally over connected devices and shares only the updates with a central server. The convergence of FL and IoT addresses key challenges across various applications, like healthcare, industrial automation, environmental monitoring, and other interactive applications. This learning environment enables intelligent, decentralized systems that respect user privacy and optimize resource usage.

2.1.1 Introduction to federated learning

Federate learning is a decentralized machine learning technique, where multiple IoT devices collaboratively train the model by keeping collected information locally. FL models process the collected information locally and only share model outputs with the centralized data server, instead of sending raw data to a central server. These decentralized models enhance data privacy and security and reduce unnecessary data transfer, and these models are particularly useful in environments like IoT, where data is distributed across numerous devices with limited energy and computational resources. The IoT encompasses a vast network of interconnected devices, sensors, and systems that collect, exchange, and act on data to enhance various aspects of our lives. From smart homes and wearable health monitors to industrial automation and smart cities, IoT has become integral to modern technology landscapes. However, the rapid proliferation of IoT devices brings significant energy challenges that must be addressed to ensure sustainable growth and efficiency.

2.1.1.1 Energy constraints in IoT environment

IoT devices are designed with energy-constrained models, and these devices face a lot of challenges, which cover battery life span, energy-starving communication, computational constraints, scalability, and environmental impacts. Many IoT devices are designed with inbuilt batteries, and this will be rechargeable. The battery replacement is impractical for the devices deployed in remote monitoring systems. Maximizing and extending battery life is critical for maintaining continuous operation, and reducing maintenance costs is a challenging task in an IoT environment. Wireless communication offers a common platform for transmitting data to central servers or cloud service providers for IoT devices. These communications need substantial energy for establishing constant data updates or real-time monitoring. The IoT devices are designed with limited processing power and memory. This design constraint creates challenges to performing complex computational tasks locally. The sheer number of interconnected devices in large-scale IoT environments impairs energy consumption issues. Efficiently managing and coordinating energy usage across these devices is an essential task for scalable IoT solutions. Carbon footprint and electronic wastes are increased due to limited and challenges in energy consumption of IoT systems. Addressing these energy challenges is essential for designing and deploying effective IoT systems. Solutions such as energy-efficient communication protocols, low-energy hardware design, and innovative data processing techniques are essential parts of ensuring the longevity, extension, and sustainability of IoT ecosystems.

2.1.1.2 Importance of energy efficiency in IoT environment

Energy efficiency is paramount in IoT ecosystems due to the inherent limitations of IoT devices and the expansive scale at which they operate. Most IoT devices, such as sensors, wearables, and smart home gadgets, rely on batteries or limited power sources. Efficient energy use extends their operational lifespan, reducing the need for frequent recharging or battery replacement, which is crucial for maintaining continuous service and reducing maintenance costs.

In large-scale deployments, such as smart cities, industrial automation, and environmental monitoring, the number of IoT devices can reach into the millions. Inefficient energy usage in such scenarios not only leads to increased operational costs but also poses significant environmental impacts due to higher energy consumption and frequent battery disposal.

Furthermore, energy efficiency directly affects the performance and reliability of IoT networks. Devices that conserve energy can operate longer and provide more consistent data streams, enhancing the overall reliability of the system. Efficient energy management also enables IoT devices to perform more complex tasks and support advanced functionalities like real-time data processing and machine learning, even with constrained resources.

Achieving energy efficiency in IoT also aligns with global sustainability goals. Reducing energy consumption and waste supports efforts to mitigate climate change and promotes the development of green technologies. Thus, energy efficiency is not just a technical necessity but also a strategic and environmental imperative in the advancement of IoT ecosystems [1,2].

2.2 Energy-efficient federated learning algorithms

2.2.1 Model compression techniques

Model compression techniques support for installing machine learning models over resource-constrained IoT devices. These techniques aim to reduce the energy, size, and computational overheads of models without expressively overall performance of energy energy-constrained environment. This section discusses the important model compression techniques.

2.2.2 Pruning-based model compression techniques in federated learning

Pruning-based model compression techniques are suitable in FL for improving energy efficiency, particularly for IoT environments with resource-constrained devices. These techniques are used to reduce the energy, size, and complexity of machine learning models for filtering less weighted parameters. This process will minimize the computational and communication overheads.

Model pruning technique involves the process of systematic elimination of unnecessary weights, nodes, or processing layers in a neural network structure to generate a more efficient and compact model. The main aim of this model is to maintain or slightly decrease the accuracy by significantly reducing the requirements of model size and computational overheads. The model pruning methods are classified into three types of pruning methods, weight pruning, layer pruning, and dynamic pruning approach.

The working principle of the model pruning technique is to remove unwanted weights from the processing networks. The main focus is to understand the important attributes to be considered for developing a suitable model. A typical approach is to identify and measure the impact of loss function for each weight value. This process can be done easily by adapting gradients that approximate the loss variation by varying the weight values. Yann LeCun creates a classic method for computing the second-order derivative for improved results.

Weighted pruning method is classified into two types: unstructured pruning and structured pruning models. The unstructured pruning technique removes individual weights in the neural model that have a small amount of impact on the model's output. The most forthright approach is magnitude-based pruning is used to remove weight value below a specified threshold level. The structured pruning approach filters entire structures rather than individual weights, which include neurons, filters, or channels. Structured pruning technique is a hardware-based method, and this leads to a more substantial reduction in computational overheads.

Layer-specific pruning technique uses a pruning process for all the layers of the neural network. This method removes less certain layers to improve the performance, and this can be safely reduced in size. Adaptive pruning method adjusts the filtering process dynamically during the training process based on the current level of performance and available resources [3]. This technique uses adaptive requirements and conditions for setting up the federated learning environment. The generalized pruning approach for model improvement is shown in Figure 2.1.

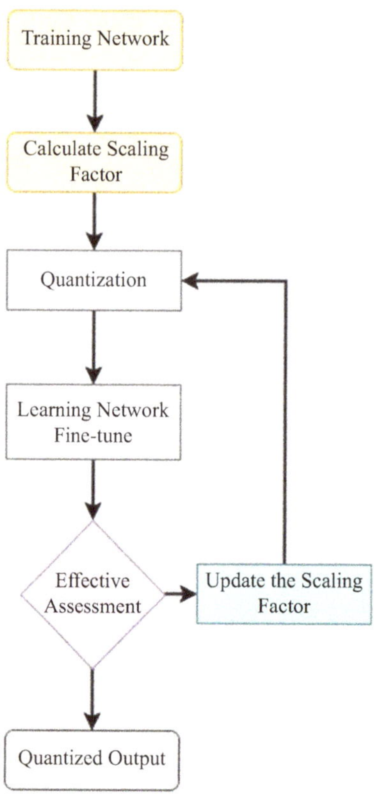

Figure 2.1 Flowchart for model pruning technique

Pruning-based model compression techniques are used to improve and achieve efficiency in the utilization of energy in federated learning for IoT environments [4]. These techniques help to conserve computational and communication resources by using federated learning more viable and sustainable in resource-constrained settings. Implementing effective pruning strategies needs careful thought of accuracy, device heterogeneity, and communication overhead.

2.3 Efficient gradient descent techniques for energy-efficient federated learning

Energy efficiency is a unique critical issue faced by FL techniques compared to traditional centralized machine learning techniques. Gradient descent is an efficient optimization method used in machine learning to adapt to meet the constraints of a distributed IoT environment. This section discusses the detailed view of efficient gradient descent techniques customized for energy-efficient federated learning:

2.3.1 Sparse gradient descent technique

Sparse gradient descent technique [5] provides a solution for addressing these challenges by reducing the size of data that needs to be communicated and processed. This section discusses the working principle of the SGD technique.

Working principle of SGD

Step 1. Select the most significant gradients for conducting global model updates. This will reduce the unwanted communication overheads.

Step 2. The selection process sparse updates can be done in two ways as follows:
- (a) Thresholding technique: Apply threshold gradient for selecting suitable gradients.
- (b) Top-K selection: The client IoT devices select the top *k* number of largest value gradients.

Step 3. The selected sparse updates are compressed for transmission and this compression process can be done by using quantization and encoding techniques.

Step 4. The central server aggregates the sparse updates by using an efficient sparse data structure.

Step 5. The sparse computation for both client and server can be done by using minimum updates, and this will reduce the computational overheads.

The sparse gradient descent technique achieves efficiency through reduced communication cost, energy efficiency, and scalability. The amount of data transmission between the client and the central server is reducing the maximum amount by transmitting only a significant number of gradients. This significant sparse selection leads to lower bandwidth usage. The energy consumption is reduced for both the client and central server by reducing the communication and computational overheads. The federated learning system can be scaled to a larger size of clients with increasing the network or central server overloads by reducing the communication overheads (Figure 2.2).

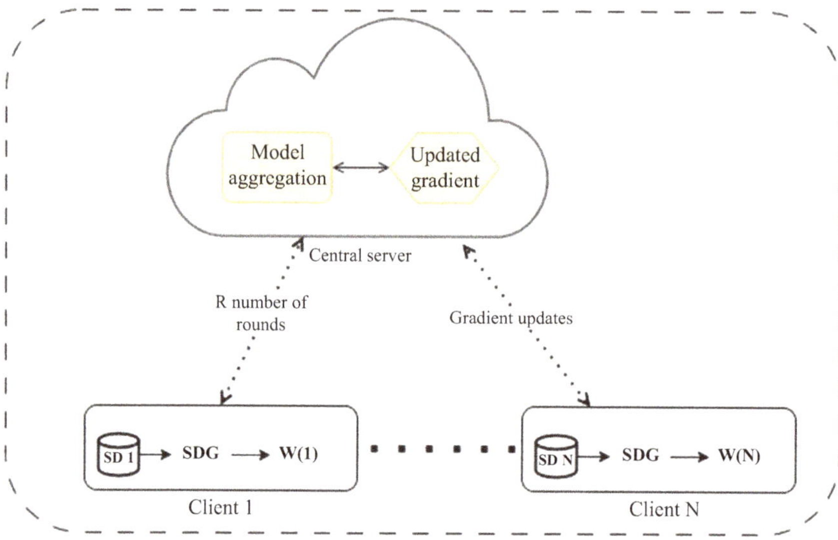

Figure 2.2 Sparse gradient descent-federated learning technique

The sparse gradient descent technique can be implemented with the following conditions: select sparsity level, handle sparse data, and model convergence. The sparsity level must be selected to balance between communication efficiency and model performance. The sparse data can be efficiently maintained by using suitable data structures and algorithms to ensure high efficiency in processing sparse data. The convergence of the model may be slowed down by sparse updates. This issue can be mitigated by using periodic full updates or adaptive sparsity techniques.

Sparse gradient descent is an efficient technique to enhance the efficiency of federate learning by reducing the communication and computational overheads. This technique achieves energy efficiency without compromising the performance of the model by focusing on the most significant updates, and it is more suitable for deployment in resource-constrained environments.

2.3.2 Quantized gradient descent technique

Quantized gradient descent (QGD) is a technique designed to improve the efficiency of gradient descent methods, exclusively for federated learning techniques. Federated learning is a machine learning technique where multiple clients collaboratively train a model by keeping the training data decentralized. Each client device computes updates to the model based on available local data and these updates are then aggregated to form a global model [6].

The QGD technique reduces the communication cost and computational overheads associated with transmitting gradients between client devices and the central server. The following section explains how QGD works and its application in energy-efficient federated learning. The QGD has two important key concepts: gradient descent and quantization. The gradient descent is an optimization algorithm used to minimize the loss function for model design by iteratively improving parameters. The quantization involved to reduce the precision of the gradients. The client device sends lower precision instead of sending full precision floating point gradients.

Procedure for quantized gradient descent technique

Step 1. Each client device computes the gradient value of the loss function based on the model attributes from the available local data.

Step 2. The computed gradients are quantized to reduce their size by using quantization techniques as follows:

(a) Uniform quantization: Each gradient values are mapped to a discrete set of values.

(b) Stochastic quantization: Gradient values are stochastically balanced with the nearest quantized level based on their proximity.

Step 3. The quantized gradients are transmitted from the clients to the central server, and this reduced size minimizes the communication overhead significantly.

Step 4. The central server receives the quantized gradients from the participating clients and aggregates them to update the global model.

Step 5. The central server may apply de-quantized aggregated gradients to restore them to higher precision for the updated model.

Step 6. The central server receives all the quantized gradients from all client devices and combines them to compute updates for the global model. The aggregation techniques can handle the precision loss used by quantization.

Step 7. The centralized server may apply a de-quantization approach to aggregated gradients to restore them to higher precision for updating the model.

Step 8. The global model is updated using the aggregated gradients, and this updated model has been sent back to the client devices for the next iteration.

QGD technique is used to reduce the communication overheads significantly by sending minimum precision gradients. The selection of lower precision gradients leads to faster communication and lower bandwidth usage. The energy consumption rate of a client device is reduced by reducing the communication load, and this will be beneficial for energy-constrained mobile or edge devices. The QGD technique enables federated learning to support for large number of client devices without increasing the communication network. The QGD technique is particularly useful for mobile and edge computing applications, IoT networks, and privacy-preserved learning applications. QGD is an efficient technique for enhancing the robustness, efficiency, and scalability of FL.

2.3.3 Federated averaging technique for energy-efficient FL

Federated averaging (FedAvg) is an essential technique of federated learning and this technique is designed to optimize the collective training outputs of machine learning models across multiple decentralized devices. This section provides a detailed explanation of the FedAvg technique. This method improves privacy and minimizes the requirement for large-scale data transfer to a central server [7,8].

FedAvg is a specific algorithm for federated learning, introduced by McMahan *et al.* [9]. This technique combines local stochastic gradient descent (SGD) on each client device with periodic model averaging on a central server.

Procedure for FedAvg technique

Step 1. The centralized server initializes the global model attributes, and these attributes are shared with all the clients.
Step 2. Each client receives the global model and trains it with local data through several iterations.
Step 3. Client devices perform local updates by using SGD or some other optimization technique to reduce the local loss function.
Step 4. Model update has been performed by combining each client update with local training by the central server.
Step 5. The central server aggregates the received model attributes from all the participating clients.
Step 6. The aggregation is done by using the weighted average method of the client updates, and these weights are proportional to the number of local training samples.
Step 7. The model weight is computed as follows:

$$W = \sum_{i=1}^{K} \frac{n_{C_i}}{N} . w_i$$

Here, C_i and n_{C_i} represents i^{th} client and the number of samples on the client. The model weight is represented as w_i for each client C_i. The total number of samples across all the clients (N) is computed as follows:

$$N = \sum_{i=1}^{K} n_i$$

Here, K indicates the number of clients.

Step 8. The updated global model has been shared back to the clients. Steps 1–7 are repeated for a maximum number of iterations or until reaching efficient convergence.

The FedAvg technique is a more energy-efficient approach compared to traditional centralized machine learning training techniques. This energy efficiency can be achieved by reducing data transfer, localized computation, communication frequency, adaptive participation, and model compression. The FedAvg technique communicates only mode parameters between client devices and the server and this will significantly reduce the bandwidth and energy.

The training process occurs on the client device using local data with distributed computational load. This decentralization approach evades the high energy consumption associated with a centralized approach.

FedAvg technique uses periodic communication with the central server for sharing the model updates. This periodic communication reduces the number of communication iterations, and this leads to minimum energy usage in network transmissions. FedAvg technique uses an adaptive participation approach with a subset of clients to reduce energy consumption by limiting the number of active devices in each round. This approach further enhances energy efficiency.

FedAvg technique is particularly suitable for scenarios to achieve data privacy and energy efficiency. Mobile edge computing applications are designed with the collaboration of smartphones, IoT devices, and wearable sensor devices. These applications are suitable for health monitoring, privacy-preserved learning, and personalized recommendations without sharing data. An advanced industrial IoT environment is designed with distributed sensors and devices for improving predictive maintenance and operational efficiency by using federated learning. Smart healthcare systems are designed to achieve train models on patient-related data without compromising privacy, enhancing diagnostic, and treatment capabilities.

FedAvg is an efficient technique in federated learning that balances local computation cost and global communication overheads to achieve energy-efficient, privacy-preserving collaborative model training. Its design principles make it highly suitable for diverse applications in distributed systems where data privacy and energy efficiency are key concerns.

2.3.4 Decentralized gradient descent technique

Traditional FL methods designed with a central server to aggregate updates come from clients, and this can introduce challenges such as a single point of failure, high communication costs, and privacy concerns. The decentralized gradient descent (DGD) technique provides a solution for these issues by eliminating the need for a central server and allows clients to communicate directly with each other.

In DGD, client devices perform local computations and share information with their neighbor devices in a network. Each client upholds its own set of model parameters and updates them based on both local data and information received from neighbor devices. This approach uses the collective computation power and data of all clients to reduce the dependency on a central server.

Working principle of DGD technique

1. Each client device initializes its own model attributes independently or common initial model.
2. Each client computes the gradient of the loss function based on its local data. The local gradient indicates, how the model parameters should be adjusted to reduce the loss.
3. The client devices exchange model attributes with their immediate neighbors in the same network. The exchanging of attributes can be done by synchronous or asynchronous.
4. Each client aggregates this information with its local gradient for the received updates from the nearest devices. This combination can be done by using simple averaging or weighted averaging.
5. Each client updates its model parameters based on the aggregated data and the update rule typically applies the following gradient descent step:

$$\gamma_{C_i}^{(t+1)} = \gamma_{C_i}^{(t)} - \alpha \nabla L_{C_i}\left(\gamma_{C_i}^{(t)}\right) + \alpha \sum_{j=1}^{N_{C_i}} \left(\gamma_{C_j}^{(t)} - \gamma_{C_i}^{(t)}\right)$$

   Here, $\gamma_{C_i}^{(t)}$ are the parameters of client C_i at the iteration t, α is the learning rate, $\nabla L_{C_i}\left(\gamma_{C_i}^{(t)}\right)$ is a local gradient, N_{C_i} is the number of neighbor devices to C_i, and $\gamma_{C_j}^{(t)} - \gamma_{C_i}^{(t)}$ represents the difference in the parameters with client C_i and its neighbor devices.
6. Steps 2–5 are repeated until the model parameters converge to a satisfactory level or maximum number of iterations.

The DGD is a more energy-efficient technique than centralized FL for several reasons. DGD reduces the communication overhead and energy consumption compared to centralized FL by minimizing the sending of updates to a central point. The local aggregation ensures energy efficiency due to aggregation updates done locally with neighbor devices. DGD allows for parallel processing across multiple clients, and this process increases the speed of training updates and reduces overall energy consumption. DGD techniques are adapting the communication frequency and topological-based network conditions for optimizing the energy usage.

DGD technique is facing the following challenges, and these issues need to be addressed to ensure energy efficiency, The selection of network topology significantly impacts the convergence rate and communication efficiency. The asynchronous network communication can lead to delays and mustiness in updates and this process directly affects the convergence and accuracy of the model. Ensuring scalability in the IoT environment by maintaining efficiency and adapted convergence is a challenging task for large size of networks with many clients. Handing client failures and ensuring the robustness of the learning process needs careful design due to the absence of a central server. The DGD technique offers a promising approach for energy-efficient FL by applying local computations and local device communications. Designing an efficient DGD algorithm requires careful consideration of network topology, communication policies, and fault tolerance mechanisms.

2.3.5 Gradient accumulation technique

Gradient accumulation is an efficient approach designed to improve the robustness and performance of training deep learning models and is more suitable for distributed settings like federated learning. Gradient accumulation is a technique where gradients are computed and accumulated over multiple mini-iterations for updating the model attributes. The gradient accumulation is useful in federated learning due to the following reasons, memory, communication, and computational efficiency. This technique achieves memory efficiency by reducing the memory footprints compared to large-size batches by accumulating gradients over several smaller batches. The frequent communication between clients and the central server increases the energy utilization and bandwidth usage in federated learning.

The gradient accumulation technique reduces the number of updates sent to the server by combining multiple gradients into a single update. Frequent computations with smaller size of batches are more efficient for resource-constrained devices than processing larger size batches. The following procedure explains the working principle of the gradient accumulation technique.

Working procedure of gradient accumulation technique

1. Each client device trains the model updates on its local data.
2. The gradients are computed and accumulated from multiple mini-batches, instead of updating each small batch.
3. The accumulated gradient is computed efficiently through an average of the gradient collected from the processed mini-batches.
4. The accumulated gradient has been sent to the central server by the accumulating Step 3. The central server aggregates the updates from all the clients to enhance the global model.

Gradient accumulation achieves energy efficiency in federated learning techniques through reduced communication overheads, efficient use of computational resources, and a balanced workload. The energy consumption is achieved for transmitting data between clients and the central server by reducing the sending of updates. This is an essential benefit for devices with limited energy life. Accumulating gradients allows IoT devices to perform more efficient computations by reducing idle times and making use of available resources. The accumulated gradient helps to balance the computational cost across devices and prevent device bottleneck issues from limited computational power. This balanced approach ensures that all devices are participating effectively.

The gradient accumulation is an efficient technique to improve the efficiency of federated learning through reduced energy consumption and communication overheads. The participating IoT devices reduce the frequency of updates sent to the server by applying accumulated gradient calculations from multiple small batches. The process of training is more efficient and sustainable.

2.4 Performance evaluation of energy-efficient techniques in federated learning

Performance evaluation for the energy-efficient techniques in FL is conducted for analyzing, based on energy consumption, model accuracy, communication overhead, and convergence time. This section discusses these metrics and provides a detailed view to illustrate the performance of different energy-efficient techniques. This evaluation is conducted for sparse models, quantization models, gradient sparsification, FedAvg, and adaptive gradient methods.

2.4.1 Energy consumption rate

The energy consumption is measured through the total energy used for IoT devices based on FL techniques. The model accuracy is calculated based on the global model accuracy from aggregated local updates. The amount of data sharing and exchange between devices and central server is measured for communication overheads. The time taken to achieve a predefined accuracy threshold for the global model is known as convergence time. The average energy consumption of different

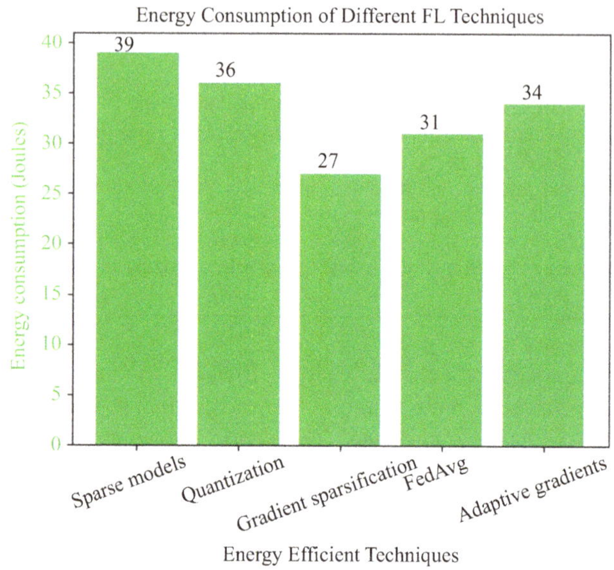

Figure 2.3 Evaluation of energy consumption of federated learning techniques

techniques during the training process is computed for a standard set of IoT devices. The evaluation of energy consumption is shown in Figure 2.3.

2.4.2 Model accuracy

The model accuracy is measured based on the incorporated energy efficiency aspect. The main focus is to balance the trade-off between model accuracy and energy consumption by ensuring the effectiveness and sustainability of the learning process. The following equation is used to measure the energy efficiency adjusted factor for model accuracy:

$$M_{\text{Accuracy}} = \text{Accuracy}_{\text{FM}} - \mu . \frac{E_{\text{Total}}}{E_{\text{Max}}}$$

Here, $\text{Accuracy}_{\text{FM}}$ is a final model accuracy of the FL training process, and E_{Total} is the total energy consumption during the federated learning process. The maximum energy consumption of training FL technique is mentioned as E_{Max}, and the scaling factor to normalize the energy consumption impact is defined as a constant factor value as μ. The above equation is used to evaluate the effectiveness of the FL process based on excessive energy consumption while achieving higher model accuracy. $\text{Accuracy}_{\text{FM}}$ of the global model obtained from the federated learning process and the high accuracy shows the better model performance. The total energy used by all participating devices in the FL process E_{Total}. The

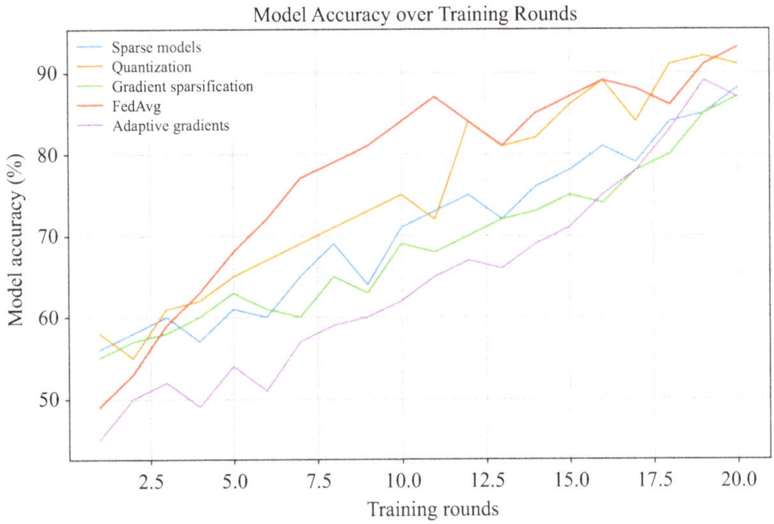

Figure 2.4 Model accuracy with different sizes of rounds

lower energy consumption indicates excellent energy efficiency. The constant factor μ is balanced by the importance of energy consumption relative to accuracy it can be adjusted based on the requirements. The normalization factor representing the maximum allowable consumption as E_{Max} to ensure the energy penalty is proportional to the maximum expected energy usage.

Figure 2.4 shows the model energy consumption is measured for sparse models, quantization models, gradient sparsification, FedAvg, and adaptive gradient methods. According to the evaluation, FedAvg and adaptive gradient technique achieve high model accuracy with minimum energy consumption. The model accuracy is systematically evaluating and optimizing the federated learning training process for energy-constrained IoT environments.

2.4.3 Communication overhead

The communication overhead is an important metric for energy consumption in federated learning. This metric will measure the amount of data shared and exchanged between IoT devices and the central server during the training process. The communication overhead can be measured to understand its influence on energy consumption. The following equation is used to measure the communication overhead:

$$\text{Communication}_{\text{Overhead}} = N_C \times U_R \times \left(M_{\text{Up}} + M_{\text{Down}}\right)$$

Here, the number of client devices is represented as N_C, and U_R denotes the number of communication rounds. The number of model updates from each client uploaded and downloaded is defined as M_{Up} and M_{Down}, respectively. Figure 2.5

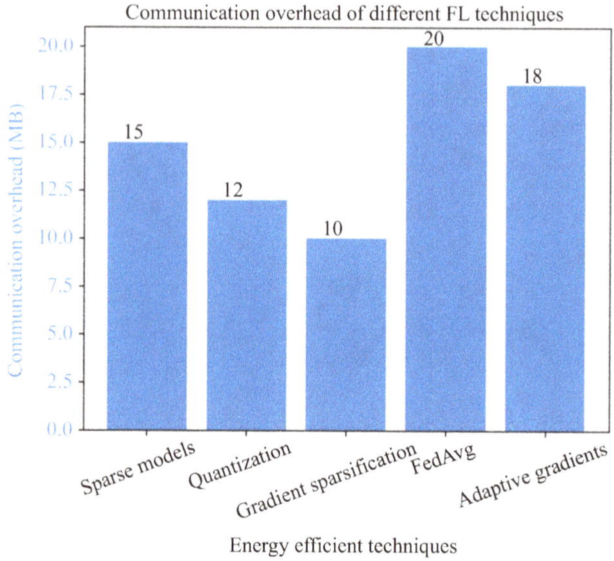

Figure 2.5 Communication overhead for federated learning algorithms

shows the evaluation result of communication overhead, and this measurement is taken from varying the number of IoT devices and the number of rounds used in each device.

2.4.4 Convergence time

Convergence time in FL techniques refers to the total number of communication rounds required for achieving global model-specific accuracy. The convergence time can be computed by using the following equation for energy-efficient FL techniques, and this can be measured based on the following factors such as local updates, communication rounds, and energy constraints of the devices.

$$T_{\text{Convg}} = F\left(\frac{T_N}{T_K.B_{\text{Size}}}, \quad T_E, \mu, \tau\right)$$

Here $F(.)$ is a function that models the relationship between the related parameters. T_N denotes the total number of data samples across all the devices. T_K and B_{Size} are the total number of participating devices and batch size of the sample, respectively. T_E is the total number of epochs per round, and the desired accurate threshold value is represented as τ. μ is the learning rate for achieving the accuracy by assigning optimal value. Figure 2.6 shows the convergence time evaluation for energy-efficient federated learning techniques.

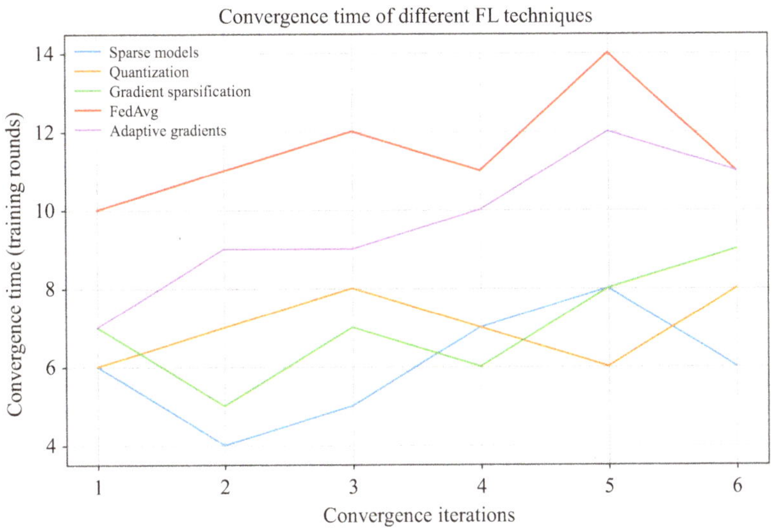

Figure 2.6 Evaluation of convergence time for federated learning techniques

References

[1] Albelaihi R, Yu LK, Craft WD, *et al.* 2022. Green federated learning via energy-aware client selection. *Proc IEEE Global Communications Conf*, pp. 13–18. https://doi.org/ 10.1109/GLOBECOM48099.2022.10001569.

[2] Battiloro C, di Lorenzo P, Merluzzi M, *et al.* 2023. Lyapunov-based optimization of edge resources for energy-efficient adaptive federated learning. *IEEE Trans Green Commun Netw*, 7(1):265–280. https://doi.org/10.1109/TGCN.2022.3186879.

[3] Abdelmoniem AM and Canini M. 2021. Towards mitigating device heterogeneity in federated learning via adaptive model quantization. *Proc 1st Workshop on Machine Learning and Systems*, pp. 96–103. https://doi.org/10.1145/3437984.3458839.

[4] Arouj A and Abdelmoniem AM. 2022. Towards energy-aware federated learning on battery-powered clients. *Proc 1st ACM Workshop on Data Privacy and Federated Learning Technologies for Mobile Edge Network*, pp. 7–12. https://doi.org/10.1145/3556557.3557952.

[5] Abdelmoniem AM, Ho C-Y, Papageorgiou P and Canini M. 2023. A comprehensive empirical study of heterogeneity in federated learning. *IEEE Int Things J*, 10(16):14071–14083. https://doi.org/10.1109/JIOT.2023.3250275.

[6] Abe Y, Sasaki H, Kato S, *et al.* 2014. Power and performance characterization and modeling of GPU-accelerated systems. *Proc 28th Int Parallel and Distributed Processing Symp*, pp. 113–122. https://doi.org/10.1109/IPDPS.2014.23.

[7] Al-Abiad MS, Obeed M, Hossain J, *et al.* 2022. Decentralized aggregation for energy-efficient federated learning via overlapped clustering and D2D communications. https://arxiv.org/abs/2206.02981.

[8] Albaseer A, Abdallah M, Al-Fuqaha A, *et al.* 2021. Threshold-based data exclusion approach for energy-efficient federated edge learning. *Proc IEEE Int Conf on Communications Workshops*, pp. 1–6. https://doi.org/ 10.1109/ICCWorkshops50388.2021.9473806.

[9] McMahan B, Moore E, Ramage D, Hampson S, and Arcas BA. Communication-efficient learning of deep networks from decentralized data. In: *Artificial Intelligence and Statistics*, PMLR, 2017, pp. 1273–1282.

Chapter 3

Federated learning frameworks and algorithms for energy-efficient IoT

Kiran Malik[1], *Kuldeep Singh Kaswan*[2], *Jagjit Singh Dhatterwal*[3] *and Rajani*[4]

Abstract

The advancements of IoT systems have brought forth higher rates of connection and innovative uses of data in several industries. Nevertheless, the growth of IoT generates new issues of energy efficiency as the simple quantity of devices increases and centralized approaches to data processing fail to provide efficient solutions for dealing with the data volumes. FL on IoT becomes a revolutionary approach to address the aforementioned challenges named as federated learning that enables the numerous IoT devices to cooperate in training a model without exchanging the raw data and thus cuts the communication overhead and energy consumption. This chapter focuses on combining FL with standards-based energy-saving IoT frameworks and discusses the fundamentals of energy control, FL architecture, and the significance of FL in managing power consumption with minimal impact on system performance.

In this chapter, the concept of FL is introduced first along with how it can be applied to IoT systems, and then the chapter focuses on the energy-efficient FL algorithms in detail. It covers various issues related to FL in IoT applications, such as resource management, security and privacy, scalability, and latency when using FL in IoT, and presents some possible solutions based on case studies and enhanced optimization methods. It also showcases the practical aspects such as smart homes, industrial IoT, and healthcare where the FL frameworks have proven their worth in terms of energy efficiency. With reference to the discussed key performance indicators and assessment techniques, the chapter provides a thought-provoking

[1]Department of Computer Science and Engineering (AIML), GL Bajaj Institute of Technology and Management, India
[2]School of Computer Science and Engineering, Galgotias University, India
[3]Department of Artificial Intelligence and Data Science, Koneru Lakshmaiah Education Foundation, India
[4]Department of Computer Science, Kalinda College, University of Delhi, India

analysis of the future trends in FL for energy-efficient IoT to identify the directions for innovations in this domain.

Keywords: Federated learning; Power management techniques; Energy-efficient IoT; Industrial IoT; Healthcare IoT systems

3.1 Introduction

The increased uptake of IoT systems across various industry segments has led to exponential connectivity of numerous devices thereby increasing power consumption. Resource-scarce IoT systems have emerged as a new discipline since power control is another significant focal point when it comes to IoT networks. These systems are developed specifically in terms of optimized hardware, power-efficient protocols, and superior power-saving mechanisms in order to reduce energy consumption as much as possible but without loss in performance. Energy control is crucial in IoT concerning applications mentioned above, like environment surveillance, homes, and industrial IoT where the number of devices can be massive and where IoT devices are required to run independently for a long time [1].

The use of batteries in IoT devices impacts the environment due to energy consumption, and the overall cost of implementing IoT solutions on a large scale poses significant challenges. Lower utilization of power thus enhances the lifespan of the IoT devices and lowers battery replacement and costs of operations. Moreover, the transition to green and sustainable technology calls for the optimization of energy consumption through smart IoT platforms. Pervasive centralized data processing in IoT has also proved to be very energy intensive as compared to IoT networks due to the high volume of data that is transmitted between IoT devices and cloud servers.

This has led to the discovery of federated learning (FL) as a potential solution to enhance energy efficiency in IoT systems. In FL, the model training is done locally at each IoT device hence there is limited data that needs to be transmitted so consuming less energy in communication and data processing. FL makes sure that the raw data will only reside in local devices and the updating model will be shared, which greatly improves the privacy and conserves energy in large-scale IoT networks [2]. This chapter examines how FL can help in managing challenges related to energy efficiency in the context of IoT systems.

3.2 Foundations of federated learning

FL has become one of the most effective means of performing model training in distributed systems such as the IoT. This section discusses fundamental ideas of FL, its structure, advantages when used in IoT, and issues that emerged in its application in IoT contexts.

3.2.1 Federated learning

Federated learning is described as a multidevice, edge-node learning technique in which a common model is learned through local computation and data privacy without sending data to a central server. In contrast to centralized learning where raw data is sent to a central server for training, FL lets each device train a local model and send only the model updates (gradients) to the central server. These updates are then combined by the server to enhance the global model and the server later presents it to numerous other devices.

This method enhances data privacy since no raw data is exported from the devices, which can be appropriate in constraining domains like healthcare and finance. Furthermore, FL minimizes the amount of information transferred over the networks which cuts on bandwidth utilization and enhances scalability. In FL, the data is not transferred to a central server; instead, only model parameters are transmitted, which facilitates data security and privacy [3].

Now let us look at FL's key parts where data remains decentralized where the data remains in devices, training where each device trains the model on data collected and then sends the updates to the server, aggregation where the server collects the updates and then refines them to the global model and finally the communication efficiency where instead of exchanging large sets of data over the networks, FL sends updates. These characteristics make FL an interesting choice for energy-efficient IoT systems as it supports big-size model updates without being a threat to data privacy or network congestion.

3.2.2 Architecture of federated learning systems

The architecture of FL systems allows for distributed learning between all the different devices, including IoT sensors, mobile phones, and edge devices. Regarding FL systems, the latter consists of the master server and several clients where the master server handles the training process while clients train local models on their respective data. These devices then transmit blocks of model updates (e.g., gradients or weights) to the server which in turn aggregates these updates to form a new global model. These are the parts of the coordination of the server, communication interfaces, and procedures and of the mechanisms for model fusion and synchronization. These components assist in guaranteeing that practicable distributed FL denotes can run in the arrangement of devices with disparate calculating strength and information transfer speed [4].

3.2.3 Benefits of federated learning for IoT

This type of learning called FL has several benefits to IoT systems but more particularly on privacy and efficiency. This has been noted to be one of the main advantages of using this type of cloud storage, particularly in a learning institution. In the IoT context, objects such as sensors and smart appliances generate big volumes of sensitive information, particularly in sectors such as healthcare and smart cities. By adopting FL, device models are created to enable aggregating and processing of private data locally within the device to reduce the threats of data leakage and to meet data protection laws [5].

Other advantages include minimizing network bandwidth as well as energy consumption. Many previous categories of machine learning used for decision-making are receptive to massive data inputs transferred to central host servers, thus exerting pressure on a network. In FL, only updates in models are shared hence the communication overhead is considerably minimized. This is more notable in IoT systems where the devices involved have restricted computational capabilities and power sources such as batteries. By reducing the number of data transfers and the amount of data that are transmitted, FL enables the devices of IoT to last longer hence making it more viable [3]. Besides, FL strengthens systems' reliability as the learning process is distributed rather than concentrating on a single point as it is in centralized systems [4].

3.2.4 Challenges in implementing federated learning in IoT

However, several issues make it difficult to adopt federated learning in IoT settings despite the advantages it offers. A major issue is the diversity of devices that people use in daily routines, including stationary and portable computers, laptops, and smartphones. Furthermore, IoT devices come in different sizes and capabilities; with differences in processing power, memory, and battery. There is also the issue of heterogeneity where some of the devices may lack the capability to handle the resource demands that come with model training and hence inconsistent model updates that affect the performance of the system. Due to such a gap, the need for new FL algorithms that will work with devices of different capabilities arises [6].

Another issue is high communication latency and limited bandwidth, which is characteristic of IoT networks. While FL decreases the volume of data transfer, the continuous exchange of model updates between devices and the central server can be slow in terms of bandwidth in a specific network. There is a need to develop proper interaction mechanisms that will reduce delay but at the same time increase coordination among the devices [4]. However, adversarial attacks and model poisoning are still potential threats. Precisely on this account, FL is sensitive to adversarial attacks since the attacker can taint the updates sent by the different decentralized devices and, thus, degrade the model performance or make it fail in critical IoT applications [7].

In conclusion, federated learning is a comprehensive solution to decentralized model training that offers numerous benefits for IoT devices in terms of privacy and efficiency in terms of energy consumption and bandwidth requirements. Nonetheless, there exist some challenges including device heterogeneity, communication delays, and security aspects that must be solved for FL to be effective in energy-efficient IoT networks.

3.3 Energy-efficient IoT frameworks

The management of energy is a major consideration in IoT systems since many of the devices are constrained with power and must operate in efficient as well as sustainable manners for extended periods. This section focuses on the fundamental concepts of energy efficiency in IoT and offers information about protocols, architecture, and techniques in making IoT devices power-efficient.

3.3.1 Key principles of energy efficiency in IoT

The primary criterion for energy efficiency in IoT is to minimize energy usage while maintaining the device's performance and communication connectivity. They involve reducing data transmissions, making the activity of sensors optimal, and conserving power even when not in use. IoT, which is power-aware, aims to optimize the trade-off between power consumption and the performance of a specific job; this is done by incorporating concepts such as scheduling, data reduction, and resource management. Another principle is adaptive resource management, which enables the optimization of IoT device consumption depending on the task at hand to prolong the device's lifespan in energy-restricted settings [8].

3.3.2 Overview of energy-efficient protocols and architectures

Several energy-efficient communication protocols and architectures have been developed to enhance the performance of IoT devices. Protocols such as Bluetooth Low Energy (BLE), Zigbee, and LoRaWAN are widely used in IoT networks for their ability to minimize energy consumption during data transmission. Additionally, lightweight protocols like MQTT and CoAP enable efficient data exchange between IoT devices and cloud servers, reducing energy costs. Architectures such as edge computing and fog computing also play a significant role in reducing latency and energy consumption by processing data closer to the devices rather than sending it to centralized cloud servers [9].

3.3.3 Energy consumption model for IoT devices

$$E_{\text{total}} = E_{\text{active}} + E_{\text{idle}}$$

where:

- E_{active} is the energy consumed during the active state.
- E_{idle} is the energy consumed during the idle state.

The energy consumption in the active state E_{active} is given by

$$E_{\text{active}} = P_{\text{active}} \times T_{\text{active}}$$

where:

- P_{active} is the power consumption during the active state.
- T_{active} is the duration of the active state.

Similarly, the energy consumption during the idle state E_{idle} is

$$E_{\text{idle}} = P_{\text{idle}} \times T_{\text{idle}}$$

where:

- P_{idle} is the power consumption during the idle state.
- T_{idle} is the duration of the idle state.

Thus, the total energy consumption becomes

$$E_{\text{total}} = (P_{\text{active}} \times T_{\text{active}}) + (P_{\text{idle}} \times T_{\text{idle}})$$

3.3.4 Duty cycle and energy efficiency

$$D = \frac{T_{\text{active}}}{T_{\text{active}} + T_{\text{idle}}}$$

The average power consumption P_{avg} over a full cycle (active + idle) is

$$P_{\text{avg}} = D \times P_{\text{active}} + (1 - D) \times P_{\text{idle}}$$

To optimize energy efficiency, the goal is to minimize P_{avg}. This leads to a fundamental energy efficiency metric:

$$\eta = \frac{\text{Useful Energy}}{\text{Total Energy Consumed}} = \frac{P_{\text{active}} \times T_{\text{active}}}{P_{\text{avg}} \times (T_{\text{active}} + T_{\text{idle}})}$$

3.3.5 Communication energy consumption

$$E_{\text{tx}} = L \times E_{\text{bit}} \times d^{\alpha}$$

where:

- E_{bit} is the energy consumed per bit.
- d is the transmission distance.
- α is the path-loss exponent (typically $2 \leq \alpha \leq 4$).

For receiving a packet of size L, the energy consumption E_{rx} is

$$E_{\text{rx}} = L \times P_{\text{rx}}$$

where P_{rx} is the power consumed during reception.

Thus, the total communication energy E_{comm} is

$$E_{\text{comm}} = E_{\text{tx}} + E_{\text{rx}} = L \times E_{\text{bit}} \times d^{\alpha} + L \times P_{\text{rx}}$$

3.3.6 Energy-efficient routing protocols

$$E_{\text{forward}} = P_{\text{tx}} \times T_{\text{tx}} + P_{\text{rx}} \times T_{\text{rx}}$$

where:

- P_{tx} and P_{rx} are the power consumption during transmission and reception.
- T_{tx} and T_{rx} are the transmission and reception times.

The total energy consumption for routing a packet from source to destination over N hops is

$$E_{\text{route}} = \sum_{i=1}^{N} \left(P_{\text{tx}}^{(i)} \times T_{\text{tx}}^{(i)} + P_{\text{rx}}^{(i)} \times T_{\text{rx}}^{(i)} \right)$$

3.3.7 Energy-efficient sleep/wake schedules

$$E_{\text{saving}} = E_{\text{idle}} - E_{\text{sleep}}$$

where:

- $E_{\text{sleep}} = P_{\text{sleep}} \times T_{\text{sleep}'}$ and P_{sleep} is the power consumption during sleep mode.

  The total energy consumption with sleep mode is then:

$$E_{\text{total sleep}} = (P_{\text{active}} \times T_{\text{active}}) + \left(P_{\text{sleep}} \times T_{\text{sleep}}\right)$$

3.3.8 Power management techniques in IoT devices

Proper power utilization strategies are crucial to enhance the life span of IoT devices, particularly, those deployed in difficult-to-reach areas. Power management techniques such as duty cycling which involves periodically powering on and off the device when not in use minimizes power consumption during the off periods. Moreover, IoT systems started using techniques like solar and kinetic energy to help in fulfilling the energy needs of a device. Some of these include dynamic voltage and frequency scaling (DVFS), where the operating frequency and voltage of a processor are adapted based on the load placed on the processor, and low-power wireless communication standards that enable less power to be used in data transfer [10].

Total energy consumption E_{total}:

$$E_{\text{total}} = \sum_{i=1}^{N} \left(P_{\text{tx}_i} \cdot T_{\text{tx}_i} + P_{\text{rx}_i} \cdot T_{\text{rx}_i} + P_{\text{comp}_i} \cdot T_{\text{comp}_i}\right) + \sum_{j=1}^{M} \left(P_{\text{idle}_j} \cdot T_{\text{idle}_j} + P_{\text{sleep}_j} \cdot T_{\text{sleep}_j}\right)$$

where:

- N is the total number of active communication tasks.
- M is the total number of idle or sleep states.

3.3.9 Terms

3.3.9.1 Communication energy

- P_{tx_i}: Power consumption during transmission for task i.
- T_{tx_i}: Transmission time for task i.
- P_{rx_i}: Power consumption during reception for task i.
- T_{rx_i}: Reception time for task i.

3.3.9.2 Computation energy

- P_{comp_i}: Power consumption during computation for task i.
- T_{comp_i}: Computation time for task i.

3.3.9.3 Idle and sleep energy

- P_{idle_j}: Power consumption during idle state for device j.
- T_{idle_j}: Time spent in idle state for device j.
- P_{sleep_j}: Power consumption during sleep state for device j.
- T_{sleep_j}: Time spent in sleep state for device j.

3.3.10 Case studies: energy-efficient IoT frameworks

The following are several real-world implementations of energy-efficient IoT frameworks that underscore the significance of these methods: For instance, smart agriculture systems employ IoT devices for soil conditions, water, and crop health, typically with limited energy consumption and leveraging energy-efficient protocols such as Zigbee for data transfer. Likewise, IoT-based sensors integrated into streetlights in smart cities apply power management strategies in regulating lighting intensity and duration depending on the conditions of darkness and traffic. These case investigations illustrate how effective IoT frameworks for energy optimization can be disseminated across different industries for sustainability enhancement and operational cost efficiency [11].

Cost- and power-aware IoT architectures are required for the stability and sustainability of connected systems, especially in areas where resources are scarce. The use of smart power management techniques, effective communication procedures, and intelligent architectures helps to maximize IoT's functionality while minimizing expenses and the usage of energy, making its applications economically and environmentally sound.

3.4 Federated learning algorithms for energy-efficient IoT

FL algorithms are oriented to allow model training across various devices without the need to collect centralized data. These algorithms are important to prevent issues of energy consumption in IoT systems since they work on principles of reducing computational and communication overheads.

$$\min_{\{w_i\}} E_{\text{total}} = \min_{\{w_i\}} \left(\sum_{i=1}^{N} \left(E^i_{\text{comm}} + E^i_{\text{comp}} \right) \right)$$

where:

- N is the total number of IoT devices.
- w_i represents the model parameters for the i-th device.

Communication energy E^i_{comm}:

The energy consumed by the i-th IoT device for communicating the model updates with the central server can be modeled as

$$E^i_{\text{comm}} = T^i_{\text{comm}} \cdot P^i_{\text{tx}}$$

where:

- T^i_{comm} is the transmission time for the i-th device to send its model update.
- P^i_{tx} is the transmission power of the i-th device.

The transmission time T^i_{comm} can be expressed as

$$T^i_{\text{comm}} = \frac{S}{B_i \cdot \log_2\left(1 + \frac{h_i P^i_{\text{tx}}}{N_0}\right)}$$

where:

- S is the size of the model update.
- B_i is the bandwidth allocated to the i-th device, N_0 is the noise power.
- h_i is the channel gain.

The complete optimization problem for minimizing energy consumption in federated learning over IoT devices is

$$\min_{\{w_i, B_i, P^i_{\text{tx}}, P^i_{\text{comp}}\}} \sum_{i=1}^{N} \left(\frac{S \cdot P^i_{\text{tx}}}{B_i \cdot \log_2\left(1 + \frac{h_i P^i_{\text{tx}}}{N_0}\right)} + \frac{D_i \cdot C_i \cdot P^i_{\text{comp}}}{f_i} \right)$$

subject to:

$$\frac{S}{B_i \cdot \log_2\left(1 + \frac{h_i P^i_{\text{tx}}}{N_0}\right)} + \frac{D_i \cdot C_i}{f_i} \leq T_{\max}, \ \forall i \in \{1, 2, \ldots, N\}$$

$$P^i_{\text{tx}} + P^i_{\text{comp}} \leq P^i_{\max}, \ \forall i \in \{1, 2, \ldots, N\}$$

3.4.1 Overview of federated learning algorithms

FL algorithms primarily involve two main steps: local training of models on individual devices and synchronization of the updated models at a central server. A few popular techniques are FedAvg where weights of local models are averaged to update the global model; a few more sophisticated techniques are FedProx and FedMA addressing concerns like clients' heterogeneity and model split. These algorithms are designed to optimize the trade-off between accuracy and communication overhead, which is important for IoT devices with limited computing power [3].

3.4.2 Energy-aware federated learning algorithms

IoT FL algorithms that consider energy are concepts that are created to reduce the energy usage of IoT devices. These algorithms also include techniques for avoiding frequent interaction between these devices and the central server as a way of conserving energy. To reduce the energy required for data transmission, methods like adaptive communication scheduling, where status updates are sent only when there is a large variation, and compression methods, which help in reducing data size, can be used. Besides, applying device-aware computations which adjust the number of computations depending on the computational capabilities of the devices can also help to improve the energy consumption more [5].

$$\min_{\mathbf{w}} \left(\frac{1}{N} \sum_{i=1}^{N} \left(L_i(\mathbf{w}) + \lambda \cdot \frac{\alpha_i \cdot E_{\text{comm}}^{(i)} + \beta_i \cdot E_{\text{comp}}^{(i)}}{E_{\text{max}}^{(i)}} \right) \right)$$

where:

- $\mathbf{w}$ represents the global model parameters to be optimized.
- N is the total number of IoT devices participating in the federated learning process.
- $L_i(\mathbf{w})$ is the local loss function for the i-th device.
- λ is a regularization parameter balancing the trade-off between model accuracy and energy consumption.
- $E_{\text{commm}}^{(i)}$ is the communication energy consumption for the i-th device during the model update.
- $E_{\text{comp}}^{(i)}$ is the computational energy consumption for the i-th device during local model training.
- $E_{\text{max}}^{(i)}$ is the maximum energy capacity of the i-th device.
- α_i and β_i are weighting factors that adjust the relative importance of communication and computational energy consumption for each device.

3.4.3 Resource allocation and optimization techniques

Managed resource utilization is another important consideration in energy-efficient FL for IoT. Subordinate schemes, for example, dynamic load balancing make it possible to distribute the computational tasks based on the capabilities of the device so that it will not be overloaded or underloaded. Practical techniques such as gradient sparsification and quantization decrease the amount of data transmitted and therefore reduce both communication overhead and power consumption. Also, federated learning algorithms use techniques to reduce the number of rounds of communication for training in order to save power but converge [4].

3.4.4 *Case studies: federated learning algorithms for energy efficiency*

It has been shown that energy-efficient FL algorithms can be effectively applied in real-world IoT deployments. For example, in the case of smart homes, energy-centric FL algorithms allow entities like thermostats or smart cameras to collaboratively learn about consumer preferences while avoiding energy wastage. Likewise, in industrial IoT, FL algorithms help fine-tune the efficiency of machines for scheduling energy-efficient maintenance and minimizing data transmission. These two case studies demonstrate the advantages of adopting FL algorithms into IoT systems to improve performance and energy consumption [11].

In general, federated learning algorithms are very effective in improving the energy efficiency of IoT systems. These algorithms help in energy-aware methods, efficient resource management, and studying real-world scenarios; they bolster efficient and sustainable IoT operations and demonstrate their versatility.

3.5 Integration of FL with energy-efficient IoT

Integrating FL with energy-efficient IoT systems is essential for achieving optimal performance and sustainability. This integration involves designing system architectures that support efficient data aggregation, processing, and communication while addressing the unique challenges of IoT environments.

$$\min_{\{w_k\}_{k=1}^{K}} \sum_{k=1}^{K} \left(\alpha_k \cdot E_k^{\text{local}}(w_k) + \beta_k \cdot C_k^{\text{comm}}(w_k) + \gamma_k \cdot P_k^{\text{update}}(w_k) \right)$$

subject to:

$$w_k^{t+1} = w_k^t - \eta \nabla F_k\left(w_k^t\right), \quad \forall k \in \{1, 2, \ldots, K\}$$

where:

- K is the number of IoT devices participating in federated learning.
- w_k represents the model parameters for device k.
- $E_k^{\text{local}}(w_k)$ is the energy consumption for local computation of the model update on device k.
- $C_k^{\text{comm}}(w_k)$ is the communication cost for transmitting the updated model from device k to the central server.
- $P_k^{\text{update}}(w_k)$ is the energy cost related to the model update process, including optimization steps and aggregation.

- $\alpha_k, \beta_k, \gamma_k$ are weighting factors that balance energy consumption, communication cost, and model update cost, respectively.
- η is the learning rate for model updates.
- $F_k(w_k^t)$ represents the local loss function for device k at iteration t.

3.5.1 System architecture for FL in energy-efficient IoT

The usual structure of integrating FL with the energy-efficient IoT environment is decentralized where many IoT devices collectively train some global model but do not exchange individual data. This architecture entails a principal server, which collects the model updates from all the devices, and edge nodes, which execute the computations. To reduce the communication overhead and power consumption in the network the structure of the architecture is designed to employ good aggregation schemes and low frequency update rates. Moreover, edge computing frameworks can also be integrated to process information with higher efficiency in terms of energy consumption [9].

3.5.2 Data aggregation and processing techniques

It is essential to note that methods related to data collection and analysis are vital to enhance FL in IoT-based systems. Coordination mechanisms include methods by which updated models are aggregated and sent back to the devices while keeping the data transmission as minimal as possible. There are methods like federative averaging (FedAvg) and federative proximal (FedProx) when dealing with asynchronous data and ensuring convergence. Techniques and measures involve the following: model quantization, which shrinks the size of updates transmitted through the network, and differential privacy methods, which improve security without a high return cost. These methods assist in maintaining a balance between energy usage and model performance [5].

3.5.3 Communication protocols and network considerations

Standard and network management strategies are crucial for implementing FL with innovative energy-saving IoT networks. MQTT and CoAP protocols are employed for sending data in an efficient way and minimizing energy usage. To avoid the wastage of energy, techniques like asynchronous updates, where devices are updated at different time periods, are used, along with an adaptive communication schedule by which the number of updates is done based on the network traffic. Another aspect of the network affecting the current system is the timely provision of adequate networks, including latency and bandwidth, to enhance reliable and effective communication between the connected devices and the server [4].

3.5.4 Case studies: FL integration in IoT systems

Real-life examples can be derived to demonstrate the use of FL in combination with IoT systems for enhanced power-saving solutions. In smart grid applications, FL algorithms allow energy meters and grid sensors to jointly learn consumption patterns with little communication, thus saving a lot of energy. In healthcare, wearable devices apply FL to enhance health monitoring models without privacy violations or high-power consumption. The following are some illustrations of how FL can be combined with energy-efficient measures to improve IoT devices' functionality and sustainability across multiple sectors [11].

Implementing federated learning into low-power IoT platforms necessitates consideration of the system architecture, data handling, and networking protocols. Positive examples illustrate the applied advantages of this integration, which can positively affect performance and sustainability indicators in various IoT contexts.

3.6 Challenges and solutions in FL for energy-efficient IoT

Some of the challenges associated with the union of FL with energy-efficient IoT systems include the following. Solving these challenges is an opportunity to use FL to the maximum for developing IoT networks' performance and sustainability.

3.6.1 Security and privacy concerns

Some of the challenges of federated learning for IoT include security and privacy. Due to FL's approach of collecting model updates from multiple devices, the data used in the updates can be leaked if inferred from the received updates. To maintain data confidentiality, other techniques like differential privacy and secure multiparty computation are used. Differential privacy masks individual contributions to model updates by adding noise, while secure multiparty computation ensures that the data is encrypted during aggregation. They assist decrease threat factors such as data breaches and unauthorized access, though they come with other disadvantages such as increased computational load and system complexity [12].

3.6.2 Scalability and latency issues

Another disadvantage of federated learning for large-scale IoT systems is related to scalability and latency problems. It also shows that as the number of devices grows, the number of models for recalculating increases too, as does the load on the central server, which may turn into a bottleneck. Some of the solutions to these problems are asynchronous update methods, where the member device updates the model on its own and does not have to wait for all devices to do the same, and hierarchical FL architecture, where the updates are centrally aggregated to the intermediate servers before reaching the central server. Such strategies can alleviate the communication overhead burden and scalability issues [4].

3.6.3 Interoperability and standardization challenges

Integration with different structures and devices for IoT makes it necessary to have interoperability and standards in FL. Federated learning also lacks standard protocols and frameworks, which can make the integration of individual implementations less effective. To overcome these challenges, there are attempts to establish specific guidelines and frameworks for FL compatible with different IoT devices and transmission methods. For developing consistent standards for smooth integration, it is crucial to have collective efforts by the industry players and standardization bodies [5].

3.6.4 Proposed solutions and future directions

Although there are several challenges associated with the use of social media, the following solutions and further research directions are being considered. Other methods to increase privacy-preserving techniques include expanding on the use of more complex cryptographic mechanisms in the computations and increasing the efficiency of the differential privacy algorithms used to protect the data. New trends in edge and fog computing are believed to solve the scalability and latency problems by decentralizing the processing burden to the source. Furthermore, it will enable the standardization and widespread adoption of federated learning and IoT systems for easier integration. Future studies could involve further extending these solutions and searching for new methods to optimize federated learning for large-scale IoT networks with low-power consumption [11].

In federated learning for energy-efficient IoT, the challenges that need to be resolved include privacy preservation, scalability, and standardization. These efforts are important in expanding the possibilities of FL to enhance the IoT performance and increase its efficiency and security.

3.7 Advanced topics in FL for energy-efficient IoT

Even as FL grows as a field, new complex areas are being developed to improve the effectiveness of FL in energy-efficient IoT applications. Such developments include adaptive federated learning algorithms, combining edge computing with FL, AI-based optimization techniques, and realistic real-world applications. To enhance the utilization of FL in IoT, a high level of understanding of these topics is essential.

3.7.1 Adaptive federated learning techniques

The adaptive FL approaches propose to improve the FL solutions and their performances according to real-world IoT conditions. Such techniques include methods of training and their possible optimization depending, for instance, on data distribution and device features. In adaptive FL, the parameters related to updation frequency, aggregation of models, and communication can be dynamically modified depending on feedback obtained from the IoT devices. For instance, federated learning with emphasizing personalization means that various devices can train specific models that are optimized for their local datasets while simultaneously participating in a global model. This is useful when dealing with the variation in the capability of different types of devices and changes in the network connectivity, thus enhancing the learning performance and power efficiency or consumption.

3.7.2 Edge computing and federated learning in IoT

The use of federated learning in conjunction with edge computing also helps to improve the performance of IoT systems. Through data processing, and model training at the edge of the network, close to the originating data source, there is a limited need to move large amounts of data over the network, thus utilizing less energy. Such integration also enables updated models to be fed back to their respective locations, which minimizes latency and enhances real-time performance. Edge processing also encompasses simultaneous data collection and processing at the edge, which can help address latency and accuracy issues for model updates while remaining energy-conscious. This can be used to support federated learning architectures that are highly scalable and ideal for numerous and vast IoT environments [13].

3.7.3 AI-driven optimization in energy-efficient IoT systems

Energy optimization is a critical factor in IoT systems, which can be achieved by incorporating various AI optimization algorithms. These techniques employ AI and machine learning in the allocation of resources, energy, and other operating parameters. For example, the reinforcement learning algorithm can change the power consumption rate of IoT devices depending on their performance and available power. Furthermore, it is possible to predict the demand for energy and schedule operations accordingly in order to save more energy. Through AI-based optimization techniques, IoT resources are managed in a smarter way leading to energy conservation and increased life-cycle of the devices [14].

3.7.4 Real-world implementations and use cases

Various applications of federated learning in IoT energy-efficient systems illustrate the effectiveness of the technique in different areas. In smart cities, federated learning is applied to enhance public transportation and smart Grids by collaboratively learning from the knowledge gathered through multiple numbers of sensors while preserving local data. In industrial contexts, it enhances predictive maintenance and energy management since it consolidates data from machinery and equipment. Medical IoT devices employ federated learning to improve patient care systems without trading off personal health data. These use cases illustrate the effectiveness of incorporating federated learning with energy conservation in practical applications [11].

The state-of-art of federated learning enhances the advancement of efficient IoT by focusing on complex aspects. These innovations not only improve the efficiency and sustainability of IoT applications but also contribute to creating better and smarter solutions, especially in practical applications.

3.7.5 Case studies and applications

FL has been integrated into energy-efficient IoT systems and has produced new solutions for various domains, including privacy and functionality. FL, by making use of decentralized data processing, allows the devices to cooperate in the model training process without disclosing the private data of their users, which guarantees their privacy while maximizing the accuracy of the model at the same time. These are especially useful for applications like smart homes, industrial IoT, healthcare, and environmental monitoring, where power management and data privacy are concerns. The following section discusses FL's practical use in these domains, showcasing how FL improves energy management and decision-making.

3.7.6 Smart homes and energy-efficient IoT

FL plays a crucial role in the development of smart homes in improving energy efficiency where multiple systems including heating, ventilation, air conditioning, and lighting are optimized. In federated learning, data from different smart home devices and sensors is combined and used locally to train models for improving prediction about users' preferences and other environmental factors. For instance, federated learning can determine patterns in heating and cooling usage, and then adjust temperature depending on occupancy, time of day, and external environment. This approach minimizes energy consumption and overall utility expenses while centralizing data to protect the user's privacy [15].

3.7.7 Industrial IoT and energy management

In industrial cases, federated learning is applied in the improvement of energy efficiency and the prognosis of equipment failure. By using federated learning at multiple connected industrial machines and sensors, information from different sources could be collected, without sharing personal information to a central computer. This allows for the creation of models to predict failures in the equipment, as well as utilizing energy in the most effective manner, and having a better way of managing the schedules for production. For example, federated learning can make use of the vibration, temperature, and usage patterns to determine the best time that a particular machinery is likely to need repairs hence minimizing the time that the machinery will be off hence saving on energy [16].

3.7.8 Healthcare IoT systems and federated learning

Facilitated learning is instrumental to healthcare IoT systems since it allows for the secure and efficient transfer of data between numerous connected medical devices and institutions. In some use cases like remote diagnosis of patients' wear, federated learning enables several devices to train models on health data and not the data itself. This helps protect the patient's identity and at the same time ensures that the diagnostic models are more correct. For instance, federated learning can be applied to make use of data collected by wearable health monitors to determine patterns in the patient's health status, thereby allowing health practitioners to develop unique treatment plans accordingly and monitor any possible developing health complications [17].

3.7.9 Environmental monitoring and smart agriculture

Federated learning is also used in environment monitoring as well as smart agriculture to enhance resource utilization and environmental efficiency. Intelligent and connected agriculture in federated learning harnesses data from numerous sensors handling the soil situation, climate, and crops for creating architectures that instruct irrigation and fertilizer management. Said localized approach makes it easier to track and allocate resources and minimize the wastage that may be incurred in the broader generalizations made in the traditional approaches. In the case of environmental analysis for decision-making, federated learning can be applied in order to analyze data from many distributed sensors and systems used to monitor and collect data for environmental indicators such as air quality, water quality, and other indicators that can help in management and planning of environmental impacts [18].

These cases prove how federated learning can be applied in the real world within different domains, showing how it can improve energy consumption and organizational performance as well as tackle privacy issues.

3.8 Performance metrics and evaluation

In the context of analyzing FL frameworks for energy-efficient IoT systems, performance indices are critical to identifying the efficiency of such systems. Various measures like energy consumption, model accuracy, and the ratio of successful inter-device communications are vital in evaluating the general performance, scalability, and sustainability of FL-based IoT systems.

3.8.1 Key performance indicators for energy-efficient IoT

KPIs are thus very useful in measuring the energy efficiency of IoT systems. These are metrics used to evaluate IoT devices, networks, and applications by analyzing their energy efficiency, battery, delay time, and data transfer rate. Key performance indicators for energy-efficient IoT are power per task, energy per bit, device availability, and network availability. For instance, the utilization of energy for IoT functionality, for example, gathering and analyzing data, is effective in defining the general efficiency of the system. KPIs also assist in measuring the impacts of power conservation techniques and resource management procedures commonly used in IoT systems.

3.8.2 Evaluation of FL algorithms in IoT systems

When comparing FL algorithms in IoT systems, several parameters should be considered, including model accuracy level, convergence time, communication load, and energy consumption. These metrics help to keep the FL algorithms in check regarding their energy efficiency and performance. For example, model accuracy is used to compare the efficiency of distributed learning, whereas convergence time reflects the time it takes for a model to achieve the best result. Training overhead refers to the amount of data transmitted among the IoT devices and central servers in the training process. An efficient approach to an IoT energy-efficient machine learning model is the minimization of communication and energy consumption for the highest accuracy [3].

3.8.3 Benchmarking and comparative analysis

Comparisons of FL algorithms in energy-conscious IoT systems and benchmarking studies require a structured assessment of multiple algorithms based on performance measurements including energy used, accuracy of models, communication costs, and scalability of the system. For instance, in the case of energy-aware FL algorithms such as FedAvg, FedProx, and Scaffold, researchers may gather data on energy consumption per communication round, the rate at which the FL model converges, and bandwidth utilization of different IoT settings.

In general, the FedAvg might have lower communication overhead but higher energy consumption since it has slower convergence rates in non-IID data. On the other hand, Scaffold might achieve faster convergence with less energy consumption but needs more intricate implementation, while FedProx strikes a balance between communication efficiency and model accuracy by considering the heterogeneity of data. For instance, Li *et al.* in their work, published in 2020 found that under conditions of varying data distributions, FedProx consumed up to 15% less energy than FedAvg, which is a standard FL algorithm.

Such data aggregation and analysis will then provide the necessary information for the organization to make informed decisions on selecting the most appropriate FL algorithm relevant to the context of the IoT system in place. Furthermore, comparative analysis allows evaluation of the potential compromise between energy consumption, accuracy, and communication costs to see whether the selected solution corresponds to sustainable development objectives. Even optimizing the FL algorithms by 10%–20% in a real-world deployment will mean cost-cutting on the energy needed for running IoT systems, especially in large-scale settings like smart cities or industrial IoT implementations. Consequently, benchmarking offers relevant knowledge to develop efficient and usable IoT systems.

3.9 Future trends and research directions

With the advancements in FL in the future, a number of emerging technologies are expected to complement FL in energy-efficient IoT systems: One interesting trend is the combination of FL with edge computing to address local computations to minimize latency and enhance real-time decision-making [19]. It reduces the energy spent in consuming the data transmitted and helps IoT devices work optimally in constrained networks. Another novel approach in the FL is the integration of blockchain technology for decentralization, which provides enhanced security and transparency in the management of distributed data [20]. To secure the FL processes and to enable IoT systems to preserve data integrity and achieve efficient energy use, the use of blockchain is beneficial.

Advancements in energy-saving IoT platforms are also in the process of changing the picture. New FL approaches are being proposed where models are updated in response to the amount of energy supplied to IoT nodes and the capability of the nodes. This solution also offers a more efficient utilization of resources and thus high scalability for big IoT networks [16]. Furthermore, optimizing communication protocols that incorporate energy considerations enables the reduction of the energy cost of frequent data transfer between IoT devices and central servers. FL deployments in IoT environments require energy-efficient protocols that assure high data accuracy, and therefore, they make FL efficient.

However, there are a few more issues and opportunities for future research in this domain. A major concern is the feasibility and practicality of scale in terms of its impact on the correctness and speed of the system for large and diverse IoT networks. Also, handling the trade-off between model accuracy and power consumption is another key research direction. Still, security and privacy concerns are paramount, especially in vast, decentralized networks. So, as the field expands and evolves over time, these issues will also create opportunities for further FL development and integration with IoT in more effective ways that are sustainable in the long run.

3.10 Conclusion

This chapter has comprehensively reviewed the integration of FL frameworks and algorithms with energy-savage IoT systems. We began by highlighting the role of energy efficiency in IoT and how FL, which brings decentralization to machine learning, can solve IoT devices' energy challenges and respect data privacy. Because of FL attributes that include the reduction of data transmission and boosting local processing, the approach is relevant in addressing energy difficulties in IoT networks.

The value and contribution of this chapter are based on illustrating how FL can benefit IoT's use cases including smart home, industrial IoT, healthcare, and environmental monitoring. For these reasons, energy-aware algorithms as well as resource optimization strategies revealed that FL can potentially save a considerable amount of energy without compromising the model accuracy and performance. From the point of view of the reader, this chapter outlines how FL can be adapted to the growth of efficient, secure, and large-scale IoT solutions. All the information presented here is crucial for the development of future IoT environments where energy consumption and functionality have to be met.

Nevertheless, there are issues like data security, heterogeneities of the IoT devices, communication latency, and scalability which are the major concerns when it comes to the implementation of FL to energy-efficient IoT. These are some of the challenges that need to be considered to achieve the maximum benefits of FL in this context.

From here on, it is envisaged that further development in FL for IoT includes an adaptive FL approach, integration with edge computing in IoT, and incorporation of AI for energy optimization. Overcoming the current challenges and using new technology opportunities will open the perspective for constructing innovative and resource-efficient IoT systems that can increase the quality of existing infrastructure globally, and follow the principles of saving energy and being environmentally friendly.

References

[1] Jayakumar H., Raha A., Kim Y., Sutar S., Lee W. S., and Raghunathan V. (2016). Energy-efficient system design for IoT devices, In *21st Asia and South Pacific Design Automation Conference (ASP-DAC)*, Macao, China, 2016, pp. 298–301, doi:10.1109/ASPDAC.2016.7428027.

[2] Lim, W. Y. B., Luong, N. C., Hoang, D. T., and Niyato, D. (2020). Federated learning in mobile edge networks: A comprehensive survey. *IEEE Communications Surveys & Tutorials*, 22(3), 2031–2063.

[3] McMahan, B., Moore, E., Ramage, D., Hampson, S., and Arcas, B. A. (2017). Communication-efficient learning of deep networks from decentralized data. In *Proceedings of the 20th International Conference on Artificial Intelligence and Statistics*, pp. 1273–1282.

[4] Kairouz, P., McMahan, B., Avent, B., *et al.* (2021). Advances and open problems in federated learning. *Foundations and Trends® in Machine Learning*, 14(1–2), 1–210.

[5] Li, T., Sahu, A. K., Talwalkar, A., and Smith, V. (2020). Federated optimization in heterogeneous networks. *Proceedings of Machine Learning and Systems*, 2, 429–450.

[6] Kaswan, K. S., Dhatterwal, J. S., Yadav, R., Malik, K., and Tripathi, A. M. (2024). Federated learning: research, challenges, and future directions. In *2024 IEEE International Conference on Computing, Power and Communication Technologies (IC2PCT)* (Vol. 5, pp. 71–76). Piscataway, NJ: IEEE.

[7] Bagdasaryan, E., Veit, A., Hua, Y., Estrin, D., and Shmatikov, V. (2020). How to backdoor federated learning. In *Proceedings of the 23rd International Conference on Artificial Intelligence and Statistics*, pp. 2938–2948.

[8] Petrov D., Kroschewski K, Mwammenywa I., Kagarura G. M. and Hilleringmann U., (2021). Low-cost NB-IoT microgrid power quality monitoring system. *IEEE Sensors*, Sydney, Australia, 2021, pp. 1–4, doi:10.1109/SENSORS47087.2021.9639641.

[9] Xia, F., Yang, L. T., Wang, L., and Vinel, A. (2020). Internet of Things. *International Journal of Communication Systems*, 33(4), e4247.

[10] Sahota H., Kumar R., Kamal A. and Huang Jing, (2010), An energy-efficient wireless sensor network for precision agriculture. *IEEE Symposium on Computers and Communications*, Riccione, Italy, pp. 347–350, doi:10.1109/ISCC.2010.5546508.

[11] Hota, A., Singh, D., Mahapatra, A., and Panda, B. (2020). Energy efficient techniques for IoT based smart agriculture. *Test Engineering and Management*, 83. 7604–7612.

[12] Shokri, R., Stronati, M., Song, L., and Shmatikov, V. (2015). Privacy-preserving deep learning. In *Proceedings of the 2015 ACM SIGSAC Conference on Computer and Communications Security*, pp. 1310–1321.

[13] Brecko A, Kajati E, Koziorek J, and Zolotova I. Federated learning for edge computing: A survey. *Applied Sciences*. 2022; 12(18):9124. https://doi.org/10.3390/app12189124.

[14] Nutakki M. and Mandava S. (2023), Review on optimization techniques and role of artificial intelligence in home energy management systems. *Engineering Applications of Artificial Intelligence*, 119, 105721.

[15] Khan Q. W., Ahmad R., Rizwan A., Khan A. N., Lee K.T., and Kim D. H., (2024). Optimizing energy efficiency and comfort in smart homes through predictive optimization: A case study with indoor environmental parameter consideration, *Energy Reports*, 11, 5619–5637.

[16] Chung K. and Lim J.-T. (2023). Machine learning for relaying topology: Optimization of IoT networks with energy harvesting. *IEEE Access*, 11, 41827–41839, doi:10.1109/ACCESS.2023.3270631.

[17] Wang R., Lai J., Zhang Z., Li X., Vijayakumar P., and Karuppiah M. (2023). Privacy-preserving federated learning for internet of medical things under edge computing. *IEEE Journal of Biomedical and Health Informatics*, 27, 2, 854–865, doi: 10.1109/JBHI.2022.3157725.

[18] Žalik, K. R. and Žalik, M. A review of federated learning in agriculture. *Sensors* 2023, *23*, 9566. https://doi.org/10.3390/s23239566.

[19] Abreha, H. G., Hayajneh, M., and Serhani, M. A. (2022). Federated learning in edge computing: a systematic survey. *Sensors*, *22*(2), 450.

[20] Lu, Y., Huang, X., Dai, Y., Maharjan, S., and Zhang, Y. (2019). Blockchain and federated learning for privacy-preserved data sharing in industrial IoT. *IEEE Transactions on Industrial Informatics*, *16*(6), 4177–4186.

Chapter 4

Communication efficiency in federated learning in IoT environment

Amutha Prabakar Muniyandi[1], L. Godlin Atlas[2], N. Deepa[3] and Mahmoud Ahmad Al-Khasawneh[4,5]

Abstract

Federated Learning (FL) has emerged as a decentralized machine learning paradigm that enhances privacy and efficiency by enabling edge devices within the Internet of Things (IoT). FL allows models to be collaboratively trained without sharing raw data, thereby preserving data privacy. However, communication overhead remains a significant bottleneck in adopting FL in resource-constrained IoT environments. This chapter delves into the challenges and strategies for improving communication efficiency in FL techniques within IoT ecosystems. It begins by identifying key sources of communication overhead, such as frequent model updates and large data payloads. The chapter then explores state-of-the-art techniques, including model compression, sparsification, quantization, and adaptive communication strategies. Special emphasis is placed on optimizing the trade-off between communication costs and model accuracy while accounting for the heterogeneity of IoT devices and networks. The chapter also highlights recent advancements in edge computing and 5G/6G technologies that complement FL by reducing latency and improving scalability. Practical applications and use cases in smart cities, healthcare, and industrial IoT are discussed to demonstrate the real-world impact of these approaches. Finally, the chapter concludes by summarizing open research directions for achieving sustainable and efficient FL systems in dynamic IoT environments.

Keywords: Federated learning; Communication efficiency; Internet of Things (IoT); Model compression; Edge computing

[1]Department of Computer Engineering, Government Polytechnic College, Madurai, India
[2]Department of Computer Science and Engineering, Bharath Institute of Higher Education and Research, India
[3]Department of Networking and Communications, School of Computing, SRM Institute of Science and Technology, India
[4]School of Computing, Skyline University College, University City Sharjah, UAE
[5]Applied Science Research Center, Applied Science Private University, Jordan

4.1 Introduction

Communication efficiency is an important factor to be considered for designing an efficient and robust federated learning (FL) technique for achieving efficiency in IoT environments, especially, for IoT devices with resource-constrained and unreliable network connectivity. This chapter provides a detailed view of the various strategies and techniques to optimize communication efficiency in federated learning and these techniques ensure minimal bandwidth usage, reduced latency, and energy consumption.

FL framework has been developed as a promising model for training machine learning approaches across decentralized IoT devices. These approaches are particularly used in the Internet of Things (IoT) environment. A large amount of data has been generated at the edge or client devices of the network. However, one of the important challenging issues to be addressed is to ensure communication efficiency in implementing federated learning in IoT ecosystems. The limited resources like bandwidth, intermittent connectivity, and heterogeneous nature of IoT devices require efficient communication protocols and approaches to optimize the overall system performance and energy consumption. Energy consumption could be reduced by adapting efficient communication protocols.

Communication efficiency in federated learning techniques is focused on design with a minimum amount of data exchanged between the client devices and the central server while maintaining or enhancing the accuracy and convergence speed of the global model. Communication efficiency is a mandatory aspect to focus on in the IoT environment due to several reasons, bandwidth constraints, energy consumption, scalability, and data privacy and security. IoT environments rely on wireless communication networks with limited bandwidth. Unwanted communications involved in the IoT environment can lead to network congestion, high latency, and increased computational overheads. Communication is a high energy consumption process for the IoT environment. The energy consumption can be reduced by minimizing the data transmission significantly and this will ensure the improved battery lifespan of devices and sustainability for IoT devices. The amount of data exchanged between IoT devices and central servers is growing with high volume, due to the increasing to IoT devices. Efficiency and robustness play an important role in achieving data security and privacy for well-organized communication protocols. The disclosure of sensitive information shared between communication devices can be achieved or minimized by reducing the frequency and size of data sharing. The system's privacy preservation capacity can be ensured through this process.

This chapter investigates the various aspects of communication efficiency in federated learning within IoT environments. This study starts by exploring data compression techniques, such as model pruning, quantization, and delta encoding. The data compression techniques are used to reduce the size of the data exchanged between clients and the server. The chapter also discusses the significance of selecting suitable communication protocols and infrastructure by including edge and fog computing architectures. The computational analysis has been conducted over the collected data and this process reduces the latency and bandwidth utilization. The adaptive communication strategies with dynamic bandwidth allocation and frequency-sharing

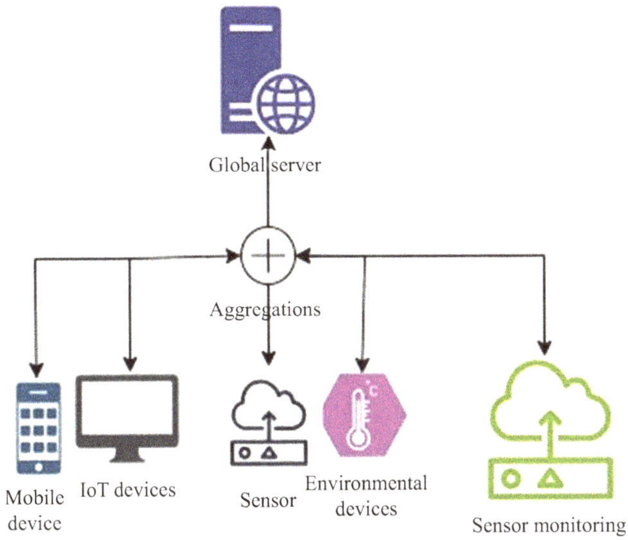

Figure 4.1 Architectural framework of aggregation process in federated learning

techniques are examined and studied to optimize the trade-off between communication overhead and model accuracy. This chapter further addresses privacy-preserved communication techniques by using secure aggregation and confidentiality approaches. This will ensure data protection by minimizing the communication costs. The final chapter presents real-world case studies and practical implementation details of how these communications are efficiently applied for various IoT scenarios (Figure 4.1). The real-time case studies are illustrated with practical challenges and solutions achieved in the FL technique for diverse IoT environments [1].

This chapter aims to provide the readers with a detailed view of the knowledge and tools used to design and implement effective FL systems through a comprehensive overview of communication efficiency in federated learning. This chapter highlights the importance of balancing communication efficiency with other critical factors like model accuracy, energy consumption, and data privacy.

4.2 Data compression techniques for achieving communication efficiency in federated learning

Data compression techniques are used to reduce the volume of data shared between IoT devices and central servers, and it is an essential aspect of improving efficiency in communication for FL [2]. This compression is essential in IoT environments for devices with limited bandwidth and energy resources. Federated learning can maintain model accuracy with minimum communication overheads by applying model compression. This section explores various types of data compression techniques that contribute to establishing efficient communication in federated learning.

4.2.1 Model pruning and sparsification

Model pruning and sparsification techniques are designed to reduce the number of insignificant weighted parameters in a model by eliminating the process. This technique helps to share and transmit smaller units of data (sparser model), which reduces communication overhead. Model pruning and sparsification techniques are powerful tools in data compression for reducing the size of machine learning models. The IoT environment is constructed with devices of limited bandwidth, computational power, and energy consumption. The model pruning and sparsification techniques are essential for achieving communication efficiency.

Model pruning refers to the process of eliminating less important parameters (such as weights or neurons) from a neural network. All the components are not contributing equally to aggregating model updates and the nonperformed components can be removed. The weighted pruning approach is designed to eliminate individual weights in the neural network, and it will create little effect on the model's outputs.

4.2.1.1 Algorithm for model pruning and sparsification

Model pruning and sparsification techniques can be systematically implemented through a sequential set of steps. The following algorithm provides the outlines for the general procedure of model pruning sparsification for applying in neural network models.

Algorithm: Model pruning and sparsification technique

---

1. Start with a pretrained network model and this training process is initialized with a predefined pruning criterion
2. Set a pruning threshold or target sparsity level
3. For each attribute, compute an importance score by using selected pruning criterion
4. Rank the attributes based on their importance scores
5. Select the attributes with the lowest scores for pruning, as follows:
   (a) Pruning all attributes below a specific threshold
   (b) Pruning a fixed percentage of attributes
6. Set the selected parameters to zero, effectively deleting them from models
7. Repeat Steps 2–6 iteratively to achieve the level of sparsity by gradually increasing the pruning threshold or target sparsity level
8. Develop a sparse matrix based on the stored pruned model. This will reduce the storage and communication cost
9. Deploy a pruned and sparse model for setting up the federated learning

---

This technique uses iterative pruning and fine-tuning processes for achieving efficiency in model updates. The pruning is carried out iteratively and fine-tuned for the next round. This process can be conducted for multiple iterations to incrementally reduce the model size to maintain performance. The pruning process is applied globally or layer-wise to improve the performance. The global pruning process selects the least important weights from the entire model and layer-wise pruning ensures that each layer maintains weight value in a proportionate way. The dynamic pruning adjusts the pruning strategy based on dynamic weight values. This adaptive approach leads to a more efficient compression process as it considers the significant weight value over time.

The model pruning and sparsification process ensures the following benefits during the training process: reduced communication overhead, low energy consumption, quick inference and training, and scalability. The communication overhead between client devices and central server in a federated learning environment is significantly reduced by sharing nonzero attributes and a pruned model. The computational overhead in pruned and sparse models requires a minimum amount, and this will lead to lower energy consumption. The smaller size of model training generally requires less computation, faster inference time, and shorter training periods. The pruning and sparsification process provides an efficient environment for federated learning across a large number of devices and this approach minimizes communication and computational overheads [3].

Model pruning and sparsification are critical techniques for achieving data compression in federated learning, particularly in IoT environments. These methods reduce communication overhead, energy consumption, and computational requirements while maintaining an acceptable level of model accuracy. As federated learning continues to be deployed across various applications, the importance of these techniques in ensuring efficient and scalable implementations will only grow (Figure 4.2).

The pruning and sparsification techniques face the following challenges and limitations during the training process. Aggressive pruning techniques lead to significant drops in model accuracy and it is crucial to find a balance between the process of compression and performance. Implementing pruning and sparsification techniques is complex for implementing in a real-time IoT environment and it requires careful designing and domain expertise. The pruning technique applies different layers of components of a model that may tolerate different levels of sparsity. The developers are facing challenges in understanding and optimizing the framework for achieving optimization in federated learning.

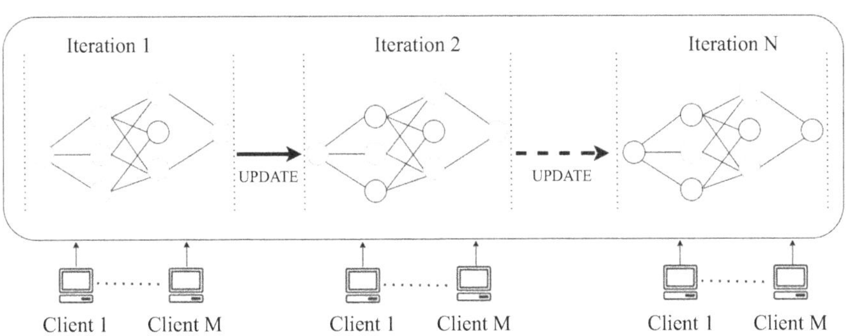

Figure 4.2 Architecture for pruning technique in federated learning

The weight-based pruning technique is designed by involving weight values for each layer. Unwanted weights are removed with magnitudes below a certain threshold level by reducing the number of nonzero attributes. This technique helps to compress the model and this leads to fewer attributes that need to be communicated. Neuron-based pruning works with like weight pruning technique at the level of neurons or entire layer. Neurons with a low contribution to the model's output are pruned, and this technique leads to a simpler and smaller model. The models are represented as sparse matrices and nonzero elements are stored and communicated. This significantly reduces the amount of data.

4.3 Quantization technique in federated learning

The decentralized learning machine learning framework is defined as federated learning (FL), and this will enable multiple client devices, such as mobile devices or edge nodes, to collaboratively train a global model without sharing their private data. This approach provides a solution for privacy concerns and reduces the need for data centralization. However, FL introduces some unique challenges based on communication efficiency and computational resource management. The model updates must be transmitted or shared frequently between client devices and a central server. The communication overhead can be reduced through strategies exclusively designed for bandwidth-limited environments.

The mapping between continuous values to discrete levels is refereeing the quantization technique. These techniques are used to reduce the precision rate for model updates for sharing data. The quantization process reduces the amount of data that needs to be communicated between client devices and server, and this process minimizes the bandwidth utilization and energy consumption rate [4].

4.3.1 Algorithm for quantization technique in federated learning

The quantization technique is used to reduce the precision of weights and activations in a neural network, thereby minimizing the amount of information that needs to be stored and transmitted. This technique is especially suitable for federated learning to minimize communication overheads and computational loads on resource-constrained IoT devices. The following section discusses the step-by-step procedure for applying quantization to model attributes in federated learning.

Algorithm: Quantization technique in federated learning

---

1. **Initialization process**
   (a) Initialize the global model δ^0 in the server side
   (b) Define quantization levels N_Q, learning rate μ, and number of communication rounds T_R. The set of client devices that participated in the quantization process is defined as $C_{i=1 \text{ to } N}$

2. **Server-side process**
   (a) For each $i = 1 \ldots T_R$ do
      (i) The current global model δ^ihas been shared with all the clients in $C_{t<N} \in C_N$
3. **Client-side process**
   (a) For each client from $C_i \in C_t$ do
      1. The local computation is performed by downloading the current global model δ^t
      2. The client device C_i performs local training over Data set of D_i for the Epochs size of M
      3. The new global model δ_i^{t+1} create from the results
      4. The quantization update of local model updates $\Delta\delta_i = \delta_i^{t+1} - \delta_i^t$ as follows:

         $$\Delta\delta_i^Q = Q_f(\Delta\delta_i)$$

      5. The quantization function $Q_f(.)$ computes the continuous model updates based on the set of discrete values defined by the quantization levels N_Q. This quantization can be done by using either quantization or non-quantization techniques
      6. The quantization update $\Delta\delta_i^Q$ is compared with previous model updates and prepared for transmission

   (b) The client device C_t transmits quantized model update $\Delta\delta_i^Q$ to central server
4. **Server-side model aggregation**
   (a) The model update $\Delta\delta_i^Q$ received from the client device C_t is aggregated with the received updates to update the global model
   (b) Dequantize the received updates $\Delta\delta_i^Q$ to approximate the original update $\Delta\delta_i$
   (c) Apply the aggregation process as follows:

   $$\Delta\delta^t = \frac{1}{|C_t|}\sum_{i \in C_t} \Delta\delta_i$$

   (d) The updates global model is generated as follows:

   $$\delta^{t+1} = \delta^t + \mu.\Delta\delta^t$$

   (e) Repeat Steps 2–4 until the maximum number of iterations T_R or the model convergences to achieve high accuracy value
   (f) The final global model δ^T is generated by the central server

---

Quantization technique introduces approximation error based on the reduction in precision and the selection of quantization levels N_Q to balance the trade-off between communication overheads and model accuracy. Additional compression techniques are used to reduce the size of transmitted data. Data security can be achieved during the transmission of data by using confidentiality techniques. The above give algorithm provides a detailed view of the implementation of the quantization technique in federated learning, and this algorithm focuses on the steps involved in quantizing and aggregating model updates to achieve communication efficiency.

4.4 Delta encoding and update pruning

Delta encoding technique transmits only the changes (deltas) in model attributes rather than the full model updates. This technique takes optimized facts from all initial stages of training and the updates for the model attributes become smaller. The delta encoding is used to encode the difference between the current model attributes and the previous trained model [5]. This will reduce the size of data to be communicated exclusively for model convergences.

- **Update pruning**: Similar to model pruning, update pruning involves sending only significant updates. Smaller updates, which are less likely to impact the model significantly, are discarded, further reducing communication overhead.

4.4.1 Algorithm for delta encoding and update pruning technique in federated learning

Delta encoding and update pruning are techniques used in FL to reduce communication overhead by transmitting only the significant changes (deltas) in model parameters and pruning insignificant updates. Below is a step-by-step algorithm for implementing these techniques in an FL setting.

Algorithm: Delta encoding and update pruning in federated learning

---

1. Initialization process
   (a) The central servers initialize the global model δ^0 and share this with all clients
   (b) Each client device C_i is initialized with its local model δ_i^0 from the global model
2. Client-side updates
   (a) Each client C_i performs local training processes by using its local data D_i and updates its model attributes. The updated local model δ_i^t at round $t \in T$
   (b) The updated $\Delta\delta_i^t$ is computed from the difference between the current local and global model,

   $$\Delta\delta_i^t = \delta_i^t - \delta^t$$

   (c) Apply encoding methods to reduce the size of the updated model need to be transmitted as follows:

(i) Apply quantization over $\Delta\delta_i^t$ for reducing precision
(ii) Apply Huffman encoding technique or other encoding techniques to reduce the size of transmitted data

(d) An optimum threshold value is set for finding which updates are significant
(e) The pruned delta $\Delta\delta_i^{t,\text{pruned}}$ is computed as

$$\Delta\delta_i^{t,\text{pruned}} = \begin{cases} \Delta\delta_i^t & if\ |\Delta\delta_i^t| \geq \tau \\ 0 & if\ |\Delta\delta_i^t| < \tau \end{cases}$$

3. Aggregation process
   (a) The central server aggregates the received pruned deltas from all the clients to create the updated global model. The aggregation process is performed as follows:

$$\delta^{t+1} = \delta^t + \frac{1}{K}\sum_{i=1}^{K} \Delta\delta_i^{t,\text{pruned}}$$

Here, K is defined as the number of participating clients' devices

4. The centralized server updates the global model δ^{t+1} and sends the updated model to all the clients. Check the global model convergence of updated next level
5. Repeat Steps 2–4 until to reach an optimum convergence rate
6. The final global model δ^T is reached once the maximum number of communication rounds completed

---

The selection of threshold value τ affects the trade-off between communication efficiency and model accuracy. The selection of a higher τ value leads to more aggressive pruning and it affects model performance. The compression techniques used in delta encoding vary based on application requirements and the device's computational capacity. The communication overhead and model accuracy have been balanced dynamically by adjusting the threshold value τ. This algorithm effectively reduces the communication overheads by transmitting only significant updates and compressing the data [6].

4.5 Gradient compression

Gradient compression techniques focus on compressing the gradients computed during backpropagation, which are then sent to the central server for aggregation.

- **Gradient clipping**: Clipping the gradients to a maximum value prevents extremely large gradients, which could lead to excessive communication.

- **Gradient sparsification**: Transmits only a fraction of the gradients, typically the ones with the largest magnitudes. The rest are either set to zero or approximated, reducing the amount of data sent.
- **Gradient quantization**: Similar to weight quantization, but applied to the gradients. It reduces the precision of the gradient values to lower the data size.

4.5.1 Algorithm for gradient compression technique

Gradient compression techniques aim to minimize the amount of data sharing between client devices and the central server during federated learning by using compressed gradient values. This process includes several sets of steps to reduce the precision of the gradients to preserve the essential information needed for model updates [7]. The following algorithm provides a detailed explanation with a step-by-step workflow for a typical gradient compression technique.

Algorithm: Gradient compression technique

---

1. Initialize the model parameter δ^0 with the central server and distribute the initial model δ^0 to all client devices
2. For each client device C_i
   (a) Collect the current model attributes for δ^t from the central server
   (b) Access the local dataset D_i and initialize batch size B_{size}
   (c) Compute local gradient $\nabla_{\text{i}}(\delta^t)$ using the local dataset D_i and the loss function $_{\text{i}}(.)$
   (d) Apply gradient compression techniques as follows:
      (i) Apply quantization to fiz the gradients to reduce precision
      (ii) Find and select the top K largest gradients
      (iii) Apply efficient encoding techniques to compress the nonzero gradients
   (e) Compute and restore error compensation based on the value of the difference between the original and compressed gradients and update it for the next iteration
3. For the central server
   (a) Collect compressed gradient value $\tilde{\nabla}_{\text{i}}(\delta^t)$ from all participating client devices
   (b) If necessary, apply the decompression process for the received gradients
   (c) Apply aggregation process over decompressed gradients to compute the global gradient as follows:

$$\nabla(\delta^T) = \frac{1}{K}\sum_{i=1}^{K}\tilde{\nabla}_{\text{i}}(\delta^t)$$

   Here K is the number of client devices participating in the communication

4. The global model is updated with model parameters δ^t by using aggregated gradients as follows:

$$\delta^{T+1} \leftarrow \delta^T + \tau.\Upsilon(\delta^t)$$

Here τ is a learning rate for the gradient compression technique

5. If the global model has converged then the process iteration is terminated. If the convergence is not achieved, then go to Step 2 and execute the next iteration

---

The dynamic adjustment of compression level based on the current state of the training process can be achieved by increasing compression in later stages. The process of compression and communication preserves security and privacy over the shared data. This technique uses an error feedback mechanism for identifying the information confidentiality and integrity loss. The above algorithm provides a detailed view of the working principle of the gradient compression technique for federated learning. The selection of compression techniques and attributes will depend on the requirements given by the applications. An optional mechanism is used for mitigating the negative impact of compression techniques through an effort feedback mechanism.

4.6 Federated dropout

Federated dropout extends the concept of dropout from deep learning to federated learning. It involves randomly dropping out a subset of model parameters during communication. The key advantage is that only a fraction of the model parameters are updated and communicated, leading to significant savings in communication costs.

4.6.1 Implementation considerations

- **Trade-off between compression and accuracy**: While data compression reduces communication costs, it may also affect model accuracy. Techniques like quantization and pruning should be carefully calibrated to balance these factors [8].
- **Energy and computation overhead**: The computational complexity of compression algorithms can impact the energy consumption of IoT devices. Therefore, choosing lightweight compression techniques is crucial for resource-constrained environments.
- **Security and privacy**: Data compression should not compromise the security and privacy of the federated learning system. Techniques like differential privacy can be integrated to ensure that compressed data does not leak sensitive information.

4.6.2 Federated dropout technique algorithm

The federated dropout technique is designed based on the dropout technique from deep learning [9]. Each training process is involved based on randomly dropping a subset of the model's attributes. This technique reduces communication costs based on transmitting and updating a portion of the model. The following algorithm discusses the steps involved in implementing the federated dropout technique.

Algorithm: Federated dropout technique

1. Initialize the global model G_{model} based on the global model architecture with initial weights W_G and set the global model attributes $M_G(W_G)$
2. Select dropout rate $D_p \in (0, 1)$, which indicates the model attribute to be dropped in each iteration
3. Select a suitable number of communication rounds as T_R
4. Client devices are selected randomly $C_{t<T}$ from the available list of client device C_T
5. Send the global model $M_G(W_G)$ to the select set of client devices C_t
6. For each client device $c_i \in C_{t<T}$
   (a) Apply dropout function to randomly drop a fraction D_p of the model attributes G_{model}. $G_{(c,\text{dropouts})}$ denotes the remaining attributes by applying the dropout function
   (b) Apply local training process with remaining attributes $G_{(c,\text{dropouts})}$ over the client local dataset D_c for the set of epochs E_c
   (c) Compute the local model updates ΔG_c based on the remaining attributes
7. Each client device c sends the local model updates ΔG_c to central server
8. Server receives all the local model updates ΔG_c from the client devices and aggregates the global updates
9. Computes the average model updates ΔG as follows:

$$\Delta G = \frac{1}{|C_t|}\sum_{c \in C_t} \Delta G_c$$

10. Updates the global attributes ΔG based on the aggregated updates ΔG

$$G_c = G_c + \Delta G$$

11. Repeat the Steps 3–10 for T_R rounds
12. The global model G_{model} has been obtained with the completion of communication rounds
13. The global model has been shared with participating client devices

The selection of $\boldsymbol{D_p}$ directly affects the trade-off between communication efficiency and model performance. Higher $\boldsymbol{D_p}$ minimizes the communication costs, and it affects the convergence rate and model accuracy. The client devices are designed with different dropout rates or strategies based on their computational cost and network structure. Dropout-based federated learning techniques are designed with differential privacy for achieving privacy by ensuring that only partially model information is shared.

The data compression techniques are used to achieve communication efficiency in federated learning, particularly for energy-constrained environments. An FL system uses strategies like pruning, quantization, delta encoding, and gradient compression can reduce communication overheads by maintaining acceptable levels of model accuracy and performance. These techniques are playing an important role in increasingly enabling scalability and efficiently distributed learning systems.

4.7 Adaptive communication techniques

The federated learning technique is designed by involving a training process for a global model across multiple decentralized devices without sharing raw data and this will preserve data privacy. The communication overhead is a critical challenge in FL due to frequent data exchange between client devices and central server. This overhead consumes high network bandwidth, and this leads to high energy consumption. Energy consumption is problematic in resource-constrained IoT devices. The adaptive communication strategies in FL are designed to address these challenges by dynamically adjusting the communication protocols based on the current system conditions.

4.7.1 Components of adaptive communication strategies

Federated learning techniques are designed with the following key components: dynamic communication frequency, client selection and scheduling, gradient compression and sparsification, adaptive learning and batch size, and asynchronous federated learning for achieving efficiency in communication. This section discusses the adaptive communication strategies for achieving communication and energy efficiency in FL techniques.

The classical traditional FL techniques use frequent communication between client devices and central server for sharing local training epochs. The dynamic communication frequency uses adaptive strategies that can reduce the frequent communication between these devices based on factors of network conditions, model convergence rate, and energy levels.

The adaptive frequency system can be implemented by using continuous monitoring of convergence and energy awareness monitoring. Quick model convergence means the frequency of communication is less. Energy awareness is a regular monitoring of IoT devices for achieving lower energy, and this can reduce the communication frequency to save battery life. The selected set of client devices participates in every round of the FL model. Adaptive client selection and scheduling techniques apply priorities based on factors like data quality, computational capacity, and energy levels. The selection and scheduling techniques can be designed by using a subset selection strategy and energy-efficient scheduling. The selection process of devices focuses on ensuring representativeness by minimizing the number of active device participants. The scheduling process is done by using a prioritized device based on available energy levels.

The management of learning rate and batch size can be adjusted to achieve energy efficiency from the current state and network conditions of participating IoT devices. The asynchronous federated learning supports achieving flexibility in communication and clients need not synchronize their updates with the central servers at the same time. This process reduces idle times and allows devices to send updates whenever they are ready.

Adaptive communication strategies are used to achieve benefits in reducing energy consumption for the IoT environment. This technique reduces communication overhead by using dynamically adjusting communication attributes and these strategies can significantly reduce the amount of data sharing. This will be more suitable for energy and bandwidth-constrained devices. The adaptive strategies are giving high priority to the energy efficiency of devices, and this strategy supports resource-constrained devices. The adaptive mechanism is more suitable for achieving scalability by efficiently managing devices involved in the larger size of the IoT environment. These techniques enhance the security and privacy of participating devices by reducing the frequency and size of communications. Applying adaptive strategies in device handling in an IoT environment, the exposure of sensitive information is minimized and system privacy is enhanced.

The adaptive strategies have a few challenges such as complexity, heterogeneity, and trade-offs. This strategy can add complexity to the system design and requires more careful attribute selection for implementing it in federated learning. Developing an adaptive communication strategy in the heterogeneous nature of IoT devices for hardware, network connectivity, and energy resources is a challenging task. The reduction of energy consumption through minimizing the communication overhead will lead to a slowdown in the model convergence rate. Balancing the trade-off between energy efficiency and model convergence is crucial for using adaptive design strategies.

The adaptive communication strategies are essential system designs for enhancing the energy efficiency of federated learning in the IoT environment. This strategy helps to manage the inherited challenges in resource-constrained devices by applying dynamic adjustment in various aspects of communication parameters.

4.8 Privacy-preserved communication techniques

Federated learning is a decentralized technique designed for multiple participants collaboratively to train a model and create updates without sharing their raw data. This approach is particularly suitable for sensitive data-handling environments like healthcare and financial applications. Achieving and preserving privacy and security between the central server and multiple client devices is an important area to concentrate on for designing an efficient FL system. This section provides a detailed explanation of privacy-preserving techniques in the framework of communication for federated learning.

4.8.1 Secure aggregation technique

The communication between client devices and the central server is a sensitive channel for sharing data, and secure aggregation is an essential technique for securing the aggregated data from all the devices. This can be achieved by using an authenticated and confidential framework such as encryption or a secure multiparty computation environment.

Encryption techniques allow secure and confidential communication between client devices and the central server and this can be implemented by using symmetric and asymmetric encryption techniques. Each client device shares its data and model updates to the server by applying cryptographic algorithms. The server can perform the aggregation process by decrypting the received updates and this will ensure the confidentiality of the individual updates that come from client devices.

A secure multiparty computation framework allows participating multiple computing parties jointly to compute a function on their inputs by achieving privacy. The client, in federated learning, uses multipart computation protocols to share encrypted model updates with the server.

The differential privacy introduces noise over the data or model updates to prevent the identification of individual participant data. This approach ensures that the output of a computation does not significantly change when a single participant's data is modified and provides a strong privacy guarantee. The client-side differential privacy is applied to each client device for adding noise over their model updates and this noise-added data is shared with the central server. This approach reduces the risk of identifying individual data points from the aggregated updates. When the server introduces noise over the aggregated model updates is known as server-side differential privacy. This approach helps to protect against inference attacks and deduce information about the individual participants.

Encrypted communication channels ensure secure data transfer between client devices and central server, and this encryption process ensures unauthorized parties cannot be intercepted or tampered with communication channels. This can be achieved by using standard encryption protocols like SSL (Secure Socket Layer) or TLS (Transport Layer Security).

The mechanism of split learning is used to divide the models into multiple segments and these segments are trained on different clients. This approach reduces the risk rate of revealing sensitive data by sharing partial model information with the server. The server preserves privacy by reducing the size of the gradients. Techniques like gradient sparsification or compression are used to reduce the risk of leaking sensitive information through model updates. The trusted execution environment provides a secure area within the protected code and data. This approach can be used on the server side for aggregating model updates without exposing individual updates to the server.

Anonymization is a technique used to prevent the association of model updates with a specific set of client devices. This mechanism can be achieved by using temporary identifiers to protect client's original identities. A strong secure environment can be established by combining multiple privacy-preserving techniques. The dual layer of protection against security attacks can be ensured by using differential privacy and secure aggregation process.

Privacy-preserved communication in federated learning is an important area of research for ensuring sensitive data remains under a protected area during the collaborative training process. The privacy techniques discussed in this section provide different levels of security and privacy for the participating clients. The selection of a suitable method depends on the specific set of requirements of the application, which includes the desired level of privacy, computational resources, and an acceptable level of accuracy loss.

4.9 Conclusion

This chapter provides a detailed view of optimizing communication for achieving energy efficiency in FL. Energy efficiency in communication is a crucial task for extending the lifespan of edge devices, minimizing operational costs, and enhancing the sustainability of federated learning deployments. Energy-efficient communication strategies comprise several key approaches, which include minimizing the frequency and size of data transmissions, using model compression techniques, and implementing efficient aggregation techniques. These techniques reduce the energy efficiency associated with data sharing between client devices and central server by carefully managing the bandwidth and computational resources.

Moreover, advanced approaches such as client selection algorithms and adaptive learning rates can further improve energy efficiency by reducing the consumption of computational resources by the client devices. This will reduce unnecessary communications. The application of asynchronous communication protocols and decentralized architecture frameworks are contributing to minimizing energy consumption by managing synchronization overhead and allowing more flexible information exchanges.

The energy-efficient communication strategies support to conserve energy utilization of IoT devices and improve the scalability and feasibility of federated learning systems, suitable for resource-constrained environments. Ongoing research and innovations in communication efficiency play an important role in achieving the full potential of IoT devices by maintaining an environmentally friendly and cost-effective ecosystem for the IoT environment.

References

[1] Hosseini M, and Mohsenin T, 2021. QS-NAS: optimally quantized scaled architecture search to enable efficient on-device micro-AI. *IEEE J Emerg Sel Top Circ Syst*, 11(4):597–610. https://doi.org/10.1109/JETCAS.2021.3127932.

[2] Hu YQ, Huang HJ, and Yu N, 2022. Device scheduling and channel allocation for energy-efficient federated edge learning. *Comput Commun*, 189:53–66. https://doi.org/10.1016/j.comcom.2022.03.008.

[3] Imteaj A, Thakker U, Wang SQ, *et al.*, 2022. A survey on federated learning for resource-constrained IoT devices. *IEEE Int Things J*, 9(1):1–24. https://doi.org/10.1109/JIOT.2021.3095077.

[4] Jararweh Y, Doulat A, AlQudah O, *et al.*, 2016. The future of mobile cloud computing: integrating cloudlets and mobile edge computing. *Proc 23rd Int*

Conf on Telecommunications, pp. 1–5. https://doi.org/10.1109/ICT.2016.7500486.

[5] Khowaja SA, Dev K, Khowaja P, *et al.*, 2021. Toward energy-efficient distributed federated learning for 6G networks. *IEEE Wirel Commun*, 28(6): 34–40. https://doi.org/10.1109/MWC.012.2100153.

[6] Kim J, Kim D, Lee J, *et al.*, 2022. A novel joint dataset and computation management scheme for energy-efficient federated learning in mobile edge computing. *IEEE Wirel Commun Lett*, 11(5):898–902. https://doi.org/10.1109/LWC.2022.3147236.

[7] Kim YG, Wu CJ, 2020. AutoScale: energy efficiency optimization for stochastic edge inference using reinforcement learning. *Proc 53rd Annual IEEE/ACM Int Symp on Microarchitecture*, pp. 1082–1096. https://doi.org/10.1109/MICRO50266.2020.00090.

[8] Kim YG, Wu CJ, 2021. AutoFL: enabling heterogeneity-aware energy efficient federated learning. *Proc 54th Annual IEEE/ACM Int Symp on Microarchitecture*, pp. 183–198. https://doi.org/10.1145/3466752.3480129.

[9] Li L, Xiong HY, Guo ZS, *et al.*, 2019. SmartPC: hierarchical pace control in real-time federated learning system. *Proc IEEE Real-Time Systems Symp*, pp. 406–418. https://doi.org/10.1109/RTSS46320.2019.00043.

Chapter 5

Energy-efficient federated learning methods for IoT environment

Amutha Prabakar Muniyandi[1], Feslin Anish Mon[2], L. Godlin Atlas[3] and Mahmoud Ahmad Al-Khasawneh[4,5]

Abstract

The rapid expansion of the Internet of Things (IoT) has led to an unprecedented surge in data generation and processing demands. Federated Learning (FL) has emerged as a promising framework for enabling collaborative model training across distributed IoT devices while preserving data privacy. Given the resource-constrained nature of IoT devices, developing energy-efficient FL techniques is crucial to ensure sustainability and prolonged device operation. This chapter provides a comprehensive exploration of cutting-edge energy-efficient methods tailored for FL in IoT environments. Key contributions include an in-depth analysis of energy consumption challenges specific to IoT-driven FL and the introduction of innovative strategies to optimize communication and computation overheads. The chapter systematically reviews and evaluates techniques such as model compression, adaptive aggregation, and participant selection. Furthermore, it examines the role of energy-aware resource allocation and edge computing in enhancing the efficiency of Federated Learning. Empirical studies and simulations are presented to demonstrate the feasibility and performance of these methods, offering valuable insights into their practical deployment. This chapter serves as a comprehensive guide for researchers and practitioners aiming to leverage Federated Learning in IoT ecosystems, fostering innovation in sustainable and intelligent IoT solutions by addressing the critical intersection of FL and energy efficiency.

Keywords: Federated learning; Internet of Things (IoT); Energy efficiency; Edge computing; Resource optimization

[1]Department of Computer Engineering, Government Polytechnic College, Madurai, India
[2]Faculty in Department of Information Technology, University of Technology and Applied Sciences, Sultanate of Oman
[3]Department of Computer Science and Engineering, Bharath Institute of Higher Education and Research, India
[4]School of Computing, Skyline University College, University City Sharjah, UAE
[5]Applied Science Research Center, Applied Science Private University, Jordan

5.1 Introduction to federated learning and IoT

The Internet of Things (IoT) connects various electronic devices for collecting information and automates across various applications. Federated learning (FL) provides an excellent solution to leverage this decentralized information while preserving privacy. Federated learning trains the models locally over connected devices and shares only the updates with a central server. The convergence of FL and IoT addresses key challenges across various applications, like healthcare, industrial automation, environmental monitoring, and other interactive applications. This learning environment enables intelligent, decentralized systems that respect user privacy and optimize resource usage.

Federated learning is a decentralized machine learning technique, where multiple IoT devices collaboratively train the model by keeping collected information locally. FL models process the collected information locally and only share model outputs with the centralized data server, instead of sending raw data to a central server. These decentralized models enhance data privacy and security and reduce unnecessary data transfer, and these models are particularly useful in environments like IoT, where data is distributed across numerous devices with limited energy and computational resources.

5.1.1 Comparison with traditional machine learning

Machine learning (ML) involves proper training models on centralized data where all the data is gathered and processed in a commonplace. These techniques require substantial computing resources and raise privacy concerns. FL decentralizes the training process by allowing models to be trained locally on individual devices where data is generated. The model updates are shared with a central server in FL, and this model enhances privacy and security. Federated learning techniques are more scalable and energy-efficient, and these techniques are more suitable for resource-limited environments.

5.1.1.1 Benefits and challenges of federated learning

Federated learning techniques support a lot of benefits and challenges. Federated learning models allow training processes conducted on local devices without transferring raw data to a centralized server. This model will enhance the privacy and security of individual devices, and sensitive information remains on the local device. FL technique can leverage the computational power of numerous decentralized devices, enabling the training process of larger models without overloading a central service. The FL models are reducing the processing time for data transfer due to handling the data locally. FL models are optimizing recourse use by utilizing the existing computational capabilities of edge devices. This will reduce the need for extensive cloud infrastructure.

Federated learning has a few challenges in real-time implementation in IoT. Frequent communication between devices leads to significant network overhead, especially for large-scale models or datasets. Variable computational power and energy resources of individual devices can lead to unpredictable training times and performance. Differences in local data distributions can cause challenges in model convergence and generalization. The inside attackers play a vital role in exploiting model updates that come from devices, which leads to indirect information leakage. Implementing FL required efficient and robust mechanisms for security communication, aggregation of model updates, and handling device-level failures. This will increase the complexity compared to traditional machine learning approaches.

Federated learning has significant advantages in terms of privacy, security, scalability, and resource efficiency. This technique introduces issues and challenges connected to communication networks, device heterogeneity, and data security and privacy that need to be carefully accomplished.

5.1.2 Intersection of federated learning and IoT

The incorporation of FL techniques with IoT-based applications represents a transformative method for handling large quantities of data collected or generated by interconnected devices. Federated learning allows IoT devices to collaboratively conduct training processes for machine learning models while keeping data in local devices, addressing privacy-related issues, and reducing the requirement of extensive data sharing.

Federated learning can improve smart city applications by enhancing disseminated data processing for traffic management, energy usage and distribution, and environmental monitoring and management, ensuring real-time sensitivity and privacy. In IoT-based healthcare applications, federated learning can defend and secure patient data while permitting collaborative model training for various medical devices and organizations, enhancing diagnostic accuracy and adapted personal-level treatment.

By leveraging federated learning, IoT ecosystems can attain sustainability between information usage and privacy, promoting innovation while solving challenges related to critical data security and efficiency [1].

5.1.3 Importance of federated learning in IoT devices

FL plays an important role in enhancing the development, functionality, and efficiency of IoT devices and this development will address the key challenges related to efficient bandwidth, data privacy, and real-time data processing. IoT devices handle sensitive information, such as personal health-related information, live location information, and financial and business transactions [2]. FL enables these devices to train locally and ensures that raw data never leaves the device. This technique pointedly reduces the risk of data breaches and improves security and privacy by managing sensitive information securely.

Traditional centralized machine learning techniques require the transfer of large amounts of data to central servers, overwhelming significant network bandwidth. FL alleviates this issue by only sharing model outputs rather than raw data, and this will make it a more efficient bandwidth utilization. This efficiency is most important for IoT ecosystems where network computing resources may be inadequate.

FL allows IoT devices to process information locally and update model output in a real-time environment, and this ability is critical for applications that require instant responses, such as autonomous vehicle monitoring systems, industrial automation applications, and smart home systems. By incorporating a real-time decision support system, FL improves the overall efficiency and performance of IoT applications [3]. FL provides scalable machine learning by using the distributed nature of IoT networks. It permits multiple devices may collaborate on the model training stage without using centralized data aggregation. This distributed method can lead to more efficient, robust, and accurate models by including diverse data sources.

In summary, federated learning is important for IoT devices for ensuring data privacy, preserving bandwidth, allowing real-time processing, and supporting scalability by applying collaborative model training. These benefits make federated learning as an essential technology for proceeding with the abilities and adoption of IoT systems.

5.1.4 Energy efficiency in IoT networks

Energy efficiency is a serious issue to be considered in the design, deployment, and operation of IoT networks. The IoT network consists of various interconnected sensor devices often operating in a diversified environment and with different levels of energy constraints.

Many IoT devices are functioning with battery power, and this will make energy efficiency essential for enhancing the operational lifetimes and reducing the maintenance requirements. Energy-efficient IoT devices are contributing to lower energy usage and reduce carbon footprint, aligning with sustainability goals. Reducing energy consumption can be achieved through lower operational costs for deploying and maintaining IoT networks.

5.1.4.1 Design strategies for energy efficiency

Designing an IoT-based network with sensor devices must have energy-efficient processors, sensors, and communication modules for minimizing energy consumption rate during operation and standby modes [4]. Implementing efficient communication protocols such as MQTT, CoAP, or LoRaWAN in an IoT environment will reduce the overhead and conserve energy during data transmission. IoT devices can enter low-power sleeping modes when idle mode and wake up periodically to perform necessary tasks, balancing responsiveness with energy conservation. Processing data locally by the device level in the network reduces the number of transmissions needed for frequent data sharing to centralized servers, and this process conserves energy and improves response times.

Energy efficiency design strategies are facing many challenges due to diverse device requirements and trade-offs with performance optimization. Achieving energy efficiency in IoT networks involves a multidimensional method that integrates hardware selection and design, communication protocols, channel section, power management strategies, and renewable and sustainable energy solutions. IoT network deployment can enhance reliability, sustainability, and cost-effectiveness while minimizing environmental impact through a prioritized energy-efficient model.

5.2 Fundamentals of energy-efficient federated learning

Federated learning technique enables multiple devices to be used collaboratively for learning a shared model without sharing raw data, ensuring privacy and security. This method is important for optimizing energy usage across various sectors by leveraging distributed data from smart grids, IoT devices, and industrial systems. The chapter investigates core concepts, algorithms, and applications, providing insights into how federated learning techniques are enhancing energy efficiency, reducing costs, and supporting sustainable practices. It serves as an essential resource for researcher scholars, design engineers, and policymakers in the energy and artificial intelligence domains.

5.2.1 Principles of federated learning

Federated learning is a decentralized method where multiple IoT devices collaboratively train the shared model by keeping their collected data [5]. This method solves privacy, security, and data governance issues by allowing data to remain in local devices. The fundamental principles of federated learning include decentralization, privacy preservation, communication efficiency, federated optimization, robustness, and fault tolerance. These principles make federated learning a powerful paradigm for applications requiring privacy, efficiency, and collaboration across distributed data sources.

5.2.1.1 Energy consumption model

Yang *et al.* [6] developed an energy consumption model for n at time slot t is expressed as follows:

$$\mathrm{Eng}_{n,t} = \alpha.\delta_{n,t}^{\mathrm{Local}} + \sum_{i=1}^{m}\sum_{j=1}^{n} \sigma.E_{i,j} \tag{5.1}$$

Here, α and σ are the coefficient factors for the energy constant for each IoT device. The energy factor for communication efficiency is measured as follows:

$$\mathrm{Eng}_{n,t}^{\mathrm{cm}} = E_{n,t}.T_{n,t}^{\mathrm{cm}} \tag{5.2}$$

Here, $E_{n,t}$ and $T_{n,t}^{\mathrm{cm}}$ are the energy consumption of transmission and communication time for each IoT device. The total energy is calculated as follows:

$$E_{n,t}^{T} = \mathrm{Eng}_{n,t} + E_{n,t}^{\mathrm{cm}} \tag{5.3}$$

They have proposed a federated learning framework for minimizing the total energy consumption for all IoT devices with latency constraints and various resource constraints. The energy minimization problem is expressed as follows:

$$\min_{n,t} \sum_{i=t}^{T}\left(\sum_{i=1}^{N} E_{n,t}^{T}\right) \tag{5.4}$$

$$0 \leq p_{n,t} \leq p_n^{\text{Max}}, \forall n \in N, \forall t \in T \tag{5.5}$$

$$f_n^{\text{Min}} \leq f_{n,t} \leq f_n^{\text{Max}}, \forall n \in N, \forall t \in T \tag{5.6}$$

$$E_{n,t}^T \leq \sigma + E_{n,t}, \forall n \in N, \forall t \in T \tag{5.7}$$

Equation (5.5) denotes the constraint for the transmission power allocation for IoT devices. Equation (5.6) defined the constraint for CPU frequency allocation and f_n^{Min} and f_n^{Max} denotes minimum and maximum frequency respectively. Equation (5.7) defines the each global round completed within the time frame , $\forall t \in T$.

5.2.2 Energy consumption in federated learning

Understanding and optimizing energy utilization is an essential task for making federated learning viable in real-world applications, especially for resource-constrained devices. The energy consumption cost is measured based on the utilization of devices for communication and computation costs. The FL techniques mainly rely on communication between devices involved in the IoT ecosystem and centralized server. This data sharing may consume high energy due to frequent or large number of updates. Techniques like model compression, quantization, and sparse updates can support reducing the amount of data transmitted, thereby saving energy. Each communicating device performs local computations for updating the model based on the collected data [7]. FL involves executing complex algorithms that consume significant computational cost and energy. Optimizing the computational cost for each instance through model pruning and efficient algorithms is important for minimizing energy consumption. Devices involved in federated learning often spend time waiting to complete other tasks. This waiting time will lead to idle energy consumption. An efficient scheduling and coordination process mitigates the unwanted waiting time by applying balanced load allocation. Federated learning techniques are subject to diverse energy requirements based on the participating devices. Adaptive energy-efficient algorithms are used for managing energy availability and capabilities of each device and this will improve the overall energy efficiency. Energy efficiency becomes an important issue for supporting federated learning by addressing the above-mentioned issues in the IoT environment.

5.2.3 Fundamental architecture for federated learning

IoT environments are designed by involving various sensor devices, and federated learning in IoT provides a global machine learning model without sharing local information with centralized servers. The architecture of the FL-based IoT environment consists of several key components and ensures effective training and privacy. This section discusses the architecture for federated learning in an IoT environment [8].

5.2.3.1 System components

The federated learning model is designed with IoT devices (clients), central server, and network infrastructure. The IoT devices are designed with local data storage, local training, and communication modules. The central server is constructed with aggregated model updates from multiple IoT devices. This will maintain a global model for updating with aggregated results. Network infrastructure facilitates communication between IoT devices and the centralized server. This process can be achieved through wireless networks and IoT communication protocols.

5.2.3.2 Architecture workflow

The central server is initialized as a global model and is distributed to each participating IoT device. Federated learning parameters are defined based on communication frequency, model architecture, and privacy-preserving designs. Each participating device is trained with the global model on its local information. This model training involves the following steps: data preprocessing, training process, and model updates.

5.2.3.3 Additional considerations

The design strategies for federated learning algorithms are mainly focused on achieving energy efficiency and fault tolerance. Energy efficiency and consumption can be achieved for optimized communication and computation power through model compression and reduced communication. Fault tolerance can be handled by continuous monitoring of offline or failed IoT devices.

Figure 5.1 shows the federated learning architecture, and this architecture ensures to connect the IoT devices, central server, and communication network. Each IoT device is connected to handle training and data privacy, and central server is used to manage global model aggregation. The communication network is used to establish a connection between devices and server. The federated learning architecture ensures that sensitive data remains in the local device for the benefit of collaborative learning.

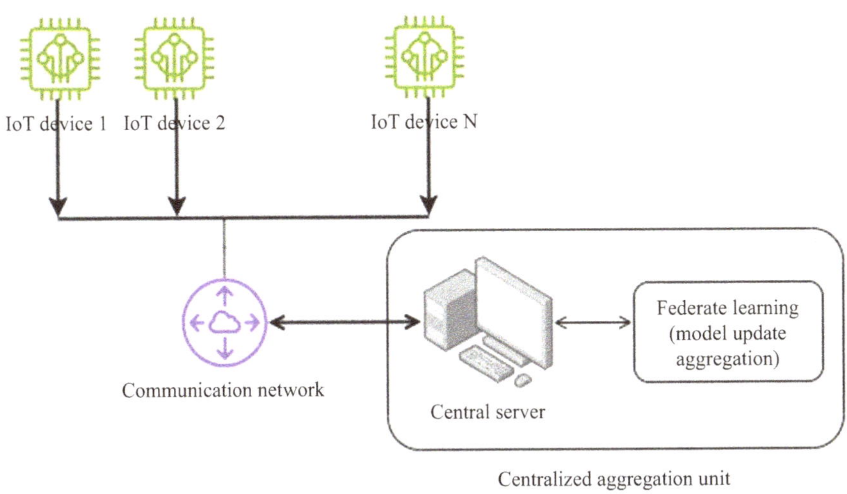

Figure 5.1 Architecture for federated learning with centralized server

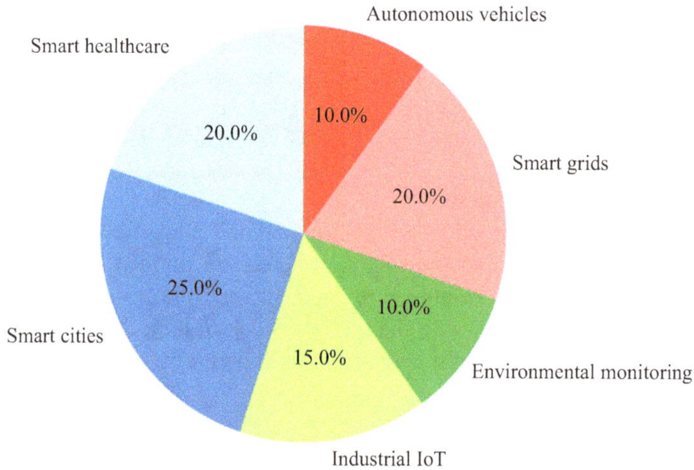

Figure 5.2 Application of federated learning in different domains

Figure 5.2 shows the federated learning application domains and smart city applications are using federated learning techniques nearly 25%. Smart grids and smart healthcare applications are supported for 20% with FL techniques. Autonomous vehicles, environmental monitoring, and industrial IoT applications are designed with FL techniques.

5.3 Architectures and algorithms for energy-efficient federated learning

This chapter investigates the design and implementation of systems and methods aimed at optimizing energy utilization in federated learning. This chapter explores fundamental architectures that support energy-efficient data processing and transmission, and this architecture enhances computational efficiency and minimizes energy consumption. This section covers strategies such as model compression, adaptive learning, and efficient communication protocols. This will provide detailed insights into how federated learning can be made sustainable and scalable solutions.

5.3.1 Architectures for federated learning in IoT

FL in the IoT necessitates specialized architectures for accommodating the unique constraints and capabilities of IoT devices. These architectures are designed for ensuring efficient, scalable, and secure model training processes across diverse and distributed IoT platforms. This section discusses some important architecture for federated learning in IoT, which includes centralized federated learning, hierarchical FL, fully decentralized FL, federated learning with edge collaboration, federated learning with split learning, and federated learning with blockchain integration.

5.3.1.1 Centralized federated learning architecture

A centralized server controls and coordinates the learning process for the connected device in the IoT environment. The locally connected IoT devices perform the computation process in the local device and send the updates to the central server. These updates will be coordinated and combined to form a globally accepted model for IoT connected environment. This architecture has some advantages and challenges. This architecture is simple to implement and manage for the connectivity of small-scale IoT devices. The architecture is potential bottlenecks and single points of failure, and this will have a high communication cost and energy consumption.

5.3.1.2 Hierarchical federated learning

This architecture introduces intermediary nodes (edge servers) placed between IoT devices and central server. The intermediary nodes are aggregating updates from nearby connected devices before forwarding them to central server. This will work based on a hierarchical structure. This architecture has reduced the communication latency and bandwidth utilization in IoT device networks. This architecture improves the scalability and fault tolerance of the participating devices. The main challenges for this architecture are increasing the complexity in managing hierarchical structures, and this structure requires efficient coordination mechanisms.

5.3.1.3 Fully decentralized federated learning architecture

This architecture eliminates the central server and enables a direct communication model for exchanging model updates with other participating devices. Gossip protocols and peer-to-peer networks are commonly used for establishing connectivity among the devices for exchanging data. This architecture will enhance the privacy and resilience to central server failures. Highly distributed and large-scale IoT networks are utilizing this architecture. This architecture ensures convergence and consistency for the global model, and this will create complex communication and synchronization.

5.3.1.4 Federate learning with cloud-edge collaboration architecture

This architecture combines cloud and edge computing network resources for balancing computational load and improving efficiency. This architecture works with the support of IoT devices to perform the initial stage of computation. The edge servers are used to handle intermediate aggregations and the cloud servers will perform the final stage of aggregations. This architecture model optimizes resource utilization and reduces network latency. This model leverages the advantage of both cloud and edge computing environments. This architecture requires efficient transposition of tasks across different layers and it needs higher implementation complexity [9].

5.3.1.5 Federate learning with split learning architecture

The model is split into segments and these segments work as a layer mechanism. Initial layers are trained with IoT devices and reaming layers are processed with central server or edge nodes. The intermediate results are shared with central server.

This architecture will reduce the data transmission volume and enhance security and privacy. This model is more suitable for resource-constrained IoT devices. This architecture requires careful design for the model-splitting process, and the potential challenge is to balance computational load across devices and servers.

5.3.1.6 Federate learning with blockchain integration architecture

This architecture utilizes blockchain technology to manage and verify the integrity of model updates. This architecture ensures a secure and transparent accumulation of updates. This will enhance the security and trust in the federated learning working process. Decentralized agreement mechanisms improve robustness and efficiency. The blockchain techniques are increasing the complexity and potential overhead. This requires efficient blockchain protocols to minimize energy consumption.

The purpose of these architectures is to balance the trade-offs between efficient computational cost, communication overhead, energy utilization, and security for making federated learning achievable and operative for diverse IoT applications.

5.3.2 Energy-efficient federated learning algorithms

Energy-efficient federated learning algorithms are crucial for optimizing the energy consumption of participating devices, especially in resource-constrained environments like IoT networks. These algorithms focus on reducing computation and communication overhead while maintaining model performance. Here are some key approaches.

Techniques such as model pruning, weight quantization, and knowledge distillation reduce the size of the model and the amount of data that needs to be communicated. This technique significantly reduces energy consumption and communication bandwidth overheads. Ensuring the compressed models retains accuracy and generalization capabilities.

The adaptive federated learning technique dynamically adjusts the frequency of communication and the number of local updates done by using the current state of the devices and network conditions. The unnecessary communications, energy consumption, and model convergence speed are reduced in this technique. Designing efficient and robust adaptive mechanisms that support diverse and changing conditions is a challenging task.

An extended version of the federate averaging (FedAvg) algorithm includes a periodic averaging technique, where model updates are combined less frequently and partial participation. According to the design specification, only subsets of devices are participated in each round. This technique reduces communication costs and energy usage for maintaining efficient performance. Managing a trade-off between model accuracy and efficient communication is a challenging task in the FedAvg algorithm.

The client selection strategy technique selects a subset of devices to participate in each training process based on their availability of energy, computational capacity, and network usage. This technique ensures that the selected subset of devices are the most capable and energy-efficient devices and extend the overall system lifetime. Designing a fair and effective mechanism for selecting devices does not follow bias in the model.

This technique follows a hierarchical structure for conducting and combining local updates through intermediate nodes to the central server. This process reduces direct communications from devices to the server. This technique consumes minimum communication costs and distributes the energy load equally across the network. Ensuring timely and efficient aggregation of information at intermediate devices to maintain model accuracy is a challenging task.

Energy-aware scheduling algorithms work based on the energy profiles of participating devices and aim to minimize peak energy usage and avoid overloading any single device. This technique optimizes energy distribution and prevents device failures. Enhance the sustainability of systems based on energy awareness. Achieving a balanced computational load and managing scheduling complexity is a challenging task in energy-aware scheduling techniques.

The federated learning with local adaptation technique combines the global mode of training with the local adapted threshold value, and this mechanism finetunes the global model for each device. This will reduce the number of communication updates. This technique minimizes communication needs for improving model performance. Maintaining the global model's generality with local model's specification is a challenging task.

By applying these energy-efficient federated learning algorithms, it is possible to achieve stability between maintaining high model accuracy and minimizing energy usage in the training process. Energy-sensitive environments are making use of federated learning algorithms more practical for a wide range of applications.

5.4 Implementation and deployment

This section provides details about the implementation and deployment of federated learning algorithms in an IoT environment. This section will discover setting up federated learning, energy monitoring and management, and case studies and practical application of FL algorithms.

5.4.1 Setting up federated learning in IoT environments

Setting up FL in IoT environments involves with set of procedures to ensure efficient, secure, and scalable deployment. IoT devices are designed with limited resources, so it is an important task to design a system with optimized computational and communication efficiency. The following subsection discusses the step-by-step guide for setting up federated learning in IoT ecosystems:

Step 1: system design and architecture

In the system design, the first task is to define the objective and requirements for the federated learning project. The second level is to identify the types of IoT devices involved in the ecosystem. Select a suitable FL architecture based on the requirements of the project. FL architectures are classified into three categories such as centralized, hierarchical, and decentralized. In a centralized system design, a central server is used to combine updates from all the connected IoT devices. Hierarchical system design works with intermediate edges servers or gateways for updating local information, and this design supports minimizing the local transactions. Devices are connected directly with each device using peer-to-peer networks.

Step 2: data preparation and handling
The local devices collect information from the IoT environment and data distribution is done across IoT devices while keeping it local to comply with privacy regulations. Use different types of techniques like differential privacy mechanisms to protect individual data points. Each data transfer is carried out by using secure communication protocols (e.g., SSL/TLS).

Step 3: model selection and training
Select a suitable architecture model for connecting IoT devices with limited computational power. Model compression techniques are implemented to reduce model size. Local training loops on IoT devices are established to update the model using local data, and the computational overhead is minimized by using efficient optimizers (e.g., SGD, Adam).

Step 4: communication protocols
Efficient communication strategies are applied to improve data-sharing efficiency by using communication protocols. An efficient communication strategy uses compression techniques for updates to reduce the communication overhead. An adaptive communication frequency technique is used to adjust the interval between updates based on the state of the network devices. The model updates come from IoT devices combined by implementing federated learning averaging (FedAvg) or other aggregation algorithms. The efficiency and robustness of aggregation methods ensure to handling of unreliable or straggling devices.

Step 5: infrastructure setup
The infrastructure setup is creating an efficient network setup by deploying edge servers or gateways to handle local aggregation and preprocessing. A central server is established for global aggregation and coordination between devices. The networking ensures reliable and secure network connections between IoT devices, edge servers, and other participating devices. Optimized network configuration is used to handle variable bandwidth and latency.

Step 6: monitoring and maintenance
This phase is used to handle the monitoring and maintenance process of devices to ensure the efficiency of IoT ecosystems. The performance of IoT devices, model accuracy, and energy consumption are tracked by accommodating monitoring tools. This process is used to identify and address the issues in real-time applications by using logging and alerting systems. In the maintenance phase, IoT devices regularly update models and software to accommodate the improvements and security patches. The system performances are evaluated and assessed periodically for necessary adjustments.

Step 7: deployment and scalability

The deployment starts from pilot deployment, and it starts with a small-scale deployment to test the system's functionality and performance. The necessary adjustments are carried out based on the gathered feedback. Gradually scale the deployment to more IoT devices for handling larger size of loads. The system stability is maintained by implementing load balancing and fault tolerance mechanisms.

Step 8: security and compliance

Federated learning technique is a local update model for centralized or decentralized server mechanisms, and this technique ensures end-to-end encryption for data transmission. A secure aggregation technique is used to protect model updates. Data protection is achieved by adhering to protection regulations such as GDPR, HIPAA, and local data privacy laws. Data audit mechanisms are used to ensure compliance and maintain transparency. The following tools and frameworks are used to achieve security and data privacy in federated learning:

- **Federated learning frameworks**: TensorFlow Federated, PySyft, Flower (a friendly federated learning framework).
- **IoT platforms**: AWS IoT, Google Cloud IoT, Azure IoT Hub.
- **Communication protocols**: MQTT, CoAP, HTTP/2.

Federated learning system in the IoT ecosystem can be implemented by the above-given steps. These steps are achieving efficient, scalable, and secure data transfer by ensuring that local data is used efficiently while upholding data privacy and optimizing resource usage.

5.4.2 Energy monitoring and management

Energy monitoring and management is an essential part of the FL system in the IoT environment, and this will ensure sustainable and efficient operation of the system. This section discussed a few key aspects to be considered for energy monitoring and management in FL for IoT environments. The energy aware and monitoring system components are organized as given in Figure 5.3.

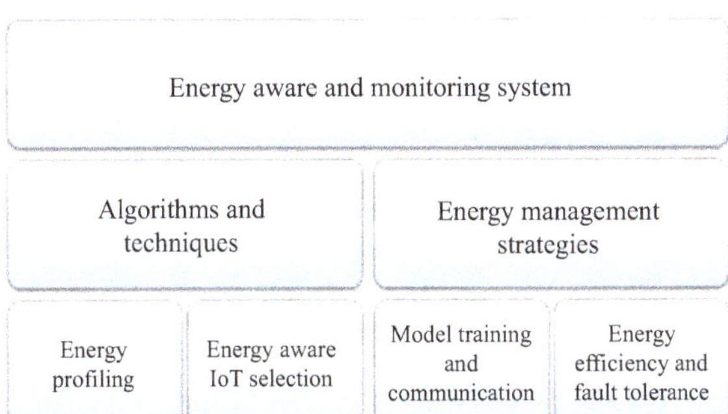

Figure 5.3 Energy monitoring and management

5.4.2.1 Energy profiling of IoT devices

A device characteristic shows the energy profile for each IoT device to understand its energy consumption patterns, computational capabilities, and battery life. The energy consumption data for each device is collected by deploying energy monitoring sensors or software tools. The aggregated energy consumption data from each IoT device to the central monitoring system for analyzing for generating auditing profiles.

5.4.2.2 Energy-aware client selection

The client device selection was conducted based on their current energy levels and historical energy consumption patterns. Tasks are evenly distributed among available IoT devices to prevent energy depletion of individual devices. The client device participation is adjusted based on their battery's current status to achieve sustainable functioning of the device over time.

5.4.2.3 Optimized model training and communication

The model training and communication are optimized by using offload heavy computations to edge servers or cloud resources for conserving device energy. To optimize the learning rate through an adaptive mechanism by adjusting the device energy levels for efficient convergence. The optimum data transmission reduces energy consumption by using energy-efficient communication protocols (e.g., MQTT, CoAP).

5.4.2.4 Energy management strategies

Energy management plays an important role in reducing energy utilization by using dynamic power modes, task scheduling, and energy harvesting. The power management for each device is dynamically adjusted based on workload and energy availability. The task scheduling process is used to train the tasks during off-peak energy consumption periods to reduce the impact of device operations. Supplement device power and extended operational during are achieved by utilizing energy harvesting techniques.

5.4.2.5 Energy-efficient algorithms and techniques

Model compression technique is employed for reducing computational loads and energy consumption during local model training. Essential model updates are only transmitted to conserve communication energy. The learning parameters are adjusted dynamically based on the device energy constraints.

5.4.2.6 Monitoring and analytics

The process of real-time monitoring continuously monitors energy consumption metrics and device health indicators as a regular monitoring process. Efficient anomaly detection algorithms are used to identify and address energy inefficiencies and device malfunctions. The system efficiency is optimized by tracking FL performance metrics.

5.4.2.7 Energy-aware system design

The energy-aware FL systems are designed with energy-efficient components, hardware, sensor components, software tools, and architectures. The device's longevity and optimum energy consumption over time are implemented by using lifecycle management strategies. Ensure energy monitoring and management tools are scalable for FL systems due to the scalability of the IoT environment.

The organizational resources are optimized by integrating efficient and robust energy monitoring and management practices into federated learning for the IoT ecosystem. This optimization process ensures extended device lifespan, minimum resource usage, and sustainable functioning by maintaining performance and data privacy standards.

5.4.3 Case studies and practical applications

The section discusses the case studies and practical applications of the FL technique in the IoT ecosystem. FL presents various practical applications in IoT environments, leveraging its capability to train models across distributed devices by preserving data security and privacy and minimizing communication costs. This section discussed a few case studies and practical applications for showing the efficiency of federated learning in an IoT environment.

Personalized healthcare monitoring systems are designed by using IoT devices such as wearable sensors and health monitors for collecting individual health information from patients. Personalized health prediction is achieved by using FL models that are directly available on users' devices. This process improves model accuracy with personalized data, reduces latency in health insights, and ensures security and privacy by keeping sensitive health data local.

Smart cities are designed based on traffic management and optimization techniques to reduce the unwanted network traffic flow. IoT sensors in traffic monitoring devices capture real-time traffic data. The FL aggregates local traffic data from various IoT devices to predict traffic patterns and optimize traffic timings. Smart city applications are reducing congestion, lowering emissions, enhancing overall transportation efficiency predicting traffic patterns, and optimizing traffic light timings.

Industrial IoT applications use sensor devices for monitoring production area energy consumption and this process comes under predictive maintenance. These IoT sensors are used to monitor industrial machinery equipment health parameters. Federated learning techniques are used in collaborative model training processes across distributed sensors to predict equipment failures and scheduled maintenance periods proactively. This process minimizes downtime, reduces maintenance costs, and enhances operational efficiency by using collected local sensor data without centralizing sensitive information.

Smart grids are used to share power for home and business applications, and smart grids are facing a lot of power losses during transmission. The IoT devices in smart meters are used to monitor the electricity usage patterns of participating users. FL technique aggregates data from smart meters for predicting energy demands and optimizing energy distribution operations. This process enhances smart grid stability, achieves load balance, and supports renewable energy integration while maintaining user privacy.

IoT devices (e.g., beacons, smart shelves) support collecting information from retail stores for tracking customer behavior for identifying customer browsing patterns and purchase history. FL techniques are applied for training models on local IoT data for predicting customer preferences and optimizing personalized marketing places. This will increase customer engagement and improve product sales rates. Individual privacy and buying preferences are maintained efficiently.

Edge computing applications support real-time video analysis through IoT devices, such as cameras and sensors, for monitoring devices. Federated learning analyzes video and image data locally on edge devices to detect anomalies, recognize abnormal object movements, monitor private area safety, or monitor safety compliance. This process reduces latency in decision-making, enhances security monitoring capabilities, and achieves data privacy by minimizing data transmission.

Telecommunication networks are automated for allocation of bandwidth and channel monitoring systems to support providing efficient network usage. The IoT devices are used to monitor network conditions in cellular networks. Federated learning collaboratively trains models over edge devices to optimize network parameters. This will improve the quality of service and predict user demand patterns. This analysis and monitoring process achieves enhanced network performance, reduces operational costs, and maintains user privacy by processing data locally.

These case studies illustrate how federated learning enables efficient and privacy-preserving machine learning applications in IoT environments. By leveraging distributed data and computational resources, FL supports diverse industries in achieving improved operational efficiency, enhanced decision-making capabilities, and compliance with privacy regulations.

5.5 Future directions and challenges

This section provides a detailed look ahead regarding the upcoming research direction for energy-efficient FL mechanisms in IoT environments. This section discusses the challenges faced by the FL mechanism that need to be addressed for extensive acceptance and effectiveness.

5.5.1 Future directions

The following future directions are focused on developing efficient FL techniques to achieve high efficiency and accuracy for prediction. To develop more efficient and advanced model compression techniques based on customer support system mode for IoT devices. These techniques are focused on reducing the computational and communication cost overhead further while maintaining model accuracy. Integrating edge computing architecture with federated learning techniques to minimize latency and improve real-time decision support system. This integration supports local data processing and model training directly on edge devices and minimizes the dependency on a centralized server. To develop adaptive and dynamic resource allocation techniques for resource allocation that support dynamically adjusted device capabilities and energy constraints. Adaptive allocation techniques are supporting to optimize the energy consumption for balancing computational loads across IoT devices. Enhanced privacy preserved techniques are supporting innovation on differential privacy and secure aggregation mechanisms to strengthen data privacy in FL. This advancement addresses privacy concerns and regulatory requirements.

Establishing industry standards and interoperability framework for FL in the IoT ecosystem facilitates seamless integration and scalability. This framework will promote collaboration and compatibility across diverse IoT environments, enabling a larger view of adoption and innovations. Developing efficient and robust algorithms that can handle heterogeneous IoT environments with diverse device capacities, network conditions, and data distributions ensures reliable performance and model convergence across a variety of IoT environments, which include dynamic changes in device participation.

5.5.2 Challenges

Federated learning-based energy-efficient framework design for IoT environment has many challenges, and the following section discusses these challenges:

> Resource constraint on IoT devices plays an important role in using federated learning systems. The IoT devices have limited computational power, memory, and battery life, which pose constraints on implementing complex machine learning algorithms. Ensuring data robustness, privacy, and security preserving mechanisms by combining sensitive data from a distributed IoT device is a challenging task.
>
> The communication cost is very high, due to the frequent access and usage of data transmission between IoT devices and central servers. Scalability and coordination in a federated learning system for the larger size of IoT environment is a complex task while maintaining synchronization and coordination. Designing an efficient algorithm with robust solutions for heterogeneous data distributions and device dynamics is a challenging task for using FL techniques.

Addressing these future directions and challenges will be essential for understanding the possibility of energy-efficient federated learning in IoT environments. Federated learning can transform data-driven applications by including advancements, strong collaboration, and maintaining a focus on privacy and efficiency. This advancement will support sustainable and responsible deployment in IoT ecosystems.

5.5.3 Research directions in energy-efficient federated learning

This section provides a detailed view of research directions in energy-efficient FL, aimed at quickly evolving to address the challenges and opportunities in the IoT ecosystem. This section discusses several promising research directions in FL-based energy-efficient algorithms.

Develop advanced techniques for compressing models by including sparse gradients, weight quantization, and low-rank factorization. Design a dynamic model adaptation by investigating algorithms that dynamically adjust model complexity and size. Develop an enhanced technique by compressing gradients and model updates to reduce communication overhead and energy utilization. Implement efficient algorithms for achieving energy efficiency through adaptive adjusting communication frequency, resource, and protocol with specific network conditions. Develop an edge-assisted FL architecture to connect edge devices and assist in model training and combination to reduce latency and enhance privacy. Generate strategies for maintaining offload computation-intensive tasks to edge servers for achieving data privacy and security. Research scholars may be focused on developing efficient and robust methods for securing aggregated model updates from distributed devices without compromising privacy. The homomorphic encryption model may be adapted for enabling secure communications on encryption in FL scenarios.

Develop an algorithm for optimizing both computation and communication energy consumption for maintaining model accuracy. Designing an approach that considers multiobjective function with energy efficiency, model accuracy, and fairness in federated learning scenarios is an essential research area for energy conservation.

Blockchain and distributed ledger technology may be extended to use for ensuring transparency, accountability, and integrity in FL usage across distributed IoT devices. A secure healthcare IoT system design may use energy-efficient FL techniques for personalized healthcare monitoring, disease prediction, and health caretaking based on information from wearable sensor devices.

The advanced research direction will contribute to making federated learning more energy-efficient, scalable, and usable for a wide range of IoT applications. The research challenges and limitations are overcome by applying advanced research areas, which include academia, industry, and policy creators.

5.5.4 Conclusion

FL signifies a transformative approach for generating and achieving an energy-efficient environment in IoT ecosystems. By decentralizing model training and keeping data local, federated learning reduces the need for extensive data transfers or sharing by using decentralized model training and keeping data in a local device. This process significantly reduces the communication overhead and energy utilization associated with traditional machine learning methods. This process is particularly not an efficient technique in IoT environments, where devices have limited computational power and battery lifespan.

Federate learning techniques can optimize both computational and energy efficiency by applying model compression, communication protocols, and adaptive resource allocation techniques. Edge computing techniques further enhance the efficiency and benefits by applying data processing and aggregation techniques closer to the data source. This will reduce latency and enhance real-time decision-making and supporting capabilities.

Federated learning addresses data security and privacy concerns by ensuring that sensitive data collected from various devices remains on the local devices. This mechanism fulfills stringent data protection regulations and fostering trust among user IoT devices. Advanced privacy-preserving techniques ensure that even combined data cannot be compromised by attackers by applying differential privacy and secure aggregation.

Federate learning-based energy-efficient techniques for IoT ecosystems face a lot of challenges, which include managing heterogeneous devices, achieving scalability, and maintaining robust security. Addressing these issues and challenges through ongoing advanced research and innovative approaches is an essential process. Federated learning offers promising advancements to connect the large amount of potential of IoT devices for promoting sustainability and data security.

References

[1] Chen MZ, Poor HV, Saad W, *et al.*, 2020. Wireless communications for collaborative federated learning. *IEEE Commun Mag*, 58(12):48–54. https://doi.org/10.1109/MCOM.001.2000397.

[2] Chen R, Li L, Xue KP, *et al.*, 2023. Energy efficient federated learning over heterogeneous mobile devices via joint design of weight quantization and wireless transmission. *IEEE Trans Mob Comput*, 22(12):7451–7465. https://doi.org/10.1109/TMC.2022.3213766.

[3] Cho YJ, Wang JY, and Joshi G, 2020. Client selection in federated learning: convergence analysis and power-of-choice selection strategies. https://arxiv.org/abs/2010.01243.

[4] da Silva JMB, Ntougias K, Krikidis I, *et al.*, 2021. Simultaneous wireless information and power transfer for federated learning. *Proc 22nd Int Workshop on Signal Processing Advances in Wireless Communications*, pp. 296–300. https://doi.org/10.1109/SPAWC51858.2021.9593160.

[5] Deng L, Li GQ, Han S, *et al.*, 2020. Model compression and hardware acceleration for neural networks: a comprehensive survey. *Proc IEEE*, 108 (4):485–532. https://doi.org/10.1109/JPROC.2020.2976475.

[6] Yang Z, Chen M, Saad W, Hong CS, and Shikh-Bahaei M, 2020 Energy efficient federated learning over wireless communication networks. *IEEE Trans Wireless Commun*, 20(3):1935–1949.

[7] Gaudette B, Wu CJ, and Vrudhula S, 2016. Improving smartphone user experience by balancing performance and energy with probabilistic QoS guarantee. *Proc IEEE Int Symp on High Performance Computer Architecture*, pp. 52–63. https://doi.org/10.1109/HPCA.2016.7446053.

[8] Gaudette B, Wu CJ, and Vrudhula S, 2019. Optimizing user satisfaction of mobile workloads subject to various sources of uncertainties. *IEEE Trans Mob Comput*, 18(12):2941–2953. https://doi.org/10.1109/TMC.2018.2883619.

[9] Hong S and Kim H, 2010. An integrated GPU power and performance model. *ACM SIGARCH Comput Archit News*, 38(3):280–289. https://doi.org/10.1145/1816038.1815998.

Chapter 6

Energy optimization for IoT communication

G. Arun Prasath[1], *S. Dinesh Krishnan*[2], *A.S. Shanthi*[3] *and Daniel Arockiam*[4]

Abstract

This chapter provides an in-depth exploration of energy optimization in Internet of Things (IoT) communication, focusing on the challenges and strategies to achieve sustainable, energy-efficient systems. It examines the complexities of IoT energy usage, taking into account a variety of device capabilities, communication protocols, and the dynamic nature of data transfer. Adaptive sensing, energy-efficient communication protocols, energy harvesting, and power control are important subjects. Practical applications in industries like healthcare, agriculture, and smart cities are examined with the incorporation of cutting-edge technology like machine learning, edge computing, and decentralized architectures. Future developments that will pave the way for robust, sustainable IoT ecosystems are also highlighted in the book: the deployment of 5G, advances in AI, and multidisciplinary partnerships.

Keywords: IoT communication; Energy optimization; Energy-efficient protocols; Machine learning; Edge computing; Energy harvesting; Sustainable IoT; Adaptive sensing; Power management; Smart cities

6.1 An overview of Internet of Things communication

The Internet of Things (IoT) has rapidly transitioned into a transformative force, which involves the interconnection of various systems and objects to facilitate the interchange of data and communication in a seamless manner. At its core, Internet of Things communication is the interchange of information between a wide variety of devices, which can include anything from sensors and actuators to complex computing systems. The overarching objective is to establish a networked

[1]GITAM School of Technology, GITAM Deemed to be University, India
[2]Department of Computer Science and Engineering, B V Raju Institute of Technology, India
[3]Department of Artificial Intelligence and Data Science, Dr. NGP Institute of Technology, India
[4]Department of Computer Science and Engineering, Amity School of Engineering and Technology, Amity University Madhya Pradesh, India

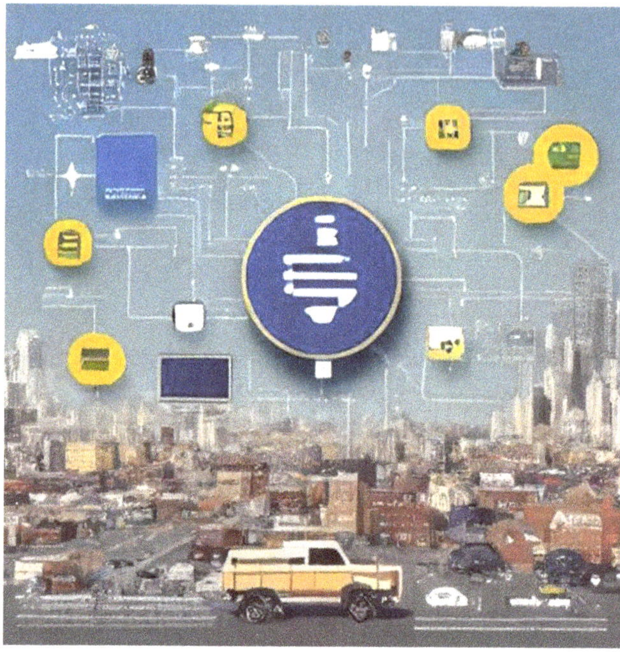

Figure 6.1 Internet of Things (IoT) with everything

environment that improves productivity, automates procedures, and makes it easier to make decisions based on accurate information. Figure 6.1 illustrates many sorts of Internet of Things (IoT) applications in real-world scenarios.

6.1.1 The importance of energy efficiency and optimization

On the other hand, this boom of connectedness comes with a burden that is inherent to it: the consumption of energy. A great number of Internet of Things devices are able to function in areas with limited resources because they rely on energy-harvesting technologies or batteries. The requirement for energy optimization in Internet of Things communication has thus become a primary priority as a consequence of this.

Developing solutions that are both sustainable and scalable requires a fundamental understanding of the dynamics of energy usage in the IoT. Recognizing the wide variety of devices that make up the Internet of Things ecosystem, each of which has its own energy profile and limits, is a necessary step in this process. Complexity and multifacetedness characterize the energy environment, which includes everything from power-hungry edge computing nodes to minuscule sensors that are installed in remote locales.

6.1.2 Overview of the challenges presented by energy consumption

There are a number of obstacles that add to the mystery of energy usage in Internet of Things communication. A few examples of these issues are the unpredictable nature of data transfer, the fluctuating processing demands, and the wide variety of communication protocols that are utilized. Energy optimization efforts are further complicated by the vast magnitude of Internet of Things deployments as well as the variety of devices.

Given these circumstances, it is absolutely necessary to conduct an exhaustive investigation into various methods of energy optimization. The purpose of this chapter of the book is to analyze these problems and provide insights into the delicate balance that must be maintained between an efficient communication system and the conservation of energy. Through an examination of the underlying principles that control energy consumption in Internet of Things communication, readers will get a foundational understanding of the concerns that are currently being discussed. This will pave the way for later chapters that will delve into specific solutions and technologies available. As we move on with this investigation, it is becoming increasingly clear that tackling energy optimization in Internet of Things communication is not merely a technical difficulty; rather, it is a crucial step toward constructing an Internet of Things ecosystem that is both sustainable and resilient. By giving careful thought to communication paradigms, device features, and upcoming technologies, we are able to plot a road toward a future in which the advantages of the IoT are utilized without sacrificing energy efficiency.

6.1.3 Challenges with the Internet of Things' energy consumption

The IoT presents a landscape of energy usage that is characterized by a wide variety of complex difficulties. These issues reflect the heart of energy optimization struggles and highlight the complexity of managing power resources across a wide variety of Internet of Things devices. The fluctuating workloads that Internet of Things devices are subjected to constitute one of the most significant issues. Internet of Things devices frequently function in surroundings that are dynamic, in contrast to traditional computing systems, which have predictable usage patterns. Sensors may remain inactive for extended periods of time, only to be activated on an irregular basis, which necessitates responses that are both prompt and efficient in terms of energy consumption during active phases. Given the irregular nature of the communication pattern, it is necessary to implement energy optimization algorithms that are flexible enough to accommodate varying levels of workload.

When it comes to the Internet of Things, the selection of communication protocols adds even another layer of complexity. Although lightweight communication protocols such as MQTT and CoAP make it possible to communicate with minimal cost, the overhead that is associated with protocol headers and control messages can considerably add to the amount of energy that is consumed. This is especially true in situations where devices often exchange small packets of data. Finding a happy medium between the usefulness and efficiency of a protocol is of the utmost importance to accomplish the objectives of energy optimization.

6.2 Differences in the capabilities of different devices

The Internet of Things ecosystems are made up of a wide variety of devices, each of which has its own set of capabilities and energy limits. It is difficult to provide a consistent strategy for energy management since every type of sensor, from low-power sensors with modest computational capacity to more robust edge computing devices, presents its own unique complications. To ensure that energy-efficient solutions are adapted to the specific demands of individual components within the Internet of Things network, it is necessary to have a comprehensive understanding of the features and constraints of each type of device; this is necessary to design strategies that cater to the heterogeneity that exists within the network. The Internet of Things (IoT) devices that are now in use are depicted in Figure 6.2.

The difficulty of energy consumption in large-scale Internet of Things deployments is made more difficult by scalability. As the number of devices that are linked to the internet increases, the complexity of managing energy resources also increases. The difficulties associated with scalability present themselves in a

Figure 6.2 IoT devices

variety of ways, including increasing network congestion, increased competition for limited bandwidth, and the requirement for effective coordination methods. There is a need for creative solutions that are capable of scaling seamlessly with the growing breadth of Internet of Things applications to address these difficulties.

A holistic strategy to energy optimization in Internet of Things communication is required to successfully navigate through these issues. It requires a comprehensive comprehension of the dynamic relationship that exists between the properties of the devices, the communication protocols, and the overarching objectives of the Internet of Things ecosystem. A detailed road map to attaining energy efficiency in the Internet of Things communication will be presented in the next chapters, in which we will delve into particular tactics and technologies geared to address these difficulties.

6.3 Energy-efficient communications

When it comes to the enormous terrain of Internet of Things connectivity, the selection of protocols is a crucial factor in defining the level of energy efficiency required. The backbone of data interchange in Internet of Things networks comprises preexisting protocols, each of which is suited to unique requirements. For the purpose of optimizing energy consumption, it is vital to have a solid understanding of their subtleties as well as the constantly changing landscape of communication protocols.

6.3.1 A brief overview of several protocols

MQTT, CoAP, and AMQP are examples of well-established protocols that are included in the landscape. Each of these protocols is meant to solve a certain component of the Internet of Things conversation. By way of example, MQTT is very effective at reducing the amount of communication overhead, which makes it acceptable for devices with limited resources. In contrast, the CoAP protocol makes use of the HTTP framework to provide RESTful communication. It is designed to accommodate interactions that are lightweight and stateless. When picking the most appropriate solution for a particular Internet of Things application, it is essential to do a thorough analysis of the advantages and disadvantages of these protocols. Internet of Things protocols are depicted in Figure 6.3.

6.3.2 Comparative analysis

The process of comparing protocols requires a careful analysis of the variables that measure their performance. In terms of overall energy consumption, the overall energy consumption of devices is impacted by metrics such as message size, connection overhead, and latency. When one has a thorough understanding of these metrics, it is easier to make decisions that are well informed and to match the protocol with the particular requirements of the Internet of Things application. In this setting, the trade-off between energy efficiency and protocol complexity becomes an important factor to take into consideration.

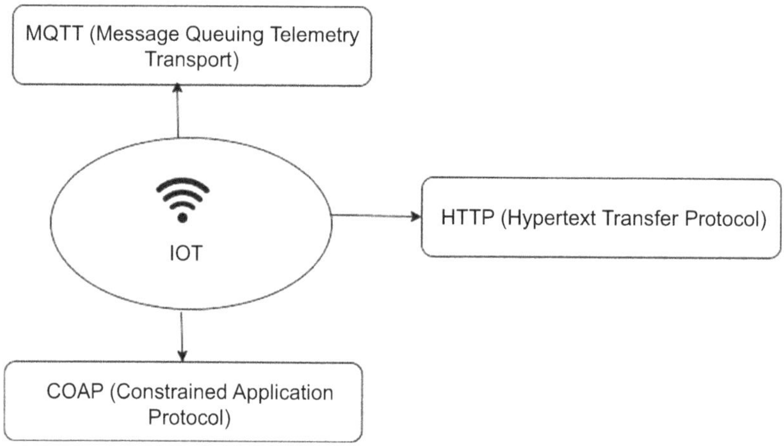

Figure 6.3 IoT protocols

6.3.2.1 New low-energy communication protocols

New protocols are being developed in response to the ever-increasing demand for low-energy communication as the IoT continues to undergo development. Protocols such as MQTT-SN (MQTT for sensor networks) and low-power wide-area network (LPWAN) technologies are becoming increasingly popular in situations where devices are required to function with a minimal amount of power. Utilizing communication patterns that have been optimized, these protocols ensure that devices are able to send data in an effective manner while simultaneously reducing the amount of energy that is consumed.

The exploration of the terrain of energy-efficient communication protocols is not only a technical undertaking; rather, it is a strategic decision that affects the overall performance and sustainability of ecosystems that are connected to the Internet of Things. In the following chapters, we will go deeper into practical considerations for protocol selection, we will examine real-world use cases, and we will highlight the role that protocols play in achieving energy optimization in Internet of Things communication.

6.3.3 Power management solutions

To successfully navigate the complexities of energy optimization in Internet of Things communication, it is necessary to conduct an exhaustive investigation of power management solutions. For the purpose of prolonging the operational lifespan of devices, improving their energy efficiency, and ensuring that power resources are used in a prudent manner, these tactics encompass a range of methodologies.

6.3.4 Data transmission in a dynamic form

One of the most important aspects of power management is the capability to make dynamic adjustments to the transmission of data. Devices are able to remain in low-power states for extended periods of time because of adaptive methods such as intermittent data reporting and transmissions that are prompted by events. Through the utilization of this strategy, the frequency of active communication is reduced, resulting in the conservation of energy and the extension of the device's total lifespan.

6.3.5 Administration of power at the device level

The management of power at the device level requires a combination of software and hardware strategies to be effectively implemented. Components that consume less power, sleep modes that are optimized, and wake-up procedures that are efficient all contribute to a reduction in overall power consumption. The difficulty lies in finding a middle ground between responsiveness and energy conservation. This involves making sure that devices are prepared to take action when it is required, while also ensuring that they remain in energy-saving states when they are not operational.

6.3.5.1 Networking that is efficient with energy

In terms of power management, the networking layer is an extremely important component. Methods such as hierarchical routing, which reduces the amount of distance that data must travel, and duty cycle, which involves equipment switching between active and sleep modes, are examples of techniques that contribute to effective energy utilization. The special requirements and limits of Internet of Things communication are addressed by these networking solutions, which are geared to satisfy the specific needs of devices that frequently operate in tough conditions.

6.3.6 Sensing that is adaptive

Adaptive sensing algorithms allow for the optimization of sensors, which are essential to a wide variety of Internet of Things applications. Sensors are able to preserve energy without affecting the quality of the data that they collect by altering their sampling rates when contextual considerations or event triggers are taken into consideration. With this adaptive technique, sensors are able to function at their highest possible efficiency, allowing them to react to changes in their surroundings while simultaneously reducing their energy usage during periods of stability.

As we continue to go deeper into the world of power management solutions, it is becoming increasingly clear that attaining energy optimization in Internet of Things communication is a task that involves multiple dimensions. Whether it be the fine-tuning of communication patterns or the optimization of the behaviors of individual devices, the tactics that are utilized need to be adapted to the particular characteristics and requirements of the Internet of Things environment. In the next chapters, we will investigate real-world implementations, case studies, and emerging trends in power management. This will provide a comprehensive understanding of the tactics that are driving energy-efficient Internet of Things connectivity.

6.3.7 Energy harvesting on World Wide Web

The quest for energy efficiency is further complicated by the incorporation of energy-collecting devices into the fabric of the Internet of Things connectivity, which brings about a revolutionary dimension. The desire for continuous gadget operation and the limits imposed by finite power sources are served by energy harvesting, which acts as a bridge between the two.

For the purpose of supplying Internet of Things devices with electrical power, energy harvesting is the process of converting ambient energy sources, such as solar radiation, vibrations, or thermal gradients, into electrical power. In circumstances in which conventional power sources, such as batteries, may be problematic or difficult to replace, this approach offers a great deal of promise.

6.3.8 Integration of Internet of Things devices

A comprehensive awareness of the features of the devices and the energy landscape in the surrounding environment is required for the seamless integration of energy harvesting with Internet of Things devices. By deploying energy-harvesting modules alongside sensors and communication components, devices are able to collect energy from their surroundings. This eliminates the need for devices to replace their batteries on a regular basis and reduces the influence that disposable power sources have on the environment.

6.3.8.1 Case studies and examples of past achievements

In the IoT, real-world case studies can illustrate the actual benefits of energy harvesting. The many uses and the potential for self-sufficient, sustainable Internet of Things ecosystems are demonstrated by these examples, which range from solar-powered sensor nodes in agricultural fields to vibration-powered devices in industrial settings. The potential of energy harvesting as a fundamental enabler of long-term applications of the Internet of Things that do not require maintenance is demonstrated by success stories.

6.3.9 Difficulties and recent developments

Despite this, there are still obstacles to overcome before energy harvesting can become widely adopted. Ongoing issues include the variability of ambient energy sources, the constraints of energy storage, and the efficiency of harvesting technology. Innovations in materials science, improvements in energy storage technologies, and breakthroughs in energy-harvesting techniques are all aimed at addressing these problems, which will move the sector toward implementations that are more resilient and reliable.

In the course of our exploration of the arena of energy harvesting in the Internet of Things communication, it has become abundantly evident that this approach is not merely a method for extending the lifespans of devices; rather, it represents a paradigm change toward sustainability and resilience in the ecosystem of the Internet of Things. Following this, the ensuing chapters will delve deeper into the complexities of energy-harvesting technologies, offering insights into their practical applications, current research, and the ever-changing environment of energy-efficient Internet of Things connectivity.

6.3.9.1 The process of optimizing sensor networks

The optimization of sensor networks has emerged as a fundamental need within the massive network of communication that defines the IoT. Sensing devices, which are frequently the fundamental elements of Internet of Things installations, provide the function of the system's eyes and ears by gathering data that is used to inform decision-making processes. The difficulty lies in ensuring that these sensors function well, striking a balance between the requirement for precise data and the limitations imposed by the limited capacity of available energy supplies.

6.3.9.2 Sensitivity to limits placed on energy resources

The sensitivity of sensors in Internet of Things networks to energy restrictions is one of their defining characteristics. Battery power or energy harvesting is the source of power for many of these businesses, which are located in inaccessible or remote areas. Therefore, to optimize sensor networks, it is necessary to take into account the distinct energy profiles of the devices that are being optimized. Therefore, it is necessary to adjust the sensing intervals, data transmission speeds, and power states to achieve a delicate equilibrium between the precision of the data and the conservation of energy.

6.3.9.3 The process of dynamically selecting and deploying sensors

The journey of optimization can be extended to include the selection and deployment of dynamic sensors. There may be variations in the amount of energy that is required for various sensing modalities, such as temperature, humidity, and motion. Sensors are chosen in an intelligent manner by adaptive techniques, taking into account the conditions of the environment or the requirements of a particular application. In addition, the deployment of sensors in a smart manner to enhance coverage while simultaneously eliminating redundant data collecting is a contributor to total energy efficiency.

6.3.10 Approaches to sensing that are adaptable

The optimization of energy use is significantly impacted by adaptive sensing strategies. These tactics entail modifying the sensing settings in accordance with the factors that are present in the situation. An example of this would be a temperature sensor in an agricultural Internet of Things deployment that might raise its sample rate during moments of essential growth and decrease it during periods of stability. Sensors have the ability to preserve energy without compromising the relevance of the data that they collect on account of their ability to constantly adjust to changing situations.

The optimization of sensor networks is not only a technological task; rather, it is a search for synergy between the accuracy of data and the conservation of energy. This practical application of these tactics will be illuminated in future chapters through the use of real-world examples and implementation scenarios. It is possible to acquire a more nuanced understanding of the complexity and opportunities of energy-efficient Internet of Things communication by investigating the ways in which sensor networks are optimized in various contexts, ranging from smart cities to industrial Internet of Things deployments.

6.4 Using machine learning to optimize energy use of resources

A significant step forward in the development of intelligent and adaptable systems is represented by the convergence of machine learning (ML) and energy optimization in IoT communication. A dynamic method to address the complex difficulties connected with energy usage in Internet of Things devices is provided by machine learning algorithms. These algorithms have the ability to recognize trends and make predictions based on data.

6.4.1 The application of predictive analytics to energy consumption

The capacity to forecast and reproduce patterns of energy usage is at the heart of machine learning's contribution to the optimization of energy use. It is possible for machine learning algorithms to estimate when devices are expected to be most active by evaluating past data. This enables preventive measures to be taken to optimize energy use. By bringing energy use in line with demand, this predictive analytics technique not only helps to reduce energy consumption but also improves the overall efficiency of IoT devices.

6.4.1.1 Intelligent algorithms for dynamic energy monitoring and management

There is a significant contribution that machine learning algorithms make to the development of intelligent, adaptable systems that are able to manage energy in a dynamic manner. Real-time data is analyzed by these algorithms, which take into account a variety of parameters including the burden of the device, the conditions of the environment, and the state of the network. Machine learning-driven systems improve energy consumption in response to the ever-changing dynamics of the Internet of Things environment. This is accomplished by dynamically modifying power states, communication frequencies, and certain other factors.

6.4.2 Computers at the edge of the network and localized decision-making

The combination of machine learning and edge computing results in the introduction of a decentralized strategy for the optimization of energy use. Making decisions at the local level is made possible by machine learning models that are put directly on edge devices. This eliminates the need for continuous contact with centralized servers. This not only reduces the amount of data that is transmitted, which helps to conserve energy, but it also improves the responsiveness of Internet of Things devices by enabling them to make quick and independent decisions at the edge.

The transformational potential of this method is brought to light by case studies and practical implementations that demonstrate the successful marriage of machine learning and energy optimization. The examples shown here demonstrate how machine learning algorithms help the development of self-aware and energy-efficient Internet of Things ecosystems. These examples range from energy-aware routing in smart cities to predictive maintenance in the industrial Internet of Things.

As we continue to explore the field of machine learning for the purpose of energy optimization, it is becoming increasingly clear that this convergence marks a paradigm shift in the manner in which IoT systems are created and operated. Further exploration of the intricacies of machine learning applications in energy efficiency will be conducted in the coming chapters. These chapters will delve into emerging trends, problems, and the expanding landscape of intelligent Internet of Things communication.

To improve energy efficiency, cloud computing and edge computing are being utilized. Computing in the cloud and computing at the edge of the network have a mutually beneficial interaction that plays a significant role in determining the energy efficiency landscape of Internet of Things communication. Creating a dynamic infrastructure that optimizes energy use across the Internet of Things ecosystem is the result of the convergence of these two paradigms, each of which possesses specific capabilities.

6.4.2.1 Putting computations in the cloud and offloading them

The cloud computing model functions as a centralized powerhouse that is able to handle sophisticated computations and jobs that require a significant amount of data. IoT devices are able to run in energy-efficient modes by offloading certain processing duties to the cloud. This reduces the amount of computation that takes place on the device itself, hence reducing the amount of power that is consumed. This strategy makes use of the scalability and processing capabilities of cloud infrastructure to disperse the computational burden in an effective manner.

6.4.3 The role of edge computing in energy-efficient Internet of Things

On the other hand, edge computing brings computation closer to the source of the data, which reduces the need for significant data transmission to centralized cloud servers. This decentralized strategy reduces the amount of delay and bandwidth that is required, which helps to protect the environment and conserve energy. Edge computing devices, which are equipped with computational capabilities, process data locally, allowing for choices to be made in real time without primarily relying on resources that are hosted in the cloud.

6.4.3.1 Optimal resource allocation and hybrid approaches to problem solving

The synergy that exists between cloud computing and edge computing extends to hybrid systems that dynamically distribute resources in accordance with the needs set forth by workload and latency. Real-time optimization of resource allocation is achieved through the use of machine learning algorithms within this hybrid architecture. These systems find a compromise between energy efficiency and computational performance by intelligently selecting where processing takes place, whether it be locally at the edge or centrally in the cloud by utilizing a distributed computing architecture.

6.4.3.2 Taking security into account when optimizing the Internet of Things

The design and implementation of systems are made more difficult by the additional layer of complexity that is added by the intertwining of energy optimization and security considerations in Internet of Things connectivity. It is absolutely necessary to find a way to strike a careful balance between energy saving and security procedures to guarantee the robustness and resilience of Internet of Things ecosystems.

6.4.3.3 Finding a middle ground between energy efficiency and security protocols

It is common for security protocols, which are necessary for protecting Internet of Things devices and data, to introduce overhead, which can have an effect on energy usage. To achieve the optimal level of balance, it is vital to select security measures that are in accordance with the particular requirements of the application, while simultaneously minimizing the amount of superfluous computational and communication overlap. Because of this optimization, devices are guaranteed to maintain their level of security without sacrificing their energy economy.

6.5 The influence of safety on the consumption of energy

When it is necessary to perform cryptographic procedures or secure data transmissions on a regular basis, the relationship between security and energy efficiency becomes more apparent. When it comes to reducing the influence that security has on energy consumption, the utilization of efficient cryptographic algorithms, safe key management systems, and adaptive security measures become essential components. Recent developments in energy-efficient security methods and lightweight cryptography have contributed to the delicate balancing act that is being performed.

6.5.1 Examples of implementations that are both safe and efficient in their use of energy

To shed light on how businesses and industries traverse the difficult landscape of implementing safe and energy-efficient Internet of Things installations, real-world case studies are utilized. There are numerous examples that demonstrate the practical practicality of these solutions, including some that demonstrate the successful integration of security measures without compromising energy efficiency. The examination of such case studies provides one with the opportunity to get insights into the sophisticated decision-making that is necessary to create a harmonic balance of energy optimization and security.

A detailed knowledge of how these components jointly contribute to the energy efficiency and security of Internet of Things communication arises as a result of the exploration of these aspects of cloud computing, edge computing, and security considerations. A full picture of the ever-changing environment of energy-optimized and secure Internet of Things systems will be provided in future chapters, which will delve into specific use cases, advancements, and emerging trends.

6.5.2 Case studies

The implementation of energy optimization tactics in Internet of Things communication in the real world reveals a rich tapestry of problems, inventions, and success stories. Case studies and actual implementations provide a view into the process by which theoretical principles are converted into tangible solutions. This provides practitioners and scholars alike with useful insights.

6.5.2.1 Making energy efficiency a reality in the healthcare industry

Through the monitoring of patients, the collection of crucial data, and the facilitation of timely interventions, Internet of Things devices play a pivotal role in the healthcare industry. When it comes to medical settings, where devices need to work continually without exhausting restricted power sources, energy-efficient communication is of the utmost importance. Case studies in the healthcare industry highlight adaptive sensing technologies, edge computing for real-time analysis, and optimal communication protocols that are suited to the specific requirements of patient monitoring and healthcare applications.

6.5.2.2 Ecologically sound agriculture: taking care of plants while conserving energy

The IoT technologies contribute to the field of smart agriculture by enabling precision farming and optimizing resource utilization. The conditions of the soil, the weather patterns, and the health of the crop are all monitored via sensors implanted in the field. Continuous data gathering is made possible by the utilization of energy-efficient communication technologies, which, when combined with energy harvesting from solar sources, eliminate the need for the devices to undergo frequent replacing of their batteries. Examples of practical implementations in agriculture illustrate the synergy that exists between environmental monitoring and deployments of the Internet of Things that are sustainable and energy mindful.

6.5.2.3 Smart cities as a means of promoting urban sustainability

Intelligent transportation systems and waste management are only two examples of the many applications that can be made possible through the implementation of Internet of Things technology in smart cities. The implementation of creative solutions is necessary to achieve energy efficiency in these various urban areas. Case examples highlight the integration of edge computing for real-time traffic management, optimal sensor networks for waste collection, and adaptive communication strategies to strike a compromise between the accuracy of data and the conservation of energy. These applications demonstrate the role that the Internet of Things plays in the development of resilient and sustainable urban ecosystems.

6.5.2.4 The Internet of Things in industry: improving productivity and safety

It is essential to have energy-efficient Internet of Things communication in industrial settings, where precision and dependability are of the utmost importance, to improve efficiency and guarantee the safety of the workers involved. The utilization of machine learning for predictive maintenance, edge computing for local decision-making, and optimized communication protocols to minimize delay in key operations are all demonstrated by practical implementations in the industrial IoT. These case studies shed light on the revolutionary effect that energy optimization has on the processes that are used in industrial settings.

6.5.2.5 Observations and insights obtained through actual deployments

An examination of the results of practical deployments reveals lessons that are of great value to the Internet of Things community as a whole. This set of lectures goes beyond merely focusing on technical concerns and delves into the complexities of project management, collaboration among stakeholders, and the adaptability of solutions to problems that are encountered in the real world. When it comes to the success of energy-optimized Internet of Things installations, factors such as scalability, interoperability, and user acceptance emerge as significant variables.

Over the course of our investigation into these case studies and practical applications, the convergence of theory and reality becomes more and more apparent. When it comes to the pursuit of energy-efficient and sustainable Internet of Things communication, the problems that were experienced and the lessons that were learned serve as a foundation for continuing refinement and innovation. Further exploration of emerging trends, continuing research, and the ever-changing landscape of Internet of Things optimization will be conducted in subsequent chapters. These chapters will be based on the rich tapestry of experiences that have been garnered from real deployments.

6.6 Future trends and directions

A dynamic environment that is formed by technology breakthroughs, evolving use cases, and the constant drive for sustainability is shown when one takes a look into the future of energy optimization in Internet of Things communication. In the world of Internet of Things energy efficiency, the examination of future trends and research paths acts as a compass, directing the path of innovation and delivering solutions to developing difficulties.

6.6.1 Incorporation of 5G and beyond technologies

The introduction of 5G and the prospects of succeeding communication technologies hold a great deal of potential for the development of energy-efficient Internet of Things connectivity. IoT applications are able to function more quickly and with greater responsiveness because of the higher data rates and lower latency that 5G networks provide. As we look to the future, it is likely that research will concentrate on utilizing these characteristics to build communication protocols that achieve the best possible balance between speed and energy conservation.

6.6.2 Improvements in artificial intelligence at the edge and decentralized processing

The development of technological advancements such as artificial intelligence (AI) and edge computing has brought about new aspects of energy optimization. Recent developments in edge artificial intelligence have made it possible to perform more complex data processing at the source, hence lowering the amount of data that must be transmitted to centralized servers. This heralds a move toward intelligent, self-aware Internet of Things ecosystems, which is made possible by the synergy between edge artificial intelligence and decentralized processing, which presents prospects for localized decision-making and adaptive energy management.

6.6.2.1 Technologies that are capable of harvesting sustainable energy

The quest for technologies that are capable of capturing energy in a sustainable manner continues to be at the forefront of research initiatives. The issues that are connected with the fluctuation of ambient energy sources are the focus of innovations in materials science, which, when combined with advancements in energy storage systems, strive to address these challenges. It is possible that in the future, there may be an integration of innovative energy-harvesting techniques, such as bioenergy harvesting or enhanced photovoltaic cells, which will further enhance the autonomy and sustainability of Internet of Things devices.

6.6.3 The Internet of Things for energy-optimized resilience and security

It is of the utmost importance to ensure both resilience and security as IoT technology becomes increasingly integrated into critical infrastructure. There is a good chance that future research lines will investigate the possibility of enhancing security measures that can be smoothly integrated with strategic energy optimization. The security landscape of energy-efficient Internet of Things communication will be shaped by the development of lightweight cryptographic algorithms that are resilient against emerging attacks and adaptive security protocols that are capable of managing evolving risks.

6.6.3.1 Design that is centered on people and the user experience

As the IoT grows more integrated into everyday life, the human-centered design of apps for the IoT is becoming increasingly prominent. It is possible that future research will investigate the behavior of users, their preferences, and their acceptance of energy-efficient Internet of Things solutions. To encourage wider adoption and improve the overall user experience, it will be essential to customize user interfaces, communication patterns, and energy optimization tactics so that they are in line with the expectations of users.

6.6.4 Collaborations spanning multiple disciplines

Collaborations between different fields are required because of the complex nature of energy optimization in Internet of Things communication applications. Expertise from a variety of disciplines, including computer science, electrical engineering, materials science, and behavioral sciences, may come together in the future to form a convergence across research directions. Through collaborative efforts, the understanding of the issues associated with energy optimization will be enhanced, which will lead to the development of holistic solutions that handle both technical and human-centric aspects.

Researchers and practitioners are prepared to begin on a journey that will be distinguished by creativity, collaboration, and a firm commitment to sustainability as they chart the future of energy optimization in Internet of Things communication. While we are venturing into the unexplored territories of emerging technologies and evolving use cases, the trajectory of energy-efficient Internet of Things communication systems will be shaped by the continuous examination of these future trends and research initiatives.

6.6.5 Applications that are industry-specific for energy-optimized Internet of Things

The application landscape of the energy-optimized Internet of Things stretches across a wide range of industries, each of which presents its own different set of difficulties and opportunities. Through an examination of the complexities of industry-specific implementations, one can gain insight into the manner in which energy efficiency is adapted to fit the particular requirements and limitations of different industries.

6.6.6 Providing care that is focused on the patient and providing precision monitoring

When it comes to the healthcare industry, energy-optimized Internet of Things communication is an essential component in the progression of patient-centered care and precision monitoring. Wearable technology and medical sensors, which are powered by limited sources of energy, make use of adaptive sensing and communication mechanisms to guarantee continuous monitoring without sacrificing the sense of comfort experienced by the patient. A further refinement of the delivery of healthcare services is achieved through the incorporation of edge computing for real-time analytics, which simultaneously improves efficiency while reducing energy consumption.

6.6.6.1 Precision agriculture and resource optimization are two aspects of agriculture

In the field of agriculture, the landscape of precision farming is being transformed by energy-efficient Internet of Things connections. Sensors that are placed in the field collect information about the state of the soil, the weather patterns, and the health of the crop. The optimization of sensor networks, in conjunction with the collection of energy from solar sources, makes it possible to implement agricultural methods that are both sustainable and autonomous. This application, which is special to the sector, not only helps to preserve energy but also makes a contribution to the optimization of resources, which in turn helps to improve total yields and reduce environmental effects.

6.6.6.2 Sustainable urban development and effective resource management are the hallmarks of smart cities

To improve urban sustainability and resource management, smart city projects make use of Internet of Things communication that is designed for energy efficiency. Internet of Things sensors that are integrated into urban infrastructure monitor traffic patterns, manage waste collection, and optimize energy use in buildings while also managing waste collection. Real-time decision-making is made easier with the convergence of cloud computing and edge computing, which also helps to reduce latency and conserve energy for the environment. The impact is not limited to operational efficiency; rather, it contributes to the development of urban places that are environmentally sensitive and sustainable for human habitation.

6.6.7 The Internet of Things in industry: improving both operational efficiency and safety

IoT communication that is effective in terms of energy consumption plays a crucial part in the industrial sector, helping to improve operational efficiency and ensure workplace safety. The ability to do predictive maintenance and real-time monitoring of machinery is made possible by industrial sensors that are connected through communication protocols that have been developed. When machine learning algorithms are deployed at the edge, they do data analysis locally to arrive at choices in a timely manner. This eliminates the requirement for continuous contact with centralized servers. This application, which is specialized to the industry, not only boosts productivity but also reduces downtime and improves worker safety.

6.6.7.1 The monitoring of the environment, with a focus on conservation and the preservation of biodiversity

Efficient use of energy Internet of Things makes a substantial contribution to the monitoring of the environment and the preservation of biodiversity. In ecosystems where devices operate remotely or in hard conditions, continuous data collection can be maintained through the utilization of adaptive communication mechanisms and the harvesting of energy from natural sources. Through the provision of useful insights regarding environmental changes, habitat health, and the overall well-being of varied ecosystems, this application contributes to conservation efforts and provides support for those efforts.

6.6.7.2 Intelligent mobility and traffic management

Internet of Things communication that is efficient in terms of energy consumption is reshaping the landscape of intelligent mobility and traffic management in the transportation sector. Vehicles that are connected to the internet and are fitted with sensors and communication modules improve both the flow of traffic and the safety of the roads. An analysis of traffic patterns and the facilitation of dynamic routing decisions are both performed by machine learning algorithms that operate in real time. This application, which is specialized to the industry, not only lessens the amount of congestion and enhances the efficiency of transportation, but it also works to lower the energy footprint that is linked with poor traffic management.

The versatility and significance of energy-optimized Internet of Things connectivity are demonstrated by these applications that are tailored to a particular industry. Practitioners and researchers contribute to the establishment of sustainable, efficient, and resilient ecosystems that span a variety of industries, including healthcare, agriculture, smart cities, industry, environmental monitoring, and transportation. This is accomplished by adjusting solutions to the specific difficulties and requirements of each sector. The IoT that has been optimized for energy consumption has a cross-cutting influence that goes beyond simple efficiency; it encourages innovation, boosts productivity, and addresses key concerns in more than one domain.

6.7 Conclusion

In the process of crossing the vast field of energy-optimized Internet of Things communication, this book has dug into the complexities of the technologies, tactics, and applications that define the landscape of connected devices. The investigation has been both exhaustive and enlightening, covering everything from the underlying principles of energy consumption concerns to the actual applications across a wide range of businesses. At the moment when we are drawing to a close on this investigation, a compilation of insights and a vision for the future are becoming apparent.

Beginning with an understanding of the significant role that the Internet of Things plays in reshaping our interconnected world, the journey began with the creation of ecosystems in which devices communicate with one another in a seamless manner to improve efficiency, enable automation, and provide information for decision-making. On the other hand, this connectivity does not come without its difficulties, the most significant of which is the requirement to maximize the efficiency of energy usage. As a result of our identification of these problems, we embarked on a multidimensional investigation of tactics, technologies, and applications in the real world that aimed to address the delicate balance that exists between connection and sustainability.

As the chapters progressed, a narrative was revealed to us that led us through the intricate concerns of energy-efficient communication protocols, power management tactics, and the incorporation of cutting-edge technologies such as machine learning, cloud computing, and edge computing. When we investigated the possibility of incorporating energy harvesting into the fabric of Internet of Things devices, we were able to harness ambient energy sources to maintain continuous operation. This was an idea that had previously been considered promising.

Real-world case studies shed light on the practical aspects of energy optimization across a wide range of industries, including healthcare, agriculture, smart cities, and industrial settings, among others. These experiences provided a testament to the revolutionary impact of energy efficiency, not just in terms of extending the lifespans of devices but also in terms of altering entire industries, supporting sustainability, and improving the quality of life.

When looking into the future, the investigation of potential future trends and research initiatives provides a picture of a landscape that is constantly changing. There is a possibility that the possibilities of energy-optimized Internet of Things communication will be redefined as a result of the integration of 5G, improvements in edge artificial intelligence, and the pursuit of sustainable energy-harvesting technologies. It is becoming increasingly important to take into account human-centered design, resilience, and security as these are the factors that will pave the way for interdisciplinary partnerships and user-centered breakthroughs.

Within the framework of applications that are special to a particular industry, we were able to observe that energy optimization is not a universally applicable endeavor but rather a customized strategy that is in accordance with the specific problems and objectives of each sector. In the realms of healthcare, agriculture, smart cities, industry, environmental monitoring, and transportation, energy-optimized Internet of Things communication has developed as a means of reshaping processes, improving efficiency, and contributing to broader sustainability goals.

As we move into the final phase of this investigation, it becomes abundantly clear that energy-optimized Internet of Things communication is not only a technical endeavor; rather, it is a journey toward a future that is more environmentally friendly, efficient, and interconnected. The foundation for revolutionary change is laid by the convergence of technology developments, new methods, and a profound awareness of the intricacies that are distinctive to the business.

The lessons that have been learned from the complexities of energy optimization will serve as guideposts for practitioners, researchers, and innovators as they continue to navigate this ever-changing terrain. The rich tapestry of information that moves the field ahead during this inquiry is collectively contributed to by the challenges that were encountered and conquered, the victories that were recognized, and the spirit of collaboration that was fostered throughout the course of this exploration.

As we come to the end of this book, we find ourselves at the brink of the junction of potential and possibility. The future of energy-optimized Internet of Things communication is not a destination but rather a journey. This journey will be characterized by continuous innovation, collaboration across disciplines, and a persistent dedication to the creation of linked ecosystems that are not just intelligent but also sustainable. The chapters in this book are merely markers on this trip, and the path forward holds the possibility of a future in which energy-efficient Internet of Things communication is not merely a goal but rather an essential component of our connected world.

Further reading

[1] K. Dev, P. K. R. Maddikunta, T. R. Gadekallu, S. Bhattacharya, P. Hegde and S. Singh, "Energy Optimization for Green Communication in IoT Using Harris Hawks Optimization," *IEEE Transactions on Green Communications and Networking*, vol. 6, no. 2, pp. 685–694, 2022, doi:10.1109/TGCN.2022.3143991.

[2] X. Liu, Z. Liu and M. Zhou, "Fair Energy-Efficient Resource Optimization for Green Multi-NOMA-UAV Assisted Internet of Things," *IEEE Transactions on Green Communications and Networking*, vol. 7, no. 2, pp. 904–915, 2023, doi:10.1109/TGCN.2021.3130075.

[3] M. M. Salim, D. Wang, H. A. El Atty Elsayed, Y. Liu and M. A. Elaziz, "Joint Optimization of Energy-Harvesting-Powered Two-Way Relaying D2D Communication for IoT: A Rate-Energy Efficiency Tradeoff," *IEEE Internet of Things Journal*, vol. 7, no. 12, pp. 11735–11752, 2020, doi:10.1109/JIOT.2020.2999618.

[4] L. Liu, A. Wang, G. Sun and J. Li, "Multiobjective Optimization for Improving Throughput and Energy Efficiency in UAV-Enabled IoT," *IEEE*

Internet of Things Journal, vol. 9, no. 20, pp. 20763–20777, 2022, doi:10.1109/JIOT.2022.3175712.

[5] G. Yang, R. Dai and Y. -C. Liang, "Energy-Efficient UAV Backscatter Communication with Joint Trajectory Design and Resource Optimization," *IEEE Transactions on Wireless Communications*, vol. 20, no. 2, pp. 926–941, 2021, doi:10.1109/TWC.2020.3029225.

[6] F. -J. Alvarado-Alcon, R. Asorey-Cacheda, A. -J. Garcia-Sanchez and J. Garcia-Haro, "Carbon Footprint vs Energy Optimization in IoT Network Deployments," *IEEE Access*, vol. 10, pp. 111297–111309, 2022, doi:10.1109/ACCESS.2022.3216377.

[7] O. Elgarhy, L. Reggiani, M. M. Alam, A. Zoha, R. Ahmad and A. Kuusik, "Energy Efficiency and Latency Optimization for IoT URLLC and mMTC Use Cases," *IEEE Access*, vol. 12, pp. 23132–23148, 2024, doi:10.1109/ACCESS.2024.3364349.

[8] A. Mondal, D. Mishra, G. Prasad and A. Hossain, "Joint Optimization Framework for Minimization of Device Energy Consumption in Transmission Rate Constrained UAV-Assisted IoT Network," *IEEE Internet of Things Journal*, vol. 9, no. 12, pp. 9591–9607, 2022, doi:10.1109/JIOT.2021.3128883.

[9] H. -T. Ye, X. Kang, J. Joung and Y. -C. Liang, "Optimization for Wireless-Powered IoT Networks Enabled by an Energy-Limited UAV Under Practical Energy Consumption Model," *IEEE Wireless Communications Letters*, vol. 10, no. 3, pp. 567–571, 2021, doi:10.1109/LWC.2020.3038079.

[10] X. Liu, Z. Liu, B. Lai, B. Peng and T. S. Durrani, "Fair Energy-Efficient Resource Optimization for Multi-UAV Enabled Internet of Things," *IEEE Transactions on Vehicular Technology*, vol. 72, no. 3, pp. 3962–3972, 2023, doi:10.1109/TVT.2022.3219613.

[11] L. Xu, X. Zhou, Y. Li, F. Cai, X. Yu and N. Kumar, "Intelligent Power Allocation Algorithm for Energy-Efficient Mobile Internet of Things (IoT) Networks," *IEEE Transactions on Green Communications and Networking*, vol. 6, no. 2, pp. 766–775, 2022, doi:10.1109/TGCN.2022.3144532.

[12] H. -T. Ye, X. Kang, J. Joung and Y. -C. Liang, "Optimization for Full-Duplex Rotary-Wing UAV-Enabled Wireless-Powered IoT Networks," *IEEE Transactions on Wireless Communications*, vol. 19, no. 7, pp. 5057–5072, 2020, doi:10.1109/TWC.2020.2989302.

[13] R. Saadat Yeganeh, M. J. Omidi and M. Ghavami, "Multi-BD Symbiotic Radio-Aided 6G IoT Network: Energy Consumption Optimization with QoS Constraint Approach," *IEEE Transactions on Green Communications and Networking*, vol. 7, no. 4, pp. 2067–2080, 2023, doi:10.1109/TGCN.2023.3281460.

[14] L. Zhang, A. Celik, S. Dang and B. Shihada, "Energy-Efficient Trajectory Optimization for UAV-Assisted IoT Networks," *IEEE Transactions on Mobile Computing*, vol. 21, no. 12, pp. 4323–4337, 2022, doi:10.1109/TMC.2021.3075083.

[15] A. Meng, X. Gao, Y. Zhao and Z. Yang, "Three-Dimensional Trajectory Optimization for Energy-Constrained UAV-Enabled IoT System in Probabilistic LoS Channel," *IEEE Internet of Things Journal*, vol. 9, no. 2, pp. 1109–1121, 2022, doi:10.1109/JIOT.2021.3079363.

[16] S. Khan, K. A. Awan, I. U. Din, A. Almogren and B. Seo-Kim, "An Adaptive Biomimetic Ant Colony Optimization with 6G Integration for IoT Network Communication," *IEEE Access*, vol. 11, pp. 95584–95599, 2023, doi:10.1109/ACCESS.2023.3310273.

[17] N. Lin, Y. Fan, L. Zhao, X. Li and M. Guizani, "GREEN: A Global Energy Efficiency Maximization Strategy for Multi-UAV Enabled Communication Systems," *IEEE Transactions on Mobile Computing*, vol. 22, no. 12, pp. 7104–7120, 2023, doi:10.1109/TMC.2022.3207791.

[18] D. Zeng, Y. Li, L. Chen, L. Gu and C. Hu, "Sensing or Transmission? Stochastic Scheduling of Energy-Harvesting Sensors Toward Zero-Carbon IoT," *IEEE Transactions on Green Communications and Networking*, vol. 6, no. 2, pp. 1132–1140, 2022, doi:10.1109/TGCN.2021.3133936.

[19] Z. Yang, P. Yue, S. Wang, G. Pan and J. An, "Energy-Efficient Optimization for RIS-Aided MIMO Covert Communications," *IEEE Internet of Things Journal*, vol. 10, no. 21, pp. 18993–19003, 2023, doi:10.1109/JIOT.2023.3265126.

[20] Y. Mi and Q. Song, "Energy Efficiency Maximization for IRS-Aided WPCNs," *IEEE Wireless Communications Letters*, vol. 10, no. 10, pp. 2304–2308, 2021, doi:10.1109/LWC.2021.3100329.

Chapter 7

Energy harvesting and energy-efficient communication protocols in IoT

Jagjit Singh Dhatterwal[1], Kuldeep Singh Kaswan[2], Kiran Malik[3], B. Tirapathi Reddy[1] and Daniel Arockiam[4]

Abstract

The chapter discusses energy efficiency as one of the key enablers in a relatively new area of IoT systems. This issue is topical because as IoT devices become more integrated into society and their everyday use, huge importance is placed on their energy consumption and management. These devices can be characterized as having scarce energy supplies, and hence there is a need to employ certain strategies to ensure that available energy is utilized fully. This chapter considers a number of different factors relating to the energy usage of communication systems in IoT contexts and the specific communication protocols, forms of data transmission, and power management that are used. This is an emphasis on how LPWAN, BLE, and Zigbee, among other energy-sensitive protocols, help to minimize energy consumption. It includes discussions on technologies of energy harvesting, including solar energy harvesting, RF energy harvesting, and thermal energy harvesting, as well as how machine learning is applied to energy management and energy optimization. The chapter also considers how the identified opportunities in energy efficiency can be complemented and optimized through the use of such innovations as edge computing and blockchain.

To this end, the chapter aims at presenting an overview of the state of the art on power management and its application to IoT communication systems. Cooperative communication strategies, adaptive transmission power control (TPC), data aggregation, and other approaches for lowering energy demands are also analyzed. To this end, the chapter provides real-world evidence of these techniques' feasibility and advantages by analyzing their application in smart homes, industrial IoT systems, and smart cities. Some of the potential issues like the impendence between

[1]Department of Artificial Intelligence and Data Science, Koneru Lakshmaiah Education Foundation, India
[2]School of Computer Science and Engineering, Galgotias University, India
[3]Department of Computer Science and Engineering (AIML), G L Bajaj Institute of Technology and Management, India
[4]Department of Computer Science and Engineering, Amity School of Engineering and Technology, Amity University Madhya Pradesh, India

power consumption and network size, security, and future trends in IoT are addressed. The chapter ends with noting that the need to foster more research and development in energy efficiency technologies and strategies will remain relevant a long time into the future. While comparing the existing approaches, the future of developments in this topic is also discussed to help enhance energy optimization in IoT communications, which in turn will help the modification and development of IoT networks to be more sustainable and efficient in the future.

Keywords: Internet of Things; LPWAN; Bluetooth low energy; Zigbee; Power consumption

7.1 Introduction

In the ever-emerging world of IoT, communication systems can be best described as the lifeline of connected items through which data is exchanged and interactions happen in various applications. There are various types and forms of IoT communication systems, which are basically the technologies and protocols that allow sensors, actuators, or any other devices to connect seamlessly. Such systems employ different communication protocols, including low-power wide-area networks (LPWAN), Bluetooth low energy (BLE), and Zigbee, as they work under the limitations of bandwidth together with the diverse capabilities of the connected devices.

Energy management is always critical in IoT systems because many IoT devices are constrained in terms of power, mainly being battery operated and installed in inaccessible places. The utilization of energy in these appliances prolongs the use of the devices, reduces expenditure on their maintenance, and conserves the environment by minimizing the amount of energy used. It has been seen that with the increasing number of connected devices in IoT networks and the increased scale of networks, energy and power management has become a critical issue in keeping the system efficient and reliable.

However, energy efficiency in IoT communication is not easy to achieve; the following challenges arise. Due to the diverse nature of IoT devices, different communication techniques and the requirement of constant data transfer, power consumption, and overall cost become a major concern. Furthermore, the objective of minimizing energy consumption is not exclusive as it can only be achieved at the cost of either data rate or latency. Solving such issues means that IoT needs to implement novel methods of power management, data transmission, and protocols so that it can function efficiently while being power-conscious. That is why this chapter is devoted to analyzing these aspects in detail to give an understanding of present-day approaches and further developments for energy optimization in IoT communication systems [1].

7.2 Energy consumption in IoT communication

Energy involvement in IoT communication proves to be an important issue that determines IoT performance and reliability. This section discusses the distribution of energy consumption in IoT devices, the effect of communication protocols on energy consumption, and the energy consumption of the different IoT components.

7.2.1 Energy consumption in IoT device

Energy usage in IoT devices is presumed from a number of activities namely data transmission, computation, and when the device is in an idle mode. Data transfer and transmission using wireless networks are demanding in terms of energy and usually take the lion's share of energy consumed in a node. The energy which is consumed in the communication depends on other factors like signal intensity, distance of transmission, and traffic load. Furthermore, writing and reading data as well as operation of computations on IoT devices also consumes power. Apparatus typically exists in active, idle, and sleep modes in which, the involved energy consumption levels are distinct. The problem is how to harmonize these modes to maximize performance and minimize power consumption.

7.2.2 Effects of using communication protocols in controlling energy consumption

A lot goes into the selection of the communication protocol mainly because it has effects on the energy consumption of IoT systems [2]. Other protocols like low-power wide-area networks (LPWAN) like LoRaWAN and NB-IoT are created in a way that will consume the least power by allowing, the least frequency of sending data and low power transmission. This was in contrast to higher data rate protocols such as the Wi-Fi and Bluetooth technologies that have heavier power consumption due to their many transmission and reception duties. Energy-efficient protocols are necessary to enhance the battery power of IoT devices and to enhance their application in diverse sectors.

7.2.3 Energy requirement in IoT sensors, actuators, and devices

There are a few different IoT parts like sensing, control, and communication that consume power in a different manner. Environmental data, which sensors pick up, might require lots of energy especially when it is carrying out several readings or detailed measurements. Another component of a smart system is actuators governing all the physical actions that respond to certain sensor data; actuators also consume energy, especially in applications that call for constant or extensive use of the actuators [3]. These functions consist of the communications modules that form the basis for data exchange but that normally consume a lot of power, particularly when active in transmitting data. Innovative power management techniques including duty cycling and TPC must be employed with a view of using the right amount of power in these components to increase the IoT device's usability time.

Such knowledge of energy distribution is useful in engineering better IoT platforms through the matching of proper protocols and the inclusion of proper power management strategies (Table 7.1).

Table 7.1 Power consumption in IoT sensors, actuators, and devices

Device type	Power consumption (typical)	Operational modes	Power-saving features	Examples
Sensors				
Temperature sensor	0.1–2 mW	Sleep, active	Low-power sleep modes	DHT22, LM35
Pressure sensor	1–5 mW	Sleep, active	Periodic sensing with wake-up timers	BMP180, MPL3115A2
Humidity sensor	1–3 mW	Sleep, active	Duty cycling	SHT31, AM2302
Light sensor	0.5–1 mW	Sleep, active	Adaptive sensing rates	TSL2561, BH1750
Motion sensor (PIR)	1–50 µW (sleep), 100 mW (active)	Sleep, active	Event-driven wake-up	HC-SR501, LHI968
Actuators				
Relay	200–400 mW	Active	Mechanical design to reduce energy	Songle SRD-05VDC-SL-C
DC motor	1–5 W	Active	Pulse-width modulation (PWM) control	Generic DC motors, L298N driver
Servo motor	0.5–1 W	Idle, active	Limited active runtime	MG996R, SG90
LED display	20–100 mW	Sleep, active	Dimming, adaptive refresh rate	OLED, 7-segment displays
Buzzer	50–200 mW	Active	Short duty cycle	Piezoelectric buzzers
Communication modules				
Wi-Fi module	60–200 mW	Sleep, active, transmit	Power-saving modes	ESP8266, ESP32
Bluetooth module	10–50 mW	Sleep, active, transmit	Low-energy communication (BLE)	HC-05, NRF52840
LoRa module	40–150 mW	Sleep, active, transmit	Duty cycle control	SX1276, RFM95
Zigbee module	15–75 mW	Sleep, active, transmit	Low-power listening	XBee S2C, CC2530
IoT gateways				
Raspberry Pi	2–5 W	Idle, active	Dynamic voltage/frequency scaling	Raspberry Pi 3/4
Arduino Uno	50–100 mW	Idle, active	Low-power modes	Arduino Uno R3, Nano
Edge devices	1–3 W	Idle, active	Data offloading to reduce energy	NVIDIA Jetson Nano, Intel NUC

7.3 Energy-efficient communication protocols

In the field of IoT, one of the important decisions is the choice of effective energy-consuming protocols for data transfer. This section deals with a number of protocols that are aimed at ensuring that communication is done efficiently with the least energy requirement (Table 7.2).

7.3.1 Low-power wide-area networks

LPWAN protocols are designed for low data rate and long range which also fulfills the requirement of IoT applications where the device is battery operated for long

Table 7.2 Energy-efficient communication protocols

Protocol	Technology type	Main features	Energy-saving techniques	Use cases
LoRaWAN	LPWAN	Long-range, low-power, suitable for large networks	Adaptive data rates, low duty cycles, sleep mode operation	Smart cities, agriculture, industrial IoT
NB-IoT	LPWAN	Narrowband, optimized for deep coverage	Reduced device complexity, optimized signaling, extended idle periods	Smart metering, wearables, smart homes
Bluetooth low energy (BLE)	Short-range	Short-range, low-power communication	Efficient connection-less communication, adaptive frequency hopping	Wearables, smart homes, health monitoring
Zigbee	Mesh network	Low-power, short-range mesh networking	Duty cycling, sleep mode, efficient mesh routing	Home automation, industrial automation
6LoWPAN	IPv6-based WSN	IPv6 for low-power devices, uses compression	Header compression, efficient packet size reduction, adaptive link-layer retransmission	Smart grids, environmental monitoring
Wireless sensor networks (WSNs)	Distributed network	Self-organizing, energy-aware routing	Energy-aware routing protocols, data aggregation, clustering for minimizing redundant transmissions	Environmental sensing, agriculture
Sigfox	LPWAN	Low power, low data rate, wide coverage	Ultra-narrowband technology, asynchronous communication, minimal data transmission	Asset tracking, smart metering, logistics
Wi-Fi HaLow	Low-power Wi-Fi	Long-range, low-power, Wi-Fi for IoT	Power-saving modes, efficient sleep-wake cycles	Smart homes, smart cities, wearables

periods of time. Two main LPWAN technologies are as follows: LoRaWAN and NB-IoT.

- LoRaWAN (long-range wide-area network): The LoRaWAN is the wireless technology used in the sub-GHz frequency bands and is chosen to support low data rate applications. It is intended to provide extended-range connectivity and at the same time low power consumption, and this is made possible through its adaptive data rate method and low duty cycle operation mode. In the LoRaWAN network, different classes of devices are provided which include Class A, Class B, and Class C devices; Class A and Class B are the battery-operated LoRaWAN devices, whereas Class C includes additional gateway nodes which are LoRaWAN devices. This is due to its network architecture which consists of end devices, gateways, and network servers that enable data transmission and reception with little power consumption.
- NB-IoT (narrowband IoT): NB-IoT is one of the cellular-based LPWAN technologies that use a licensed spectrum that can offer good connectivity even in adverse conditions. H consent is used to transmit small volumes of data at long and irregular intervals which improves power consumption in contrast to cellular technologies. NB-IoT utilizes a narrowband channel, and its benefits encompass extended coverage, low latency, and high energy efficiency making it applicable to most IoT applications [4].

7.3.2 Wireless sensor networks

Wireless sensor networks (WSNs) are formed of a number of sensor nodes deployed in an area to measure physical or environmental parameters [5]. These networks are based on energy-conserving communication protocols, such that sensor nodes have to be replaced with fresh batteries only after a significantly long interval of use. Other methods that are used include data fusion, sleep management, and adaptive wake-up protocols that help in reducing the amount of energy used. Some of the well-known protocols already developed for WSNs include directed diffusion, which increases energy efficiency through efficient data routing, and LEACH (low-energy adaptive clustering hierarchy), which organizes activated nodes in less amount.

7.3.3 Bluetooth low energy

Bluetooth low energy or BLE is a wireless transmission interface that was developed with the intention of being used in applications that require low energy and low power. It functions in the 2.4-GHz Industrial Scientific and Medical band and has a power-optimized data transfer. In the BLE, the data are transmitted periodically using a technique called advertising while the device is in a low-power mode at other times. These modes of communication are less energy consuming than continuous communication protocols. BLE is used vastly in fields such as wearable devices, health monitors, and smart home products.

7.3.4 Zigbee and 6LoWPAN

Zigbee: Zigbee is a protocol currently used for communications in the Personal Area Network with low power and low data rate requirements. Moreover, it operates in the 2. of 4GHz Industrial, Scientific, and Medical (ISM) band and mesh networking that makes it possible to enhance the connectivity range and communication reliability while consuming energy. Zigbee's low energy consumption is realized through its possession of sleep modes and its capacity for forming meshes.

6LoWPAN (IPv6 over low-power wireless personal area networks): 6LoWPAN helps to run IPv6 communication on the low power, low data rate as in the case with IoT. It has approaches in header compression and packet fragmentation to help in the transmission of IPv6 packets over limited bandwidth networks. This protocol is suitable for mesh networking and for combining with other IPv6-based networks; it increases energy efficiency by decreasing the overhead corresponding to the communication.

7.4 Energy harvesting techniques in IoT

Energy harvesting techniques are very useful to increase the working time of IoT devices by utilizing the ambiance energy. These techniques help introduce the concept of reducing the conventional battery system and making IoT far more maintenance-free. This section provides an overview of some of the major ways of energy harvesting together with their interfacing with IoT devices as illustrated in Figure 7.1.

7.4.1 Solar energy harvesting

Solar energy collection involves the utilization of photovoltaic cells to trap the sunlight with the aim of producing electricity. This technique is most suitable for effecting IoT devices intended to operate in outdoor or well-lit conditions. Solar cells are devices that change light into electrical power with the ability to drive devices directly or charge batteries for later use. Solar energy harvest enables IoT use cases like weather monitoring kiosks and sensors used in the smart farming industry [6]. The performance of the solar collection is relative to aspects such as light intensity, angle of incidence, and the photovoltaic materials applied.

7.4.2 Transmission energy or radio frequency energy harvesting

Radiofrequency (RF) energy harvesting harnesses electromagnetic waves from different forms of RF signals including radio, television, and cell signals and converts them to useful electrical energy. This technique makes use of RF signals present in all corners of today's society to charge low-power IoT devices, especially in areas where there is a congestion of RF signals such as busy cities. RF energy harvesting systems employ the utilization of rectifiers which help in the conversion of the captured RF signals into DC power. RF energy harvesting can supply power continuously; however, it is a significant disadvantage to have less

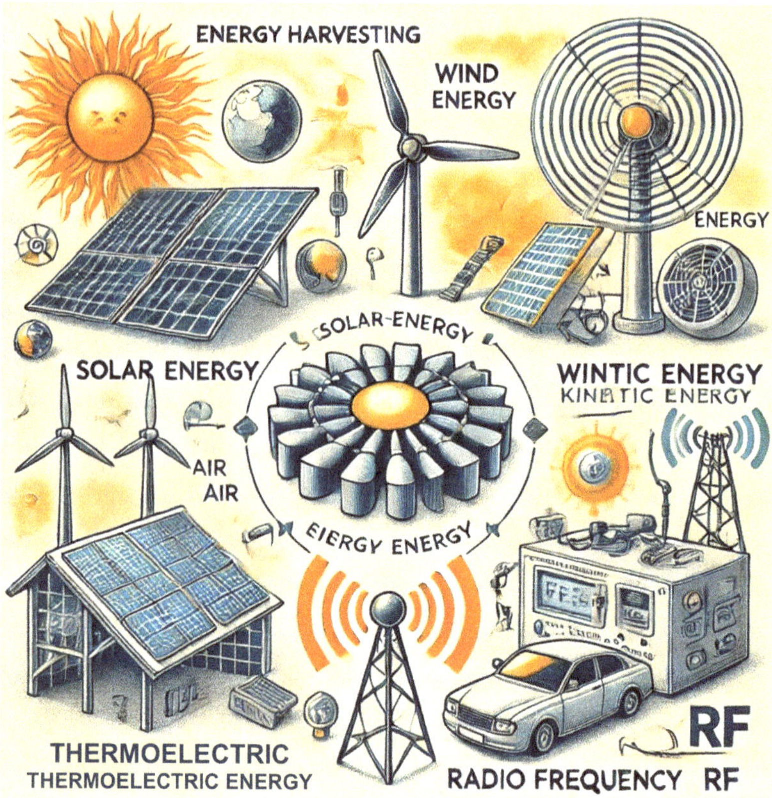

Figure 7.1 Energy harvesting techniques

efficiency compared with the strength and frequencies of the signals. Vibration and thermal energy conversion Smart material Smart structures and sensors 10%–15% of the energy generated is converted to usable power.

Vibration energy harvesting utilizes piezoelectric materials or electromagnetic generators to convert mechanical vibrations into electrical energy. This method is used for IoT devices installed in the environment with a stable level of vibrations, for instance, industrial equipment or car engineering. Thermal energy includes using discarded heat from industrial applications or environmental temperature fluctuation to produce electricity with the help of thermoelectric generators. Vibration and thermal energy can also be used to provide additional power to the IoT devices, and this can help increase the level of its operation without having to rely on additional external sources of energy.

7.4.3 Combining energy harvesting with IoT devices

To incorporate energy scavenging strategies in IoT devices, it is essential to use various power sources to enhance the efficiency of the devices by increasing their lifetime. For this integration, there is a need for optimal energy management systems, wherein power generation, storage, and utilization are made. For instance, IoT devices may utilize energy harvesting to recharge batteries rarely while still running constantly. Sophisticated algorithms can also identify available energy sources and prioritize consumption based on the requirements of the device in the IoT network hence increasing efficiency in IoT systems.

Energy harvesting has a central role in self-sustaining IoT systems since it enables the expansion and improvement of sustainability for IoT systems. Using solar, RF, vibration, and thermal energy IoT devices could become more independent from the traditional energy sources and perform more operations on their own. Synchronization of these techniques with energy-efficient IoT designs also increases operational efficiency while also increasing the overall lifespan of the gadgets and decreasing the need for maintenance. With more research and better development on the technologies capable of improving harvesting technologies, the chances for better IoT networks that are self-sustaining increases and the future of smart systems in different fields in the future looks bright. All these advancements will dictate the future of energy-efficient IoT technologies all across the globe.

7.5 Energy-efficient data transmission techniques

The use of energy-efficient data transmission mechanisms is critical in the IoT system to enable improvement in its capacity and durability. These methods are focused on managing the energy put into use in transmitting data over the network, and this is very important in terms of costs and battery usage. Some of them are adaptive power control, data aggregation, and the use of advanced schedule methods.

7.5.1 Adaptive transmission power control

Adaptive TPC is one of the essential techniques for minimizing energy consumption in IoT networks. Adaptive TPC works by changing the transmission power of a device with respect to the distance to the receiver and may be the quality of the channel. Thus, TPC can increase or decrease the link power to the lowest level to maintain the link quality in communications between the adjacent nodes at a distance. This approach reduces unnecessary energy consumption that would be experienced if the device were to transmit at a more powerful constant rate. For instance, if an IoT device is in near proximity to the receiver, the power may be low; whereas, in the instance that the IoT device is farther away or in a weak signal area, the power can be high. This real-time adjustment minimizes energy consumption in general, maximizes battery longevity, and improves the sustainability of IoT networks.

7.5.2 Data aggregation and compression

Another method that is very crucial in handling data in IoT systems is data aggregation and compression to minimize energy consumption in the system when transmitting data. Data aggregation is the process of combining data derived from one or many sources with the objective of presenting it in simpler forms before transmission. This helps in reducing the number of packets that are transported within the network thus reducing the overall communication load and power utilization. For example, in case the sensor network is set up for monitoring an environmental parameter, aggregation might entail the collation of readings from various sensors into a consolidated report. Compression also enhances the efficient consumption of energy since data is compressed to a smaller format hence reducing the size of packets in the frame. It is possible to use Huffman coding for the compression of data or run-length encoding to shrink the size of data to process. Through the use of these techniques, IoT systems are able to minimize bandwidth consumption and time taken during the transmission process and thereby save on energy.

Algorithm 1 Data Aggregation and Compression in IoT Networks

Input: IoT sensor data $D = \{d_1, d_2, ..., d_n\}$ from n devices
Output: Compressed and aggregated data C
Initialize $C \leftarrow \emptyset$ ▷ Set to store compressed data
Set aggregation period T ▷ Time window for data aggregation
Set compression threshold e ▷ Threshold for data compression
for each aggregation period $t = 1$ to T **do**
    Collect data D_t from all devices within period t
    Aggregate data $A_t \leftarrow Aggregate(D_t)$ ▷ Aggregate data across all devices
    Apply compression function: $C_t \leftarrow Compress(A_t, e)$
    Add C_t to the final compressed dataset C
end for
return C

7.5.3 Duty cycling and sleep scheduling

Duty cycling and sleep scheduling are techniques incorporated to control the states of IoT devices to optimize energy consumption. Duty cycling is therefore a cyclic ON–OFF operation of devices depending on the activity of the device or system. Active periods are still periods where the device operates while in sleep mode, the device shuts down all but the most necessary components to save energy. Sleep scheduling goes beyond this by selectively putting into the low power sleep mode, devices at times when activity is expected to be low. For instance, a temperature sensor that detects temperature change in the smart home may only be active at a particular time let us say every hour while it spends the rest of the time in sleep mode. This approach lowers the amount of time devices spend in power-hogging states thus conserving energy and battery life.

7.5.4 Cooperative communication strategies

Some of the cooperation communication strategies include the collective efforts of several IoT devices in sending and receiving information as well as saving power

[7]. Some of the examples of cooperative schemes include cooperative relaying and network coding which helps the devices to share resources and help in the transmission of data. Cooperative relaying is a type of system where a device with signal strength assists in forwarding information from other devices with relatively weaker signals thus minimizing the number of times the information is transmitted. This means the incorporation of data from different sources with the same transmission leading to better resource use of the network and fewer disasters that require retransmission. Through the application of the described cooperative strategies, IoT networks will be more efficient, dependable, and energy-wise, thus being powerful and necessary for large-scale IoT service applications.

7.6 Machine learning for energy optimization

Several ML-based techniques have been applied as energy management strategies in IoT systems. In an IoT network, through the integration of AI/ML, better decisions can be made on reducing energy consumption hence increasing efficiency. AI/ML systems help in predictive energy management where through the collection of data and analysis of this data to determine the energy demands and usage in the future. For instance, by using predictive models, the usage rate of energy can be studied in relation to the time of the day and season with the aim of forecasting when energy usage is more likely to be high. To accurately predict energy needs there are many machine learning techniques that can be applied, these entail regression analysis, time series forecasting, and anomaly detection. These predictions assist IoT systems in taking advanced measures in the use of energy, for instance, reducing power usage during periods of low demand or seeing ways of avoiding wastage of energy. This of course works to supplement energy efficiency and application to improve cost reduction and sustainability.

7.6.1 RL for energy-efficient routing

Reinforcement learning is one of the machine learning techniques that aim at utilizing and improving decision-making via consecution through the environment. Applying RL in the context of IoT it is possible to create energy-efficient routing protocols. Due to the fact that routing decisions are considered in terms of actions and rewards, the RL algorithms will be able to choose the appropriate routes that will correspond to the least energy consumption while transmitting data with reliability. For example, an RL-based routing algorithm may change routing paths due to the real-time information regarding the condition of the links, the battery status, and/or the cost of transmission to the destination node. Thus, it aids in managing network traffic and also in increasing the longevity of IoT devices through efficient energy consumption [8].

There are several clustering algorithms for energy efficiency in IoT networks as presented below.

Energy-aware clustering algorithms have been developed with the intent of enhancing energy utilization of IoT networks by grouping devices into logical clusters and controlling their interactions within these clusters in an efficient manner. In such algorithms, one of the nodes known as cluster head is meant to be chosen depending on powers for instance to conduct data gathering and interaction with other clusters. This decreases the number of messages necessary to be exchanged by specific devices and is useful in ensuring that energy utilization in the system is well distributed. These algorithms also have the added advantage of rotating the role of cluster head among devices; this helps in preventing a specific device from being overloaded thereby increasing the overall lifetime of the network. Energy-aware clustering techniques prove to be beneficial in the efficient use of resources, less communication, and improved scalability of IoT systems [9].

Integrating machine learning algorithms in energy optimization enables them to predict the IoT systems' management and improve the routing strategies as well as clustering. These approaches utilize complex matrices to decide on energy saving, extension of device life, and enhanced network performance, thus leading to sustainable IoT operations.

7.7 Energy-efficient network design

7.7.1 Topology control for energy conservation

Topology control is a mechanism where the nature of topology needed in a certain area is involved with regard to power use in the network and general performance. Another way of conserving energy is by changing the network topology for instance, identifying which of the nodes have to be operational and which ones need to be put to sleep. These are methods such as controlling transmission power to avoid overlapping and interference with other signals and hence reduce the energy used for communication. For example, in WSNs, topology control algorithms transpose the network topology with the current energy levels, network conditions, and communication needs [10]. This kind of dynamic adjustment is useful in increasing the network lifetime as well as achieving better energy management.

7.7.2 Energy-aware routing protocols

Energy-aware routing protocols are developed to ensure that the route taken by the data packets passes through the network in a prudent manner to consume minimum energy. These protocols incorporate energy in their routing algorithms to make energy evenly distributed across the nodes. For example, LEACH (low-energy adaptive clustering hierarchy) routing and its derivatives prefer to utilize more energy-rich nodes in constructing its routing path to obviate the early drainage of nodes. Moreover, energy-aware routing may incorporate such factors as energy per offered packet or residual battery energy; using them, it is possible to forward packets along optimal energy paths so that a network life cycle is maximized.

These are clustering and hierarchical network structures. Clustering and hierarchical network structures improve energy efficiency through node organization in clusters headed by a cluster head node. This configuration minimizes the number of direct transmissions with the base station or the sink node. While cluster heads collect data from their corresponding cluster members and are the only nodes responsible for the physical transmission of information to the sink, they offload much of the communication burden and hence save energy. Hierarchical approaches can also work slightly better in terms of energy efficiency since its numerous clusters are broken down into chains, with the data sent between them up and down the chain, as it improves network scalability.

7.7.3 Network coding for energy efficiency

With network coding a node is allowed to encode data before transmitting and this will greatly improve the efficiency of the network and reduce power consumption. Different from running data in its original format, network coding allows nodes to mix together several data packets into one packet before transmitting them. This approach leads to a reduction in the number of transmissions needed, the amount of data that is transmitted over the network, and energy utilization. Network coding seems to be highly effective, especially in higher redundant networks or in networks where data have to be transmitted over several paths resulting in both energy conservation and overall improved performance.

For this reason, the present strategies highlighted here for energy-efficient network design are instrumental for IoT communication system operations. Reducing the consumption of energy and improving the durability of IoT networks can be achieved by topology control, energy-aware routing, clustering, and network coding. Use and integration of such techniques would ensure that IoT systems adopt measures to ensure that the systems are more sustainable, pull down on operational costs, and prolong the usage of the network. Some of these approaches tend to work best on one hand with energy efficiency while at the same time may not affect or compromise the networks' ability to perform well. In general, these concepts outlined above, are an example of major progress made in the search for more effective means of IoT communication [11].

7.8 Edge computing for energy optimization

7.8.1 Role of edge computing in reducing energy consumption

Edge computing is an emerging computed model that aims to process data closer to the source of data generation rather than concentrating on the cloud server. It greatly minimizes the transmission of data across a long distance to the data centers or cloud platform, hence, reducing the energy consumed in data transmission. The savings in data and information exchange do more than just save the available bandwidth; it also helps to save the energy used by the communication infrastructure. Moreover, edge computing deals with data processing locally, thus excluding delay and optimizing performance, which is essential for applications that require immediate analysis. This suggested that edge computing helps to conserve overall energy in IoT systems by cutting down the amount of data that has to be transmitted over the network [12].

Computation shifting arises where instead of sending data to centralized data centers for preprocessing, analysis, and post-processing, data processing is directly carried out locally by the devices, or edge servers which are nearer to the data. This strategy reduces the pressure of transferring raw data to remote cloud servers for processing as the process is power costly and time consuming. Calculations on edge devices are carried out locally and these enable them to determine the exact data required to be transferred to the cloud, this is after analyzing data in real time. This not only reduces the energy that is used during the data transmission but also speeds up the applications that require real-time processing such as the monitoring systems, control systems, and the decision-making systems. The reason behind shifting computation is that it saves power by minimizing dependence on the cloud and by making better utilization of the resources in the edge.

7.8.2 Energy-efficient data processing at the edge

As far as optimization of energy consumption in data processing at the edge level is concerned, it is personalized by utilizing algorithms and hardware that would consume very limited energy while handling or processing data. Data collection, data sampling, and data preprocessing are some of the approaches utilized at the edge layer to minimize data traffic to the cloud layer. Also, edge devices are provided with lower power consumption, integrated low power risks, and power-saving hardware circuits which are able to complete computational operations with less power consumption. These optimizations also assist in saving of energy in addition to improving the reliability and speed of the system. As mentioned earlier, energy-efficient processing is another way through which edge computing guarantees sustainable functionality of IoT systems while at the same time delivering real-time performance [13].

7.9 Blockchain technology for energy optimization in IoT

Blockchain has been widely used in IoT systems to enable energy optimization to be efficient decentralized, secure, and transparent. Currently, when implementing blockchain with IoT networks, the effectiveness of energy management is improved, and it is possible to conduct the exchange of energy resources between individuals, maintain secure interaction, and make decentralized decisions.

7.9.1 Blockchain-enabled energy management systems

The IoT energy systems have therefore improved through the help of blockchain technology. Smart grid systems that utilize blockchain have the benefit of recording energy generation, utilization, and trade in a decentralized, transparent, and nonmodifiable manner. Through the incorporation of blockchain in IoT-based energy management systems, energy buyers and sellers, or producers and consumers, enable direct energy trading through efficient distribution of resources and proper energy balance. It also optimizes the overall energy system since it depends less on central authorities and helps minimize energy wastage while at the same time facilitating the monitoring of energy resources.

7.9.2 Advanced energy system (AES) decentralized energy trading and microgrids

Blockchain's application in decentralized energy trading and microgrids is significant because it enables transactions between energy providers and consumers without third-party intervention. Localized systems of energy distribution can be called microgrids, and they have the possibility to use blockchain to enhance their control over energy flows. Smart contracts utilizing blockchain can support the automatic trading of energy between the participants to sell or buy excess energy at appropriate times. This helps in increasing the uptake of clean energy resources, enhancing the stability of the electrical network, and lowering the overall energy utilization by making supply and demand correspond in real time.

7.9.3 Blockchain-enabled secure and energy-efficient IoT networks

Blockchain acts as the reinforcement layer to IoFT by increasing the reliability of sensitive information in addition to the security of the overall network system. In efficient IoT networks for energy consumption, blockchain plays the role of reducing security threats that are associated with data alteration and management [14]. Based on the properties of the blockchain, IoT devices can communicate in a reliable fashion without the need for a control authority which in turn lowers energy consumption associated with communication overhead. However, blockchain can also be combined with low-energy consensus algorithms like, for example, proof of stake (PoS) or practical byzantine fault tolerance (PBFT) to minimize the energy usage of IoT networks.

7.10 Case studies in energy optimization

Energy management is a critical factor that helps achieve higher levels of sustainability and effectiveness of IoT systems. This section introduces practical scenarios that highlight how energy-efficient technologies can make a difference in different applications, such as smart homes, industrial IoT, and smart cities. These examples explain how IoT can be applied practically to reduce energy consumption. Smart homes that focus on energy conserve IoT objects to efficiently manage power in the home through the use of automatic control and monitoring. Smart thermostats, lighting, and appliances that contain sensors can sense occupancy and adjust energy consumption through optimization of occupancy habits. For example, smart thermostats provide management of temperature depending on the number of people in the house and outside weather conditions, thus ensuring that people save on energy while at the same time enjoying their preferred temperatures.

In the same way, through the utilization of renewable energy systems like solar systems for electricity generation and energy storage in batteries, smart homes minimize the dependence on grid systems. Cost reduction and resource conservation remain the primary connotations associated with these technologies. Energy efficiency on the IIoT is created by intelligent sensor networks combined with AI-based predictive analysis for maintenance [15].

Through the constant supervision of the machinery and the identification of the areas that require optimization, the IIoT systems help the factories address the issue of excessive energy consumption. Otherwise, smart analytics using big data and artificial intelligence will be able to determine when some equipment needs to be serviced or optimized to prevent energy losses due to faulty machines. Real-time monitoring also makes it possible for factories to move energy consumption to different times during off-peak times to save more resources. It not only reduces cost but also decreases the ecological impact of manufacturing industries as well. Several smart cities apply IoT solutions for controlling energy consumption in structures in the city. For instance, in smart street lighting where the brightness automatically adjusts according to traffic information collected through sensors, the power consumption is brought down greatly. In addition, smart grids and IoT-based traffic management systems efficiently manage the distribution of energy and fuel consumption. Also, the charging stations of electric vehicles or EVs in smart cities employ dynamic pricing strategies to regulate the power demands in smart cities, which create a sustainable urban environment. Most of these measures provide not only improved energy efficiency but also a qualitative improvement in urban living conditions.

7.11 Challenges and future directions

Some of the challenges are associated with energy-efficient communication within the IoT context while others are challenges that can be met and lead to new future trends in the IoT systems.

Security versus energy efficiency trade-offs: Another interesting aspect of IoT communication is the problem of security and energy consumption trade-offs in efficient IoT applications. Many IoT devices have relatively simple processors, and their batteries are not easy to replace; therefore, simple and efficient security measures take a lot of power to implement. Secure transmission techniques, encryption, and authentication procedures are very much time and energy-consuming, leading to a trade-off between security and power consumption. The research should continue how to develop light but effective security systems with maximum and efficient utilization of the available device resources.

Scalability challenges in large IoT networks: This is more so considering that as the number of IoT networks increases, there is always a challenge in scaling the network. As the size of the network increases, it presents a higher traffic load, higher energy utilization, and even more complicated protocols. Evaluating energy-efficient techniques to be sustainable for large-scale IoT networks is a difficult task. The energy needs of hundreds, if not thousands of interconnected devices means that algorithms for control, data flow management, and resource utilization have to be sophisticated. Solutions like dynamic energy management, clustering, and hierarchy of networks may be the future scalable solutions in IoT.

Future trends in energy-efficient IoT communication: Higher levels of incorporation of energy efficiency in IoT communication in the coming future look forward to the impact of AI and machine learning, edge computing, and blockchain. Energy embedded in predictive AI-based energy management and continuous instantaneous control and optimization of network parameters can easily be cut down to the barest minimum. Through edge computing, data processing will be done nearer to where the data originates from reducing energy consumption in data transfer. The use of blockchain on IoT in the proposed solution addresses the decentralization, energy consumption, security of transaction, and trust of IoT networks. All of these trends are capable of transforming the existing IoT communication systems by providing solutions to existing problems as well as future developments.

7.11.1 Conclusion

This chapter is devoted to where the author discusses methods and approaches to IoT systems energy saving, which define the lifespan and costs of IoT devices. As the instance of IoT networks and devices increases day by day, more emphasis has been given to their deployment for future smart applications such as smart cities, better industrial automation, and home automation applications, then the need to optimize energy consumption is a must. Some of the topics sampled in this chapter include energy-efficient communication protocols such as LPWAN, Zigbee ML algorithms used in predicting energy usage to help in energy conservation, and edge computing that helps reduce energy usage through offloading computations near data sources. Furthermore, it explores energy scavenging systems like photovoltaic/power-by-light, RF technologies that will allow a device to be powered in a perpetual manner by the ambient surroundings.

As a result, the chapter stresses the need to properly manage energy in the IoT systems for its scalability and sustainability and provides useful recommendations for the developers and researchers. Possible mechanisms, such as adaptive TPC, clustering algorithms, and blockchain-based energy management systems are discussed in terms of their effects on power consumption and network performance. Nevertheless, some difficulties are still present: the conflict of interest between energy density and security, the ability to create large networks with such systems, and the capacity to provide a smooth and effective performance during energy-saving periods. In the future, the integration of AI technology, edge computing, and renewable energy sources are expected to be able to mitigate these challenges hence leading to efficient energy utilization in the IoT systems. From this chapter, the reader acquires useful knowledge on how to mitigate existing challenges and enhance energy optimality in IoT communication networks.

References

[1] Xu, L. D., He, W., and Li, S. (2014). Internet of Things in industries: A survey. *IEEE Transactions on Industrial Informatics*, 10(4), 2233–2243.

[2] Li, X., Niu, J., Kumari, S., Wu, F., Sangaiah, A. K., and Choo, K. K. R. (2018). A three-factor anonymous authentication scheme for wireless sensor networks in Internet of Things environments. *Journal of Network and Computer Applications*, 103, 194–204.

[3] Kumar, L. P. D., Grace, S. S., Krishnan, A., Manikandan, V. M., Chinraj, R., and Sumalatha, M. R. (2012). Data filtering in wireless sensor networks using neural networks for storage in cloud. *IEEE International Conference on Recent Trends in Information Technology*, 2012, 202–205.

[4] Zulkifli, C. Z., and Noor, N. N. (2017). Wireless sensor network and Internet of Things (IoT) solution in agriculture. *Pertanika Journal of Science & Technology*, 25, 91–100.

[5] Liu, H., Bolic, M., Nayak, A., and Stojmenovic, I. (2008). Taxonomy and challenges of the integration of RFID and wireless sensor networks. *IEEE Network*, 22(6), 26–32.

[6] Deepu, C. J., Heng, C. H., and Lian, Y. (2016). A hybrid data compression scheme for power reduction in wireless sensors for IoT. *IEEE Transactions on Biomedical Circuits and Systems*, 11(2), 245–254.

[7] Dev, K., Maddikunta, P. K. R., Gadekallu, T. R., Bhattacharya, S., Hegde, P., and Singh, S. (2022). Energy optimization for green communication in IoT using Harris Hawk's optimization. *IEEE Transactions on Green Communications and Networking*, 6(2), 685–694.

[8] Vermesan, O., and Friess, P. (2013). *Internet of Things: Converging Technologies for Smart Environments and Integrated Ecosystems*. Gistrup: River Publishers.

[9] Maddikunta, P. K. R., Gadekallu, T. R., Kaluri, R., Srivastava, G., Parizi, R. M., and Khan, M. S. (2020). Green communication in IoT networks using a hybrid optimization algorithm. *Computer Communications*, 159, 97–107.

[10] Sathish Kumar, L., Ahmad, S., Routray, S., *et al.* (2022). Modern energy optimization approach for efficient data communication in IoT-based wireless sensor networks. *Wireless Communications and Mobile Computing*, 2022(1), 7901587.

[11] Serrano, M., Barnaghi, P., Cousin, F. C. P., Vermesan, O., and Friess, P. (2015). Internet of Things semantic interoperability: Research challenges, best practices, recommendations and next steps. *European Research Cluster on the Internet of Things (IERC)*, 9(2), 18–35.

[12] Jo, D., and Kim, G. J. (2016). ARIoT: Scalable augmented reality framework for interacting with Internet of Things appliances everywhere. *IEEE Transactions on Consumer Electronics*, 62(3), 334–340.

[13] Babar, S., Mahalle, P., Stango, A., Prasad, N., and Prasad, R. (2010). Proposed security model and threat taxonomy for the Internet of Things (IoT). In International Conference on Network Security & Applications (CNSA), vol. 89, pp. 420–429. Berlin: Springer.

[14] Frustaci, M., Pace, P., Aloi, G., and Fortino, G. (2017). Evaluating critical security issues of the IoT world: Present and future challenges. *IEEE Internet of Things Journal*, 5(4), 2483–2495.

[15] Kim, D. Y., and Jung, M. (2016). Data transmission and network architecture in long-range low-power sensor networks for IoT. *Wireless Personal Communications*, 92(2), 445–458.

Chapter 8

Energy consumption and efficiency in federated learning (FL) for IoT

Kuldeep Singh Kaswan[1], Jagjit Singh Dhatterwal[2], Kiran Malik[3] and K. Babu[4]

Abstract

Federated learning (FL) can be therefore described as a revolutionary technique within machine learning deemed specific for the Internet of Things (IoT) context due to its focus on privacy and communication overhead. FL differs from traditional machine learning as it does not centralize data, instead, the training process is performed by multiple IoT devices while simultaneously keeping data local and the global model is learned collaboratively. This method forms a way of solving some problems like bandwidth limitation, energy utilization, delay, expandability, and heterogeneous data in IoT systems. Communication paradigms are critical and sensitive in FL for IoT and therefore require effective management. Loosely coupled IoT networks have been defined to have particular requirements for bandwidth management, energy conservation, and real-time data processing that have motivated better techniques. Issues such as model compression (pruning, quantization), gradient compression, and adaptive communication methods play a central role in improving communication rates. Life management strategies such as energy-conscious communications procedures and optimum distribution of units also contribute to the endeavor.

The decision of architecture for FL in IoT like decentralized and hierarchical tends to affect communication effectiveness. A wide spectrum of application scenarios, including smart homes and cities, health care, and self-driving vehicles, raises the problem of efficient communication management. It deals with security/privacy issues such as secure aggregation to means that communication efficiency will not be used at the expense of privacy by using differential privacy. From the

[1]School of Computer Science and Engineering, Galgotias University, India
[2]Department of Artificial Intelligence and Data Science, Koneru Lakshmaiah Education Foundation, India
[3]Department of Computer Science and Engineering (AIML), GL Bajaj Institute of Technology and Management, India
[4]Department of Computational Intelligence, SRM Institute of Science and Technology, India

current trends, there is a likelihood of enhancing their use of artificial intelligence or more of machine learning for further enhancement, deploying the use of 5G systems, and coming up with other techniques, learning from the existing drawbacks. This abstract emphasizes the continued development of research and innovations toward the achievement of better communication efficiency of FL for IoT while desiring to achieve the best of both worlds with limited space and resources in the ever-expanding connected world.

Keywords: Data privacy; Resource management; Energy consumption issues; Secure aggregation techniques

8.1 Introduction

Federated learning (FL) is a novel approach to machine learning wherein several devices or decentralized origin of datasets jointly train a mutual model while protecting data privacy. In contrast to the centralized learning approach in which data is collected to a main server for the purpose of model training, FL works in a manner where data stays at the edge devices [1]. On the contrary, the local models are trained locally on each device, and only model updates usually the gradients or the weights are shared with the other devices through a central server for averaging. This approach to training decentralized is especially beneficial for applications that require stringent privacy since the data is not transferred around but instead learned by various units, thus improving the privacy and security of an application [2].

FL is very pertinent to the Internet of Things (IoT) because it is a learning process that can be undertaken on any IoT device that is collecting massive data. Even for these devices that have less processing power and small memory, local data can help in training a global model. As shown, FL has the potential to facilitate collaborative learning along with maintaining the privacy of data which makes it useful for different IoT use cases starting from home automation, healthcare, industrial IoT, and self-driving cars.

The IoT or the connected world of technology devices has brought about the generation of intelligent technologies that involve the integration of the billions of devices that have the capability to sense, process, and even take actions on data. Such IoT systems exist in different fields such as smart cities, health, industries, and transport. Sensors, cameras, and other connected actuators produce vast quantities of data on a regular basis, so necessitating efficient data processing techniques for the delivery of rich and valuable intelligence and to enable real-time decision-making accordingly.

However, the centralized data processing paradigm, which structures data processing in a distinct facility, is frequently unprofitable and does not work for IoT systems for several reasons, including massive data volumes, limited bandwidth, and security issues. Federated learning is a remedy to this by allowing data to be processed on different IoT gadgets without necessarily having to transfer the data to a server that is central. Thanks to FL, IoT systems can learn efficiently and at a large scale extract information from those connected devices while respecting data privacy [3].

This chapter has highlighted how communication efficiency is a crucial aspect of federated learning and more so when it comes to the integration of IoT systems. In FL, there might be a huge cost of communication between the central server and the edge devices especially in large-scale IoT networks with limited bandwidth resources. There is also a need to reduce the frequency of passing data between worker nodes so that the global model can perform well.

Many aspects can be upgraded in FL for IoT, and the enhancement of communication efficiency is a good reason. First, it decreases the pressure on the network bandwidth, which is perceived to be a main constraint in IoT scenarios. Second, it saves power for IoT devices; these are mostly battery-powered devices and are characterized by restricted power capacity [4]. Last but not least, it also prevents latency for timely analysis and decision-making in key IoT-related applications. Thus, efficient communication in FL is critical to the real-world application of this technology in IoT systems [5].

Nevertheless, the efficiency of communication in federated learning for IoT systems has some drawbacks to be managed. One of the first concerns, thus, is the lack of homogeneity in IoT devices when it comes to their processing power, memory, or networking capabilities. These differences can cause shifts in the training process, making some of the device's inability to achieve the communication FL needs. The other challenge is the trade-off between the rate of communication and achieving the best performance of the model. Decreasing the rate of update frequency or size as well as the amount of information that has to be communicated to the central server can reduce the communication cost yet it also reduces the rate of convergence of the global model and thus the performance. Also, IoT networks are usually characterized by unpredictable connectivity, meaning that the lines of communication between the devices, as well as the server, may be severed, which will have a negative effect on the FL process.

However, the issues of privacy and security broaden the problem even further. It is also a fairly nontrivial task to design communication protocols where the communication costs are also low while naturally preserving high privacy guarantees like differential privacy. These considerations must be faced to create new methods that can allow for improving at the same time communication efficiency, model accuracy, and privacy [6].

8.2 Fundamentals of federated learning in IoT

8.2.1 Definition and core concepts of federated learning

FL is a distributed machine learning approach that empowers several devices or nodes, called clients, to jointly learn a model while maintaining the training data locally. This is different from the more conventional lawyer approach called centralized machine learning in which data from multiple sources is collected to a central server for training. FL is especially useful in situations where the security of data is an issue or where it may be impossible to transfer massive amounts of information to a central server based on problems of bandwidth or latency [7].

In FL, every client has its own local model, learns from its data, and then works only with updates of models (for example, gradients or weights) on the central server or an aggregator. Specifically, the intermediate results obtained from these clients are sent to the central server that synthesizes them to derive a global model, which can then be sent back to the clients for another round of training. This process of iteratively calculating continues until the model acquires the desired or required level of accuracy.

8.2.2 How FL differs from traditional machine learning in IoT

It must be stressed that federated learning is quite distinctive from machine learning in general and from the IoT perspective in particular. In conventional BM-SDI, data collected from various IoT devices are normally accumulated and stored in a large-scale data warehouse where the training of the model is done using this accumulated data. These issues include centralization of the system, privacy, control, security, and scalability, which become more important as most of the IoT devices produce and consume large volumes of data that are often sensitive.

To curb these worries, FL makes the training process more decentralized. Even though the presented FL approach is theoretically less accurate and requires more communication compared to centralized approaches for IoT, where devices are frequently constrained of resources and can work in areas where they have asynchronous connections. FL as discussed above preserves the data locally on the devices while only sharing the model updates, and thus, it ensures that the data is not leaked to other unauthorized individuals and it reduces the communication overhead involved in sending large datasets [8]. It also perfectly complements the edge computing concept, which is a way of moving the computations closer to the data source to optimize the performance of IoT systems (Table 8.1).

8.2.3 Architecture of FL in IoT environments

The architecture of FL in IoT environments typically involves three main components: the IoT devices (also referred to as the client devices), the center or hub (or referred to as the aggregator), and the network that is in charge of the connection of the two.

- *Client devices*: These are the IoT devices that create and gather data. They employ each device to learn a local model on the data provided and sporadically send model delta to the central server. Since IoT devices are inherent and we have considered that the models can be of several types, the local models may be of different complexity depending on the device's computational capacity and the type of data it produces.
- *Central server (aggregator)*: This means that the central server is accountable for collecting the updates of the model from the clients available.

Table 8.1 Differences between federated learning (FL) and traditional machine learning (ML)

Aspect	Traditional machine learning in IoT	Federated learning in IoT
Data handling	Centralized data collection on a server for training	Decentralized data remains on devices; only model updates are shared
Privacy	Requires data aggregation, increasing privacy risks	Preserves privacy by keeping data local
Communication	Data transmission to the central server, leading to high bandwidth usage	Model updates are transmitted, reducing communication overhead
Scalability	Scalability is limited by central server capacity and network bandwidth	More scalable as data stays on devices, reducing load on the central server
Energy consumption	Higher energy consumption due to data transmission and central processing	Lower energy consumption due to localized computation and less frequent communication
Model training	Centralized training on a global dataset	Distributed training across devices, with models aggregated on a central server
Latency	Higher latency due to data transmission and centralized processing	Lower latency by processing data locally, reducing network dependency
Security	Centralized data storage is vulnerable to breaches and attacks	Enhanced security as data stays on individual devices
Adaptability to heterogeneous devices	Limited adaptability; relies on uniform data preprocessing	Better adaptability; handles diverse data sources and device capabilities
Fault tolerance	Centralized system can be a single point of failure	Decentralized approach enhances fault tolerance, as learning continues even if some devices fail
Resource utilization	High resource demand on central server and network infrastructure	Distributed resource utilization across IoT devices
Data transfer overhead	Significant data transfer from devices to server	Minimal data transfer; only model updates are communicated
Implementation complexity	Easier to implement with a single, centralized system	More complex implementation due to distributed architecture
Use cases	Suitable for smaller-scale IoT deployments	Ideal for large-scale IoT networks, such as smart cities, healthcare, and industrial IoT

This aggregation is commonly done via algorithms such as federated averaging (FedAvg), in which the server calculates the weighted average of the models' updates with weights proportional to the data sizes used for training by the clients. The model comes back to the clients for further training hence forming the feedback loop until the model comes to a certain convergence level.

- *Communication network*: It enables the clients on the various models to update the central server with the latest models being developed. In many IoT applications, this network forms a wireless interface such as Wi-Fi, Bluetooth, or cellular networks. The effectiveness of the CL system is significantly dependent on the quality of the connectivity through the fluency of the network; often it results in constrained connection, increased power demand, and poor exclusion of some of the clients. Some of the issues that the design of the FL in IoT needs to consider include heterogeneity in the IoT devices, non-IID data distribution, and the need to establish an efficient communication protocol that is not too burdensome for the IoT devices. Furthermore, the architecture has to be resilient to certain failures of the network or even individual devices for the global model to be able to converge.

8.2.4 Data privacy and security in FL for IoT

Another important reason for using FL in IoT scenarios is the improvement of data privacy degree. This means that we do not have the risk of data breach that is common when sending the data to a central server that is held on the device. But at the same time, FL adds new privacy and security issues, which should be solved to maintain the system's reliability.

$$\bar{g} = \frac{1}{N}\sum_{i=1}^{N}\left(g_i + \mathcal{N}(0,\sigma^2)\right)$$

where:

- N is the number of participating IoT devices.
- g_i is the local gradient from the i-th device.
- $\mathcal{N}(0,\sigma^2)$ represents Gaussian noise with a mean of O and variance σ^2, added to each local gradient to ensure privacy.

Here even though FL reduces the necessity to transfer raw data and hence minimizes privacy leakage; the model updates that are being sent by the client can still pose some privacy leakage risks. For instance, model gradients can be reverse-engineered in some circumstances to gain specific information regarding the used training data. Some of the potential solutions to this risk include differential privacy and secure multiparty computation (MPC). Differential privacy puts noise into the model updates before they are sent limiting the ability of others to retrieve information about specific samples in the set. Secure MPC, on the other hand, is an extension of MPC but computer in a such manner that the inputs of the different parties remain private to the parties [9].

The FL systems also suffer from attacks known as model poisoning attacks whereby the clients supply the FL system with wrong update models, which reduce the efficiency of the global model. To counter such attacks sound aggregation methods, anomaly detection, and client authentication are used. These measures help to maintain the integrity of the model and stay true to the global setting even when faced with adversarial actions.

8.3 Challenges of communication in FL for IoT

FL has been identified as one of the most successful methods of deploying machine learning in distributed environments such as the IoT. FL preserves a number of privacy advantages due to the possibility of model training decentralization across a range of devices. However, incorporating FL with IoT is a bit more complex due to challenges in communication. In this section, we explore the issues common in the communication process of FL in the IoT context such as limited bandwidth, high energy use, high latency, scalability issues, and heterogeneity in data.

Another major constraint in IoT networks is the available bandwidth that throttles when FL is performed. Specifically, IoT targets several locations which in turn require common wireless protocols like Wi-Fi, Bluetooth, or cellular network. These protocols are in general said to have a rather restricted bandwidth which determines the amount of data that one node can transmit to another. In the case of FL, whenever devices need to communicate with the central server to receive the update to the model, the issues of bandwidth come into the picture and can cause a delay. This challenge is even more complicated when there are many devices trying to transmit at the same time when the network is congested with IoT devices. To overcome this, some suggestions have been made such as model compression, gradient sparsification, and periodic communication but they are costly in terms of model accuracy and convergence rate [10].

$$B_{\text{required}} = \sum_{i=1}^{n} \left(\frac{D_i}{T_i} \right)$$

where:

- B_{required} represents the total required bandwidth in the IoT network.
- D_i is the data size generated by the ith IoT device.
- T_i is the time interval for data transmission from the ith IoT device.
- n is the total number of IoT devices in the network.

8.3.1 Energy consumption issues

Another important concern in IoT-based FL is energy consumption. Most of the IoT devices are driven by batteries and other energy sources and therefore have restricted energy capability. The communication process in FL especially the continuous exchange of model updates is known to be energy-demanding, thus causing quick battery drain. This is a big challenge as energy efficiency for IoT devices is very important in the long run. Possible solutions associated with this challenge include the following: Limited numbers of communications, efficient management of resources, and proper utilization of energy-saving communication protocols. However, the main challenge in attempting to achieve this is to optimize the number of messages and the energy expended, especially in large-scale IoT applications in areas that may not be easily accessible.

$$E_{\text{total}} = E_{\text{train}} + E_{\text{comm}} + E_{\text{idle}}$$

where:

- $E_{\text{train}} = P_{\text{train}} \times T_{\text{train}}$ is the energy consumed for local training, with P_{train} being the power consumption during training, and T_{train} being the duration of training.
- $E_{\text{comm}} = P_{\text{comm}} \times T_{\text{comm}}$ is the energy consumed for communication, with P_{comm} being the power consumption during communication, and T_{comm} being the duration of communication.
- $E_{\text{idle}} = P_{\text{idle}} \times T_{\text{idle}}$ is the energy consumed during idle periods, with P_{idle} being the power consumption during idle state, and T_{idle} being the duration of the idle state.

8.3.2 Latency and real-time data processing needs

Latency or the time taken for data transmission is an important factor when it comes to the implementation of FL in IoT networks especially in applications that need a fast response time. Low throughput can hamper the model update coordination resulting in slowed down model convergence time and less than optimal performance. In real-time use cases like self-driven automobiles, health care, and industrial control systems, latency can be costly. Latency is a key problem associated with IoT networks where the majority of the networks employ long-range communication protocols. Overcoming this challenge has to do with fine-tuning the communication interface, the use of edge computing to minimize the distance of data transfer, and the FL algorithms with suitably low latency that enable the completion of the overall training process even in circumstances of update lateness [3].

$$L = \frac{D}{B} + \sum_{i=1}^{n} \left(C_i + \frac{M_i}{B} \right)$$

where:

- D is the size of the data being processed.
- B is the available network bandwidth.
- C_i is the computation time at each IoT device i.
- M_i is the size of the model update from each device i.
- n is the total number of IoT devices.

The problem of scalability becomes a significant issue that influences the IoT-based FL especially as the number of participating devices is very large. Traditional approaches to building machine learning models suffer from a communication overhead that grows with the size of the network as the system grows, hence, poor update coordinating and convergence. Solutions for large-scale IoT networks become challenging when bandwidth and energy constraints arise—particularly when IoT devices transmit the results of their local models to a central server. Also, it is difficult to achieve equal accuracy defined in the model across a heterogeneous network of devices with different CPU and network resources. Methods such as hierarchical FL wherein the local gradients are first computed for some rounds and then combined during the same at intermediate nodes before being sent to the server have been put forward to solve the scalability issue. However, these solutions should be well designed to not introduce extra layers of indirection and communication overhead to the system [11].

$$C(N) = O(N \times S_{\mathrm{m}} \times f)$$

where:

- $C(N)$ is the total communication cost in the network.
- N is the number of IoT devices participating in the FL process.
- S_{m} is the size of the model update transmitted by each device.
- f is the communication frequency (i.e., how often model updates are transmitted).

Inter-device data distribution is an aspect that is unique in IoT networks, and which is well described by the data heterogeneity concept. IoT devices capture data from a variety of environments and thus the collected data are non-IID. This heterogeneity is a problem because the central server has to combine models that were trained using drastically different datasets. This can lead to the problem of model bias and the phenomenon where all models tend to be worse than the best. Furthermore, different distributions of data can increase communication problems since the devices with unusual data have to almost constantly communicate to check on the model. Dealing with the problem of data heterogeneity necessitates creating reliable FL methods that would incorporate non-IID data while minimizing the required communication rounds. Other strategies have been developed including personalized FL for instance, where models are designed unique to each device; however, such strategies make communication processes even more complex [5].

8.4 Communication efficiency techniques in FL

Due to these features, FL has received increasing interest as a technique for distributed machine learning in which the data remains decentralized. However, achieving high levels of communication efficiency is still a big problem even more so in IoT systems due to constraints in bandwidths, power, and computational resources. To meet this challenge, several approaches have been designed to enhance the process of communication in FL. This section looks into the following methods of addressing the challenges of distributed deep learning: model compression, gradient compression, decreasing communication frequency, client selection, and model aggregation.

These are techniques that are used to make the federated learning process possible yet compress the models that are to be transferred between IoT devices and the central server. One of the techniques is pruning, which refers to the process of shedding unimportant weights or neurons within a neural network thereby making the model less complex and small in size. In this way, pruning can substantially reduce the communication overhead because only the most important aspects of the model need to be sent between the parts of the system.

Quantization reduces the communication costs even lower by only keeping a part of the model parameters that are quantized. Rather than the traditional 32 floating point formats for the model weights, these can be quantized in certain lower-level formats such as 8 or even 1 bit. This as a result reduces the amount of data that is required to be transmitted across the networks without much impacting the results of the model. By applying these techniques, it is possible to reduce significantly the overall communication traffic between the devices connected to the server. Existing studies by combining the pruning and quantization methods have found that there are enormous benefits to reducing communication costs while the compromise made in terms of accuracy was not drastic. In FL, gradient exchange between the server and IoT devices is one of the primary reasons for the area's communication congestion. Gradient compression techniques have been developed to mitigate this overhead through compression of the gradients before they are transmitted. Some of them include gradient quantization, gradient sparsification, gradient coding, and so on.

In this method, small gradient values are set to zero, hence transmitting only the most crucial values of gradients. This method is actually very beneficial in cutting down on communication load but at the same time does not compromise on model quality. The simplest approach is perhaps top-k sparsification whereby only the largest "*k*" gradients are sent back to the server. As for gradient quantization, which is another approach, the gradients' precision is lowered similarly to the model quantization. When both of these approaches are used, one is able to achieve a substantial decrease in the overhead incurred. For instance, it has been shown that gradient sparsification can make communication costs up to 90% cheaper with minimal effect on the model quality.

The other way of improving the communication efficiency in FL is by decreasing the number of interactions that take place between the IoT-connected devices and the server. Some of the strategies of communication are time based whereby devices report back to the server at specified intervals of time as opposed to constant reporting. This approach brings down the number of communication rounds hence conserving resources such as bandwidth and energy. Adaptive communication goes one step further and varies the communication within the learning process based on the current state of the learning process. For instance, in the case of a low convergence rate, the devices may be required to transmit at a slower rate, and in contrast, during the critical phase, the transmission rate may be higher. It makes it possible to use the available resources far better and reduces the amount of pointless information exchanged.

Interaction patterns target who should be included in a round of communication instead of targeting all the clients, and there are different client selection strategies. This approach will significantly lower the communication overhead since everyone in the company will not be receiving and responding to emails from people in another department. It is also evident that different criteria can be employed for client selection such as the devices, quality of the data, and networks among others.

For example, gadgets that have a better network connection or data containing better samples may be selected whereas devices that have weak connections or low power supply may be rejected. Also, to accomplish a balance between communication efficiency and model performance, one can use strategies such as Random/any client selection, or selection based on client importance. Thus, on the basis of carefully chosen clients, the communication load could be balanced well and the overall working efficiency of the FL process could be greatly improved. Consequently, it has been found that optimization of the client selection process can result in about a 30% reduction in the communication costs without having to impact the model performances.

Otherwise, model aggregation is a core process in FL by which updates received from multiple devices are used to create a global model. The most typical approach to aggregation is federated averaging (FedAvg) when the server computes the mean of the model updates coming from the devices. However, variations of this approach have been developed to take the communication efficiency of the system to even another level. Sparse model aggregation for instance aims at aggregating only the more important updates thus minimizing the amount of data transferred from the server to the devices. Furthermore, hierarchical aggregation is done at intermediate levels in the network and thus puts less pressure on the main server. To this end, these highly sophisticated aggregation procedures assist in reducing the amount of data to be communicated while at the same time guaranteeing the worldwide model to be as efficient and stable as possible. Thus, increasing the model's comprehensiveness is (HttpStatus) possible by applying different methods of model aggregation to increase communication efficiency in large IoT networks.

8.5 Resource management in FL for IoT

In particular, considering the applicability of FL in the context of the IoT, the question of resource management is intrinsically important due to the limited computational, energy, and communication capabilities of IoT devices. This section discusses the various strategies and approaches that mitigate these challenges with emphasis on optimal resource use, energy-conscious communication procedures, dynamic usage of resources, and the key trade-offs in communication and model accuracy.

8.5.1 FL systems: resource management

Optimal deployment of resources in FL systems is important, especially in the IoT context where clients, for instance, have limited processing powers and energy capabilities. The allocation process involves the process of mapping and partitioning different computational tasks and data processing loads, in a manner that results in effective and efficient utilization of the available resources without complicated energy consumption patterns and communication overhead. When it comes to efficient resource allocation one technique that can be used is known as adaptive client selection. In this method, clients (IoT devices) are selected depending on the resource availability and the network and only clients having adequate resources are chosen to participate in FL at any one time. It also leads to cost-effectiveness due to the reduced chances of having systems that have a congested flow of information or slow flow of information flow.

Another technique for load balancing is that the FL tasks are scattered among all the participating devices and there is no single device that is overloaded. Load balancing is thus suitable to be implemented through edge computing where instead of running all computations on constrained IoT hubs, some computations can be offloaded to proximal edge servers. This approach is useful in reducing the load of processing on each IoT device, especially given the fact that they are usually resource constrained.

8.5.2 Energy-efficient communication protocols

One of the most important concerns in IoT is energy efficiency because IoT devices are most commonly battery-powered and should last longer. In the context of FL, communication of devices with the main server (or rather edge nodes) can be power-consuming, this is especially true in the cases where constant updates are needed. To solve this, energy-efficient communication protocols have been designed. These protocols prove effective in reducing the energy that is used in passing information since it works to reduce the frequency, size, and time of communication that is done.

Gradient sparsification is one of the approaches used in this method where only the most important information concerning the updates in the model is sent between the various devices and the server. Due to filtering only the required updates, the communication load is minimized and therefore energy is saved. The third approach is to transmit compressed updates and the style of compression is called model compression. Methods such as quantization and pruning can help solve this problem by decreasing the number of bits that need to be transmitted thus saving energy without any compromise on the model USED.

Furthermore, asynchronous communication protocols can also improve energy consumption since some of the devices can also communicate with the server at different intervals depending on their status and the network status. This decreases dependency on the need to equally time synchronize all the devices, a process that consumes a lot of power on a large IoT network.

8.5.3 Dynamic resource management as well as adaptive systems

In FL for IoT applications, it is imperative to employ dynamic resource management schemes due to the fluctuating nature of the network and resource conditions in IoT networks. It is noteworthy that these dynamic characteristics involve adaptive systems by constantly endorsing the states of networks and devices and fine-tuning resource usage and data transfer protocols.

For example, to carry out the adaptive FL, it is possible to change the learning process according to the current bandwidth and energy of the devices connected to the network. If the network conditions are bad then the system may decrease its frequency of communication or go for a low-power protocol. On the other hand, when there is an availability of resources, the communication frequency in the system can be enhanced to enhance the learning process. It also guarantees that the FL system can work propitiously depending on the conditions in a way that maximizes resource utilization and depletes energy resources unnecessarily.

The second aspect of dynamic resource management pertains to the FL process to the decision that is made depending on the current scenario regarding the participation of the devices. Devices with low energy or weak connectivity can be removed from the training process for some time or their contribution during the computations can be given less priority to make sure that the performance of the entire system is not affected by the poor-performing devices.

8.5.4 Trade-offs between communication efficiency and model performance

Findings have shown that getting improved CE in FL-IoT solutions is usually accompanied by compromises with model accuracy. For example, decreasing the rate of exchange of the data/updates between server and clients lowers the energy consumption as well as bandwidth; however, the convergence rate of the model, and its accuracy, might be affected. Hence, organizations need to balance these factors effectively to enjoy the best results possible.

Adaptive communication strategies are one way of handling this trade-off where the communication system varies the communication rate with the learning process of the target. For instance during the early stages of model updates, when the size of the updates is large and frequency high, less communication needs to be made. However, as the model converges and the updates become smaller, communication frequency could be increased to better fine-tune the model without much increase in the consumption of resources.

Client prioritization is another strategy we can use; this is because devices that have important contributions towards the improvement of the model are usually considered important and therefore are given more priority concerning communication. This means that the most relevant updates are always sent to the server regardless of the contribution that some of the devices may have on the improvement of the model. In this way, there is a good trade-off between the communication overhead and the accuracy of the model itself for the FL systems, as well as for allowing IoT devices to contribute to learning without overwhelming them.

Therefore, toward effective management of resources in FL for IoT, it is crucial to consider efficient management of resources, low energy consumption during communication, and adaptability of the system. The three important aspects can be managed and controlled properly, and the trade-off between communications and model performance can be better achieved to make FL systems efficient for IoT systems even in constrained resources.

8.6 Communication protocols and architectures for FL in IoT

FL in the IoT context implies challenges and options for efficient communication of federated learning bases. The problem of how to achieve scalable federated learning for thousands of IoT devices with different computational resources and connectivity lies in the efficient communication between the devices. This section discusses the communication issues and constraints that affect FL performance in IoT settings based on current communication protocols, decentralized FL structures, peer-to-peer communication, hierarchical structure, and hybrid structures.

8.6.1 An overview of existing communication protocols

Considering the FL for IoT, the communication protocols are crucial in defining the performance of model training and updates. As mentioned above, HTTP and MQTT are widely used due to their simplicity and the fact that they are supported by most IoT networks. However, these protocols may not be efficient for performing a high rate of round/iteration communication and low latency that is required in the FL.

Hypertext Transfer Protocol (HTTP) comes as a standard protocol for Web-based applications; however, it may increase overhead because of its stateless and large header and is not suitable for tremendous data change in FL. While, on the other hand, the Message Queuing Telemetry Transport (MQTT) is a protocol that is appropriate for the low-bandwidth and high-latency networks that are prevailing in the IoT milieu. Because of its publish-subscribe model, updates can be easily broadcasted hence eliminating frequent polling in the Internet of Things, which saves bandwidth.

Some of the new developments that have been introduced are Federated Learning Communication Protocol (FLCP), which has been developed to improve communication on FL and they use strategies like differential compression and efficient aggregation. These protocols are specific to FL due to the decision parameters that arise from big models, and continuous updates.

8.6.2 Decentralized FL architectures and their impact on communication

FL architectures are constructed almost fully decentralized to avoid the problems associated with a central server which implies relatively low communication rates. In decentralized FL, the intercommunication among the nodes (client) takes place independently without the involvement of a central server and instead of using this all the model updates are exchanged directly with other nodes.

One can imagine that this approach greatly helps to minimize the communication overhead and latency because all the nodes can communicate directly without the need for an intermediate aggregator server. Additional techniques like gossip protocols in which the nodes exchange information randomly with a selected subset of nodes could also be employed for the advancement of scalability and, in general, the robustness of the decentralized FL.

However, the decentralized architectures also pose some issues like managing the synchronization over multiple models and dealing with the adversity of having "evil" nodes. Some of the challenges mentioned above can also be solved by protocols commonly used in decentralized FL; they usually provide mechanisms for consensus and validation to keep the global model up-to-date even without a central coordinator.

8.6.3 Peer-to-peer communication models for FL

In this regard, peer-to-peer (P2P) communication models are checked since they provide a direct way of sharing information between the IoT devices engaged in FL. In P2P FL, the nodes interact with their fellow nodes and not through the assistance of a central server. With this model, one might hope to minimize communication latency as well as enhance autonomy and reliability, as the system is much less vulnerable to any particular point of failure.

In P2P models, there are strategies like direct information exchange by broadcasting data and the updating of models with message passing and adjusting the parameters by combining information. This approach is beneficial in the sense of making better use of network resources which assists in faster convergence of the learning process whereby the update propagates through the network.

Nevertheless, P2P models are also associated with some issues connected with networks' stability and security. The challenge in handling consistency across several nodes that implement learning protocol and correct aggregation of updates in a P2P network is challenging. These difficulties and challenges entailing the use of complex and sophisticated features which further need complicated algorithms and protocols to effectively govern this federated learning process and uphold its reliability.

8.6.4 Hierarchical and hybrid FL architectures

Dependent and mixed systems incorporate both centralized and decentralized characteristics with the aim of achieving an optimal level of communication while at the same time paying attention to matters of implementation. The updates can be propagated from the local nodes to intermediate servers or clusters that gather the updates and send them to a central server while in other cases, the updates are collected at the central server before the updates are forwarded to other servers or clusters.

There is less communication between nodes and the central server that is needed by this multilayer approach for aggregation and coordination by intermediate servers. It also provides scalability since the nodes are grouped into clusters and each cluster is controlled by an intermediate server thus reducing the communication load on the main server.

Hierarchical and decentralized structures work in parallel with one another by importing benefits from each kind of structure. For instance, a combination of a central hub and a hierarchical structure with a central server is responsible for an initial aggregation and coordination of messages as well as P2P interaction in clusters as a means of minimizing the inter-cluster traffic.

8.7 Use cases of FL in IoT with communication efficiency

FL is very relevant to smart homes, and smart cities by improving the efficiency of communication without compromising on privacy. In smart homes, numerous IoT devices, for example, thermostats, security cameras, and smart speakers produce a huge number of data. The conventional cloud-based machine learning models would call for the transmission of such big data to a single server, which can be sequential and also poses several issues of privacy. These problems are, however, addressed by FL as the models are trained locally on the devices, and only update parameters, which translates to less data being exchanged [12].

In the structure of smart cities, where there are many sensors and devices that acquire such parameters as environmental conditions, traffic conditions, and public safety states, each communication focuses on model updates rather than data transfer. For instance, FL can be applied in traffic management systems where the system learns traffic patterns and adjusts the traffic signals without sharing the details data with the central servers. These practices of training them locally decrease the bandwidth requirement and optimize the urban IoT networks [5].

8.7.1 Healthcare IoT systems

The healthcare IoT systems also greatly benefit from the FL due to the strict privacy requirements needed for the communication of medical data. Smart devices, for instance, wearables and health sensors, capture patient-level data which can be used to train machine learning models for early health risk prediction. FL also allows for the development of strong model architectures for the right kind of patient health care since data remains residual at its point of origin [13].

For instance, in a hospital chain, FL can help train models that estimate the patient's condition or provide prescriptions without accumulating the patients' records in a common database. This not only fosters improved efficiency in communicating but also results in data protection's conformity to legal protocols such as HIPAA (Health Insurance Portability and Accountability Act) [14].

8.7.2 Industrial IoT applications

As for FL's role in IIoT application, the key parts lie in enhancing communication efficiency and facilitating complicated manufacturing and process control. Connected industrial IoT devices transmit a huge stream of data regarding the working conditions and health of industrial equipment or control systems, productivity rates, and product quality. FL empowers model development for such applications as predictive maintenance and real-time analysis without moving giant data chunks [15].

For instance, in a factory environment, FL can improve models that detect gear failure or find the most appropriate timetable for manufacturing with the assistance of local data from different machines. This approach also reduces the volumes of data that are passed to the central server hence reducing the communication overhead and thus leading to an increase in the efficiency of industries [16].

Autonomous vehicles have been one of the hottest topics of discussion in the transportation systems of IoT.

Self-driving cars heavily use data from several sensors and this data is usually processed in real time to enable the car to make driving decisions as well as be safe on the road. FL promotes communication effectiveness as it lets vehicles perform model re-training and updating using the received data from their own sensors as well as from other vehicles' sensors. This decentralized approach helps to decrease the amount of data transmitted to central servers and this is important because of the volume and velocity of the data especially in autonomous driving scenarios [17].

Furthermore, edge computing has a significant role to play in this regard as it provides the mechanism for handling the data near its source which makes a good combination with FL. For instance, in the case of an autonomous vehicle, the inert computation can be performed locally as well as other vehicles can contribute towards enhancing the models without the cloud server more away than needed. This way of organizing communication decreases latency, decreases the costs of communication, and guarantees real-time decision-making for safety-critical activities [18].

8.8 Security and privacy considerations in FL for IoT

Security and privacy preservation are very important in FL for IoT settings because IoT is generally associated with the collection of people's personal information. FL, by design, interconnects learning across multiple devices and devices while keeping the raw data decentralized. However, it does so in a decentralized fashion which leads to issues for security and privacy. Here, the authors elaborate on vital areas of security and privacy in FL for IoT, such as the secure aggregation procedures, differential privacy, communication-efficient privacy-preserving methods, and case studies and practical applications of the concepts developed in the chapter.

8.8.1 Secure aggregation techniques

Thus, it is crucial to use secure aggregation approaches to prevent the leakage of users' information while learning in the federated systems. In FL, different IoT devices cooperate to learn a global model while they do not exchange their raw data. Instead, only the averaged model parameters (e.g., gradients or weights) are exchanged with a central server. However, such aggregated updates may lead to exposure of information related to the data of the devices if it is not well protected.

Homomorphic Encryption is one of the oldest classes of cryptographic techniques that can be applied to protect the process of data aggregation. It makes it possible for computations to be made directly on ciphertext without having to decrypt the data first. For instance, such values as gradients can be encrypted and the sum of the encrypted values can be computed by the central server and the decrypted data will contain the correct update for the model. This technique makes it possible for the server to perform certain computations that are necessary while at the same time, it never gets to see the raw data being processed.

Another type of solution is secure MPC in which a function is computed over inputs of multiple parties but the inputs remain private. MPC can be applied in the context of FL in a way that masks each device's contribution in aggregating model updates. Thus, the main drawback of MPC is the problem of calculation and the increase in its complexity in conditions of limited resources of IoT devices.

Trusted execution environments (TEEs) like Intel's SGX offer the micro-architecture of a safe zone for computations to be performed without interferences from the other components of the system. This is important because TEEs can be used to privately collate the updates that need to be made to models in an environment that is safe from such vices as tampering or eavesdropping. Despite the high level of security assurance provided by TEEs, their integration may be challenging and may necessitate hardware backing.

8.8.2 Differential privacy in federated learning

Differential privacy (DP) is an effective methodology for ensuring that persons' privacy is preserved routinely by adding noise to the data or calculations. In the case of FL, DP can be used to make it possible for individual devices to contribute their data while concealing some critical details.

LDP means adding noise directly to the data before it is transmitted to the central server to preserve the privacy of the users. Each IoT device independently distorts its data which means that even if it is intercepted or analyzed, the contribution from each device cannot easily be determined. To protect privacy, one can add noise in model updates with the help of techniques like the Laplace mechanism or Gaussian mechanism.

Another place where it is possible to apply global differential privacy is in the aggregation phase; the target is to add some noise to the received model updates to be shared with the central server. This makes sure that the final model which is updated with the updates originating from many devices has the guarantee of privacy. Some of the challenges herein are; Too much noise means reduced privacy but at the same time, it affects the performance of the global model.

The integration of DP into the more general learning framework of FL poses several challenges, so its incorporation needs to be designed so as not to lead to privacy loss and compromise the models' accuracy. Some methods like privacy amplification by subsampling may be employed to get better privacy protection as per the requirement while not drastically negative impacts on the model accuracy.

8.8.3 Communication-efficient privacy-preserving methods

Communication overhead in FL is always important bearing in mind that FL operates in IoT systems where bandwidth and energy are scarce resources. While there occurs a scenario where one needs to either protect the privacy of the messages or ensure the communication efficiency of the messages, balancing between the two is usually difficult. Several methods address this:

Gradient compression methods minimize the amount of data that is exchanged between devices and a central server. Methods such as quantization include the reduction of accuracy in which gradients are conveyed and sparsification includes only transfer of crucial gradients to reduce the data size while addressing the privacy issue. Besides, secure aggregation with compression incorporates compression techniques into secure aggregation. To avoid leakage of the gradients, the amount of data that needs to be communicated is compressed before encryption and the gradients are measured before being aggregated securely to decrease the total number of data transmitted in communication.

Federated learning with asynchronous updates or FLAU enables every device to update the global model independently thereby requiring minimal interaction. It does facilitate in controlling communication overhead and the method can be used conjointly with secure aggregation to maintain privacy. From protocols like Secure Aggregation Protocols and Communication-Efficient Differential Privacy Protocols, it is evident that there is a concern with the amount of data that is exchanged during the process as well as the privacy of clients. Such protocols are meant to operate within the context of IoT devices' limited resources.

8.8.4 Examples and practical application

Several implementations and some case studies are considered to depict the use of security and privacy methodologies in FL for IoT.

- Google's federated learning framework: Google has practiced federated learning on its Gboard application for better prediction of keys without incurring a breach of user's privacy. To prevent leakage of individual user data, the framework uses safe aggregation methods while differential privacy methods are used to protect the user data in model updates.
- OpenMined's PySyft: PySyft is a Python-based open-source library ofLOY for implementing private computation mechanisms such as federated learning, differential privacy, and secure MPC. This has been applied in several real-world applications to show how these methods facilitate the protection of privacy while at the same time promoting efficient communication in federated systems.
- IBM's federated learning platform: There is a federated learning platform in which IBM has implemented secure aggregation and differential privacy for

increasing privacy levels in collaborative learning. There have been studies done on the platform in the context of industrial IoT deployments which highlight the importance of the platform in guaranteeing privacy and security in addition to high communication rates.

8.9 Performance evaluation and metrics

Hence, the performance evaluation of FL for IoT focuses on evaluating how the system performs the coordination of communication and how it optimally performs the classification with concentrative accuracy, efficiency, and centrality of resources. The present section discusses basic evaluation metrics for the overall information exchange, the communication cost vs. accuracy issue, benchmarking strategies considering the various IoT applications and scenarios, and the use of simulation platforms and real-world experimentation resources.

8.9.1 Key performance indicators of communication efficiency

Therefore, it is imperative to select certain KPIs that would allow the comparison of the FL's efficiency in the context of IoT to reveal the extent to which its communication is effective and would employ the resources to the optimal degree. Key performance indicators include:

- Communication overhead: The total of information that is exchanged between the devices and the main control unit. This comprises the size of model updates, frequency of communication, and data that need to be transmitted. But higher work in progress means higher communication overhead indicating a waste and thereby a non-efficient process.
- Bandwidth utilization: The optimization of the bandwidth during the transfer of data. This one shows how well the available bandwidth is used and is dependent on data compression, among other things, as well as protocol overhead.
- Latency: The decisions on how long it takes to send data from one device to another as well as the time it takes to process data in the server. Less delay is important to enhance real-time applications since it directly translates to quicker model updates and efficiency for the users.
- Energy consumption: The energy which is utilized by the devices engaged in the communication process. The corresponding communication methodologies should not be energy consumptive while some IoT devices are likely to have batteries.
- Resource utilization: The effectiveness in utilization of its resources including the processing power and memory as well as storage. Communication techniques should not have a direct negative effect on these resources.
- Scalability: The boost in the level of devices the system supported without much decline in performance. Scalability criteria refer to ways or strategies

that facilitate the determination of the extent of the IoT network and the communication methods employed to improve scalability.

8.9.2 Trade-off between accuracy and the load experienced in communication

In federated learning, there has been observed a trade-off between the network model's performance and communication complexity. This has been achieved by evaluating of effects of communication strategies on both the quality of the model and communication needs.

Accuracy metrics: Some of the familiar measures of accuracy are model accuracy, precision, recall or sensitivity, and F1 measure. These metrics assess how the global model performs on the data that it has not seen before or in other words how generalizable or overfit the global model is.

- Communication load metrics: The types of measures related to the load of communication are the amount of data transmitted, the rate of updates, and the total time spent on communication. All these metrics assist in quantifying the communicational cost that is incurred by various strategies.
- Trade-off analysis: To investigate the impact of changes in the current communication strategies (i.e., data compression, the frequency of updates) on the accuracy of a chosen model. This involves making comparisons on the performance of developed models from different communication restrictions.
- Cost–benefit analysis: Analyzing the costs and benefits of the different approaches to communication with the argument that, given a limited channel of communication, it is better to give more accurate information or receive it rather than using the channels of communication to exchange a lot of information that may not be necessary. Such analysis defines the right balance between accuracy and time as to when best to implement a particular approach.

8.9.3 Establishing a reference for communication effectiveness in various IoT applications

Benchmarking is a process, where the performance of communication strategies that have been implemented in IoT use case scenarios is evaluated and compared against one another.

- Smart homes: Assessment of communication effectiveness in contexts using smart devices, security systems, and energy usage.
- Healthcare IoT: Evaluating communication approaches and considerations in cases like remote patient monitoring and wearable health devices, etc.
- Industrial IoT: Discussing strategies of communication effectiveness in control and automation of the industry, maintaining productivity during equipment failures, and good planning of supply chains.
- Smart cities: Benchmarking various methods of communication for smart structure, transportation, and environmental applications.

Benchmarking metrics:

- Communication latency: This indicates the level of latency that various applications that utilize the cloud computing solution would experience as a means of determining real-time performance.
- Data throughput: Assessment of the amount of data that can be managed at one time for processing and transmission.
- Scalability: Evaluation of how many communication strategies are implemented for growing numbers of devices and amount of data.
- Case studies and comparisons: Analysis of the case and comparison of the effectiveness of the applied communication methods in various IoT scenarios. This assists in defining effective and appropriate solutions for particular applications.

8.10 Conclusion

FL is becoming a groundbreaking solution in the process of increasing the number of efficient interoperable communication in the IoT domain. The best example of such a shift in the paradigm from conventional machine learning to FL is the quest to embrace decentralized data while at the same time addressing issues of privacy and security. The incorporation of FL in contemporary IoT systems clearly points out that data communication techniques in any IoT system are bound by the issues of bandwidth, energy, delay, and scalability. Some of the core ideas of FL such as its architecture and how data is processed are critical in surmounting the challenges posed by IoT scenarios. Optimization of resource utilization and minimization of the data transmission overhead can be achieved by the use of efficient communication techniques which include model compression, gradient sparsification, and adaptive communication. Thus, the application of AI and ML for enhancing the communication between the FL systems and their users is growing in importance as the field progresses. 5G and beyond reflects the development of the communication capabilities that can contribute to more complex and effective FL.

However, there are issues that still persist for instance the problems of scaling up the system and dynamic management of the resources. In fact, future research should be aimed at investigating other potential approaches and using the existing literature to fill gaps in the knowledge about the subject to improve the effectiveness of communication in FL for IoT. Examples of RL applications and discussions of real-world deployments accentuate the research's real-world applicability and stress how emerging FL approach can drastically reshape the vast IoT areas, from smart homes and healthy living to self-driven automobiles and Industry 4. 0. FL for IoT communication is a nascent yet ongoing process in the process of achieving the most efficient way of communicating through the technology. If it is to continue to do what it can to seek solutions that have not yet been seen and try to solve already existing problems, then it will be possible to open up many more possibilities and take IoT technology to a newer level.

References

[1] Dhatterwal, J. S., Kaswan, K. S., and Preety. (2021). Intelligent agent based case base reasoning systems build knowledge representation in COVID-19 analysis of recovery of infectious patients. In *Applications of Artificial Intelligence in COVID-19* (pp. 185–209). Singapore: Springer.

[2] McMahan, B., Moore, E., Ramage, D., Hampson, S., and Arcas, B. A. (2017). Communication-efficient learning of deep networks from decentralized data. In *Artificial Intelligence and Statistics* (pp. 1273–1282). PMLR. https://proceedings.mlr.press/v54/mcmahan17a.html.

[3] Kairouz, P., McMahan, H. B., Avent, B., *et al.* (2021). Advances and open problems in federated learning. *Foundations and Trends in Machine Learning, 14*(1–2), 1–210. https://doi.org/10.1561/2200000083.

[4] Dhatterwal, J. S., Kaswan, K. S., and Kumar, N. (2023). Telemedicine-based development of M-Health Informatics using AI. In *Deep Learning for Healthcare Decision Making* (pp. 159–178). Gistrup: River Publishers.

[5] Li, X., Wu, Y., and Zhou, X. (2020). Federated learning for smart cities: A survey and research directions. *ACM Computing Surveys, 53*(4), 1–34. https://doi.org/10.1145/3386362.

[6] Wang, S., Tuor, T., Salonidis, T., *et al.* (2021). Adaptive federated learning in resource-constrained edge computing systems. *IEEE Journal on Selected Areas in Communications*, 39(1), 137–152. https://doi.org/10.1109/JSAC.2020.3020604.

[7] Kaswan, K. S., Dhatterwal, J. S., and Nayyar, A. (2024). *Digital Personality: A Man Forever Volume 2: Technical Aspects*. Boca Raton, FL: CRC Press.

[8] Bingu, R., Adinarayana, S., Dhatterwal, J. S., Kavitha, S., Patnala, E., and Sangaraju, H. R. (2024). Performance comparison analysis of classification methodologies for effective detection of intrusions. *Computers & Security, 143*, 103893.

[9] Chithaluru, P., Singh, A., Dhatterwal, J. S., *et al.* (2023). An optimized privacy information exchange schema for explainable AI empowered WiMAX-based IoT networks. *Future Generation Computer Systems, 148*, 225–239.

[10] Lim, W. Y. B., Luong, N. C., Hoang, D. T., *et al.* (2020). Federated learning in mobile edge networks: A comprehensive survey. *IEEE Communications Surveys & Tutorials*, 22(3), 2031–2063. https://doi.org/10.1109/COMST.2020.2986024.

[11] Yang, Q., Liu, Y., Chen, T., and Tong, Y. (2019). Federated machine learning: Concept and applications. *ACM Transactions on Intelligent Systems and Technology (TIST), 10*(2), 1–19. https://doi.org/10.1145/3298981.

[12] Konecny, J., McMahan, H. B., Yu, F. X., Richtárik, P., Suresh, A. T., and Bacon, D. (2016). Federated learning: Strategies for improving communication efficiency. arXiv preprint arXiv:1610.05492.

[13] Ramaswamy, S., Smith, J., and Wang, S. (2021). Privacy-preserving federated learning for healthcare IoT systems. *Journal of Biomedical Informatics*, *118*, 103733. https://doi.org/10.1016/j.jbi.2021.103733.

[14] Smith, T., Brown, A., and Nguyen, H. (2022). Enhancing healthcare data security and efficiency with federated learning. *IEEE Access*, *10*, 16321–16333. https://doi.org/10.1109/ACCESS.2022.3150022.

[15] Deng, L., Li, L., and Liu, Y. (2020). Industrial IoT applications with federated learning: Challenges and opportunities. *IEEE Transactions on Industrial Informatics*, *16*(12), 7900–7908. https://doi.org/10.1109/TII.2020.3028071.

[16] Zhang, Z., Liu, J., and Yang, X. (2021). Optimizing industrial IoT systems with federated learning: A review and case studies. *Sensors*, *21*(15), 5067. https://doi.org/10.3390/s21155067.

[17] Chen, M., Ma, Y., and Song, L. (2021). Federated learning in autonomous vehicles: efficient data aggregation and privacy preservation. *IEEE Transactions on Intelligent Transportation Systems*, *22*(5), 3172–3182. https://doi.org/10.1109/TITS.2020.3028471.

[18] Zhao, Y., Zhou, M., and Li, Z. (2021). Edge computing and federated learning for autonomous vehicles: Integration and applications. *IEEE Internet of Things Journal*, *8*(3), 1972–1983. https://doi.org/10.1109/JIOT.2020.3031194.

Chapter 9

Adapting federated learning-based AI models to dynamic cyberthreats in pervasive IoT environments

S. Tamizharasi[1], *P. Rubini*[1], *S. Saravana Kumar*[1] *and Daniel Arockiam*[2]

Abstract

In recent times, with the greater technological advancements, there has been a growing wave of cyberattacks potentially impacting various business networks and organizations. Even a simple cyberattack may significantly affect the business value of various organizations. Furthermore, the dynamic nature of the cyberthreats creates the requirement for continuous monitoring, adaptation, and vigilance. On the other hand, digital connectivity at present has become so ubiquitous, thereby the significance has become overstated. Some of the most common cyberthreats involve phishing attacks, ransomware, malware, and advanced persistent cyber-threats. In this context, the traditional cybersecurity protocols are effective to some extent but it is often complicated to maintain a secure environment with the emerging dynamic threats imposed by malicious actors. Hence, due to the increasing risk of dynamic cyberthreats, it has become crucial to seek innovative solutions to enhance security measures. Here comes the role of artificial intelligence in meeting the pressing needs of cyberthreats. Artificial intelligence, specifically the machine learning models has emerged as a cutting-edge solution for cybersecurity. The effective implementation of AI models in cybersecurity enables the appropriate analysis of large amounts of data, using which we can identify patterns and make more informed decisions in real time. Finding various AI models can assist in the detection and prevention of numerous cyberthreats effectively. Some of the significant benefits of employing AI models for cyberthreats detection include advanced threat detection, anomaly detection and behavior analysis, dynamic threat prevention, adaptive authentication, and many more. Furthermore, the design and implementation of various AI models for threat detection offer robust solutions and act as a resilient protocol against the ever-growing landscape

[1]School of Engineering and Technology, CMR University, India
[2]Department of Computer Science and Engineering, Amity School of Engineering and Technology, Amity University Madhya Pradesh, India

of cyberthreats. This chapter explores various AI models to predict emerging dynamic cyberthreats and to ensure continuity and stability in their operations. This chapter also assesses the performance of every AI-based model with real-time datasets and explores the more efficient and suitable model to deal with cyberthreats.

Keywords: Cyberthreats; Prediction models; Artificial intelligence; Machine learning

9.1 Introduction

The growing revolution in technology enables cyberthreats to impact businesses every day. A wave of cyberattacks is happening daily at a rate more frequent than in previous years due to the tremendous growth of digital platforms and big data [1]. To be more specific, the increase in global connectivity, data outsourcing, and vast usage of cloud services form the major cause for the cyberattacks than in the past. In simple terms, cyberthreats represent an indication that a malicious user is trying to attain unauthorized access over the network to inject cyberattacks. A cyberthreat may range from a small piece of suspicious mail to a chunk of malicious code that may lead to denial of service and data breaches. Malware, social engineering and phishing attacks, man-in-the-middle attacks, denial-of-service attacks, password attacks, and injection attacks are some of the examples of cyberattacks. In general, cyberthreats represent a malicious act that can lead to disruption in digital life and damage the data [2].

Usually, cyberthreats are caused by trusted users within an organization or from third-party users at remote locations. Some of the possible sources of cyberthreats include cybercriminals, hackers, national-state actors, and insider threats. The majority of the cyberthreats are caused by malicious intent, while few are made by ethical hackers and they have positive or neutral intentions. Understanding the motivation behind various cyberthreats forms the most vital step in their prevention measures. Using strong passwords, developing advanced email security tools, and antivirus protection measures are some of the basic critical measures that can prevent the occurrence of cyberthreats. At an advanced level, most of the business sectors rely on security-awareness training programs, multifactor authentication mechanisms, network security protocols, and other endpoint security measures for the protection of security threats. However, the development and implementation of state-of-the-art mechanisms for threat detection and incident response will enable efficient detection of cyberthreats in real time. Further, these mechanisms enable us to isolate the threats and thereby minimize the amount of damage it causes to the system or we can prevent it completely. This is where exactly the role of artificial intelligence (AI) comes in managing the cyberthreats [3].

The effective implementation of AI models will assist in faster threat detection and smarter remediation activities. Cyberthreat intelligence is another efficient way through which AI models are adopted to collect, evaluate, and analyze network information to predict cyberthreats. There are many significant ways in which AI models could be adopted for the identification and prevention of cyberthreats. This chapter clearly outlines the various AI models that could be adopted for the prevention of cyberthreats. The core idea behind the prevention of dynamic cyberthreats using AI-based models will be explored and analyzed in detail. Some of the significant benefits of employing AI models for cyberthreats detection include advanced threat detection, anomaly detection and behavior analysis, dynamic threat prevention, adaptive authentication, and many more. Furthermore, the design and implementation of various AI models for threat detection offer robust solutions and act as a resilient protocol against the ever-growing landscape of cyberthreats. The major focus will be on dynamic cyberthreat risk assessment, where the AI models will be applied to imitate the actual cyberthreats through the submission of queries to the systems or programs. Through which the vulnerabilities associated with the system can be assessed. Finally, the most effective dynamic cyberthreat risk assessment models will be discussed in detail.

9.2 Dynamic cyber risk assessment

Most organizations today are concerned with cybersecurity associated with their digital assets because of increasing cyber risks and data breaches. The most robust and efficient cybersecurity measures are essential for the protection of the organization's digital assets. However, a 100% risk-free cyber environment is daunting but it is not an impossible factor. Dynamic cyber risk management is an efficient way through which one can identify the vulnerabilities associated with an organization's security posture and enable us to allocate resources for efficient mitigation [4]. Dynamic cyber risk assessment converges code security, vulnerability scanning, and penetration testing to analyze the security of web-related applications, digital assets, and networks. The core idea behind the dynamic cyber risk assessment is that it enables the cybersecurity team to perform the role of stimulated cyber criminals and analyze the system defense from an expert perspective. This is made through a complete examination of a system's vulnerability and potential threats [5]. Through this process, we can easily identify the security of the data and web applications and we can pinpoint the area of improvement. This process further provides a clear picture of the digital environment and provides future risk scenarios. As a result, the process of cyber risk management will become more inclusive, sustainable, and advantageous to everyone. However, the process of efficient dynamic cyber risk assessment requires more advanced tools and technologies. Leveraging the benefit of advanced techniques such as efficient AI-based models will result in the following insights:

- The threats that are expected to spread over various sectors could be identified easily.
- The rate of speed at which the potential cyberthreats can impact the organizations will be controlled.
- Several opportunities will be provided on future risk assessment.

- Even the higher severity risks can be predicted with modeling of low-likelihood scenarios.
- Assist in efficient handling of unforeseen security threats and taking appropriate actions.

In addition, the adoption of AI-based models also enables organizations to make quick decisions and respond to threats immediately. Thereby offering a safe digital environment to the end users.

9.2.1 Four different aspects of cyber risk assessment

The assessment of cyberthreats includes four different aspects, which are listed below:

1. Identification of assets and determining their significance to the organization.
2. Efficient identification of security gaps and vulnerabilities.
3. Identification of potential risks.
4. Establishment of potential impacts.

As mentioned above, the process of cyber risk assessment includes four different aspects. The first step is to identify the organization's digital assets, and this may include data, network, or workforce. Once the resources are identified their values should be assessed. This includes analysis from the aspect of the impact of loss of an asset. Through the identification of the significance of assets, the protection mechanisms can be prioritized [6,7]. In any network, the attackers mainly focus on the weakness of the system. Because they exploit this gap to acquire access to the network, data, and system. Hence, in the next step, all the potential flaws and vulnerabilities associated with the system should be identified. This will significantly help us to mitigate the risks. Once the vulnerabilities associated with the system are identified the next is to determine their potential risks. Through the identification of all possible threats, we can take efficient actions to mitigate the risks. Finally, the last aspect is to determine the potential impact of the losses. Usually, the impact of the losses will fall under three categories such as integrity, confidentiality, and availability. This will allow the organization to respond and mitigate the risks easily.

The appropriate use of AI models will significantly help businesses by enhancing their risk assessment strategies and standard security measures. Exploring more advanced AI-based risk assessment tools will help in the provision of actionable insights for companies' risk assessment, enabling them to create powerful cybersecurity strategies and more informed decisions [8].

9.2.2 Necessity of AI models in dynamic cyber risk assessment

The adoption of AI models is necessary to enhance the safety and integrity of sensitive data and systems. In general, AI in dynamic risk assessment will refer to the use of AI algorithms to analyze and evaluate distinct kinds of risks associated with the system in a more systematic manner. The synergy between AI and dynamic cyber risk assessment leads to a forward-looking perspective, where these technologies become instrumental in the protection of digital assets and assuring the longevity of organizations' infrastructure. Through the use of AI algorithms, we can model the patterns related to real-world hacking and this will help us to uncover the potential threats and security vulnerabilities. This will act as a precautionary measure for the organizations [9,10]. Such that they can address the significant risk associated with the sensitive data and they can improve their overall security mechanisms. Further, regular dynamic risk assessments with AI models will help organizations stay up to date on emerging threats and they can upgrade their systems, networks, and applications. A more resilient and stable digital environment will be provided to the organizations as well as their end users. Some of the significant benefits of adopting AI models for dynamic cyber risk assessment include real-time monitoring and rapid response, enhanced accuracy and reliability, scalability, cost-efficiency, efficient resource utilization, customization and tailored assessment, predictive insights, reduced downtime, and business continuity. Also, the conventional risk assessment models are inherently static and they deal with numerous complications in dealing with the landscape of dynamic cyberthreats. Whereas the adoption of AI models provides a transformative level of adaptability. This is because these models continuously learn from the data in real time then refine and adjust to the risk assessment in a constant manner. By harnessing the potential of AI organizations can proceed forward with complex regulatory requirements in a more confidential manner. Because of these reasons, AI has become the most vital component when it comes to cyber risk assessment and mitigation [11,12].

9.3 AI-based models for dynamic cyber threat detection and management

In the context of AI for cyber risk management, there exist numerous models and approaches that assist in effective cyberthreat detection and management. Some of the significant AI models that assist in the prevention of fraudulent activities in a more timely and automated manner are explored and discussed in detail [2,3,13–17]. The various AI models discussed in this section not only help in cyber risk management but also contribute to more resilient and secure digital ecosystems.

9.3.1 AI-based artificial neural network model for cyber threat detection

An artificial neural network (ANN)-based cyberthreat detection model is presented in this section. The use of the ANN algorithm converts the multitude of security events into individual event-based profiles. A deep learning-based detection technique is used to enhance the threat detection process. A detailed architecture of the working of the ANN-based cyberthreat detection system is illustrated in Figure 9.1, and it works based on a model presented in the study [18].

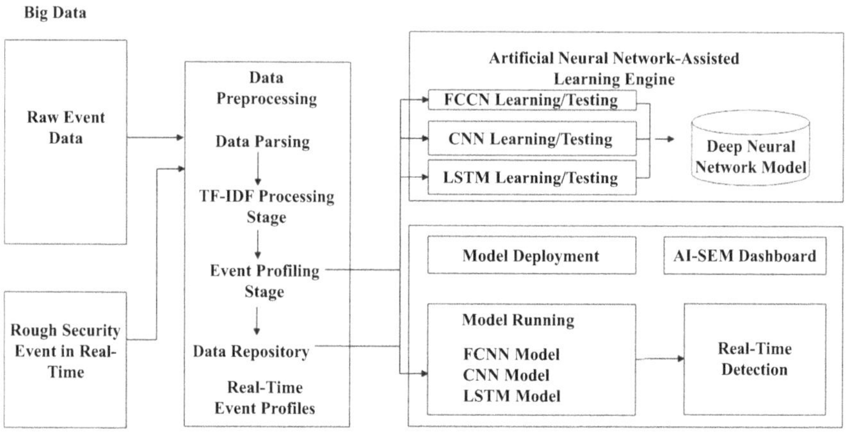

Figure 9.1 AI-based artificial neural network model for cyber threat detection

The first step associated with the architecture is the preprocessing phase. This phase is also called event profiling. During this phase, the raw data is transformed into concise input, which in turn will be provided as input to deep neural networks. The next stage is the data preprocessing phase, where the process of data normalization and data aggregation with parsing are performed consecutively within the system. The output measures such as event datasets, event profiles, and event vectors are generated at each stage, which forms an input to the next stage. Further during the data preprocessing phase, the raw security events are converted to the deep learning engine input data during the system operation in real-time detecting network intrusions. The third is the AI-based learning engine, which includes the ANN networks for modeling purposes. Each network is associated with the identification of the accurate model. The last module is the real-time threat detection phase, where the ANN model is used mechanically for the classification of security raw events. The recognized true alerts will be displayed through the dashboard for the security analysts.

9.3.1.1 Event profiling method for preprocessing

The event profiling module includes data aggregation, TF-IDF normalization, and data decomposition. The process of identification of profiling method for representation of large data will enable summarization of meaningful information from event data and that can be used as an input for the deep learning model. A real-time dataset can be used to deal with various streaming events across the world and through this statistical event sets are generated. The core idea behind this approach is to acquire the occurrence information, such that the other events can also concurrently occur with it. After the successful collection of the events, every event will be mapped into one event set using a sliding window at predefined intervals. Such that there is a possibility that the sliding window will allow the overlapping of the log over the numerous profiles. Thus, a method of concurrency-based pattern is used to acquire the deterministic features for true positive events. This is due to the reason that the ordering of the events may change slightly based on unpredictable situations. In real time, the change of sequences will be first reflected in IPS by system resources, networks, and processes. Hence, the use of a concurrency-based method permits the standardization of the gap of changeable order. At each time, the window slides with respect to the predefined time interval, every raw data related to the window will be combined into numerous event sets using source address and destination address. In this way, a number of datasets are generated for one window time. This operation will be continuously performed on the learning data. Next is the process of TF-IDF data normalization. During this phase, each unique event will be transformed into a representation that is most appropriate for the classifier and learning algorithm. The technique of vector space is used for this process. This method is often used for the development of intrusion detection models. Here, the intrusion prevention system (IPS) event patterns will be extracted from IPS events and each event will be converted into a vector. The event sets with similar concurrency will always be present at nearby locations in the vector space. Thus, the event set includes a set of occurred events. A statistical TF-IDF-based technique is used for indexing the events based on their significance. Thus, the numerical value associated with frequently occurring events will have a low weight and the event that occurs very rarely will have an increased weight. Based on this factor, a TF-IDF matrix is constructed. Where the rows represent the number of event sets and the columns represent the number of events present in the data collection.

The next step is the transformation of the event profile, where event vectors will be transferred into event profile data. Initially, the resemblance of the entire dataset is calculated along with the basepoint set. The key concept behind this data preprocessing process is to minimize the higher dimensionality measure through the calculation of cosine similarity across every data in the collection. The event patterns are then characterized using k points and cosine similarity matrices. The k basepoints are fixed based on the event vectors that occur very rarely across the dataset. The resultant matrix obtained from every event and k basepoints will be given as input to the FCNN, CNN, and LSTM neural network algorithms.

9.3.1.2 Artificial neural network-based learning engine

This module comprises three different algorithms such as FCNN, LSTM, and CNN, and all these three collectively form the EP-ANN. A fully convolutional neural network (FCNN) is the most used deep learning network where every node will be fully connected to every node of the next layer. Though the layers in the FCNN model are fully connected to each other, each layer has its own weights that are distinct and specific, which will not be shared by every node in the network. Some of the various parameters such as the amount of hidden layers, activation function types, and output class relating to each layer are dynamically configured, to begin with the initial setup. In this architecture, we make use of multilayer perceptron (MLP) models with 11 layers. This comprises one input layer, one output layer, and nine hidden layers. The leaky rectified linear unit is selected as an activation function. The SoftMax function along with the cross-entropy cost function forms the output layer. To train this model, the preprocessed data is given as an input and it comprises a learning rate of 0.001. The parameter configuration measures are tuned to take up to 1000 epochs.

The next is the convolutional neural network (CNN) model. This algorithm is mainly used to deal with spatial data. The input layer in the CNN model includes 2D or 3D arrays that match the pixel value relating to information pertaining to the image. The key layers include max-pooling layers and convolutional layers. The functionality of the convolutional layer is to receive an input and it is consoled with the help of filters to deliver ongoing data that will be given as an input to the next layers. Due to the reason that the convolutional layer includes a set of filters, a feature map will be produced for every filter and the data related to the feature maps are then aggregated to provide the output data. The CNN model designed in this chapter includes one input layer, max-pooling layers three, four convolutional layers, and one output layer with a fully connected layer. Subsampling is made by the front three convolutional layers, followed by max-pooling layers. A dropout layer is placed in front of every convolutional layer excluding the last one.

Next is the long short-term memory neural network (LSTM) model. The LSTM model is used to assess the temporal correlations across the event profiles. The model includes input, output, and a forget gate. The design includes 1–8 multilayers with *N* hidden layers. Several dynamic configurations are used to enrich the performance of the proposed model.

9.3.1.3 Real-time cyber threat detection

The three neural network models FCNN, CNN, and LSTM models are implemented in real time to detect the cyberthreats using various real-time datasets such as NSLKDD, CICIDS2017, and some of the real-time datasets [2,3] are used for simulation and assessment of real-time cyberthreat detection and analysis. The data visualization is done initially and then the model is deployed to predict the evolving cyberthreats across various systems.

9.3.2 Natural language processing-based architecture for dynamic cyber risk assessment

The overall objective of this framework is to identify and profile emerging cyberthreats in an automated manner. This framework is mainly implemented across social networks to predict and prevent malicious activities. Furthermore, it works based on the Natural Language Processing (NLP) techniques. This objective is attained through the effective implementation of four different solutions:

1. Continuous monitoring and collection of posts from important people and organizations on Twitter to predict unknown terms and malicious activities.
2. Implementation of machine learning and NLP algorithms to detect terms that are most likely to be a threat and to discard them.

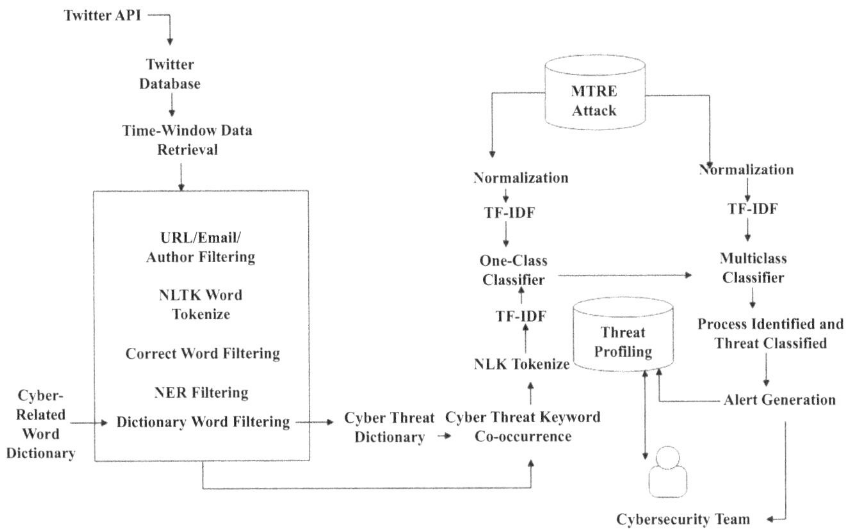

Figure 9.2 NLP-based dynamic cyber-risk assessment model

3. Leveraging most likely a tactic used by identified threat MITRE ATT&CK techniques.
4. Generation of timely alerts regarding new or emerging threats along with its objective confined to the risk. Predicting how quickly the threat can evolve right from the time of identification.

The detailed solution architecture pertaining to this objective is illustrated in Figure 9.2. The working of this model is based on the approach given in [19]. Furthermore, the various modules associated with the architecture are discussed in detail below:

9.3.2.1 Logistic Twitter API

This module is responsible for Twitter data collection and inserting them across the database systems for further processing. An open-source data collection engine called Logstash is used for the data collection process. The user profiles are selected based on suggestions given by cyberthreat intelligence analysts and entities.

9.3.2.2 Tweet database

The next module is the Tweets database. During this phase, the data collected from the Logstash Twitter plugin is stored across the elastic research database. Elastic research is an active component of the elastic stack and provides nearby analytics and search results for all types of data.

9.3.2.3 Time-window data retrieval

The first step associated with this module is data collection. In consideration of a particular time range, this module collects the Twitter mess to offer a continuous threat detection and alert system. The time range here is the sliding time window that considers the end time for the previous time range and the start time for the next time range. The Twitter messages in turn follow the unknown word selection that will be described in upcoming modules.

9.3.2.4 Unknown word selection

The major goal of this module is to detect unknown words or terms that appear across the messages collected from Twitter. Through further analysis, the name of the emerging threat can be analyzed easily. A term is called unknown only if it passes through an unknown word selection pipeline, which includes various procedures such as stop-words and punctuation filtering, NLTK word tokenize, Normalization URL/E-mail/Author filtering, and Dictionary and Named entity recognition. Because of the reason that text messages across the social network are written using various shortcuts and meanings, normalization techniques are used in this architecture. It has been analyzed through the tweets that the 47 terms are written in 124 distinct forms. The Twitter messages stored across the tweet database will have the complete Twitter post. Sometimes it also contains mention of other URLs, e-mails, and users. In this context, this architecture includes certain terms that can result in false positives. The next component is the NER filtering. After the analysis of the tweets, it has been observed that among the unknown words, there are various organizations like Google and Microsoft. These terms should be eliminated as they do not include any threat names. Natural entity recognition (NER) is the most essential task in NLP. NER deals with information extraction and processes structured and unstructured data to detect expressions that refer to organizations and people. Thus, using NER, this framework reduces the possibility of unknown words. The next component is dictionary word filtering. It filters out the terms that occur in cyberthreats and cyber-related word dictionaries. In the end, the Twitter posts are processed effectively during this stage and the list of unknown terms are identified.

9.3.2.5 Cyberthreat keyword co-occurrence

The next module associated with this architecture is cyberthreat keyword co-occurrence. The unknown words identified during the previous module are given as input to this stage. The objective here is to avoid unknown words that just occurred as a result of misspelling. Every identified unknown word is referred against the cyberthreat dictionary in Twitter posts for their presence. Such that any type of cyberthreat that relates to the unknown word can be identified easily. The output associated with this module includes unknown terms that relate to minimal one cyberthreat dictionary term along with the Twitter messages.

9.3.2.6 NLK tokenize and pro stemmer

In general, a simple typo or grammatical mistake associated with the sentence may result in the interpretation of the wrong meaning associated with the terms. For example, the two words democracy and democratic have different meanings. Thus, it is essential to identify the mis-occurrence of the words. This process is made through a comparison of the root of these words. Porter's streaming algorithm is used to identify the root of the words [5]. This algorithm is deployed for every word associated with the tweets that are acquired through the previous steps. The unknown terms acquired from the previous step along with respective tweets in a stemming format form the output of this module.

9.3.2.7 TF-IDF

The next module is the term frequency-inverse document frequency (TF-IDF). It converts the text documents acquired from the MITRE attack and CK corpus and Twitter messages to a vectorized representation model. Which can be given as an input for both single and multiple-class machine learning models to make efficient predictions. The output associated with this module included a well-trained single-class and multiclass classifier that can predict cyberattacks more efficiently.

9.3.2.8 One-class classifier

The next module associated with the system is a one-class classifier. Before this module, all the other modules were mainly focused on the identification of emerging cyberthreats based on names and unknown words. This module enables the selection of threats concerned with the tweet messages whose data is more likely to be related to malicious actions. The one-class classifier is implemented to attain this objective. As a result, suspicious activities are identified as an output of this phase.

9.3.2.9 Normalization

Normalization is the next module associated with this framework, and it is intended to merge words that mean the same thing but they are misspelled and written in various forms. The normalization procedure used in Step 4 is used here.

9.3.2.10 Multiclass classifier

The objective of this module is to identify MITREATT and CK tactics that are used by tweet messages given by the one-class classifier described in our previous subsection. Linear support vector machine [20], random forest [21], multinomial naive Bayes, and logistic regression [22] are some of the standard models used for benchmarking purposes. A 10-fold cross-validation method is used for benchmarking purposes. Furthermore, 14 different classes trained based on the cyberthreat tactics are provided as an output of this model.

9.3.2.11 Process identified and classified threats

The threat identified by the multiclass classifier is given as an input to this phase. This information is further forwarded to the threat profiling database. This module performs data enrichment-related activities through data aggregation processes. Some of the count attributes that come from tweets are detected during this phase, which acts as additional evidence to threat alerts with a greater number of favorites, replies, followers, retweets, and mentions. The attributes such as date/time, threat name, threat tactic ID, mentions count, reference URL, favorite count, followers count, and retweet count will be identified, and it will be inserted into the threat profiling database. These attributes form the output related to this phase.

9.3.2.12 Alert generation

Alert generation is the final step associated with the architecture. The objective of this module is to generate alert messages for cyberthreat analysis based on the most recently identified cyberthreats. Once the threats are appropriately identified by the machine learning model the alert messages will be generated and the required preventive actions will be taken.

In this manner, the NLP-based cyberthreat detection model identifies the cyberthreats across social networking platforms.

9.3.3 Federated learning and blockchain-based architecture for dynamic cyber risk assessment

Blockchain is a decentralization-based technique that works based on an immutable ledger. Blockchain techniques are often merged with federated learning approaches as they are subject to attacks in an untrusted computing environment. During the data aggregation phase, the federated learning-based models are prone to huge amounts of security risks. This is where exactly the role of blockchain comes into play. The decentralized nature of blockchain when integrated with federated learning can prevent many cyberattacks. A detailed architecture of a blockchain-based federated learning approach for cyberthreat detection and prevention is given in Figure 9.3. The architecture discussed in this section works based on the model given in [23].

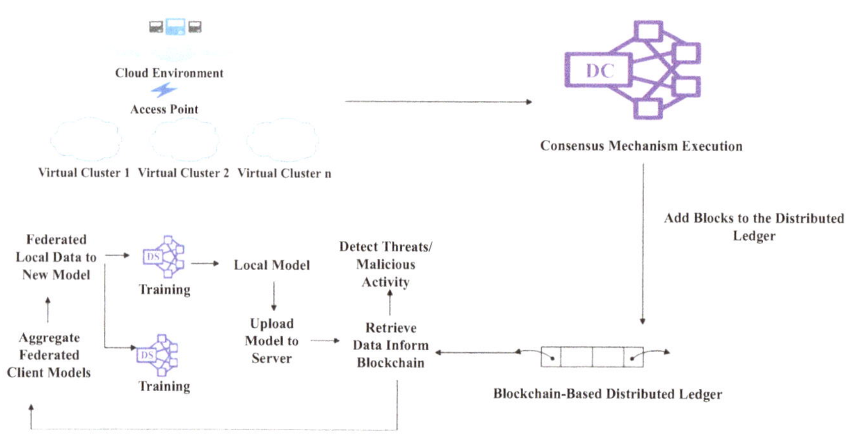

Figure 9.3 Federated learning-based dynamic cyber threat detection model

9.3.3.1 Permissioned blockchain-based solutions

Multiparty data sharing across IoT applications forms the most significant challenge and it leads to several issues. Through the appropriate implementation of the permissioned blockchain model, a private multipart data model sharing system is given in this section. Mainly two major solutions are proposed for the effective implementation of this approach, which are listed below:

1. Multiple channels are required for the learning process associated with multiple global models.
2. Next, is the global model state tree.

The aggregation of the local models is updated and stored across the blockchain network. The blockchain-based federated learning approach involves two major entities: base station and faulty replica. There exist five different phases across the blockchain platform through which the transaction occurs. Initially, the user requests for a transaction. Here, a transaction may indicate access to a file stored across a blockchain-based distributed ledger. This process occurs during the request phase. The next involves the pre-prepare phase. The system gets prepared for the access. During this phase, the system looks for the particular block in which the data is stored. Next in the preparation phase, the data requested by the user is accessed and it is validated during the validation phase. Once the validation is completed successfully the data will be given to the users. All the transactions taking place at the local nodes will be modeled using the federated learning model. The local model will be trained based on the input data and then the test model will be evaluated. All the fetched client models are then aggregated and then fed into the server for the detection of threats. Using the federated learning algorithm, this framework will efficiently identify the malicious and normal activities associated with the system. The detailed architecture related to the working model is illustrated in Figure 9.3.

9.3.3.2 Permissionless blockchain-based solutions

The permissionless blockchain-based model allows the person to perform various tasks without any restrictions. No permissions are required for user access and the user can also join as a validator in this model. A permissionless blockchain-based federated learning model can offer privacy-preserving efficient solutions to the users. The implementation of this architecture model will enhance the user experience and provide improved privacy and security measures. Furthermore, some of the various threats that arise during the implementation of the federated learning models and how the ongoing research works can overcome these challenges are tabulated and discussed in Table 9.1.

9.3.4 Generative AI-based models for dynamic cyberthreat detection

Generative AI forms the most vital and powerful tool across various domains including cybersecurity. The appropriate use of generative AI will assist cybersecurity

Table 9.1 List of possible vulnerabilities that occur in federated learning-based models with preventive solutions

Threat model	Solution proposed to overcome the threats
Differential attack	An optimized version of the federated soft-impute algorithm will overcome this threat [24] A solution based on a federated peer-to-peer approach will overcome this threat that works on random updates of subpots will overcome this attack. This approach will not take any conservators [25]
Privacy leakage attack	Blockchain-based reinforcement learning approaches will resolve this attack [26]
Byzantine attack	Solutions based on analysis of a small fraction of updates will resolve this attack. The conventional approaches will make an analysis of the whole update [27] Secure and privacy-preserving federated learning with blockchain-based solutions can resolve this issue [28] An adaptive federated learning-based solution with a digital twin can resolve the issue [29]
Adversarial attack	The effective implementation of deep neural networks will resolve this issue [30] The effective convergence of self-normalizing neural networks and Feed-forward neural networks will resolve this attack [31] An efficient approach based on differential privacy with distinct levels of granularity will resolve the issue [32] Robust and efficient boundary-based optimization models will resolve the issue [33] An efficient approach for the identification of critical features based on saliency maps will resolve the issue [34]
Gray box attack	An enhanced classifier-based solution with an attacking generator will solve this issue [35] Deep reinforcement-based learning approach for the protection of botnet detectors from adversarial attacks will solve this issue [36]
Poisoning attack	The effective convergence of Reject on Negative Impact and TRIM techniques will resolve this issue [37] Federated learning algorithms with trimmed optimization using multiple keys will resolve this issue [38] An effective approach to prevent the upload of unimportant data will resolve the issue [39] A combination of microaggregation with Gaussian mixture models will resolve this issue [40] A decentralized blockchain-based approach using Ethereum and smart contract techniques will effectively detect poisoning attacks [41] The convergence of two techniques, federated generative adversarial network (FedGAN) and generative adversarial network (GAN), will resolve the issue [42]
Black box attack	The effective use of zero-order optimization can prevent this threat easily [43]
Jamming attack	Approaches based on the dempster-shafer theory assisted client group optimization method will resolve this issue [44]

(Continues)

Table 9.1 (Continued)

Threat model	Solution proposed to overcome the threats
Inference attack	The effective implementation of privacy-preserving federated learning will solve this issue [45] The effective implementation of local differential privacy technology will solve the issue [46] Developing a model that learns only the features related to a particular task will solve the issue [47] The efficient use of federated extreme gradient boosting schemes can help identify this threat easily [48]
Shilling attack	It can be prevented through the use of four novel features from the gradient matrices [49]

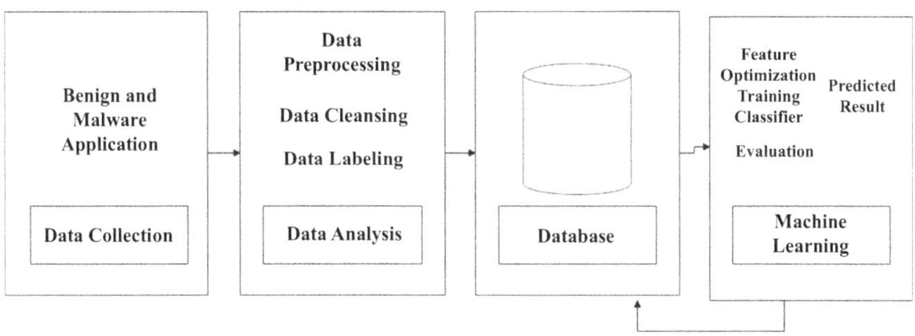

Figure 9.4 Generative AI-based model for cyberthreat detection and analysis

researchers and industrialists in acquiring new insights that help them in threat detection and response. It will also assist in improved detection and response mechanisms for cyberthreats, help develop simulation of realistic attack scenarios, and help the creation of efficient next-generation cybersecurity professionals.

A generic model of generative AI in cyberthreat detection is illustrated in Figure 9.4. In short, the generative AI model consists of four modules which include data collection, data analysis, database management, and machine learning. Initially, the data is collected from the benign and malware applications through the data collection module. Once the data is collected, it is then forwarded to the data analysis module for the analytics process. All the data collected will be labeled, cleaned, and preprocessed for removal of noise and other unwanted contents. Once these processes are completed, it is then forwarded to the database module. All the data collected for the analysis processes will be stored in this database. Then from the database, the machine learning algorithms are applied to process the data in the database. For a generative AI model to be implemented effectively, we can make use of any kind of machine learning algorithm that suits well for the scenario. From a cybersecurity context, most of the deep learning models are used for data analysis processes. The one major difference between the conventional and generative models is that it acts as a white box model providing the necessary information regarding the predicted output. Whereas, the conventional AI model acts as the black model has no idea regarding the predicted output. In the machine learning module, the algorithms are applied initially for the evaluation of the data. Then the training and the testing model is built with the dataset for prediction purposes. Once the model is built the features associated with the models are optimized to acquire better performance measures. The prediction result indicates the possibility of the occurrence of cyberthreats, and it will be notified to the security professionals and end users based on the emergency constraints.

9.4 Role of various other AI models in threat intelligence

Malware and cyberthreats remain to be an inevitable consequence for organizations and individuals. This is due to the reason that attackers are constantly coming with their techniques to avoid detection. This section describes the impacts of dynamic cyberthreats and various challenges associated with their detection and mitigation processes using various AI models.

In general, artificial intelligence is growing fast due to its immense potential and it is also noticeable that it plays a major role in working with cyberthreat intelligence. Some of the various AI models and their applications in cyberthreat detection are described in precise detail.

9.4.1 Deep learning models

Some of the various kinds of deep learning models such as CNNs, LSTMs, and recurrent neural networks (RNNs) are some of the widely used models for cybersecurity, and it can be useful in identifying visual indicators of cyber risks. In deep learning-based models, the first layer is provided with the input that passes across the various layers associated with the network. Each layer includes a function and a scale that differs with the change in input order and eventually produces the output. The output provided defines the predicted possibility of cyberthreats. Malware, social engineering threat detection, phishing attacks, denial-of-service attacks, insider threats, data breaches, and advanced persistent threats are some of the possible threats that could be effectively identified and prevented while adapting deep learning-based models.

9.4.2 Reinforcement learning

Reinforcement learning is a kind of machine learning-based model that is often used as a cyber defense strategic measure. Practically, cyberthreats are more dynamic, stealthy, and adaptive, which makes their detection highly a complex process. Furthermore, cyberattackers often revise their strategies and implement new threats and vulnerabilities that can break the detection systems. To deal with these uncertainty measures, the technique of reinforcement learning-based models is widely used in cybersecurity. In a reinforcement learning model, the agents are allowed to learn the feedback from the network and a series of outcomes from its actions. Through this, they can easily identify anomalous patterns, detect vulnerabilities, and prioritize the alerts.

9.4.3 Large language models

Large language model (LLM) is a kind of artificial intelligence-based model most useful in the detection of cyberthreat intelligence. They help do various cybersecurity-related tasks such as loc extraction, summarization, and TTP extraction. These models are capable of understanding and generating human-like texts, which make them highly versatile and most suitable to deal with the processing of unstructured data.

9.4.4 Bayesian networks

Bayesian networks are the most popular machine learning model in cybersecurity because they have the potential to overcome data limitations. In general, Bayesian networks work based on hypothesis probability and observed evidence. This involves updating the likelihood of the security threat across the cybersecurity. For example, using Bayesian networks we can build a network model using which we can assess the likelihood or possibility of the occurrence of cyberattacks. This is carried out based on the available evidence.

9.4.5 Decision trees

Decision trees are a kind of machine learning model now used to identify the characteristics of known cyberthreats. Based on the predictions made from the decision tree models are built that are used in efficient classification of new cyberthreats. For example, through the effective implementation of decision tree-based models, we can identify features relating to a particular kind of malware and these features could be used to find out the new instances of the malware.

9.5 Important factors to be considered when applying AI models for dynamic cyber risk assessment

Before the implementation of AI models for cybersecurity, there exist various parameters that organizations need to consider to acquire its complete advantages. Also, this will evade unpredictable outcomes and optimize the number of resources spent on various cyberthreat intelligence-based operations. The various factors that need to be considered before implementing AI models for cybersecurity include the following:

1. Data quality: Ensuring the data quality forms the most important factor. Because the quality and accuracy of the training data determine the rate at which inaccuracies and biases can be generated during threat analysis.
2. Ethical considerations: Ethical aspects concerning AI remain an open challenge due to which its application can be suppressed sometimes. Sometimes the AI-driven tools can also be used for malicious purposes impacting the

overall objective of the organization. Hence, various ethical aspects relating to AI implementation should be considered seriously before its implementation.

3. Model selection: The next important factor is the model selection. The process of selecting the most appropriate framework or model for a particular cybersecurity use case can ensure the most optimal performance.
4. Human AI collaboration: Establishing a proper balance between human expertise and AI-driven tools forms a vital component in the creation of the most efficient and robust cyberthreat intelligence measure.

9.6 Conclusion

There is no doubt that artificial intelligence and machine learning approaches are growing rapidly and they are continually evolving. On the other hand, the growth of digital technologies enables increased risk of cyberthreats. There is a crucial need to explore efficient solutions for growing cyberthreats. AI-based models form the most efficient solutions that help to build the threat models through which we can establish resilience against emerging cyberthreat-related challenges. The effective implementation of AI models for cybersecurity prevents numerous vulnerabilities and automates threat detection and response mechanisms. It can even lead to a safe data ecosystem and provide a robust IT infrastructure. In short, adapting AI models for dynamic cyberthreat detection may result in various advantages, and some of them may include cost reduction, improved accuracy, improved scalability, and many more. This is because the use of AI-based models can efficiently analyze the network traffic logs, user behaviors, system logs, and threat intelligence feeds through which they can offer proactive defense mechanisms and detect various indicators associated with the threats that may even escape from the human eye. However, some of the considerable challenges such as bias, overreliance on AI models, misinterpretation of errors, data unavailability, and cybersecurity skill gaps are some of the factors that prevent active implementation of AI models for dynamic cyberthreat detection. This area could be explored more in the future to reap the maximum benefits to all aspects of the cybersecurity ecosystem.

References

[1] Shaukat, K., Luo, S., Varadharajan, V., Hameed, I. A., and Xu, Y. "Cyber threat detection using machine learning techniques: A performance evaluation perspective." *2020 International Conference on Cyber Warfare and Security (ICCWS)*. Piscataway, NJ: IEEE, 2020.

[2] Lee, J., Park, H., Lee, H., and Kim, J. "Cyber threat detection based on artificial neural networks using event profiles." *IEEE Access*, 7 (2019): 165607–165626.

[3] Yuan, S., and Wu, X. "Deep learning for insider threat detection: Review, challenges and opportunities." *Comput. Secur.*, 104 (2021): 102221.

[4] Zhang, D., Wang, T., Jin, Y., and Pan, Y. "Physical safety and cyber security analysis of multi-agent systems: A survey of recent advances." *IEEE/CAA J. Automat. Sin.*, 8(2) (2021): 319–333.
[5] Liang, H., Liu, Y., Li, X., Tang, Q., and Chen, Z. "Dynamic evaluation of drilling leakage risk based on fuzzy theory and PSO-SVR algorithm." *Future Gener. Comput. Syst.*, 95 (2019): 454–466.
[6] Ganin, A. A., Quach, P., Panwar, M., and Linkov, I. "Multicriteria decision framework for cybersecurity risk assessment and management." *Risk Anal.*, 40(1) (2020): 183–199.
[7] Wu, W., Kang, R., and Li, Z. "Risk assessment method for cyber security of cyber physical systems." *2015 First International Conference on Reliability Systems Engineering (ICRSE)*. Piscataway, NJ: IEEE, 2015.
[8] Amin, Z. "A practical road map for assessing cyber risk." *J. Risk Res.*, 22(1) (2019): 32–43.
[9] Zio, E. "The future of risk assessment." *Reliab. Eng. Syst. Saf.*, 177 (2018): 176–190.
[10] Zhu, Q., Li, Y., Gao, H., and Yan, M. "Extended multilevel flow model-based dynamic risk assessment for cybersecurity protection in industrial production systems." *Int. J. Distrib. Sens. Netw.*, 14(6) (2018): 1550147718779564.
[11] Zhang, Q., Li, Y., Zhao, X., and Wang, H. "A fuzzy probability Bayesian network approach for dynamic cybersecurity risk assessment in industrial control systems." *IEEE Trans. Ind. Inform.*, 14(6) (2017): 2497–2506.
[12] Peng, Y., Chen, M., Zhang, J., and Liu, S. "A model-data integrated cyber security risk assessment method for industrial control systems." *2018 IEEE 7th Data Driven Control and Learning Systems Conference (DDCLS)*. Piscataway, NJ: IEEE, 2018.
[13] Jiang, T., Li, X., Yang, J., and Zhou, F. "BFLS: Blockchain and federated learning for sharing threat detection models as cyber threat intelligence." *Comput. Netw.*, 224 (2023): 109604.
[14] Ferrag, M.A., Mukherjee, M., Derhab, A., and Nguifo, E.M. "Edge-IIoTset: A new comprehensive realistic cyber security dataset of IoT and IIoT applications for centralized and federated learning." *IEEE Access*, 10 (2022): 40281–40306.
[15] Tian, P., Luo, H., Huang, J., and Xiao, Y. "Towards asynchronous federated learning-based threat detection: A DC-Adam approach." *Comput. Secur.*, 108 (2021): 102344.
[16] Tuor, A., Kaplan, S., Hutchinson, B., Nichols, J., and Robinson, S. "Deep learning for unsupervised insider threat detection in structured cybersecurity data streams." *Workshops at the 31st AAAI Conference on Artificial Intelligence*, 2017, pp. 224–231.
[17] Balusamy, B., Subramanian, S., and Baskaran, R. "A secured access control technique for cloud computing environment using attribute-based hierarchical structure and token granting system." *Int. J. Netw. Secur.*, 19(4) (2017): 559–572.

[18] Lee, J., Kim, J., Kim, I., and Han, K. "Cyber threat detection based on artificial neural networks using event profiles." *IEEE Access, s*7 (2019): 165607–165626.

[19] Marinho, R., and Holanda, R. "Automated emerging cyber threat identification and profiling based on natural language processing." *IEEE Access*, 11 (2023): 58915–58936.

[20] Tarzanagh, D.A., Farooq, M., Bacha, S., and Hameed, A. "Transformers as support vector machines." arXiv preprint *arXiv:2308.16898* (2023).

[21] Shao, Z., Ahmad, M.N., and Javed, A. "Comparison of random forest and XGBoost classifiers using integrated optical and SAR features for mapping urban impervious surface." *Remote Sens.*, 16(4) (2024): 665.

[22] Wu, J., Braverman, V., and Lee, J.D. "Implicit bias of gradient descent for logistic regression at the edge of stability." In: *37th Conference on Neural Information Processing Systems*, 2024, pp. 74229–74256.

[23] Ferrag, M.A., Mukherjee, M., Derhab, A., and Rauf, A. "Federated deep learning for cyber security in the Internet of Things: Concepts, applications, and experimental analysis." *IEEE Access*, 9 (2021): 138509–138542.

[24] Yang, J., Fu, C., and Lu, H. "Optimized and federated soft-impute for privacy-preserving tensor completion in cyber-physical-social systems." *Inf. Sci.*, 564 (2021): 103–123.

[25] Yu, S., Chen, X., Zhou, Z., Gong, X., and Wu, D. "When deep reinforcement learning meets federated learning: Intelligent multitimescale resource management for multiaccess edge computing in 5G ultradense network." *IEEE Internet Things J.*, 8(4) (2021): 2238–2251.

[26] Wang, Y., Su, Z., Zhang, N., and Benslimane, A. "Learning in the air: Secure federated learning for UAV-assisted crowdsensing." *IEEE Trans. Netw. Sci. Eng.*, 8(2) (2021): 1055–1069.

[27] Jebreel, N., Blanco-Justicia, A., Sánchez, D., and Domingo-Ferrer, J. "Efficient detection of Byzantine attacks in federated learning using last layer biases." In: *Proc. Int. Conf. Modeling Decisions Artif. Intell.* Cham: Springer, 2020, pp. 154–165.

[28] Wang, Q., Guo, Y., Wang, X., Ji, T., Yu, L., and Li, P. "AI at the edge: Blockchain-empowered secure multiparty learning with heterogeneous models." *IEEE Internet Things J.*, 7(10) (2020): 9600–9610.

[29] Sun, W., Lei, S., Wang, L., Liu, Z., and Zhang, Y. "Adaptive federated learning and digital twin for industrial Internet of Things." *IEEE Trans. Ind. Inform.*, 17(8) (2021): 5605–5614.

[30] Song, Y., Liu, T., Wei, T., Wang, X., Tao, Z., and Chen, M. "FDA3: Federated defense against adversarial attacks for cloud-based IIoT applications." *IEEE Trans. Ind. Inform.*, 17(11) (2021): 7830–7838.

[31] O. Ibitoye, O. Shafiq, and A. Matrawy, "Analyzing adversarial attacks against deep learning for intrusion detection in IoT networks." In: *Proc. IEEE Global Commun. Conf. (GLOBECOM)*, 2019, pp. 1–6.

[32] B. Hitaj, G. Ateniese, and F. Perez-Cruz, *"Deep models under the GAN: Information leakage from collaborative deep learning."* In: *Proc. Conf. Comput. Commun. Secur. (ACM SIGSAC)*, 2017, pp. 603–618.

[33] M.M. Hassan, M.R. Hassan, S. Huda, and V.H.C. de Albuquerque, "A robust deep-learning-enabled trust-boundary protection for adversarial industrial IoT environment," *IEEE Internet Things J.*, 8(12) (2020): 9611–9621.

[34] H. Qiu, T. Dong, T. Zhang, J. Lu, G. Memmi, and M. Qiu, "Adversarial attacks against network intrusion detection in IoT systems," *IEEE Internet Things J.*, 8(13) (2021): 10327–10335.

[35] Y. Xu, X. Zhong, A.J. Yepes, and J. H. Lau, Grey-box adversarial attack and defence for sentiment classification. *arXiv preprint arXiv*:2103.11576 (2021).

[36] G. Apruzzese, M. Andreolini, M. Marchetti, A. Venturi, and M. Colajanni, "Deep reinforcement adversarial learning against botnet evasion attacks," *IEEE Trans. Netw. Service Manage.*, 17(4) (2020): 1975–1987.

[37] M. Fang, X. Cao, J. Jia, and N. Gong, "Local model poisoning attacks to Byzantine-robust federated learning." In *Proc. 29th Secur. Symp. (USENIX Secur.)*, 2020, pp. 1605–1622.

[38] Z. Ma, J. Ma, Y. Miao, X. Liu, K.-K.-R. Choo, and R. Deng, "Pocket diagnosis: Secure federated learning against poisoning attack in the cloud," *IEEE Trans. Services Comput.*, 15(6) (2021): 3429–3442.

[39] B. Cetin, A. Lazar, J. Kim, A. Sim, and K. Wu, "Federated wireless network intrusion detection." In: *Proc. IEEE Int. Conf. Big Data (Big Data)*, 2019, pp. 6004–6006.

[40] A.K. Singh, A. Blanco-Justicia, J. Domingo-Ferrer, D. Sánchez, and D. Rebollo-Monedero, "Fair detection of poisoning attacks in federated learning." In: *Proc. IEEE 32nd Int. Conf. Tools Artif. Intell. (ICTAI)*, 2020, pp. 224–229.

[41] M.H.U. Rehman, A.M. Dirir, K. Salah, E. Damiani, and D. Svetinovic, "TrustFed: A framework for fair and trustworthy cross-device federated learning in IIoT," *IEEE Trans. Ind. Informat.*, 17(12) (2021): 8485–8494.

[42] R. Taheri, M. Shojafar, M. Alazab, and R. Tafazolli, "Fed-IIoT: A robust federated malware detection architecture in industrial IoT," *IEEE Trans. Ind. Informat.*, 17(12) (2021): 8442–8452.

[43] P.-Y. Chen, H. Zhang, Y. Sharma, J. Yi, and C.-J. Hsieh, "ZOO: Zeroth order optimization based black-box attacks to deep neural networks without training substitute models." In: *Proc. 10th ACMWorkshop Artif. Intell. Secur.*, 2017, pp. 15–26.

[44] N. Mowla, N.H. Tran, I. Doh, and K. Chae, "Federated learning-based cognitive detection of jamming attack in flying ad-hoc network," *IEEE Access*, 8 (2019): 4338–4350.

[45] M. Hao, H. Li, X. Luo, G. Xu, H. Yang, and S. Liu, "Efficient and privacy enhanced federated learning for industrial artificial intelligence," *IEEE Trans. Ind. Informat.*, 16(10) (2019): 6532–6542.

[46] L. Melis, C. Song, E.D. Cristofaro, and V. Shmatikov, "Exploiting unintended feature leakage in collaborative learning." In: *Proc. IEEE Symp. Secur. Privacy (SP)*, 2019, pp. 691–706.

[47] Y. Liu, Z. Ma, X. Liu, *et al.*, "Boosting privately: Federated extreme gradient boosting for mobile crowdsensing." In: *Proc. IEEE 40th Int. Conf. Distrib. Comput. Syst. (ICDCS)*, 2020, pp. 1–11.

[48] Z. Li, J. Liu, J. Hao, H. Wang, and M. Xian, "CrowdSFL: A secure crowd computing framework based on blockchain and federated learning," *Electronics*, 9(5) (2020): 773.

[49] Y. Jiang, Y. Zhou, D. Wu, C. Li, and Y. Wang, "On the detection of shilling attacks in federated collaborative filtering." In: *Proc. Int. Symp. Reliable Distrib. Syst. (SRDS)*, 2020, pp. 185–194.

Chapter 10

Hybrid security for IoT networks: from traditional security solutions to AI security

Rajeev Goyal[1], Samta Jain Goyal[1], Madhavi Dhingra[1], Shyam Sunder Gupta[1] and Daniel Arockiam[1]

Abstract

The Internet of Things (IoT) is a growing network of physical objects that are connected to the Internet and can communicate with each other. The security of IoT devices and networks is of paramount importance, as they can be vulnerable to cyberattacks, data breaches, malware, and other security threats. The increasing number of security threats, such as cyberattacks, data breaches, and privacy concerns, has highlighted the importance of ensuring the security and privacy of IoT networks. A hybrid security framework that combines traditional security solutions with machine learning and AI-based security solutions is designed to address the unique security challenges posed by IoT networks. The hybrid framework can provide a high level of protection for sensitive data and help to prevent unauthorized access or theft. In addition, it can also provide comprehensive security coverage and efficient utilization of computational resources.

Keywords: IoT; Security framework; Artificial intelligence; Cybersecurity

10.1 Introduction

The Internet of Things (IoT) refers to the growing network of physical objects that are connected to the Internet and can communicate with each other. These objects include everything from smart home devices to industrial equipment, has the ability to collect and transmit data, enabling new applications and services that can improve efficiency, productivity, and quality of life [1]. Figure 10.1 shows the opportunity for the use of IoT in different fields.

However, the widespread adoption of IoT has also raised significant security concerns. The vast number of connected devices and the complexity of IoT

[1]Department of Computer Science and Engineering, Amity School of Engineering and Technology, Amity University Madhya Pradesh, India

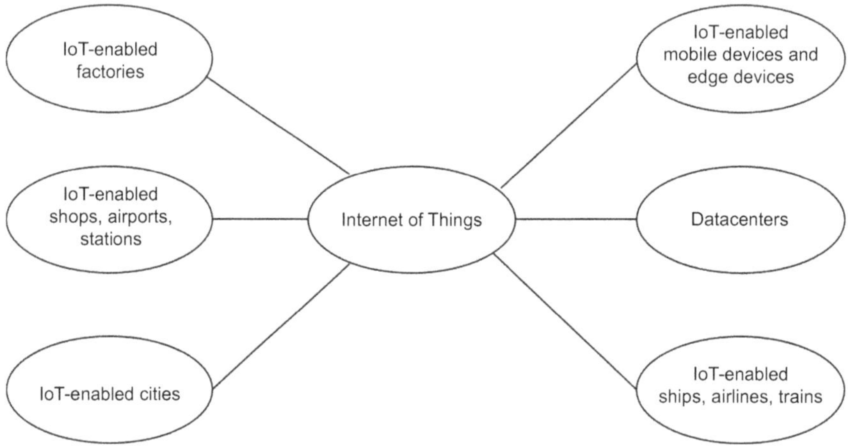

Figure 10.1 Internet of Things opportunities

networks make them vulnerable to cyberattacks, data breaches, and other security threats. To address these challenges, a hybrid security framework that combines traditional security solutions with machine learning and AI-based security solutions is needed [2].

10.1.1 Definition of IoT

IoT refers to a network of physical objects that are connected to the Internet and can communicate with each other. These objects, which are embedded with sensors, software, and other technologies, can collect and transmit data to enable new applications and services [3].

10.1.2 Importance of IoT security

The security of IoT devices and networks is of paramount importance, as they can be vulnerable to cyberattacks, data breaches, and other security threats. These threats can have serious consequences, including the compromise of sensitive data, the disruption of critical services, and even physical harm in certain cases. Therefore, ensuring the security of IoT is essential for realizing the full potential of this technology [4].

10.1.3 Need for a hybrid security framework

Traditional security solutions, such as firewalls and intrusion detection systems (IDSs), are not always effective in securing IoT networks due to their complexity and diversity. Machine learning and AI-based security solutions offer new and promising approaches to securing IoT, but they are not yet mature enough to replace traditional security solutions entirely. Therefore, a hybrid security framework that combines the strengths of both traditional and AI-based security solutions is needed to ensure the security and privacy of IoT devices and networks [5].

10.2 IoT security challenges

10.2.1 Overview of IoT security challenges

IoT security challenges arise due to the vast number of interconnected devices, the diversity of devices, and the lack of standardization in IoT networks. These challenges can include cyberattacks, data breaches, malware and viruses, privacy concerns, and a lack of standardization [6].

10.2.2 Cyberattacks and data breaches

Cyberattacks and data breaches are one of the most significant IoT security challenges. IoT devices are often connected to the Internet and have weak security measures, which make them easy targets for attackers. Cyberattacks can lead to data theft, denial-of-service attacks, and even physical harm in some cases.

For example, in 2016, the Mirai botnet attack used IoT devices to launch a distributed denial-of-service (DDoS) attack on a DNS provider, resulting in widespread Internet disruptions [6].

10.2.3 Malware and viruses

Malware and viruses can infect IoT devices, compromising their security and privacy. Malware can spread through IoT networks, causing significant damage to the network and the devices connected to it.

For example, the BrickerBot malware was designed to permanently disable vulnerable IoT devices, causing significant damage to the devices and the network [7].

10.2.4 Privacy concerns

Privacy concerns arise due to the collection and transmission of personal data by IoT devices. As these devices become more pervasive, they can collect a vast amount of sensitive data, such as location data, health data, and personal preferences, which can be exploited by attackers.

For example, in 2018, researchers discovered that a popular smartwatch was leaking sensitive user data, including location data and email addresses, due to poor security measures.

10.2.5 Lack of standardization

The lack of standardization in IoT networks creates security challenges, as different devices may have different security protocols and vulnerabilities. This makes it difficult to develop standardized security measures that can be applied across the entire network.

For example, a study by the Open Web Application Security Project found that many IoT devices had poorly implemented security features, such as weak passwords and lack of encryption, which made them vulnerable to cyberattacks [7].

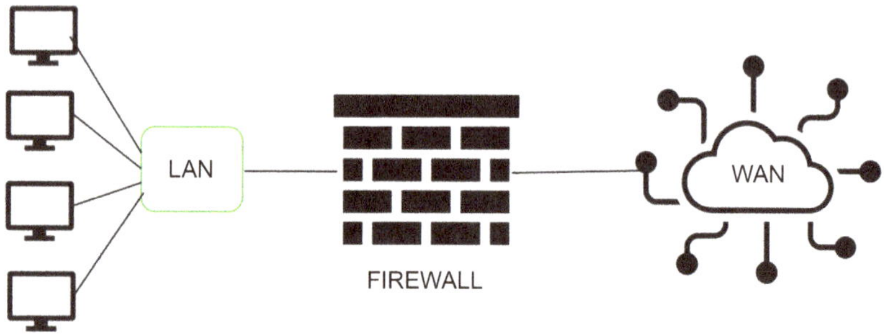

Figure 10.2 A firewall protects a number of computers on a LAN against unauthorized access

10.3 Traditional security solutions

10.3.1 Overview of traditional security solutions

Traditional security solutions have been used for years to secure networks and devices. These solutions include firewalls, IDSs, and encryption technologies. These solutions have been effective in securing networks and devices but are not always effective in securing IoT networks due to their complexity and diversity [4].

10.3.1.1 Firewalls

Firewalls are one of the most common security solutions used to protect networks from external threats. Firewalls act as a barrier between the internal network and the external network, blocking unauthorized access to the network. As shown in Figure 10.2, Firewalls can be used to filter traffic based on IP addresses, protocols, or ports.

However, firewalls are not always effective in securing IoT networks because IoT devices often use nonstandard communication protocols, making it difficult to filter traffic based on IP addresses or ports [4].

10.3.1.2 Intrusion detection systems

IDSs are used to detect and prevent unauthorized access to the network. IDSs work by analyzing network traffic for signs of unauthorized access or malicious activity. IDS can be used to detect anomalies in network traffic, such as unusual traffic patterns or unauthorized access attempts [8]. See Figure 10.3.

However, IDS may not be effective in securing IoT networks because IoT devices often generate large amounts of data, which can make it difficult to detect anomalies in network traffic [9].

10.3.1.3 Encryption technologies

Encryption technologies are used to protect data by encoding it to make it unreadable to unauthorized users. Encryption can be used to protect data at rest or

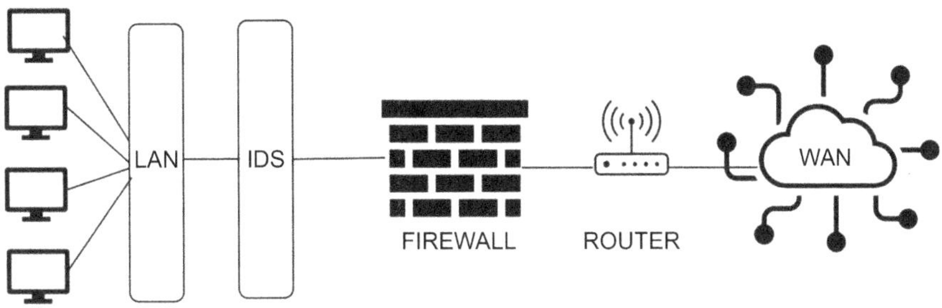

Figure 10.3 Intrusion detection systems (IDS)

in transit. Encryption can also be used to authenticate users or devices by using digital certificates or public key infrastructure (PKI).

However, encryption technologies may not be effective in securing IoT networks because IoT devices often have limited processing power and memory, making it difficult to implement strong encryption algorithms.

10.3.2 Encryption and decryption

Encryption is the process of converting data into a coded language to prevent unauthorized access or theft. Encryption is a crucial security measure for IoT devices, as it can protect sensitive information and prevent cybercriminals from stealing data.

Encryption can be used to protect data both at rest and in transit. At rest, encryption refers to the encryption of data that is stored on a device or server, while in transit encryption refers to the encryption of data as it is sent over a network.

One of the most common encryption techniques used in IoT devices is Advanced Encryption Standard (AES). AES is a symmetric encryption technique that uses a shared key to encrypt and decrypt data. AES is considered to be highly secure, as it uses a block cipher method to encrypt data, making it resistant to brute-force attacks (Figure 10.4) [10].

Decryption is the process of converting encrypted data back into its original, readable format. Decryption requires a decryption key, which is used to unlock the encrypted data. Decryption keys are typically kept secret and only shared with authorized users or devices.

In IoT networks, encryption and decryption can be used to protect data and authenticate users or devices. For example, encryption can be used to protect data transmitted between IoT devices, while decryption keys can be used to authenticate users or devices attempting to access the network.

Overall, encryption and decryption are critical components of a hybrid security framework for IoT networks, as they can provide a high level of protection for sensitive data and help to prevent unauthorized access or theft (Figure 10.5) [11].

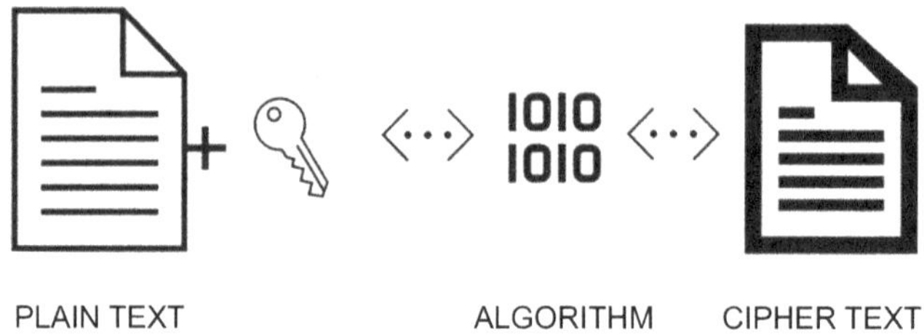

Figure 10.4 Encryption process

Figure 10.5 Decryption process

Overall, traditional security solutions can provide some level of security for IoT networks, but they are not always effective in securing these networks due to the complexity and diversity of IoT devices and networks. To address these challenges, a hybrid security framework that combines traditional security solutions with machine learning and AI-based security solutions is needed (Table 10.1).

10.3.3 Machine learning and AI-based security solutions

Machine learning and AI-based security solutions are becoming increasingly popular in IoT security due to their ability to analyze large amounts of data and detect anomalies or suspicious behavior in real time. These solutions can be used to detect and prevent cyberattacks, malware, and other security threats.

Machine learning and AI-based security solutions can be trained on large datasets to recognize patterns and identify potential security threats. These solutions can also be programmed to learn from past incidents and adapt to new security threats (Table 10.2) [12].

One example of a machine learning-based security solution is anomaly detection. Anomaly detection uses machine learning algorithms to identify unusual patterns in network traffic or device behavior. If an anomaly is detected, the security solution can trigger an alert or take action to prevent the security threat [13].

Another example of an AI-based security solution is behavioral analysis. Behavioral analysis uses AI algorithms to analyze user or device behavior and detect suspicious activity. If suspicious behavior is detected, the security solution can trigger an alert or block access to the network.

Table 10.1 Comparison between encryption and decryption [33]

Parameter	Encryption	Decryption
What is	It is a process of converting normal data into an unreadable form. It helps you to avoid any unauthorized access to data.	It is a method of converting the unreadable/coded data into its original form.
Process	Whenever the data is sent between two separate machines, it is encrypted automatically using a secret key.	The receiver of the data automatically allows you to convert the data from the codes into its original form.
Location of conversion	The person who is sending the data to the destination.	The receiver receives the data and converts it.
Example	An employee is sending essential documents to his/her manager.	The manager is receiving the essential documents from his/her employee.
Use of algorithm	The same algorithm with the same key is used for the encryption–decryption process.	The only single algorithm is used for encryption and decryption with a pair of keys where each use for encryption and decryption.
Major function	Transforming humanly understandable messages into an incomprehensible and obscure form that cannot be interpreted.	It is a conversion of an obscure message into an understandable form that is easy to understand by a human.

Table 10.2 Difference between traditional techniques and advanced techniques

Security measure	Traditional techniques	Advanced techniques
Authentication and access control	Passwords and username combinations	Biometric authentication, multifactor authentication
Encryption and decryption	Advanced Encryption Standard (AES)	Homomorphic encryption, blockchain encryption
Firewalls and intrusion detection/prevention systems	Traditional firewalls and intrusion detection/ prevention systems	Machine learning algorithms, behavior analytics
Secure communication protocols	HTTPS, SSL/TLS	SSL, Datagram Transport Layer Security (DTLS)
Firmware and software updates	Regular updates to patch vulnerabilities	Over-the-air (OTA) updates, secure boot process

Machine learning and AI-based security solutions can also be used for authentication and access control. For example, facial recognition technology can be used to authenticate users attempting to access a network or device. Voice recognition and biometric authentication can also be used for access control [14].

Overall, machine learning and AI-based security solutions are important components of a hybrid security framework for IoT networks. These solutions can provide real-time detection and prevention of security threats and help to improve the overall security posture of IoT networks.

Anomaly detection is a machine learning-based security solution that detects unusual patterns or behavior in network traffic or device behavior. Anomaly detection works by analyzing large amounts of data and identifying patterns that deviate from normal behavior. These deviations can be indicative of a security threat, such as a cyberattack or malware infection.

Anomaly detection algorithms can be trained on large datasets of normal network traffic or device behavior. These algorithms learn to recognize patterns and behaviors that are considered normal and then flag any patterns or behaviors that deviate from the norm as potential security threats [15].

There are several types of anomaly detection techniques, including statistical-based, machine learning-based, and rule-based methods. Statistical-based methods use statistical models to detect deviations from normal behavior. Machine learning-based methods use algorithms to learn from historical data and identify patterns of normal behavior. Rule-based methods use predefined rules to detect deviations from normal behavior.

Anomaly detection can be used in various ways in IoT networks. For example, anomaly detection can be used to detect and prevent cyberattacks, such as distributed denial-of-service (DDoS) attacks or SQL injection attacks. Anomaly detection can also be used to detect malware infections, as malware often exhibits unusual behavior on a device or network.

Overall, anomaly detection is a critical component of a machine learning and AI-based security solution for IoT networks. By identifying and flagging unusual behavior, anomaly detection can help to prevent security threats and improve the overall security posture of IoT networks [16].

10.3.4 Predictive modeling

Predictive modeling is a machine learning-based security solution that uses historical data to predict future security threats. Predictive modeling algorithms can be trained on large datasets of historical security incidents and network behavior to identify patterns and predict future security threats [17].

Predictive modeling can be used to detect and prevent a wide range of security threats, such as cyberattacks, malware infections, and data breaches. By analyzing historical data, predictive modeling can identify patterns and behaviors that are indicative of security threats, allowing security teams to take proactive measures to prevent these threats.

One example of a predictive modeling-based security solution is threat intelligence. Threat intelligence uses historical data to identify patterns of behavior associated with known security threats, such as malware or phishing attacks. This information can be used to identify and block potential security threats before they can do damage [18].

Another example of predictive modeling is machine learning-based IDSs. IDS uses machine learning algorithms to analyze network traffic and detect suspicious behavior that may indicate a security threat. By identifying security threats in real time, IDS can help to prevent cyberattacks and other security incidents.

Predictive modeling can also be used for risk assessment and vulnerability management. By analyzing historical data, predictive modeling can identify areas of weakness in an IoT network and provide insights on how to mitigate these vulnerabilities before they can be exploited.

Overall, predictive modeling is an important component of a machine learning and AI-based security solution for IoT networks. By using historical data to predict future security threats, predictive modeling can help prevent security incidents and improve the overall security posture of IoT networks [19].

10.3.5 Threat intelligence

Threat intelligence is a machine learning-based security solution that uses historical data to identify patterns of behavior associated with known security threats, such as malware or phishing attacks. Threat intelligence can be used to identify and block potential security threats before they can do damage.

Threat intelligence involves gathering and analyzing large amounts of data from a variety of sources, including public and private databases, social media, and dark web forums. This data is then analyzed using machine learning algorithms to identify patterns and behaviors associated with known security threats.

Threat intelligence can be used to provide real-time information on emerging security threats, allowing security teams to take proactive measures to prevent these threats. Threat intelligence can also be used to provide insights into the tactics and techniques used by cybercriminals, helping security teams to better understand the threat landscape [20].

One example of a threat intelligence-based security solution is a threat intelligence platform (TIP). A TIP is a centralized platform that aggregates and analyzes threat intelligence data from a variety of sources. The TIP can then provide real-time alerts on emerging security threats, allowing security teams to take proactive measures to prevent these threats (Figure 10.6).

Another example of threat intelligence is a security information and event management (SIEM) system. A SIEM system uses machine learning algorithms to analyze network traffic and identify potential security threats. By using threat intelligence data, an SIEM system can provide real-time alerts on emerging security threats and help security teams quickly respond to these threats.

Overall, threat intelligence is an important component of a machine learning and AI-based security solution for IoT networks. By using historical data to identify patterns of behavior associated with known security threats, threat intelligence can

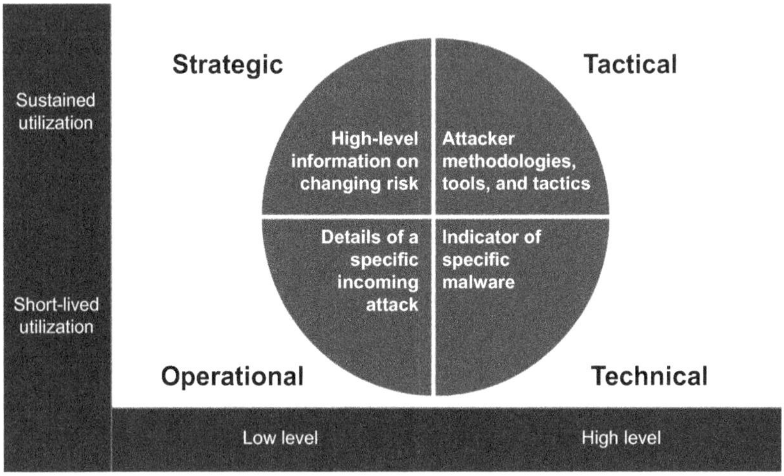

Figure 10.6 Types of cyberthreat intelligence

help to prevent security incidents and improve the overall security posture of IoT networks [21].

10.3.6 Behavioral analytics

Behavioral analytics is a machine learning-based security solution that uses algorithms to detect anomalies in user and device behavior within an IoT network. By analyzing patterns of user and device behavior, behavioral analytics can identify potential security threats in real time.

Behavioral analytics can be used to detect a wide range of security threats, including insider threats, phishing attacks, and malware infections. By analyzing user behavior, behavioral analytics can identify deviations from normal patterns of activity, such as unusual login times or access to sensitive data [22].

One example of a behavioral analytics-based security solution is user and entity behavior analytics (UEBA). UEBA uses machine learning algorithms to analyze patterns of user and device behavior and detect potential security threats. By analyzing user behavior, UEBA can identify potential insider threats, such as employees accessing sensitive data outside of normal working hours.

Another example of behavioral analytics is anomaly detection. Anomaly detection uses machine learning algorithms to identify deviations from normal patterns of behavior within an IoT network. By analyzing network traffic and device behavior, anomaly detection can identify potential security threats in real time.

Overall, behavioral analytics is an important component of a machine learning and AI-based security solution for IoT networks. By analyzing patterns of user and device behavior, behavioral analytics can help to identify potential security threats and improve the overall security posture of IoT networks [23].

10.4 Hybrid security framework for IoT

10.4.1 Overview of hybrid security framework

A hybrid security framework for IoT combines the strengths of traditional security solutions, machine learning and AI-based security solutions, and other advanced security technologies to create a comprehensive security system for IoT networks.

The hybrid security framework for IoT is designed to address the unique security challenges posed by IoT networks. It provides multiple layers of security that work together to detect and prevent security threats, while also ensuring the integrity and confidentiality of data transmitted across the network [24].

The hybrid security framework typically includes a combination of the following security solutions:

1. Traditional security solutions, such as authentication and access control, encryption and decryption, and firewalls, which provide a strong foundation of security for the IoT network [25].
2. Machine learning and AI-based security solutions, such as anomaly detection, predictive modeling, and threat intelligence, which use advanced algorithms to detect and prevent security threats in real time.
3. Other advanced security technologies, such as blockchain, which can be used to ensure the integrity and confidentiality of data transmitted across the IoT network.

By combining these different security solutions, the hybrid security framework for IoT provides a comprehensive and multilayered approach to IoT security. This approach helps to address the unique security challenges posed by IoT networks, such as the large number of connected devices, the diversity of devices and communication protocols, and the high volume of data transmitted across the network.

Overall, a hybrid security framework for IoT is an important step towards securing IoT networks and protecting sensitive data transmitted across these networks. By combining the strengths of traditional security solutions, machine learning and AI-based security solutions, and other advanced security technologies, the hybrid security framework provides a powerful and comprehensive approach to IoT security [26].

10.4.2 Combining traditional and AI-based security solutions

The hybrid security framework for IoT combines traditional security solutions with machine learning and AI-based security solutions to provide a more robust and comprehensive security system for IoT networks.

One example of combining traditional and AI-based security solutions is using firewalls and anomaly detection together. Firewalls are a traditional security solution that provides a barrier between the internal network and the external world, while anomaly detection uses machine learning algorithms to identify deviations from normal patterns of behavior within the network. By combining these two solutions, the hybrid security framework can identify and prevent security threats in real time while also preventing unauthorized access to the network [27].

Another example is combining authentication and access control with predictive modeling. Authentication and access control are traditional security solutions that ensure that only authorized users can access the network, while predictive modeling uses machine learning algorithms to analyze patterns of user and device behavior to identify potential security threats. By combining these two solutions, the hybrid security framework can prevent unauthorized access to the network while also detecting potential security threats in real time.

Overall, combining traditional and AI-based security solutions in the hybrid security framework for IoT provides a more robust and comprehensive security system for IoT networks. By using multiple layers of security that work together to detect and prevent security threats, the hybrid security framework helps to address the unique security challenges posed by IoT networks and ensure the integrity and confidentiality of data transmitted across the network [28].

10.4.3 Implementation and deployment

Implementing and deploying a hybrid security framework for IoT requires careful planning and execution. The following are some key steps that can help ensure the successful implementation and deployment of a hybrid security framework for IoT:

1. Identify the security requirements: The first step in implementing a hybrid security framework for IoT is to identify the security requirements of the network. This includes identifying the types of devices and communication protocols used in the network, as well as the types of data transmitted across the network.
2. Select the appropriate security solutions: Based on the security requirements identified in Step 1, select the appropriate traditional security solutions, machine learning and AI-based security solutions, and other advanced security technologies to be included in the hybrid security framework.
3. Integrate the security solutions: Once the appropriate security solutions have been selected, they need to be integrated into the IoT network. This requires configuring the security solutions to work together seamlessly and ensuring that they are compatible with the existing devices and communication protocols used in the network.
4. Train and test the security solutions: Before deploying the hybrid security framework in the live network, it is important to train and test the security solutions to ensure that they are functioning properly and can detect and prevent security threats in real time.
5. Deploy the security solutions: Once the security solutions have been trained and tested, they can be deployed in the live network. This requires careful monitoring of the network to ensure that the security solutions are functioning as intended and are providing the required level of security.
6. Continuous monitoring and updates: The final step in implementing and deploying a hybrid security framework for IoT is to continuously monitor the

network for security threats and update the security solutions as needed to ensure that they remain effective against new and evolving security threats [29].

In conclusion, implementing and deploying a hybrid security framework for IoT requires a multistep process that involves identifying the security requirements, selecting the appropriate security solutions, integrating the solutions, training and testing the solutions, deploying the solutions, and continuously monitoring and updating the solutions. By following these steps, organizations can effectively secure their IoT networks and protect the sensitive data transmitted across these networks.

10.4.4 Monitoring and maintenance

Once a hybrid security framework for IoT has been implemented and deployed, it is important to monitor and maintain the system to ensure its continued effectiveness. The following are some key considerations for monitoring and maintaining a hybrid security framework for IoT:

1. Regular security assessments: Conduct regular security assessments to identify any vulnerabilities or weaknesses in the system. This includes reviewing the effectiveness of the security solutions and identifying any potential security threats.
2. Ongoing training and education: Provide ongoing training and education to personnel responsible for monitoring and maintaining the security framework. This includes educating personnel on the latest security threats and techniques for addressing them.
3. Patch management: Regularly update and patch the security solutions to ensure that they are protected against the latest security threats. This includes monitoring vendor websites for security updates and patches and applying them as needed.
4. Incident response planning: Develop and maintain an incident response plan that outlines the steps to be taken in the event of a security breach. This includes identifying the personnel responsible for responding to security incidents, outlining the steps to be taken to contain the incident, and documenting the incident for future analysis.
5. Monitoring tools: Use monitoring tools to continuously monitor the IoT network for security threats. This includes using tools to monitor network traffic, detect anomalies in user and device behavior, and identify potential security threats.
6. Regular backups: Regularly back up critical data stored on the IoT network to ensure that it can be recovered in the event of a security breach or other system failure [30].

By implementing these monitoring and maintenance practices, organizations can ensure the ongoing effectiveness of their hybrid security framework for IoT and protect the sensitive data transmitted across the network.

10.4.5 Case study: hybrid security framework for a smart home IoT network

As the number of smart home devices continues to grow, so too does the need for robust security solutions to protect these devices and the sensitive data they transmit. To address this need, a hybrid security framework was implemented for a smart home IoT network. The hybrid security framework included both traditional security solutions and machine learning and AI-based security solutions [31].

As seen in Figure 10.7, the traditional security solutions included firewalls, IDSs, and antivirus software. These solutions were integrated with the smart home devices and communication protocols used in the network and were configured to work together seamlessly to provide comprehensive security coverage.

The machine learning and AI-based security solutions included anomaly detection, predictive modeling, and threat intelligence. These solutions were trained using data collected from the smart home network and were able to detect and prevent security threats in real time.

The hybrid security framework was deployed in the smart home IoT network and was continuously monitored and maintained to ensure its continued effectiveness. Regular security assessments were conducted to identify any vulnerabilities or weaknesses in the system, and the security solutions were regularly updated and patched to protect against the latest security threats [32].

In addition, ongoing training and education was provided to the personnel responsible for monitoring and maintaining the security framework, and an incident response plan was developed and maintained to ensure a quick and effective response in the event of a security breach.

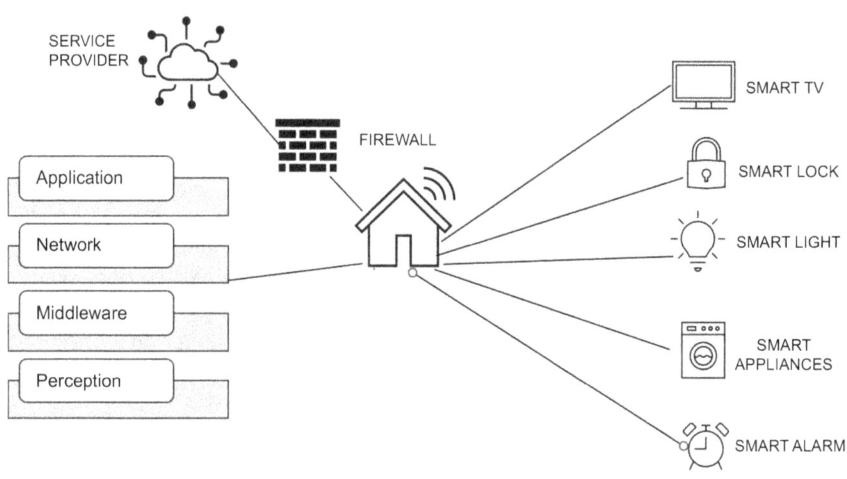

Figure 10.7 Smart home architecture

As a result of the hybrid security framework, the smart home IoT network was able to achieve a high level of security, protecting both the smart home devices and the sensitive data transmitted across the network. The hybrid security framework was also able to adapt to new and evolving security threats, ensuring that the smart home IoT network remained secure and protected against potential attacks.

10.4.6 Summary of the importance of IoT security

The increasing use of IoT devices in various domains, including healthcare, smart homes, transportation, and industrial automation, has led to the generation and transmission of large amounts of sensitive data across networks. This data includes personal, financial, and business information, making it an attractive target for cybercriminals. Therefore, ensuring the security of IoT networks has become critical to prevent data breaches, cyberattacks, and privacy violations.

10.4.7 Advantages of a hybrid security framework

A hybrid security framework that combines traditional security solutions with machine learning and AI-based security solutions can provide several advantages in securing IoT networks. It can enable a proactive approach to security by detecting and preventing security threats in real time. It can also provide comprehensive security coverage that can adapt to new and evolving security threats. A hybrid security framework can also enable the efficient utilization of computational resources by combining different security solutions that work together seamlessly.

10.4.8 Future directions for IoT security research

As IoT networks continue to expand, there is a need for continued research in IoT security. Some areas that require further attention include the development of more advanced machine learning and AI-based security solutions, the standardization of security protocols and frameworks, and the implementation of secure communication protocols. Additionally, research is needed in the areas of secure device identity management and secure firmware updates. Finally, the development of regulations and policies that mandate the implementation of robust security solutions in IoT networks is also necessary to ensure the security and privacy of users.

10.5 Conclusion

In conclusion, the rapid growth and expansion of IoT networks have created an urgent need for robust security solutions. The increasing number of security threats, such as cyberattacks, data breaches, malware, and privacy concerns, has highlighted the importance of ensuring the security and privacy of IoT networks. A hybrid security framework that combines traditional security solutions with machine learning and AI-based security solutions can provide several advantages in securing IoT networks, including real-time detection and prevention of security threats, comprehensive security coverage, and efficient utilization of computational resources. However, there is a need for continued research in IoT security to address challenges such as standardization of security protocols, secure device identity management, and the development of regulations and policies. By implementing a hybrid security framework and continuing to invest in research, we can ensure that IoT networks remain secure and protected against potential attacks, thus enabling us to fully realize the benefits of the IoT revolution.

References

[1] Al-Fuqaha, A., Guizani, M., Mohammadi, M., Aledhari, M., and Ayyash, M. (2015). Internet of Things: A Survey on Enabling Technologies, Protocols, and Applications. *IEEE Communications Surveys & Tutorials*, 17, 2347–2376.

[2] Mohy-Eddine, M., Guezzaz, A., Benkirane, S., and Azrour, M. (2023). An Efficient Network Intrusion Detection Model for IoT Security Using K-NN Classifier and Feature Selection. *Multimedia Tools and Applications*, 82, 23615–23633.

[3] Gubbi, J., Buyya, R., Marusic, S., and Palaniswami, M. (2012). Internet of Things (IoT): A Vision, Architectural Elements, and Future Directions. arXiv, abs/1207.0203.

[4] Aslan, Ö., Aktuğ, S. S., Ozkan-Okay, M., Yilmaz, A. A., and Akin, E. (2023). A Comprehensive Review of Cyber Security Vulnerabilities, Threats, Attacks, and Solutions. *Electronics*, 12, 1333.

[5] Alotaibi, B. (2023). A Survey on Industrial Internet of Things Security: Requirements, Attacks, AI-Based Solutions, and Edge Computing Opportunities. *Sensors (Basel, Switzerland)*, 23, 7470.

[6] Su, J., Vargas, D. V., Prasad, S., Sgandurra, D., Feng, Y., and Sakurai, K. (2018). Lightweight Classification of IoT Malware Based on Image Recognition. In *2018 IEEE 42nd Annual Computer Software and Applications Conference (COMPSAC)* (pp. 664–669).

[7] Wu, X., Duan, R., and Ni, J. (2024). Unveiling Security, Privacy, and Ethical Concerns of ChatGPT. *Journal of Information and Intelligence*, 2, 102.

[8] Zhu, S., Deng, X.-H., Zhang, W., and Zhu, C. (2023). Image Encryption Scheme Based on Newly Designed Chaotic Map and Parallel DNA Coding. *Mathematics*, 11, 231.

[9] Rahmani, H., Shetty, D., Wagih, M., *et al.* (2023). Next-Generation IoT Devices: Sustainable Eco-Friendly Manufacturing, Energy Harvesting, and Wireless Connectivity. *IEEE Journal of Microwaves*, 3, 237–255.

[10] Dworkin, M., Sonmez Turan, M., and Mouha, N. (2023). Advanced Encryption Standard (AES), Federal Inf. Process. Stds. (NIST FIPS), National Institute of Standards and Technology, Gaithersburg, MD, https://doi.org/10.6028/NIST.FIPS.197-upd1.

[11] Zhang, F., Guo, Y., Pu, M., *et al.* (2023). Meta-Optics Empowered Vector Visual Cryptography for High Security and Rapid Decryption. *Nature Communications*, 14, 1946.

[12] Moustafa, N., Keshk, M., Debie, E. S., and Janicke, H. (2020). Federated TON_IoT Windows Datasets for Evaluating AI-based Security Applications. In *International Conference on Trust, Security and Privacy in Computing and Communications. 2020 IEEE 19th International Conference on Trust, Security and Privacy in Computing and Communications (TrustCom)* (pp. 848–855).

[13] Lu, T., Wang, L., and Zhao, X. (2023). Review of Anomaly Detection Algorithms for Data Streams. *Applied Sciences*, 13, 6353.

[14] Ravikumar, K. K., Surendhar, P., Rubi, J., Jyothi, G., Ambikapathy, A., and Vasuki, R. (2022). Human Computer Interface Application for Emotion Detection Using Facial Recognition. In *2022 IEEE International Conference on Current Development in Engineering and Technology (CCET).*

[15] Tiwari, A., Dhiman, V., Iesa, M. A. M., Alsarhan, H., Mehbodniya, A., and Shabaz, M. (2021). Patient Behavioral Analysis with Smart Healthcare and IoT. *Behavioural Neurology*, 2021, 4028761.

[16] Deng, H., and Li, X. (2022). Anomaly Detection via Reverse Distillation from One-Class Embedding. In *2022 IEEE/CVF Conference on Computer Vision and Pattern Recognition (CVPR)* (pp. 9727–9736).

[17] Ashraf, I., Park, Y., Hur, S., *et al.* (2023). A Survey on Cyber Security Threats in IoT-Enabled Maritime Industry. *IEEE Transactions on Intelligent Transportation Systems*, 24, 2677–2690.

[18] He, K., Kim, D. D., and Asghar, M. R. (2023). Adversarial Machine Learning for Network Intrusion Detection Systems: A Comprehensive Survey. *IEEE Communications Surveys & Tutorials*, 25, 538–566.

[19] Kuhn, M., and Johnson, K. (2013). *Applied Predictive Modeling*. Berlin: Springer Science & Business Media.

[20] Sun, N., Ding, M., Jiang, J., *et al.* (2023). Cyber Threat Intelligence Mining for Proactive Cybersecurity Defense: A Survey and New Perspectives. *IEEE Communications Surveys & Tutorials*, 25, 1748–1774.

[21] Gunder, A. (2022). Security Monitoring and Management based on the Use of IBM QRadar SIEM System. *Modern Information Security*, 2, doi:10.31673/2409-7292.2022.020614.

[22] Agarkar, A., Karyakarte, M., and Agrawal, H. (2020). Post Quantum Security Solution for Data Aggregation in Wireless Sensor Networks. In *2020 IEEE Wireless Communications and Networking Conference (WCNC)* (pp. 1–8).

[23] Dhaygude, P., Dhulshette, N., Ganjale, O., Sawant, U., and Navghare, P. (2023). A Review Paper on Different Deep Learning Methodologies for User and Entity Behavior Analytics (UEBA). *International Journal of Research Publication and Reviews*, 4, 3757–3762.

[24] Liu, Z., Zhou, Y., Xu, Y., and Wang, Z. (2023). SimpleNet: A Simple Network for Image Anomaly Detection and Localization. In *2023 IEEE/CVF Conference on Computer Vision and Pattern Recognition (CVPR).*

[25] Martinez, L. S. (2022). *Behavioral Analytics*. Encyclopedia of Big Data.

[26] Moustafa, N., Keshk, M., Debie, E. S., and Janicke, H. (2020). Federated TON_IoT Windows Datasets for Evaluating AI-based Security Applications. In *2020 IEEE 19th International Conference on Trust, Security and Privacy in Computing and Communications (TrustCom)* (pp. 848–855).

[27] Liu, Z., Zhou, Y., Xu, Y., and Wang, Z. (2023). SimpleNet: A Simple Network for Image Anomaly Detection and Localization. In *2023 IEEE/CVF Conference on Computer Vision and Pattern Recognition (CVPR)* (pp. 20402–20411).

[28] Saeed, S., Suayyid, S. A., Al-Ghamdi, M. S., Al-Muhaisen, H., and Almuhaideb, A. (2023). A Systematic Literature Review on Cyber Threat Intelligence for Organizational Cybersecurity Resilience. *Sensors (Basel, Switzerland)*, 23, 7273.

[29] Zheng, Z., Xie, S., Dai, H., Chen, X., and Wang, H. (2018). Blockchain Challenges and Opportunities: A Survey. *International Journal of Web Grid Services*, 14(4), 352–375.

[30] Tan, X., Zhang, Y., Cao, J., Sun, K., Zhang, M., and Yang, M. (2022). Understanding the Practice of Security Patch Management across Multiple Branches in OSS Projects. In *Proceedings of the ACM Web Conference 2022*.

[31] Flores, M., Heredia, D., Andrade, R., and Ibrahim, M. (2022). Smart Home IoT Network Risk Assessment Using Bayesian Networks. *Entropy*, 24, 668.

[32] Aslan, Ö., Aktuğ, S. S., Ozkan-Okay, M., Yilmaz, A. A., and Akin, E. (2023). A Comprehensive Review of Cyber Security Vulnerabilities, Threats, Attacks, and Solutions. *Electronics*, 12, 1333.

[33] Deb, K., and Jain, H. (2014). An Evolutionary Many-Objective Optimization Algorithm Using Reference-Point-Based Nondominated Sorting Approach, Part I: Solving Problems with Box Constraints. *IEEE Transactions on Evolutionary Computation*, 18, 577–601.

Chapter 11

Secure data protection in federated learning for IoT

Jagjit Singh Dhatterwal[1], Kuldeep Singh Kaswan[2], Kiran Malik[3], Sumit Singh Dhanda[4] and K. Babu[5]

Abstract

Federated learning (FL) when introduced into the Internet of Things (IoT) offers remarkable progress in terms of distributed intelligence, which is harmed by remarkable privacy and security concerns. In Chapter 1, the writer starts with a brief description of IoT and the security challenges that come with it before introducing FL with the main aim of making data more private by keeping it decentralized. The basic concepts of FL are explained as well as its differences to more conventional methods of machine learning for IoT networks as well as the advantages it comes with. That is why the chapter is devoted entirely to privacy issues that can be attributed directly to FL, including data privacy threats and possible attacks, including inference and model inversion attacks. It then looks at several measures of reducing these privacy risks. From the security perspective, the threats included adversarial attacks, compromise of model update systems, and participants with malicious intents. The review of state-of-the-art methods for privacy protection, including differential privacy, homomorphic encryption, and secure multiparty computation (MPC), is conducted for their applicability to FL-IoT. Additionally, the chapter also includes security measures such as strong aggregation techniques, the adoption of the blockchain in FL, and the incorporation of TEEs. Real-life examples of privacy and security in FL are also presented in the form of paradigms such as healthcare, smart cities, and industrial IoT. The discussion goes further to some regulatory and ethical implications which include corresponding with the data privacy laws as well as some ethical considerations. Last but not least, future directions for privacy preservation in FL and novel

[1]Department of Artificial Intelligence and Data Science, Koneru Lakshmaiah Education Foundation, India
[2]School of Computer Science and Engineering, Galgotias University, India
[3]Department of Computer Science and Engineering (AIML), GL Bajaj Institute of Technology and Management, India
[4]School of Computer Science and Engineering, IILM University, India
[5]Department of Computational Intelligence, SRM Institute of Science and Technology, India

advancements that would define the future of FL security in IoT networks are further discussed in this chapter.

Keywords: Adversarial attacks; Federated learning; Security vulnerabilities; Homomorphic encryption

11.1 Introduction

The Internet of Things (IoT) is the interconnection of devices, sensors, and systems that are embedded in our everyday lives and able to connect and exchange data for the purpose of creating value from various applications ranging from smart homes to industrial automation systems [1]. Nevertheless, the developments in the capabilities of IoT devices have created major security issues. Such devices normally work in environments with less computational capacity, and in many circumstances, the devices do not have well-implemented security measures, thus making them prone to various attacks including data theft, denial of service attacks, and unauthorized access. The IoT networks added even more problems because the number of connected devices is diverse and large, making it challenging to maintain data security across such a large range of devices and platforms. Security is now of utmost importance due to data sensitivity that is characteristic of IoT devices' production data for instance health records and critical infrastructure data [2].

Federated learning (FL) is identified to be suitable and feasible to address the issues of data privacy and security in IoT [3]. Also, FL contrasts with other centralized machine learning models whereby data has to be collected and processed in a central server. FL empowers the training of machine learning models in edge devices [4]. This keeps data on the local pieces of equipment, which contributes to the low vulnerability of getting a hostile takeover of data and the like. FL aggregates model updates from multiple devices, and prevents any sensitive information from leaked to other entities during the process of training. This method is especially useful in IoT space where data protection and security collective characteristics are highly valued [5].

However, similar to any other learning approach, federated learning applied in IoT comes with its own set of privacy and security problems. However, when the updates of the model are aggregated from many devices, the system is still vulnerable to different adversarial attacks wherein the intention of the attackers is to manipulate the learning process with wrong information. Furthermore, even if data stays at local devices, the transmission of the model updates in the network might be exposed to the attack or manipulated if not encrypted sufficiently. The need to protect the privacy of the data and the updates of the model is thus a significant determinant of FL to IoT applications. The significance of these aspects cannot be overemphasized since the absence of federated learning systems may have adverse effects, for instance, data breaches and vulnerable systems on which the said advantages are meant to be granted [6].

The main purpose of this chapter is to discuss the existing and potential privacy and security issues in federated learning in the IoT context. It will extend the discussion on the FL, FL system potential threats and risks, privacy-preserving methods, security approaches that can be incorporated into the FL system, and FL case studies for IoT real-world applications. In concluding this chapter, the reader will develop a clear vision of the need to incorporate enhanced security and privacy enforcement within federated learning systems for IoTs while at the same time getting an evaluation of the current issues and research findings in this area.

11.2 Fundamentals of federated learning

FL is a machine learning technique in which multiple client devices or local servers with their own data samples can learn a model cooperatively without sharing the data. Unlike a traditional centralized learning model in which the data is gathered in a central server for training, FL allows data to stay on the devices that produced it but coordinate model training across the network. This decentralized approach also solves major privacy issues since the data is stored on devices, reducing the potential for hacks and data protection regulation compliance [3].

The fundamental concepts of FL are data local processing, local model updating, and privacy protection. In this setup, each device learns the updates to the model on its data and only those updates are exchanged back to a central server, which applies it to update its version of the model. This process is iterative, and the global model is updated several times through localized training and newer model integration.

11.2.1 Federated learning differs from traditional machine learning

Thus, federated learning largely differs from conventional machine learning in terms of data and model training. In a traditional approach to machine learning, data is collected from a variety of sources and stored in a centralized location such as a data center to create the model. This approach presents several privacy issues, especially in cases where personal information is involved such as medical records or account data as it attracts more vulnerabilities to hacking or cyber criminals due to centralized data.

Conversely, FL deploys the training process in a decentralized network, where models can be trained in the devices that produce data. This effectively eliminates the contamination of data to a central server hence minimizing the likelihood of data leakage. Also, FL is inherently built to be invariant to data heterogeneity, and it can work on the non-i.i.d data distribution across various devices, which is inherent to the IoT setting. This is done through techniques such as federated averaging, where model updates from different devices are averaged to provide an average global model (Table 11.1).

Table 11.1 Federated learning (FL) differs from traditional machine learning (TML)

Aspect	**Traditional machine learning (TML)**	**Federated learning (FL)**
Data storage	Centralized: data is collected and stored in a central server.	Decentralized: data remains distributed across multiple devices.
Data privacy	Requires transferring data to a central location, raising privacy concerns.	Data never leaves the local devices, enhancing privacy.
Training process	The model is trained on a centralized dataset at a single location.	The model is trained across multiple devices, and only model updates are shared.
Scalability	Limited by the size and capacity of the central server.	More scalable as it can leverage distributed devices without moving data.
Communication overhead	Lower communication overhead as all data is in one place.	Higher communication overhead due to the need for frequent updates from multiple devices.
Security concerns	Vulnerable to data breaches and attacks on the central server.	Requires additional security mechanisms to protect model updates and prevent malicious attacks.
Infrastructure requirements	Requires a powerful central server for storing and processing data.	Relies on distributed infrastructure, reducing the need for centralized resources.
Data heterogeneity	Assumes homogeneous data, often preprocessed uniformly.	Handles heterogeneous data from different devices, which may have different distributions and formats.
Computation location	Computation is centralized at the server.	Computation occurs locally on each device, reducing the need for centralized processing.
Latency and real-time updates	Delays may occur due to data transfer to a central server.	Enables real-time updates on local devices, with periodic global model aggregation.
Model personalization	Models are typically generalized for all users.	Allows for personalized models tailored to specific devices or users.
Energy consumption	Higher energy consumption at the central server.	Energy consumption is distributed across multiple devices.
Regulatory compliance	More challenging to comply with data protection regulations (e.g., GDPR) due to centralized data storage.	Easier to comply with regulations since data stays on local devices.
Deployment complexity	Easier deployment with centralized infrastructure.	More complex deployment due to the need to coordinate multiple devices.
Risk of data bias	Risk of bias if the central dataset is not representative of all users.	Reduces bias by training on diverse datasets across different devices.

11.2.1.1 Components and architecture of federated learning

The architecture of federated learning consists of several key components: The central server, client devices, and especially communication protocols.

- Central server: Therefore, the central server manages and guides the entire training system. It is used to start the global model and also plays the coordinating role in the communication of Client devices. It also makes model updates from the clients, adds them together, and uses them to update the overall model of the server [7].
- Client devices: These are the entities distributed in structure at decentral, for example, smartphones or IoT devices or edge servers that contain the local data and are involved in the training phase. Every client performs the updates for the global model using data inherent to it, and all it sends to the central server are the suggested update parameters, not the data themselves.
- Communication protocols: The general communication process needs to be efficient as well as secure in the framework of FL. To this effect, protocols are formulated to ensure that the model updates are transferred securely from the clients to a central server or vice versa and in the process leveraging on differential privacy or secure aggregation methods among others to enhance data protection. The FL process typically follows a cyclical flow: The baseline model is shared at the central server to the respective clients, training of the model occurs locally and the improved models are sent back to the server where the different updates are combined to improve the global model.

11.2.1.2 Benefits and challenges of FL in IoT

Federated learning offers several benefits, particularly in the context of IoT:

- Enhanced privacy: The principle of FL ensures that data is not transmitted to centralized servers hence achieves the best results in the applications that prioritize the privacy of information such as the healthcare application [8].
- Reduced latency and bandwidth usage: FL eliminates the need for data to be sent to a central server and hence the data transfer consumes lesser network bandwidth and has less latency compared to the other traditional modes of data transfer, which is very important for the reduced resources that are available in IoT devices.
- Scalability: FL can be efficient in the scalability across various devices, which is perfect for IoT-based networks with a massive population where centralized processing would not be viable.

However, FL also introduces several challenges:

- Data heterogeneity: The data that IoT devices produce may be generally heterogeneous and they possibly could not be identically distributed. This heterogeneity can prove to be challenging when training the model as it may necessitate intricate aggregation methodologies to guarantee that the global model performs well on all devices.

- Communication overhead: While FL minimizes the requirement of raw data exchange, the procedure of disseminating model updates may create a large volume of communication traffic in extensive networks.
- Security risks: Hence, with the help of FL achieves privacy FL is not free from security risks. The source data for training the model may contain bad data, entered by malicious participants, or adversarial attacks can be delivered to the global model. Therefore, adequate security measures must be put in place to minimize the above risks.

11.3 Privacy concerns in federated learning for IoT

FL can be described as a novel technology of the ML that provides the devices with the ability to cooperatively train models with no raw data. This is more so in the IoT environment where large data volumes are produced incessantly most of which are of sensitive nature. However, as it seems to offer a great solution, FL also raises major privacy issues that need to be solved for it to be both secure and trustworthy.

11.3.1 Data privacy in IoT networks

In IoT networks, devices are producers and consumers of massive data which encompass personal and sensitive data. This approach is a centralized technique of doing machine learning, centralizing this data on a single server raises a significant privacy concern. Federated learning addresses the transparent risk by keeping the data only on the devices and thus decreasing the disclosure of private details. But even in FL, there are still many opportunities for privacy violations, for instance, due to the necessity to regularly exchange information between the devices and the servers, including model update information. Essentially, the metadata, the gradients, or possibly the model parameters that are exchanged in those updates might contain information about the underlying data that needs to be protected; thus, privacy preservation is a major issue in FL concerning IoT.

$$P(M(D_1) \in S) \leq e^{\epsilon} \cdot P(M(D_2) \in S) \tag{11.1}$$

where:

- D_1 and D_2 are two datasets differing by only one element,
- M is a randomized algorithm (or mechanism) applied to the datasets,
- S is any possible output of the mechanism, and
- ϵ (epsilon) is the privacy parameter, controlling the level of privacy, with smaller values providing stronger privacy guarantees.

11.3.2 Privacy risks in federated learning models

What FL avoids but does not completely solve is the privacy issue. A most basic requirement, it should be noted, might be that models trained in the federation can still assimilate and memorize specific features from the local databases. This is often described as unintended memorization, where for instance, the training of a global model may result in the model having snippets of information belonging to a specific device that can be retrieved by anyone. Furthermore, the process of training and aggregating models in FL can be vulnerable for privacy issues like data reconstruction where the adversaries seek to construct the original data from the shared model updates.

$$\epsilon = \log\left(\frac{\Pr[\mathcal{M}(D_1) = O]}{\Pr[\mathcal{M}(D_2) = O]}\right) \tag{11.2}$$

where:

- ϵ is the privacy loss parameter, indicating the level of privacy,
- $\mathcal{M}$ is the mechanism (e.g., the federated learning model update process),
- D_1 and D_2 are neighboring datasets (differing by one individual's data), and
- $\Pr[\mathcal{M}(D) = O]$ is the probability that the mechanism $\mathcal{M}$ produces output O when applied to dataset D.

11.3.3 Potential attacks on privacy in FL

There are several privacy threats that can be explained in the context of FL for IoT, which are explained below. For example, in Inference attacks, the attacker gets the ability to infer information concerning the train data from the trained model or its updates. Another serious threat is the so-called model inversion attacks where the malicious parties utilize the gradients or the model parameters to recreate the input data thus violating privacy. In addition, in a cooperative learning environment such as FL, the adversaries can perform poisoning attacks where they feed the training with incorrect information that results in the development of wrong models that may disclose personal information.

11.3.4 Techniques for enhancing privacy in FL for IoT

To avoid such invasion of privacy, different methods have been suggested and are also under development. Of all the approaches, differential privacy is the most commonly discussed one, in which data or model updates are perturbed to prevent the identification of the specific data points that are contributing to the training process to be of potential interest to a malicious party. Another technique is called homomorphic encryption in which processing of the information can be done without decryption, and thus the information shall remain private all the time. They also use secure MPC to allow for the computation of parties' data that must remain private to individual parties. Moreover, privacy improvement is incorporated in federated averaging like applying secure aggregation protocols to protect individual contributions to model updates during the aggregation process in FL for IoT.

$$f'(x) = f(x) + \text{Lap}\left(\frac{\Delta f}{\epsilon}\right) \tag{11.3}$$

where:

- $f(x)$ is the original function applied to the data x,
- $f^{'}(x)$ is the function output with added noise,
- $\mathrm{Lap}(\frac{\Delta f}{\epsilon})$ is the noise drawn from the Laplace distribution with scale parameter $\frac{\Delta f}{\epsilon}$,
- Δf is the sensitivity of the function $f(x)$, representing the maximum change in the output when a single data point is added or removed, and
- ϵ is the privacy budget, controlling the trade-off between privacy and accuracy.

11.4 Security challenges in federated learning for IoT

Several security issues emanate from the incorporation of FL in the IoT. The IoT devices are inherently weak because of their lower computational ability, highly distributed structure, and poor security standards most of the time. These vulnerabilities are not alien to federated learning systems for the simple reason that the architecture of FL exposes a relatively larger attack surface, making it prone to several security threats. Some of its questions are data integrity, confidentiality, and trust in the participating devices. By integrating IoT's large network with FL's distributed model, the risks of unauthorized access to the network, data manipulation, or attacks on the learning process multiply significantly.

11.4.1 Adversarial attacks on FL

The security challenges in FL in IoT comprise adversarial forms of attack. These attacks could be in the form of poisoning attacks and evasion attacks. In poisoning attacks, the adversaries maliciously compromise the shared dataset and or the parameters updated by other participants or provide wrong information that reduces the accuracy of the model. For example, a few malfunctioning IoT devices could feed false information to the FL process so resulting in wrong predictions or biased results throughout the network. Evasion attacks, in contrast, imply that the adversaries work with the input data so that the global model will make wrong predictions in the inference phase. Due to this, it is hard to monitor and curb these adversarial actions as one can blend in with other well-intending parties/entities [9].

$$w_{t+1} = w_t + \eta \cdot \left(\frac{1}{N} \sum_{i=1}^{N} \Delta w_i^t + \alpha \cdot \Delta w_j^{\mathrm{adv}} \right) \tag{11.4}$$

where:

- w_{t+1} is the updated global model,
- η is the learning rate,
- N is the number of participating clients,
- $\Delta w_j^{\mathrm{adv}}$ is the adversarial update sent by the malicious client j, and
- α is the weight or impact of the adversarial update.

11.4.2 Security vulnerabilities in FL model updates

These new changes in the model of federated learning mean that there is another layer of insecurity. FL is based on the assumption that multiple participants send updates to contribute towards the construction of the global model, thus a malicious participant is capable of sending updates that may be detrimental to the construction of the global model. Such updates could be as innocent as the "backdoor" trick where the model is changed slightly in such a way that it becomes malicious under certain conditions, or the poisoning attempts aimed at the general weakening of the model's performance. There is no unified administration in FL, which makes the identification of these attacks challenging; the use of more conventional security solutions such as encryption might not be sufficient to address these threats. To control these risks, there are various measures like having robust aggregation mechanisms recommended securely [10].

11.4.3 Protecting against malicious participants in FL

As mentioned earlier, containing participants with ill intentions in federated learning is a complex process, and it entails the following strategies. First, the use of reliable aggregation approaches can assist in eliminating some of the noisy updates that reflect possible malicious actions. There exists a set of algorithms such as Krum and Byzantine-robust aggregation methods, which protect against adversarial inputs by accommodating most of the benign updates, giving no place to outliers [11]. Furthermore, using secure MPC will also enable the data and model updates to be protected in case some of the parties are controlled by the attackers. Another approach has to do with applying blockchain technology to record model updates and learning process steps to create an immutable record. These measures, then, along with constant observation and using alarms for out-of-the-normal range results, offer real improvement to the security of federated learning in IoT.

The trimmed mean $\widehat{m}$ is computed as follows:

- Sort the model updates: $\mathcal{M}_{\text{sorted}} = \{m_{(1)}, m_{(2)}, \ldots, m_{(n)}\}$, where $m_{(i)}$ denotes the i-th smallest update.
- Trim a percentage of the smallest and largest values. Let τ be the trimming percentage, then trim $\lceil \tau \cdot n \rceil$ updates from both ends of the sorted list.
- Compute the mean of the remaining updates:

$$\widehat{m} = \frac{1}{n - 2\lceil \tau \cdot n \rceil} \sum_{i=\lceil \tau \cdot n \rceil + 1}^{n - \lceil \tau \cdot n \rceil} m_{(i)} \tag{11.5}$$

Here, $\lceil \cdot \rceil$ denotes the ceiling function, which rounds up to the nearest integer.

11.5 Privacy-preserving techniques in federated learning

Data privacy and security are inevitable in FL-IoT to guarantee that the data of clients do not leak, while models are updated collectively. Most IoT devices produce personal and sensitive data, and therefore privacy should be preserved when using FL frameworks. Some mechanisms that have been created to deal with privacy issues in FL include differential privacy, homomorphic encryption, secure MPC, and federated averaged with privacy augmentation.

11.5.1 Differential privacy in FL for IoT

Differential privacy is a formalism that makes it possible to keep the privacy of each record while training the model's gradients or data. In the context of FL for IoT, differential privacy plays a part in preserving the privacy of an individual device during the training of the model since no individual device contribution can be distinguished from the overall model updates. This approach also reduces inference attacks where the attacker tries to derive other information out of the model. Differential privacy provides advantages in IoT networks that produce personal information such as in the healthcare or smart housing setting [12].

11.5.2 Homomorphic encryption in FL

It makes computations possible to be done directly on encrypted data without the need to decrypt them. In FL, this technique allows IoT devices to contribute their part in training models while protecting their raw data. The updates sent to the other devices are securely encrypted before they are sent to the central server where the encrypted updates can undergo operation and the result encrypted is then sent back to the devices. This makes sure that the data is only decrypted when it is being used hence making sure that the data is more secure. However, homomorphic encryption is a strong tool for conquering privacy issues in FL although it incurs computational costs, which can be problematic on the constrained IoT gadgets [13].

11.5.2.1 Krum aggregation function:

Given $\mathcal{M} = \{\mathbf{m}_1, \mathbf{m}_2, \ldots, \mathbf{m}_N\}$ as the set of model updates from N participants, where each $\mathbf{m}_i$ is a vector representing the update from participant i, the aggregated model update $\mathbf{m}_{agg}$ is calculated as follows:

- Compute pairwise distances: compute the Euclidean distance between each pair of model updates:

$$d_{ij} = \|\mathbf{m}_i - \mathbf{m}_j\|_2 \text{ for } i \neq j \tag{11.6}$$

- Calculate distance sums: for each model update $\mathbf{m}_i$, compute the sum of distances to all other model updates:

$$\text{sum}_i = \sum_{j \neq i} d_{ij} \tag{11.7}$$

- Select the Krum update: identify the update $\mathbf{m}_i$ with the smallest sum of pairwise distances. This update is considered the least affected by outliers.

$$\mathbf{m}_{\text{agg}} = \mathbf{m}_k \text{ where } k = \underset{i}{\text{argmin}}\,\text{sum}_i \tag{11.8}$$

11.5.3 Secure multiparty computation in FL

Another method employed to safeguard privacy in FL is secure MPC, which is a technique that enables multiple parties to collectively perform a computation over inputs of the multiple parties, without revealing the input to the other parties in the computation. In IoT-based FL or federated learning, MPC helps all the devices to train a single model with the cooperation of other devices without sharing data among them. This is made possible by the use of cryptographical techniques that enable only the final output, for instance, the aggregated model to be shared with the public and other individuals' inputs to remain hidden. MPC is more beneficial, especially in the case where data sensitivity is paramount, and therefore applicable for industrial IoT where data belonging to different industries cannot be disclosed [14].

$$\text{Aggregated Update} = \frac{1}{N}\sum_{i=1}^{N} \text{Update}_i \tag{11.9}$$

where:

- Aggregated Update is the result of securely aggregating updates from multiple participants.
- N is the total number of participating devices or parties.
- Update $_i$ is the update from the i-th participant.

11.5.4 Federated averaging with privacy enhancements

Federated averaging is one of the typical methods in FL in which local models from IoT devices are averaged to build a unified model. To increase privacy in this process several steps can be applied, including gradient clipping and noise addition. These improvements mentioned above ensure that, in the aggregated model, no individual device has an excessively prominent or distinguishable effect. The privacy of FL is also a crucial issue as federated averaging combined with differential privacy or secure aggregation protocols can help to enhance the system's privacy [15].

11.6 Security mechanisms in federated learning for IoT

FL is rather new, especially to IoT, and thus, its security has to be paramount as the technology progresses in implementation. In this section, various security measures used in FL for IoT are discussed comprehensively as explained below: strong aggregation mechanisms, blockchain mechanism, TEE, and FL with encrypted model update.

11.6.1 Robust aggregation techniques in FL

In FL, the most important operation of the system is the accumulation of local model updates while deciding about the overall security of the system. Efficient methods of aggregating the updates are specially constructed to prevent the adverse effects of the betrayal updates. One of them is Krum, along with Trimmed Mean, both of which were developed to minimize the impact of outliers in the averaging process. For instance, Krum chooses the update that is the most similar, in terms of the distance, to the other updates. This means throwing away a certain percentage of the highest and lowest averages before averaging [11]. It also strengthens the FL system against attacks for instance model poisoning, in which operators might want to manipulate models in a way that would affect their performance significantly.

11.6.2 Blockchain for secure federated learning

Blockchain technology also presents the possibility for FL systems to create a decentralized and secure ledger of information which acts as a secure record-keeping base for the aggregation of the models. As for the application of FL in blockchain, blockchain can also be used to store and verify the model update whereby all the transactions are thus traceable and secure [16]. Due to blockchain's ability to guard against fraud and provide reliable methods for independently verifying and validating the changes in models, they can successfully automate the overall federated learning process with the help of smart contracts. It also provides safety for the exchange of information while also strengthening the reliability of the system.

11.6.3 Trusted execution environments for FL

Trusted execution environments (TEEs) are secure areas within a processor that guarantee the confidentiality and integrity of computations. Special TEEs, like Intel's SGX or ARM's TrustZone that were mentioned in section TE, can be utilized in FL to shield data throughout the model training and aggregation phases. The computations can be carried out in TEEs, which affords a space for processing without leaving the safety of TEEs that are free from the rest of the system; hence, the model and data are kept safe from the attacks as noted by [17]. Attached to the isolation of federated learning processes, TEEs increase the FL framework's overall security since even if the environment is invaded, the secure enclave will not be affected.

11.6.4 Federated learning with encrypted model updates

Privacy preservation appears to be significantly critical in protecting the communication channel between the federated clients and the central server through encryption. HE for example is a technique through which computations may be made on encrypted data without necessarily decrypting the data. This implies that model updates can be accurately computed over several nodes without revealing the data or even the updates [18]. Homomorphic encryption is another safeguard that protects the privacy of the information even when it undergoes aggregation. Another form of encryption can be used to protect the federated learning process, for instance, secure MPC, which is used to compute a function where multiple parties contribute but none of them gets to see the others' inputs.

11.7 Case studies and real-world implementations

In the field of healthcare, federated learning is a new concept to accomplish model training from the patient data without compromising the patient data privacy. Healthcare IoT devices include wearable health monitors and smart medical equipment among others, and they are producers of large volumes of sensitive information [7]. The centralized model of data processing as it is used in conventional mainframe computing is vulnerable to unauthorized user access and other forms of fraud. To reduce these risks, FL allows for model updates rather than data accumulation with the training done locally on the device.

11.7.1 Privacy and security in federated learning for healthcare IoT

One of the applications is using FL to make predictions about the further health conditions of patients with the help of data from wearable gadgets [8]. Two of the original proposals of FL have been used for training models concerning the prediction of cardiovascular incidents based on data from several distributed sensors. In this case, differential privacy approaches are applied to prevent the data used for training from leaking patient's specific information. Model updates that are communicated between the local devices and the central server are protected using homomorphic encryption, to ensure confidentiality of the data.

11.7.2 Federated learning in smart cities: privacy and security perspectives

Great numbers of IoT devices in smart cities include traffic cameras, sensors of the environment, and smart meters to improve urban management and services. Federated learning is continuously implemented to process information from such gadgets without the need to gather it in one place. It is for example possible to use FL to improve traffic conditions based on some lights and camera data without disclosing the footage.

Privacy in smart cities is of paramount importance because these networks store, receive, and analyze considerable information about people's lives and whereabouts. FL addresses this by the fact that raw data is kept locally while on the shared parts, only models' updates are shared. Confidentiality of data is maintained throughout aggregation and model update operations using methods such as MPC and federated averaging with privacy-preserving methods. Further, to guarantee the purity and originality of the model updates, ideas of the blockchain are expected to be incorporated to record the data used as well as the training process.

11.7.3 Security challenges in industrial IoT federated learning

In IIoT, federated learning is used to improve the reliability of predictions for maintenance and process control as well as protect industrial data. However, IIoT systems pose such a threat since there are fatal consequences of the data and model's incorrect information. For instance, an adversary might feed wrong model updates into the system that subsequently hampers the efficiency of the predictive maintenance mechanisms, resulting in expensive machinery breakdowns.

To be able to effectively address these issues, suitable security measures have to be put in place. Some methods include anomaly detection and robust aggregation algorithms that help in determining and resolving any impact that may come out of adversarial model updates. Also, to ensure data security in transit, the use of secure communication protocols is adopted in communicating between IoT systems and their central servers. Encryption and access control mechanisms provide a solution to this problem in that only entities that have been permitted access can offer information for federated learning sessions.

11.7.4 Case study: federated learning for smart homes with privacy and security considerations

Smart homes form an emerging market in which federated learning is used to improve voice-activated home functions and convenience while maintaining confidentiality. For instance, FL is employed in creating customer-specific home automation solutions depending on data gathered from smart home appliances like thermostats, lights, and security cameras.

An example of an application of FL is in enabling power management of smart homes. The FL models leverage information obtained from smart meters and home appliances to detect users' preferences in consumption and alter energy settings to reflect the same. Data privacy is considered kept as users' data are not granted beyond their homes. Thus, local models are trained, and the updates are sent to enhance the global models. Such practices as differential privacy and federated learning with encrypted model updates preserve the privacy of the data.

11.8 Regulatory and ethical considerations

The General Data Protection Regulation (GDPR) is regarded as one of the most robust and strict data privacy laws that influence the application of FL in IoT systems to a vast level. GDPR requires organizations to assure the privacy of the data and respect the data subjects' corresponding rights. Regarding FL in IoT, it implies adopting techniques that take into consideration data minimization, purpose limitation, and data subjects' rights.

11.8.1 GDPR and data privacy regulations impact on FL for IoT

Firstly, federated learning is inherently compatible with GDPR as data are processed and do not have to be centralized. FL preserves raw data on local devices and sends only updates on models or some statistical parameters. This way makes sure that an organization does not expose personal data. But GDPR is not only about applying technologies; it also needs strong policies and procedures for the proper protection of the data at all stages of processing. These are as follows: getting prior consent from the user, user information about the usage of data, and protecting data through data protection by design and by default.

However, GDPR comprises the right of the individual to object to the processing of the data, the right to erasure of the data, and the right to receive his/her data. These rights when applied in a system that utilizes federated learning can be cumbersome to apply as it requires methods on how to manage and erase data across the network while still preserving the model consistency.

11.8.2 Ethical concerns in federated learning for IoT

Important ethical issues concerning the implementation of federated learning for IoT do not stop at the legal perspective. Specific ethical considerations include, whether the models are equitable, to what extent the decision-making process is obvious, and possible unknown prejudices. As FL is based on models trained from data coming from different sources, there can be an issue whereby local biases are accumulated in the model's outputs. To address these issues some constant measures would be needed to promote fairness, accountability, and transparency in the FL process.

Moreover, federated learning requires building trust with participants due to the way it is implemented. Ethical implementation includes: making sure that the participants bear the intervention standard of data and the training of models. The adoption and use of machine learning therefore requires transparency relating to how the models are trained, how the data is secured, and how the results are disseminated to build trust among stakeholders and users.

A different one is the risk of the misuse of the federated learning models that may pose a threat to privacy. At the same time FL can improve privacy, the possibility of misuse of the technology is possible. It is as equally important that federated learning systems are engineered to be resistant to malicious use cases and adversarial conditions in order to be implemented ethically.

11.8.3 Compliance with privacy laws in IoT federated learning

It is thus apparent that relying on privacy laws in the federated learning of IoTs is a complex business. Apart from GDPR, there are other acts of law for instance the California Consumer Privacy Act (CCPA) and the Health Insurance Portability and Accountability Act (HIPAA) that may apply depending on the context or location where the application of the technologies will occur.

Any organization adopting FL for IoT operations must guarantee that the organization's systems align with the Data Protection Acts since the system should facilitate data subject rights, which encompass data access, correction, and deletion. This includes the information architecture of federated learning environments where different data access and deletion procedures are compliant with legal frameworks.

Furthermore, privacy has to be audited and assessed from time to time to ensure that it is in compliance with the laws in place. This covers a range of factors such as how data is gathered, analyzed, and disseminated, and relevant control to be installed to guarantee data accuracy and security.

11.8.4 Implement FA ethically

To ensure the ethical implementation of federated learning in IoT, several strategies should be adopted:

- Transparency and communication: provide a clear understanding of how the federated learning systems work, how the data is protected, and how the models are trained. Make users of the smart systems able to easily read about data processing and model training, and always make them have control of data.
- Bias mitigation: propose methods that will ensure the reduction of biases in the federated learning models. This also involves ensuring that the models being used are of a fair nature and that there is a proper assessment of fairness and that there are adequate measures of handling any identified bias.
- Adversarial attack prevention: add precautions to prevent the adversarial effects on the federated learning systems. These are issues such as using very credible aggregation techniques and secure communication methodologies to protect against any vices.
- Stakeholder engagement: consult with the users, regulators, and ethical committees to ensure that the federated learning systems are ethical and address all the ethical issues to do with privacy and security.
- Continuous monitoring and improvement: design guidelines for federated learning system maintenance to identify opportunities for its enhancement. Updating and revisiting policies and practices in an organization ought to be regular but should be done in response to new challenges in the privacy and security of data and information assets and to ensure that the organization complies with the current regulations and ethical trends.

11.9 Future directions and emerging trends

FL is still in its early stages, and thus as developments are made, increasing amounts of solutions are being implemented for privacy-preserving in federated learning. The most significant of the developments is differential privacy which quantifies the privacy loss by adding noise to the obtained data or model updates in a manner that hides an individual's contribution while maintaining the overall trend. The mechanisms of differential privacy are even more developed, and this is important to make a better trade between privacy and utility as the data collected in IoT situations is of different sensitivity levels.

11.9.1 Advances in privacy-preserving federated learning

Hierarchy of homomorphic encryption schemes: Another key advancement in homomorphic encryption is a technique developed in cryptography whereby computations can be carried out on the encrypted data without prior decryption. This technique is still being fine-tuned for lesser computational overhead; thus, making it more relevant and implementable to resource-limited IoT devices. Secure MPC is also emerging and allows multiple parties to conduct computations over all the inputs submitted by the parties while being hidden from third parties. These methods are being incorporated into FL frameworks with a view of improving the security of data shared within the frameworks while at the same time maintaining collaborative learning concepts.

Machine learning and artificial intelligence are crucial for the enhancement of the security risks of FL [1]. There are ongoing works on the application of AI-based methods for detecting suspicious changes or updates of models which possibly imply such threats as poisoning attacks or model inversion. Such systems utilize ML algorithms to observe data flow and identify patterns and state estimations in real time to detect and prevent threats.

Further, new automated approaches for adversarial training are being developed whereby models are trained with typical inputs and also with adversarial examples to improve their resilience to attacks. This is proactive since it aids in constructing FL systems that are robust to different adversarial interference thereby enhancing security. AI and ML are also employed to create real-time protective strategies and countermeasures to newer threats that can occur in federated learning systems ([4] *Electrification*).

Several developing technologies are on the waitlist to improve the security of federated learning systems. The use of a distributed ledger in the form of blockchain is being investigated for it can offer secure and tamper-proof registers of models' new changes and data exchanges. Due to the integration of FL and blockchain technology, it is possible to log all the processes, which are carried out during collaborative learning, and guarantee that they are secure from unauthorized changes. This integration can also enable smart contracts to govern privacy and security compliance requirements within federated learning solutions.

It is important to mention TEEs, which are, for example, Intel's SGX or ARM's TrustZone, as the solution for creating secure enclaves for computations. TEEs guarantee that even if the FL server itself, or some of the participating nodes are malicious, the computations will be kept within a safe space. Moreover, there have been improvements in the secure hardware platforms to enable FL operations with improved security for the data and the models going through the process.

Concerning the future prospects, the following tendencies could be identified for federated learning in IoT networks in further work. Multiplication of controlled end devices and data sources: FL systems are going to face more and more IoT devices. This will provide FL with significant support in terms of distributed computing and optimization algorithms for efficient scalability while taking into consideration the issues of privacy and security.

It is believed that more adoption of edge computing with FL will be observed to update data more near the source. This integration will help to decrease the latency and increase the efficiency of FL systems in the Internet of Things applications such as self-driving cars and smart power stations.

In addition, cross-domain collaborations will be required for the progressive development of FL technology. All stakeholders in this and other similar spaces including academia, industry, and regulatory agencies will push for the formulation of standard practices, code of ethics, and processes for engraining the principles of FL, security, and privacy seamlessly in IoT systems.

11.10 Conclusion

This research work on the thematic area of "Integration of FL in IoT" offers what can be considered a revolutionary way of managing the huge number of data produced by IoT devices in a way that ensures privacy and security. Chapter 4 has focused on the most important aspects of privacy and security in FL for IoT and the peculiarities and prospects of their interaction. FL diversifies from conventional machine learning in the sense that it permits the decentralization of data processing and hence presents less exposure to privacy violations which is characteristic of centralized data storage. However, it also comes with fresh types of risks including adversarial attacks and the risk of model updates by a malicious party. To overcome these challenges, the use of strong privacy-preserving methods such as differential privacy, homomorphic encryption, and secure MPC has to be adopted in addition to secure features such as blockchain and a TEE. It is seen that the case studies depicted here illustrate how FL can be implemented in different IoT contexts including healthcare and smart cities along with addressing privacy and security concerns in large-scale applications. Furthermore, the regulatory and ethical factors highlighted raise concern about the need to adhere to data protection laws and ethics in IU to safely and responsibly implement FL in IoT systems. Finally, when considering future advancements, developments in AI, ML, and secure technologies pave the way for solutions to the problems arising with FL in IoT. Further investigations and development are needed for more effective and efficient secure federated learning methods that can support IoT networks' growth in the future. Finally, the authors conclude that the integration of FL in the growth of IoT largely depends on the achievement of a better balance between privacy and security as the foundation for the IoT which is to be built progressively to be more secure and credible.

References

[1] Kaswan, K. S., Dhatterwal, J. S., Kumar, N., and Lal, S. (2023). Artificial intelligence for financial services. In *Contemporary Studies of Risks in Emerging Technology, Part A* (pp. 71–92). Leeds: Emerald Publishing Limited.

[2] Sicari, S., Rizzardi, A., Grieco, L. A., and Coen-Porisini, A. (2015). Security, privacy and trust in Internet of Things: The road ahead. *Computer Networks*, *76*, 146–164. https://doi.org/10.1016/j.comnet.2014.11.008.

[3] Baliyan, A., Dhatterwal, J. S., Kaswan, K. S., and Jain, V. (2022). Role of AI and IoT techniques in autonomous transport vehicles. In *AI Enabled IoT for Electrification and Connected Transportation* (pp. 1–23). Singapore: Springer Nature.

[4] Kaswan, K. S., Dhatterwal, J. S., and Kumar, A. (2023). *Swarm Intelligence: An Approach from Natural to Artificial*. New York: Wiley.

[5] Li, T., Sahu, A. K., Talwalkar, A., and Smith, V. (2020). Federated learning: Challenges, methods, and future directions. *IEEE Signal Processing Magazine*, *37*(3), 50–60. https://doi.org/10.1109/MSP.2020.2975749.

[6] Yang, Q., Liu, Y., Chen, T., and Tong, Y. (2019). Federated machine learning: Concept and applications. *ACM Transactions on Intelligent Systems and Technology (TIST)*, *10*(2), 1–19. https://doi.org/10.1145/3298981.

[7] Dhatterwal, J. S., Kaswan, K. S., and Preety. (2021). Intelligent agent-based case base reasoning systems build knowledge representation in COVID-19 analysis of recovery of infectious patients. In *Applications of Artificial Intelligence in COVID-19* (pp. 185–209) Singapore: Springer Nature.

[8] Dhatterwal, J. S., Kaswan, K. S., and Kumar, N. (2023). Telemedicine-based development of M-health informatics using AI. In *Deep Learning for Healthcare Decision Making* (pp. 159–178). Gistrup: River Publishers.

[9] Bagdasaryan, E., Veit, A., Hua, Y., Estrin, D., and Shmatikov, V. (2020). How to backdoor federated learning. In *Proceedings of the International Conference on Artificial Intelligence and Statistics (AISTATS)*, pp, 2938–2948. Retrieved from https://proceedings.mlr.press/v108/bagdasaryan20a/bagdasaryan20a.pdf.

[10] Sun, Z., Kairouz, P., Suresh, A. T., and McMahan, B. (2019). Can you really backdoor federated learning? *Advances in Neural Information Processing Systems (NeurIPS)*, pp. 2515–2525. Retrieved from https://papers.nips.cc/paper/2019/file/f8b976b7b7253ed2b410c0122e8b1cc3-Paper.pdf.

[11] Blanchard, P., El Mhamdi, E. M., Guerraoui, R., and Stainer, J. (2017). Machine learning with adversaries: Byzantine tolerant gradient descent. In *Advances in Neural Information Processing Systems (NeurIPS)* (pp. 119–129). Retrieved from https://papers.nips.cc/paper/2017/file/f4b9ec30ad9f68f89b29639786cb62ef-Paper.pdf.

[12] Abadi, M., Chu, A., Goodfellow, I., *et al.* (2016). Deep learning with differential privacy. In *Proceedings of the 2016 ACM SIGSAC Conference on Computer and Communications Security* (pp. 308–318). https://doi.org/10.1145/2976749.2978318.

[13] Gentry, C. (2009). A fully homomorphic encryption scheme. Stanford University. Retrieved from https://crypto.stanford.edu/craig/craig-thesis.pdf.

[14] Bonawitz, K., Ivanov, V., Kreuter, B., *et al.* (2017). Practical secure aggregation for federated learning on user-held data. In *Proceedings of the 2017 ACM SIGSAC Conference on Computer and Communications Security* (pp. 1175–1191). https://doi.org/10.1145/3133956.3133982.

[15] McMahan, H. B., Moore, E., Ramage, D., Hampson, S., and Arcas, B. A. Y. (2017). Communication-efficient learning of deep networks from decentralized data. In *Artificial Intelligence and Statistics* (pp. 1273–1282).

[16] Xu, J., Xu, Q., Li, Y., and Jiang, Y. (2019). A survey on blockchain-based federated learning. *Journal of Computer Science and Technology*, *34*(6), 1094–1111.

[17] Costan, V., and Devadas, S. (2016). Intel SGX explained. In *2016 IEEE Symposium on Security and Privacy*. Retrieved from https://scholar.google.com.

[18] Gentry, C. (2009). Fully homomorphic encryption using ideal lattices. In *Proceedings of the 41st Annual ACM Symposium on Theory of Computing* (pp. 169–178). https://doi.org/10.1145/1536414.1536440.

Chapter 12

Case studies and application for energy-efficient federated learning in IoT

M. Nalini[1], *S. Jayasri*[1], *S. Nagammai*[1] *and Daniel Arockiam*[2]

Abstract

The purpose of this case study is to demonstrate how energy-efficient federated learning (FL) may be applied to improve the sustainability of distributed machine learning inside the Internet of Things (IoT) ecosystem. Because IoT devices have limited energy resources, traditional FL in IoT environments frequently faces difficulties, necessitating the development of improved methods. This research looks at several energy-saving strategies, including lightweight model architectures, adaptive resource management, and communication-efficient algorithms. We show how these methods may be applied in real-world IoT contexts, leading to longer-lasting devices and more efficient networks without sacrificing the accuracy of the learning models, through realistic applications and simulations. The results emphasize how crucial it is to incorporate energy-conscious techniques into FL systems to guarantee scalable and long-lasting IoT installations.

Keywords: Federated learning; Energy efficiency; Internet of Things (IoT); Edge computing; Machine learning on IoT; Smart healthcare; Smart cities; Traffic management

12.1 Introduction

An explosion of data is being generated at the edge of the network due to the growth of Internet of Things (IoT) devices. By enabling decentralized machine learning across various devices, protecting data privacy, and minimizing the need for centralized data storage, federated learning (FL) provides an answer. However, the resource limitations common to IoT devices such as low processing power, limited battery life, and limited communication bandwidth hinder FL's adoption in

[1]Electronics and Instrumentation, Sri Sairam Engineering College, India
[2]Computer Science Engineering, Amity University, India

IoT environments. Energy-efficient federated learning techniques have been developed to address these issues, with an emphasis on maximizing IoT device energy use throughout the FL process.

With an emphasis on a smart home setting, this case study investigates the use of energy-efficient federated learning in a practical Internet of Things setting [1]. To save energy consumption without reducing learning performance, the study looks into a number of techniques, such as adaptive resource management, effective communication protocols, and model compression. The outcomes show that these methods may significantly boost IoT device battery life without affecting the federated learning model's accuracy and durability.

The case study's conclusions highlight how energy-efficient federated learning has the potential to revolutionize IoT networks by making machine learning solutions scalable and sustainable. The implementation of these tactics in many Internet of Things scenarios, like smart cities, healthcare, and industrial automation, may result in notable progress in the efficacy and efficiency of IoT systems, opening the door for a wider acceptance of FL in settings with limited resources.

12.2 Application

The goal of the developing discipline of energy-efficient FL in the context of the IoT is to lower the energy consumption related to machine learning tasks that are dispersed among multiple IoT devices.

The following are some important methods and applications:

1. Hybrid model for energy-efficient intelligent transportation systems (ITS)
2. Multiagent federated reinforcement learning (MARL)
    - Horizontal federated reinforcement learning (HFRL)
    - Vertical federated reinforcement learning (VFRL)
    - Green IoT infrastructure

12.2.1 Hybrid model for ITS with low energy consumption

The suggested hybrid architecture builds an ITS that is scalable and energy-efficient by fusing green IoT technology with federated learning. The essential elements are as follows: IoT devices sensor-equipped cars and roadside apparatuses participate in federated learning and gather traffic data. By eliminating the requirement for data transport to central servers, this allows data processing at the edge, saving bandwidth and energy. Federated learning framework IoT devices work together to train a common model without sharing raw data. Devices are used for local model training, a central server handles model aggregation, and devices receive the global model back. In addition to protecting privacy, this lowers energy consumption during data transfer [2]. Eco-friendly IoT infrastructure: The ITS is driven sustainably by renewable energy sources, such as electric vehicle charging stations and solar-powered roadside devices. As a result, there is less dependency on fossil fuels, and the transportation system becomes greener.

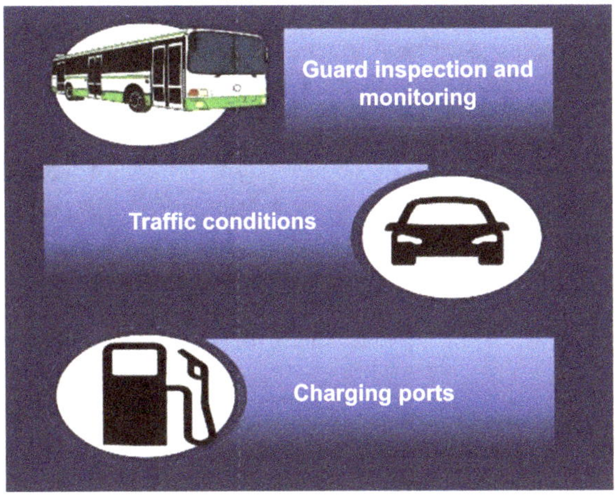

Figure 12.1 Energy intelligence for transportation system

The hybrid model optimizes energy use using a number of techniques. Locality of data: Federated learning reduces data transit and related energy costs by enabling edge processing. Route optimization: To optimize routes in real time and lower emissions and fuel consumption, machine learning examines traffic patterns. Integration of renewable energy: By reducing the need for fossil fuels, IoT devices and infrastructure are powered by solar, wind, and other green energy sources. Using IoT devices and federated learning, this scalable and adaptable architecture creates an energy-efficient ITS while protecting user privacy. Figure 12.1 shows the case study on smart cities shows that the hybrid model is workable in an actual setting.

12.2.2 Multiagent federated reinforcement learning

In this framework, agents operate in either horizontal or vertical arrangements:

Horizontal federated reinforcement learning (HFRL): Here, agents are geographically distributed but face similar decision-making tasks. They independently learn from their environments and share model updates rather than raw data, improving learning efficiency and policy optimization. Vertical federated reinforcement learning (VFRL): In this setup, agents interact with a shared environment but have limited visibility of the state. Each agent's actions influence the global environment, and they receive local rewards based on their observations, adding complexity to the learning process.

Multiagent federated reinforcement learning (MARL): The concepts of federated learning and reinforcement learning are combined to enable multiple agents to learn collaboratively while maintaining data privacy. In situations like driverless cars, where several agents must coordinate their efforts to maximize safety and traffic flow, MARL is very helpful. While addressing issues like nonstationarity and scalability in dynamic situations, strategies like adaptive client selection and effective communication are essential for improving the performance of MARL systems.

A customized framework called horizontal federated reinforcement learning (HFRL) combines the ideas of reinforcement learning (RL) and FL to improve the effectiveness of numerous agents learning in distant contexts while protecting data privacy.

Important ideas in HFRL agent distribution: Although agents in HFRL are dispersed geographically, they must make comparable decisions. Every agent functions inside its own environment, collecting information on its own and using reinforcement learning to try to optimize its policy. Data privacy is addressed by HFRL, which enables agents to gain knowledge from their local data without disclosing it to a central server. Agents share model updates rather than raw data, which lowers the possibility of data leaks [3]. Collaborative learning: By combining their experiences, agents work together to increase the efficiency of their learning. Each agent can converge towards optimal policies faster than they could separately thanks to this collective knowledge.

Sample effectiveness: When it comes to reinforcement learning, agents frequently need a lot of interactions with their surroundings in order to learn well. This problem is addressed by HFRL. Through the sharing of insights and model parameters, HFRL facilitates faster learning.

Application scenarios: HFRL is very helpful in the following situations where several agents function independently but in comparable environments: Autonomous vehicles: Autonomous vehicles are capable of sharing information about traffic patterns with one another to enhance overall navigation techniques and learning the best driving tactics based on local traffic conditions.

Smart grids: Distributed energy resources can share methods for energy distribution and consumption while optimizing their operations based on local demand. Robotics: To increase their overall efficiency, multirobot systems can learn to coordinate their activities in jobs like warehouse automation or search and rescue. Difficulties: Despite its benefits, HFRL has difficulties with things like the following: Nonstationarity: Because environments are dynamic, it is possible for nonstationary conditions to arise, which makes learning more difficult for agents as they adjust to shifting circumstances.

Communication overhead: Even though HFRL eliminates the need to transport raw data, there is still overhead associated with communicating model updates, especially in contexts with limited connectivity.

In conclusion, Figure 12.2 shows the HFRL is a promising strategy that focuses on protecting privacy and fostering cooperative learning among agents performing related tasks to improve reinforcement learning capabilities in distributed contexts.

12.2.3 Vertical federated reinforcement learning

A framework known as vertical federated reinforcement learning (VFRL) combines reinforcement learning with federated learning to allow numerous agents with various observation and action areas to work together to learn in a shared

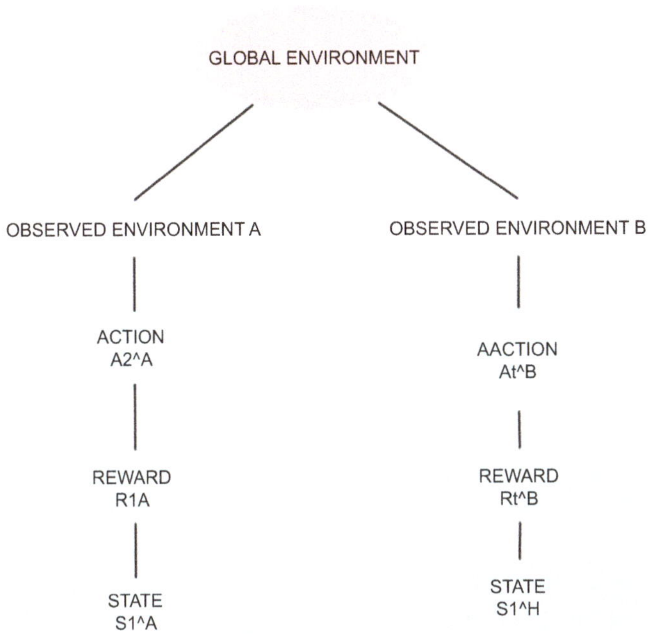

Figure 12.2 Global environment

environment while maintaining data privacy. Agents engage with a global environment E in VFRL, but before acting, each agent Fi gets a local partial observation Oi [4]. The salient features are as follows: The global state space S and action space A is made up of the sum of the state/observation and action spaces of all agents, which may vary (Oi $\neq$ Oj, Ai $\neq$ Aj). The same global environment, E (Ei = Ej = E), governs all agency operations.

The global state space ($\sum$Oi = S) is formed by the collective local observations of agents. Unlike horizontal federated learning, which divides datasets vertically by features, VFRL splits agents based on their local state spaces as viewed from the global environment. In VFRL, two categories of agents are defined: (1) Agents focused on making decisions: They can use their local state and action spaces to engage with the surroundings. (2) Agents focused on providing support: Without coming into close contact with the environment, provide supplemental knowledge to aid in decision-making. Agents can work together to learn by exchanging experiences using VFRL without sacrificing privacy. It can be used in situations such as driverless cars when agents need to coordinate their activities to maximize global objectives despite having restricted visibility.

12.2.4 Green IoT infrastructure

Eco-friendly Internet of Things infrastructure: The networking, software, and hardware elements that support environmentally friendly and energy-efficient

Internet of Things systems are collectively referred to as the "green IoT infrastructure." Among the crucial components of green IoT infrastructure:

Energy-efficient hardware low-power IoT devices: IoT nodes and sensors are designed with energy-efficient processors, memory, and radio components to decrease power consumption. Low-power wide-area network (LPWAN) technologies, such as NB-IoT and LoRaWAN, are two examples.

Energy harvesting: By scavenging ambient energy from sources like solar, thermal, vibration, or radio frequency, IoT devices with energy harvesting capabilities can lessen their dependency on batteries. Green data centers: IoT cloud infrastructure can have a lower carbon footprint by being designed with high-density servers, effective cooling systems, and renewable energy sources.

Green data analytics: Developing machine learning algorithms and data processing pipelines optimized for energy efficiency to extract insights from IoT data with minimal computational overhead. Virtualization and containerization: Leveraging virtualization technologies to consolidate workloads and enable dynamic resource allocation, improving utilization and reducing energy waste.

Low-power wide-area networks (LPWAN): Low-power LPWAN technologies like LoRaWAN and NB-IoT enable long-range, low-bitrate IoT connectivity with minimal power requirements, ideal for battery-powered devices. Sustainable software energy-aware middleware: IoT middleware platforms that optimize resource allocation and task scheduling to minimize energy usage while meeting performance requirements.

Software-defined networking (SDN): SDN enhances overall efficiency by enabling dynamic optimization of network resources and protocols to adjust to shifting energy availability and traffic patterns. Fog/edge computing: By processing IoT data using edge devices closer to the source, less data needs to be transmitted to the cloud, saving network energy. Integration of renewable energy IoT devices with built-in solar panels can be used as solar-powered IoT nodes to collect energy from the sun and run without the need for batteries or grid power.

Wind-powered base stations: This technique lessens dependency on grid electricity by using wind turbines to power cellular base stations and LPWAN gateways. Hybrid energy systems: combining energy storage with a variety of renewable energy sources, such as solar and wind, to deliver dependable, environmentally friendly power for Internet of Things infrastructure. IoT systems can dramatically lessen their environmental effect while retaining functionality and scalability by implementing these green solutions.

Nevertheless, issues with energy storage, effective data processing, and coordinated administration of diverse green infrastructure still need to be resolved.

12.2.5 Smart home automation

The way we maintain energy efficiency in our houses is being revolutionized by smart home automation. We can optimize energy use while maintaining privacy by utilizing federated learning approaches and integrating IoT devices. The main ideas and advantages of federated learning in the Internet of Things for energy-efficient smart home automation will be discussed in this chapter. Smart home appliances and energy savings: In smart homes, IoT devices are essential for improving energy efficiency. These networked gadgets gather information, pick up user behaviors, and modify their functions to save energy consumption [5]. One of the main contributions of IoT devices is as follows: gathering data in real time on user behavior, environmental factors, and energy use gaining knowledge of user preferences and making adjustments to maximize energy use by combining different home systems, such as security, lighting, and HVAC security for unified, effective operation. Smart home IoT gadgets: Federated learning for smart home automation that preserves privacy. By using federated learning, decentralized Internet of Things devices can train models collectively without sending raw data to a central server. Federated learning is a collaborative machine learning technique.

This methodology protects the privacy of data while enabling the development of precise, customized models. The following is how the federated learning method for smart home automation operates: A global model is initialized by a central server and disseminated to participating IoT devices. Every IoT device computes a local model update and trains the model with its local data. The central server receives the local update from the IoT device and combines it with updates from all the devices to modify the global model. The cycle is repeated until convergence, with the updated global model being transmitted back to the IoT devices. Federated learning preserves privacy while utilizing the combined intellect of Internet of Things devices by storing data locally on devices and only exchanging changes to the model. Advantages of federated learning for energy-efficient smart home automation: There are numerous important advantages of integrating federated learning and IoT devices in smart home automation.

Improved performance: Federated learning makes it possible to create personalized models that adjust to the preferences of specific users, increasing their performance and level of happiness. Added value: As smart home systems get smarter, they can learn important things from IoT data and open up new possibilities. Federated learning increases the precision and effectiveness of energy management models by utilizing a variety of IoT data sources. Flexible scalability: Scalability is improved by parallel processing among several IoT devices without putting too much strain on a central server. Considerable energy savings: Research indicates that in comparison to conventional systems, smart appliances, HVAC, security systems, and thermostats can cut energy use by 12%–34%.

Energy-saving measures derived from automated smart homes IoT-enabled smart home automation, along with federated learning, is a promising way to increase energy efficiency without compromising privacy. Through data collection, user preference learning, and operational adaptation, these systems can drastically cut down on energy use and environmental effects. Future developments in federated learning and IoT will likely lead to even more advancements in intelligent in sustainable home automation.

12.2.6 Smart grid management

The term "smart grid management" describes how digital technology is incorporated into the conventional electrical system to improve the sustainability, dependability, and efficiency of energy distribution. With the use of two-way communication between utilities and customers, this updated grid makes it possible to monitor and control energy flow in real time. The integration of renewable energy sources, enhanced demand response, and increased grid resilience against outages are all made possible by the smart grid. Important elements of advanced metering infrastructure (AMI) for smart grid management: Smart meters that offer real-time data on electricity consumption are part of AMI. Utilities are able to track use trends, identify power outages, and have direct conversations about energy use with customers thanks to these meters. This transparency can result in cost savings for consumers by enabling them to more efficiently regulate their energy consumption.

Reaction schemes demand response programs, which let utilities modify customer energy use during times of peak demand, are made possible by smart grids [6]. Utilities can avoid overloads and preserve the stability of the grid by offering incentives to customers to minimize their usage during certain periods. This is especially crucial when incorporating fluctuating renewable energy sources like solar and wind. Distributed energy resources (DER) resources, such as battery storage systems and rooftop solar panels, can be integrated with the smart grid.

By producing and storing energy locally, these resources can lessen the need for centralized power plants and increase the resilience of the grid. Efficient management of these resources is essential to maximize energy distribution and save expenses. Smart grid management's advantages: Increased reliability is achieved as smart grid technologies enable faster identification and isolation of outages, ensuring a more dependable electricity supply. When there are disturbances, automated systems can redirect electricity, reducing downtime and guaranteeing that vital services continue to run in an emergency. Enhanced effectiveness: Smart grids increase overall efficiency by minimizing transmission losses and optimizing energy flow. Accurate energy supply and demand matching can be achieved by improved load forecasting and management made possible by real-time data analytics.

Sustainability of the environment: Reducing greenhouse gas emissions is made easier by the smart grid's ability to integrate renewable energy sources. Global sustainability goals are supported by smart grid management, which facilitates cleaner energy production and energy efficiency. Customer self-determination: Smart grid technologies give customers the knowledge and resources they need to control how much energy they use. Customers may monitor their consumption patterns, modify usage during peak hours, and even engage in energy trading with smart meters and mobile applications.

This results in cost savings and increased involvement in energy management. An important development in the production, distribution, and use of electricity is smart grid management. Reliability, efficiency, and sustainability are improved by smart grids through the use of digital technologies and mutual communication. The adoption of smart grid technology will be essential for meeting future energy demands and tackling the difficulties posed by climate change as the energy environment continues to shift

12.2.7 Predictive maintenance in industrial IoT

IoT predictive maintenance employs sensors, data analytics, and machine learning to anticipate when equipment is likely to break. It is a proactive approach to equipment repair. IoT predictive maintenance reduces costs and downtime by allowing maintenance to be planned only when necessary by continuously monitoring the health and performance of the equipment. Important elements of IoT sensors and devices for predictive maintenance: Sensors measure parameters like vibration, temperature, and energy usage to keep an eye on the condition of the equipment. Data transmission [7]: A central cloud-based system receives sensor data wirelessly for analysis. Central data storage: Analytics can see trends and anticipate problems thanks to the storing of historical sensor data. Machine learning algorithms examine sensor data to find hidden patterns and anticipate equipment problems before they arise. This technique is known as predictive analytics.

IoT predictive maintenance examples production: IoT-enabled factory equipment keeps an eye on temperature, energy consumption, and vibration. Analytics provide targeted maintenance by anticipating problems like bearing wear or motor overheating. Wind farms: Gearboxes, blades, and wind speed are all monitored by sensors on wind turbines. Potential issues such as bearing wear are detected by predictive algorithms prior to their influence on power generation. City infrastructure: Internet of Things sensors track the flow and pressure in pipes, anticipating obstructions and identifying leaks before they cause problems. Power plants: Temperature, pressure, and vibrations are tracked on machinery such as turbines and transformers. Analytics make preventive maintenance possible by forecasting possible breakdowns. IoT predictive maintenance benefits enhanced use of assets: Anticipating problems helps to save downtime and makes remote asset management more efficient.

Extended asset life: Early problem detection keeps equipment from breaking down and prolongs its life. Increased output and smoother manufacturing lines are the results of preventing failures. Lower maintenance costs: The total cost of maintenance is decreased by preventing needless repairs and malfunctions. Enhanced technician productivity: IoT identifies issues, freeing personnel to concentrate on specific fixes. In conclusion, IoT predictive maintenance uses machine learning, data analytics, and sensors to anticipate equipment breakdowns before they happen. IoT predictive maintenance maximizes asset utilization, prolongs equipment life, boosts productivity, and lowers costs by enabling proactive maintenance.

12.2.8 Smart agriculture

IoT, AI, robotics, and other cutting-edge technologies are integrated into smart farming, or smart agriculture, to improve farming productivity, sustainability, and efficiency. It seeks to maximize crop output and quality while maximizing resource use. Instances of intelligent farming precision: Agriculture enables farmers to administer water and fertilizers precisely when needed by using sensors to measure soil temperature, moisture content, and nutrient levels. Drones: Used for crop monitoring, these aerial vehicles collect information on soil and plant health, allowing for prompt remediation. Automated machinery: By completing tasks without human assistance, autonomous tractors and harvesters lower labor costs and boost productivity. Smart greenhouses: They optimize growth conditions, use less energy, and increase agricultural yields through the use of sensors and climate control systems.

12.2.9 Traffic management system

To increase farming production, sustainability, and efficiency, smart farming, also known as smart agriculture, integrates IoT, AI, robotics, and other cutting-edge technology. It aims to maximize resource utilization while maximizing agricultural yield and quality. Examples of intelligent agriculture precision: Agriculture uses sensors to assess the temperature, moisture content, and nutrient levels of the soil, allowing farmers to apply water and fertilizers precisely when needed [8]. Drones: Applied to crop monitoring, these unmanned aerial aircraft provide data on plant and soil health, enabling timely restoration.

Automated machinery: Self-sufficient tractors and harvesters save labor expenses and increase output by executing tasks without human intervention. Smart greenhouses: By utilizing sensors and temperature control systems, they maximize growth conditions, consume less energy, and boost agricultural yields.

Dynamic message signs (DMS): Enable better route planning by informing drivers in real time about traffic patterns, collisions, or road closures. Electronic toll collecting: By automating toll collecting, systems such as E-ZPass improve traffic flow and minimize wait times at toll booths. With the use of sensors and cameras, incident detection systems automatically detect accidents or malfunctions, allowing emergency services to respond quickly. Together, Figure 12.3 explains the technologies that improve urban mobility and make transport systems safer and more effective.

12.2.10 Healthcare management system

Features and advantages of the healthcare management system (HMS): An all-inclusive software program called HMS automates and simplifies a number of healthcare operations processes. It combines information from several departments, including that of physicians, patients, lab results, medical supplies, insurance, bills, appointments, and reports. Here are some essential attributes and advantages of an HMS: Invoicing offers a variety of payment methods to cut down on human labor and improve the clinic's standing. Permits the instantaneous verification of insurance eligibility. Patient scheduling provides many alternatives for scheduling that enable doctors and patients to communicate effectively. Uses notifications, follow-

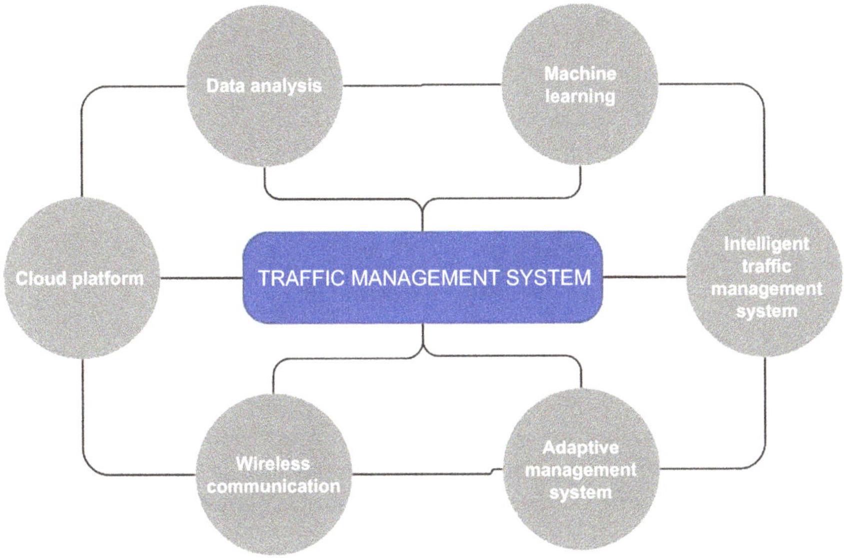

Figure 12.3 Traffic management system

ups, and reminders to assist in keeping track of appointments and medical records [9]. Reporting and analytics for data employs cognitive analytics to find gaps in performance. Support for clinical decision-making makes sure clinical and operational decision-making procedures are accurate and efficient. Information security puts in place centralized measures to fend against security risks including cyber-attacks and illegal access. An edge over competitors establishes the hospital as a cutting-edge medical facility of the future. Patient contentment aids in obtaining excellent ratings by offering an exceptional patient experience. All of this data is gathered by an HMS and is available to authorized people in all departments in a single, digital location. Figure 12.4 raises total patient care and satisfaction, decreases errors, and increases communication.

12.2.11 Environmental monitoring

To determine the effects of both natural processes and human activity, environmental monitoring entails evaluating and analyzing environmental conditions. It includes a range of kinds, such as Environmental monitoring types: Air quality monitoring: This technique helps to track air pollution levels and inform public health measures by measuring pollutants such as PM2.5 and PM10 using sensors. Water quality monitoring involves routinely analyzing bodies of water to find pollutants, protecting aquatic habitats, and providing clean drinking water. Monitoring soil: Assesses the quality and degree of pollution of the soil, which is important for managing ecosystems and agriculture. Noise monitoring: To control noise pollution, sound levels in cities are measured. As an example, air quality sensors are installed in urban areas to continuously measure pollution levels.

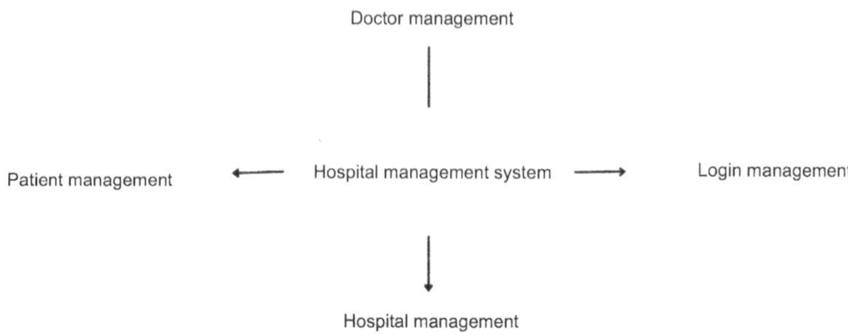

Figure 12.4 Hospital management system

Environmental authorities use water testing kits to examine the quality of river water. Relevance monitoring: The environment is essential for maintaining human health, safeguarding ecosystems, and efficiently managing natural resources.

12.3 Case study

12.3.1 Implementing federated learning in a smart home IoT network

Background:
An increasing number of IoT gadgets, including security cameras, speakers, thermostats, and more, are being added to "smart" houses. Large volumes of data are produced by these devices, and this data can be utilized to optimize network performance, enhance user interfaces, and enable customized services. Concerns with privacy, latency, and bandwidth arise from the requirement that this data be transferred to a central server for processing in traditional centralized machine learning techniques.

Challenge:
To minimize bandwidth usage, cut latency, and improve the intelligence of a smart home Internet of Things system without compromising customer privacy.

Objective:
Implementing a FL system within an IoT network for smart homes is the aim of this case study. It allows for collaborative learning across devices without requiring raw data sharing with a central server.

Approach:
System agriculture:
Devices: The system is made up of a variety of Internet of Things (IoT) devices, each with local computing power, including speakers, cameras, and smart thermostats.

Edge nodes: Certain gadgets function as edge nodes, gathering information from neighboring smart home devices.

Central server: Although it does not obtain raw data from the devices, a central server manages the federated learning process.

12.3.1.1 Federated learning workflow

Local model training: Every Internet of Things device gathers local data and uses it to train a machine learning model. For instance, temperature data from a smart thermostat may be used to train a model that forecasts consumer comfort levels.
Model consolidation: The locally trained models are transmitted to the central server, where federated averaging and other approaches are used to aggregate them into a global model.
Update on the model: After receiving the aggregated parameters, the global model is updated and delivered back to the IoT devices for additional local training.
Process iteratively: Iteratively repeating this approach allows the global model to improve over time based on contributions from every device.

12.3.1.2 Security and privacy

Data privacy: Since raw data never leaves the device, user information is kept confidential.
Encryption: To avoid manipulation or eavesdropping, communication between devices and the central server is encrypted.
Differential privacy: To further protect user data, techniques like differential privacy can be used to introduce noise into model updates.

Implementation (smart thermostat use case):
Data: Historical usage patterns, user preferences, and temperature readings.
Local model: Every thermostat develops a model based on user behavior and outside variables (such as the weather) to forecast the ideal temperature settings.
Global model: To produce a global model that more accurately forecasts the ideal settings for diverse circumstances, the central server compiles the models from every thermostat.
Result: As the system learns to anticipate users' demands without compromising privacy, users experience increased comfort with lower energy use.
Enhanced accuracy of the model: Compared to models trained on individual devices or centralized models trained on shared raw data, the global model performs better in terms of anticipating user preferences and optimizing energy consumption.
Enhanced privacy: Because their data stays on their devices, users are less likely to have privacy worries and are therefore more inclined to trust the system.
Reduced bandwidth usage: The bandwidth needed for communication is greatly decreased because only model updates rather than raw data are sent. The ability to scale Because federated learning is scalable, more devices can join the network without overburdening the communication channels or the central server.
Contact overhead [10]: Since there is less data transfer required than with traditional systems, there may be some overhead associated with the need for frequent contact between devices and the central server.

Model aggregation complexity: Combining models that have been trained on many devices can be challenging, particularly if the data distributions on those devices differ considerably (i.e., non-IID data).

Device heterogeneity: Different IoT devices may be capable of processing information differently, which could impact the training procedure. It can be required to use strategies like model compression and effective training methods to support devices with lower processing capacity.

Conclusion:

Federated learning in an IoT smart home system offers a workable way around the problems with latency, bandwidth, and privacy that come with centralized machine learning techniques. Enabling safe model aggregation and local model training allows smart homes to improve their intelligence and responsiveness without sacrificing user privacy. This case study illustrates how federated learning may revolutionize IoT networks and open the door to more effective and safe solutions.

12.3.1.3 Energy optimization in HVAC system using federated learning

Background:

In smart buildings, HVAC (heating, ventilation, and air conditioning) systems are some of the biggest energy users. Improving occupant comfort and cutting energy use requires optimizing their operation. Centralizing HVAC control, however, can be energy-intensive and fails to take into consideration the distinctive features of different buildings.

Challenge:

The challenge is to use less energy in HVAC systems without relying on energy-intensive centralized control systems, all the while preserving occupant comfort.

Goal:

Integrate federated learning into HVAC systems throughout a number of smart buildings to maximize energy efficiency, cut expenses, and preserve comfort levels.

Approach:

The architecture of the system:

HVAC Systems: The HVAC system in every building is outfitted with sensors and local processing units for monitoring and regulating air quality, humidity, and temperature.

Building management system (BMS): The BMS is in charge of the building's overall energy management.

Central coordinator: To maximize HVAC performance throughout the network, a central server compiles models from various buildings.

Federated process for learning: Local model training: The HVAC system in each building uses data from its users to train a model that predicts the best configurations for both occupant comfort and energy efficiency.

Model aggregation: A central coordinator receives the local models, which are then combined to create a global model that aids in the optimization of HVAC settings throughout all buildings.
Iterative process: New information is continuously added to the global model. Data from the buildings, thereby increasing its accuracy.
Adaptive control: By using real-time data, the global model enables HVAC systems to be controlled adaptively, which lowers energy usage.
The comfort of occupants: The system makes sure that energy savings do not come at the expense of comfort of occupants.

Finding:
Energy reduction: Optimal HVAC performance results in significant energy savings.
Increased comfort: Because environmental requirements are predicted more precisely, occupant comfort is either maintained or even increased.
Lower expenditures: More efficient HVAC operation results in lower energy expenditures for building operators.

12.3.1.4 Optimizing electric vehicle charging networks with federated learning

Background:
Energy management has both opportunities and challenges with the growing popularity of electric vehicles (EVs). To prevent grid overloads, lower energy prices, and guarantee the effective use of renewable energy sources, EV charging network optimization is essential [11]. However, energy-intensive and privacy-risky centralized data processing for EV charging optimization can be used by EV owners.

Challenge:
To limit system stress, lower energy costs, and protect user privacy by optimizing EV charging schedules and energy distribution.

Objective:
To improve energy distribution and charging schedules, save energy consumption, and maintain grid stability, use federated learning to an EV charging network.

Approach:
1. System architecture:
EV charging stations: that have local processing capacity installed to assess energy consumption and charging trends.
EVs: Every car tracks its own usage patterns, energy requirements, and charging habits.
Without gaining access to raw data, the Central Server manages the FL process by combining local models from charging stations.
2. Federated learning workflow:
Local model training: To anticipate the best charging periods and energy needs, charging stations use data from connected EVs to train local models.

Model aggregation: To generate a global model that can be utilized to improve the entire network, local models are transmitted to the central server and combined.
Iterative improvement: To increase accuracy and efficiency, the global model is repeatedly improved as additional data is gathered.

3. Energy efficiency:
Load balancing: By distributing the load among charging stations, the global model lowers peak demand and guarantees the effective use of renewable energy.
Cost reduction: The model lowers energy expenditures for grid operators as well as EV owners by optimizing charging schedules.

Result:
Optimized charging: By distributing energy more effectively, the EV charging network lowers peak loads and total energy usage.
Preservation of privacy: Since raw data never leaves the charging stations, the information of EV owners is kept private.
Reduced energy expenses: Both customers and operators experience reduced energy expenses as a result of optimized charging schedules.

Considerations:
Different charging requirements: Model aggregation is complicated because EVs have varying charging requirements.
Real-time decision-making: To properly manage charging schedules, the FL system needs to be able to make choices in real time.
Scalability: Without sacrificing effectiveness, the system must be able to accommodate an increasing number of EVs and charging stations.

12.3.1.5 Federated learning in IoT-smart home device

Background:
The way that gadgets communicate with consumers and one another is being completely transformed by the IoT. Voice-activated assistants, cameras, thermostats, and other smart home appliances are becoming commonplace and are gathering enormous volumes of data. However, the investigation of alternate strategies has been prompted by worries about data security, privacy, and the overhead associated with sending data to the cloud for centralized machine learning models.

With FL, a decentralized method, every IoT network device, or node, locally trains a machine learning model using its own data [12]. A central server then receives updates from the local models rather than the raw data. The updates are combined by this server to produce a global model, which is subsequently distributed to every device for additional local training.

Objective:
To use federated learning to increase a smart home energy management system's (EMS) prediction accuracy while protecting user privacy.
Scenario:
Thousands of homes throughout the city now have smart thermostats installed by a company. To optimize energy consumption, these devices learn from the weather,

everyday routines of users, and electricity pricing. The company wants to increase these devices' energy-saving predictions without sacrificing customer privacy.

Implementation of federated learning:

1. Data collection:
Every thermostat gathers information on occupancy, preferred temperatures, and trends in energy use.

2. Local training:
Using its data, each device trains a local neural network model. Recurrent neural networks (RNNs), for instance, can be used to forecast the ideal thermostat settings based on historical.

3. Model updates: Every thermostat periodically transmits sits model updates such as weights or gradients to a central server. For privacy, no raw data is transferred from the device.

Global model aggregation: These changes are combined by the central server to form a global model. The changes are merged using methods such as Federated Averaging.

Model distribution: Every thermostat receives a return copy of the global model. After that, each device keeps training the model locally while utilizing the information gathered from other devices.

Continuous learning: By repeating this process, new data may be gathered, and local models can be improved over time, leading to an improvement in the global model.

Results:

Enhanced predictability accuracy: The varied data from all devices helped the global model become more accurate, which resulted in more effective energy-saving suggestions.

Improved privacy: By keeping user data on their devices, privacy issues were addressed.

Decreased communication costs: Compared to conventional centralized methods, the network overhead was greatly decreased because only model updates were sent.

Scalability: As more devices were added, the system expanded effectively, and each one improved the performance of the model as a whole.

Challenges:

Non-IID data: To prevent biases, careful model aggregation procedures were needed because the data distribution among devices was not uniform or independent.

Device heterogeneity: The federated learning algorithm had to be adjusted because different devices had different computational capacities and data quality.

Communication delays: Asynchronous update mechanisms were necessary since network latency sometimes slowed down the model updating process.

Conclusion:

Federated learning leveraged the pooled knowledge of dispersed Internet of Things devices to give a strong framework for enhancing smart home energy management systems. Because it preserves user privacy and minimizes the need for large-scale data transfer, this method is perfect for Internet of Things settings. Subsequent research endeavors could concentrate on enhancing communication effectiveness and tackling obstacles associated with diverse device types.

12.3.1.6 Federated learning in IoT smart healthcare monitoring

Background: The healthcare industry is utilizing the IoT to gather real-time data on patients' vital signs, physical activity, and other health indicators. Examples of these linked devices include wearable sensors, smart medical devices, and mobile health applications [13]. As more people use these devices, there is a greater need to use the data they acquire for individualized treatment plans, early diagnosis, and predictive analytics. Significant obstacles, meanwhile, include worries about patient privacy, data security, and the bandwidth needed to send enormous volumes of health data to centralized computers. FL presents a solution by allowing the training of machine learning models without sharing the actual data directly on the devices or local nodes, such as clinics or hospitals. Sensitive patient data is instead kept private and aggregated by sending only model updates to a central server.

Objective: to create a prediction model that, while protecting patient privacy and reducing data transfer costs, can be used to identify early indications of cardiac abnormalities using data from wearable heart monitors.
Scenario: Thousands of people who are at risk of cardiovascular ailments now have wearable cardiac monitors thanks to a healthcare provider. These devices monitor vital signs, physical activity, and ECG data continually. The objective is to create a machine learning model that can anticipate possible cardiac events in advance, allowing for prompt intervention [14]. In order to preserve patient privacy, the provider hopes to accomplish this without sending the raw ECG data to a central server.

Implementation of federate learning:
Information gathering: Every wearable gadget gathers ECG information, heart rate, levels of physical activity, and many pertinent health indicators from the individual.
Local training: All wearables use the data they gather to locally train a machine learning model, like a convolutional neural network (CNN) for ECG analysis. The model's goal is to identify trends that could point to heart problems.
Model updates: The gadget updates its model on a regular basis and sends the changed weights to a central server. Most notably, no raw ECG data is sent.
Aggregation of the global model: To produce a better global model, the updates from all devices are combined by the central server. The model parameters are often combined using federated averaging.
Model distribution: All wearable devices subsequently receive a return copy of the global model. With its local data, each device keeps improving the monitoring.
Results:

Increased predictive accuracy: By utilizing the variety of data accessible on all devices, the global model is able to anticipate cardiac irregularities with more accuracy.
Enhanced privacy: By keeping patient data on local devices, healthcare standards like HIPAA are complied with and privacy concerns are addressed.
Decreased communication costs: The method dramatically lowers bandwidth utilization by just delivering model updates as opposed to raw data.
Personalized healthcare: By customizing the global model to each patient's unique requirements, each device allows for more individualized therapy and monitoring.

Challenges:
Data heterogeneity: Because patient conditions vary, each device collects data differently, which makes it difficult to efficiently aggregate the model updates.
Device variability: The consistency of local model training may be impacted by the disparities in processing power among wearables.
Communication latency: The promptness of global model updates may be impacted by model update communication being delayed in remote or low-bandwidth locations.

Conclusions: In IoT healthcare contexts, federated learning offers a potent method for creating predictive models that improve patient care while protecting privacy. The healthcare practitioner can develop a reliable and accurate model that scales across thousands of patients without sacrificing data security by utilizing local data on wearable devices. This case study shows how federated learning may revolutionize IoT-enabled healthcare by making personalized, effective, and safe medical monitoring and diagnostics possible.

12.3.1.7 Federated learning in IoT system for smart grid management

Overview: The use of FL in an IoT-based smart grid system is investigated in this case study [15]. Optimizing energy distribution and consumption in a smart city while protecting user privacy about energy usage data is the main goal.

Context: An IoT-enabled smart grid system that incorporates many smart meters from residential, commercial, and industrial buildings is a feature of a smart city. To forecast demand, optimize energy distribution, and effectively manage the grid, these smart meters gather real-time data on energy consumption. However, there are privacy problems associated with centralizing this data for analysis, since it may reveal private information about the habits and actions of individuals. Furthermore, bandwidth constraints make it difficult to transfer massive volumes of data from thousands of smart meters to a central server.

Problem statement: Conventional methods of managing smart grids rely on centralized data collecting, which presents challenges because of concerns about privacy and the inefficiency of managing large volumes of data. Creating a predictive model that can maximize energy management while protecting user privacy and without overloading the network infrastructure is the difficult part of the job.

1. **Federated learning framework:** Using data from individual smart meters, the smart grid system's federated learning technique trains local prediction models for energy use. Every smart meter processes its own data and makes local modifications to the model. Then, a central server receives these local model updates—not the raw data.
2. **Model aggregation:** To create a global model that represents the patterns of energy usage throughout the whole smart grid, the central server collects the local model updates from every smart meter. The smart meters can then use this global model to enhance their forecasts and optimize energy use on a local level.
3. **Data security and privacy:** The federated learning technique greatly lowers the possibility of disclosing private user information by guaranteeing that only model changes are sent. To ensure that no user's energy usage can be deduced from the model updates, additional privacy protection measures including differential privacy are used.
4. **Constant learning and adaptation** [16]: As fresh data is produced by smart meters, the global model is updated continuously, guaranteeing that the system adjusts to shifting patterns of energy usage over time. With this method, the smart grid can react in real time to variations in demand and dynamically modify the distribution of energy.

Result:

Better energy management: Better load balancing and less energy waste were made possible by the federated learning system's ability to estimate energy demand more accurately. Improved User Privacy: By optimizing energy distribution without gathering or centralizing sensitive user data, the smart grid was able to uphold consumer confidence and adhere to privacy laws.

Scalability: With effective communication and little load on the network, the system managed the large-scale deployment throughout the smart city.

Challenges:

Communication cost [17]: Even though federated learning minimizes the need for data transfer, there is still some communication cost involved in sending updates to the model, especially when deploying on a wide scale. A Variety of Data Sources Ensuring the global model adequately reflected the varying usage patterns was tough due to the disparate features supplied by the smart meters located around the city.

Model convergence: One of the main challenges was making sure that, despite the variety of the data, the variety of the data, the global model converged efficiently and produced trustworthy predictions. Global model converged efficiently and produced trustworthy predictions.

Result:

Federated learning in IoT systems, particularly in smart grid management, presents a promising solution to the challenges of data privacy, security, and scalability. This case study illustrates how federated learning can be leveraged to improve energy management in a smart city while preserving the privacy of individual users. The approach can be extended to other domains where IoT devices generate sensitive data that cannot be easily centralized.

12.3.1.8 Federated learning in IoT system for autonomous vehicles

Overview:
The application of FL in an IoT system for a fleet of self-driving cars is examined in this case study [18]. The main objective is to guarantee data privacy and minimize communication costs while improving the machine learning models that are utilized for autonomous driving's real-time decision-making.

Context:
A business drives a fleet of self-driving cars across several cities. To navigate, identify impediments, and make judgments about how to drive in real time, these cars rely on machine learning models. Numerous sensors (cameras, LIDAR, radar, etc.) on vehicles continuously produce enormous volumes of data. Improving the models that power decision-making processes needs this data. Centralizing this data for model training, however, presents a number of difficulties:
Data privacy: Concerns regarding the privacy of the people and places that the sensors are recording are raised when sending raw data to a central server. Limitations on bandwidth: Due to the massive amount of data collected by the sensors, sending it all to a central server is not practicable.
Latency: Centralizing data can result in delays that impair the operation of the cars. Real-time updates are essential to autonomous driving.
Problem statement:
The difficulty lies in enhancing the performance and accuracy of the machine learning models used in autonomous cars while resolving issues with data privacy, cutting down on bandwidth use, and guaranteeing real-time updates.

Solution:

1. **Federated learning framework:** Using the information gathered from its sensors, each autonomous car develops a local machine learning model. Tasks like object detection, traffic sign recognition, and route planning may be included in this model. The car only sends the updated model parameters (gradients) to a central server as opposed to sending raw sensor data.
2. **Centralized model aggregation:** To create a more comprehensive global model that takes advantage of the varied data gathered across various driving situations (such as various cities and weather conditions), the central server collects the model updates from every car. All cars then receive this global model back, allowing them to retain locally relevant information while still benefiting from collective learning.
3. **Data security and privacy**: The method greatly lowers the danger of privacy breaches by only transmitting model changes rather than raw data. Sophisticated methods such as safe aggregation and homomorphic encryption

are employed to guarantee that the model updates conceal any private information about the people or places that the car sensors have recorded.

4. **Constant learning and adaptation:** As more data is gathered by the vehicles, the global model is updated regularly. This makes it possible for the fleet to adjust to altered driving circumstances, such as modifications to traffic patterns, weather, or road conditions [19]. Additionally, by learning from the experiences of other vehicles in the same city, the federated learning system enables individual vehicles to quickly adapt to local conditions.

Enhanced model accuracy: By learning from a wider range of driving scenarios, the autonomous cars' decision- making models were able to be improved by the federated learning system without the need for centralized data storage.
Enhanced privacy: To address privacy issues, the method made sure that sensitive data, such as pictures of pedestrians or certain locations, stayed close to the car.
Decreased bandwidth usage: The system dramatically decreased the quantity of data that needed to be transferred over the network by only transmitting model changes as opposed to raw data.
Real-time adaption: The system made it possible for the models of the cars to get updates in real time, which helped them quickly adjust to changing or unforeseen road conditions.

Challenges:
Enhanced model accuracy: The federated learning system was able to enhance the autonomous cars' decision-making models without the need for centralized data storage by learning from a broader range of driving circumstances.
Enhanced privacy: The strategy ensured that sensitive data, including images of pedestrians or specific places, was kept close to the car to meet privacy concerns.
Reduced bandwidth usage: By broadcasting only model updates rather than raw data, the system significantly reduced the amount of data that needed to be carried over the network. Real-Time Adaptation: The system allowed the automobile models to get updates in real time, enabling them to instantly adapt to unexpected or changing road circumstances.

Conclusions:
Federated learning is a viable way to improve the machine learning models that are employed in autonomous cars while resolving important issues with bandwidth, privacy, and real-time performance. The viability and advantages of federated learning in an IoT system are illustrated by this case study, which focuses on autonomous driving. The method can be used for additional Internet of Things applications where privacy and instantaneous decision-making are crucial.

12.3.1.9 Dynamic resources allocation in federated learning systems

Background:
The company in charge of setting up and overseeing smart city infrastructure in a sizable metro region is called Smart City Inc. A wide range of IoT devices,

including smart meters, connected cars, environmental sensors, and traffic cameras, are part of the infrastructure [20]. Massive volumes of data are continuously generated by these devices, and these data are used for many different purposes, such as public safety, energy usage optimization, pollution monitoring, and traffic control. Smart City Inc. made the decision to use FL to train machine learning models directly on IoT devices, eliminating the requirement to centralize data, to improve these applications. Through the use of federated learning, a model may be trained locally on each device using its own data. Only the model updates need to be shared with a central server, which then compiles the updates to enhance the global model.

Challenge:
There were several obstacles to overcome when implementing federated learning in an IoT setting.
Resource restrictions: The computing power, memory, and battery life of Internet of Things devices are constrained. Devoting resources to machine learning tasks may jeopardize their core purposes (such as real-time processing and sensor data collection).
Heterogeneity: The hardware capabilities, network connectivity, and data availability of the IoT devices differed greatly. It became challenging to divide up the learning assignments through the devices as a result.
Dynamic environments: The IoT devices' ambient circumstances and usage patterns are subject to constant change. For instance, during peak hours, a traffic camera may receive a lot of data, but at night, it may receive less.
Communication overhead: To update models, federated learning necessitates regular communication between devices and the central server. Excessive communication can shorten battery life and clog networks because of the bandwidth and energy restrictions of IoT devices.
To overcome these obstacles, Smart City Inc. put into practice a dynamic resource allocation plan designed specifically for federated learning in an Internet of Things setting: Adaptive Resource Allocation: Based on the workload and battery life of the Internet of Things devices, an intelligent resource management system was created to distribute computing resources in a dynamic manner. Devices having higher resources, for instance, might be assigned more FL tasks, whereas devices with fewer resources might be asked to contribute less frequently.

Solution:
Priority-based work scheduling: The importance of the data and the function of the device in the IoT network were taken into consideration while ranking the tasks. For instance, resource allocation gave priority to public safety monitoring equipment (such as security cameras) above nonessential data collection equipment.
Monitoring and feedback in real time: To continuously evaluate the functionality and resource consumption of Internet of Things devices, a monitoring system was put into place. To guarantee that devices stayed within their operating bounds, the system offered feedback for dynamic resource allocation adjustments.

Result:

The IoT system saw notable gains after implementing dynamic resource allocation for federated learning.

Improved model accuracy: By effectively utilizing data from a variety of IoT devices, the FL framework produced more reliable and accurate models for use in traffic control and pollution monitoring, among other applications.

Enhanced resource efficiency: By ensuring that Internet of Things devices worked within their resource limitations, the adaptive allocation system led to a 25% gain in battery life and a 30% decrease in computing overhead.

Decreased communication costs: By reducing communication costs by 40%, the hierarchical FL structure and model compression approaches helped to ease network congestion and free up bandwidth for important operations.

Scalability: There was no discernible drop in performance or resource consumption when the system was expanded to support thousands of IoT devices.

Conclusion:

Federated learning in its Internet of Things network, Smart City Inc. was able to optimize the performance of smart city apps and make optimum use of scarce resources. This case study demonstrates how dynamic resource management can help smart city efforts achieve better results and more efficient operations by addressing the special difficulties presented by federated learning in IoT contexts.

12.3.1.10 Smart IoT system for energy management in commercial building

Background:

Green Tech Enterprises Sector: Real Estate for Commercial Use.

Where: New York City Structure.

Dimensions: 200,000 sq ft.

Challenge: Monitoring and optimizing energy usage across several levels and departments is difficult, and there is a high cost and consumption of energy.

Solution:

NYC's Green Tech Enterprises is the manager of multiple commercial buildings. They suffered from high utility bills, uneven energy use across departments, and little visibility into how energy was being utilized despite efforts to reduce energy consumption. Traditional energy meters in the building only supplied basic consumption statistics; however, these were not sufficient for in-depth analysis and optimization.

Objective:

Cut your energy use by 20% overall. Boost energy use tracking in real time. Find and fix inefficiencies in the way that various departments consume energy. Include renewable energy sources and make sure they are used effectively.

Solution:

To put in place an intelligent Internet of Things-based EMS, Green Tech Enterprises teamed up with a technology supplier. The following were components of the system. Smart Meters and Sensors: To gather data on electricity consumption in real time, smart energy meters were installed in each department and on each level. To keep an eye on the temperature, humidity, and occupancy levels, more sensors were added.

Centralized IoT platform: A centralized IoT platform received all of the data from sensors and smart meters. Facility managers were able to examine previous data and track energy usage in real time with this tool.

Automated control systems: By integrating with the building's lighting and HVAC systems, the Internet of Things platform optimized energy use by automatically adjusting settings based on occupancy and outside circumstances. Predictive analytics was employed by the Internet of Things system to forecast patterns of energy usage and suggest changes. It also prevented expensive downtime by anticipating possible equipment faults. Integration of renewable energy: Solar panels were mounted on the building's roof. The energy generated was monitored by the IoT system, which also made sure it was saved in batteries for later use or used efficiently.

Implementation:

Phases of the implementation were completed. Installing sensors and smart meters is phase one.

Phase 2: Linking the IoT platform to the current building management infrastructure.

Phase 3: Automation features and predictive analytics are implemented.

Phase 4: Integration and installation of solar panels. To guarantee that facility managers and employees could operate the new system efficiently, training sessions were held for them.

Outcome:

Energy reduction: Compared to the original target of 20%, the building's overall energy consumption was decreased by 25%.

Cost savings: Green Tech Enterprises saw a 30% decrease in utility expenses, which translated into substantial cost savings.

Enhanced efficiency: The Internet of Things system detected a number of inefficiencies, like lights and air conditioning units operating in vacant spaces and made automated adjustments to cut down on waste.

Improved monitoring: Facility managers could now make better decisions since they had immediate access to comprehensive energy usage data.

Sustainability: By reducing the building's dependency on the grid, the incorporation of solar energy helped to achieve sustainability objectives.

Challenge:

Complexity of integration: It was difficult and required specialized solutions to integrate the IoT system with older building management systems.

Data security: Ensuring the IoT system's security was crucial, requiring strong cybersecurity defenses.

User adoption: To guarantee that facility managers and employees made the most of the system's potential, training, and change management were essential.

Conclusion:

Green Tech Enterprises were able to improve operational efficiency and lower energy expenses and consumption thanks to the smart IoT EMS. The potential of IoT technology to revolutionize energy management in commercial buildings is illustrated by this case study.

12.3.1.11 Federated learning in IoT for manufacturing predictive maintenance

Background:

Global Manufacturing Inc. is the company.

Sector:

Manufacturing location: Factories across the globe creating predictive maintenance models for a variety of widely dispersed IoT devices without centralized data collecting is a challenge.

Problem statement:

Global Manufacturing Inc. manages a number of factories that are outfitted with a variety of IoT gadgets to track environmental factors and equipment performance. To cut downtime and maintenance expenses, the corporation sought to apply predictive maintenance to every facility. However, due to bandwidth constraints, data privacy concerns, and the sheer volume of data, gathering and centralizing data from these geographically dispersed sensors presented considerable hurdles.

Objective:

Create models for predictive maintenance that can be used in various factories. Steer clear of centralized data collecting to safeguard sensitive information. Reduce the amount of bandwidth used and the requirement for large-scale data transfers. Make sure there is little to no human intervention needed as the predictive models get better over time.

Solution:

By using federated learning, Global Manufacturing Inc. was able to train predictive maintenance models locally on IoT data from each factory, eliminating the need to send that data to a central server. The following elements were engaged in the solution:

Local IoT device training: Using data from each factory, the sensors and edge computing units among other IoT devices educated local predictive maintenance models. These models used operational data, such as temperature, vibration, and usage patterns, to forecast when maintenance was needed for machines.

Model aggregation: Updates (model parameters) from the locally trained models were periodically forwarded to a central server. After combining the updates, this server produced a global model that got better with every local training cycle.

Global model distribution: After being updated, the global model was returned to each plant and further refined using local data. This process made sure that the model remained accurate and relevant for the unique characteristics of each location. Data privacy was preserved since only model parameters rather not raw data were shared. This was essential to ensuring adherence to local data protection laws.

Efficiency optimization: The federated learning strategy minimized bandwidth utilization and increased system efficiency by utilizing local processing resources and limiting data transfers.

Implementation:

The implementation was carried out in phases:

Phase 1: Pilot testing in a single factory, with an emphasis on expensive machinery that requires regular maintenance.

Step 2: Expand to more factories with a range of machinery and surroundings.

Stage 3: Cycles of continuous improvement, during which the global model was updated and dispersed on a regular basis.

Step 4: Implementing the solution in all factories across the globe. To oversee and guarantee the smooth functioning of the federated learning process, local IT teams received technical training.

Outcome:

Increased predicted accuracy: When compared to the prior centralized model, the federated learning model produced a 15% increase in predicted accuracy. It was successful in spotting possible equipment problems before they happened.

Decreased downtime: A 20% decrease in equipment downtime resulted in considerable cost savings and improved operational effectiveness.

Data privacy compliance: Since no raw data was moved outside of the manufacturing grounds, the federated learning approach guaranteed adherence to local data privacy laws.

Reduced bandwidth usage: The organization cut its bandwidth expenses by 25% by doing away with the requirement to send massive amounts of raw data.

Scalability: The global model improved continuously as it learned from various operational situations, and the solution was effectively scaled across all worldwide facilities.

Challenge:

Model convergence: The federated learning algorithm needed to be carefully tuned to guarantee that the global model converged and performed well across all factories.

Local data diversity: To balance the impact of each local model, adaptive strategies were needed due to the diversity in data quantity and quality between plants.

System integration: Data scientists, IT specialists, and manufacturing operations teams have to work together to integrate the federated learning framework with the current IoT infrastructure.

Conclusions:

Global Manufacturing Inc. found a creative way to overcome the difficulty of deploying predictive maintenance across geographically dispersed plants by adopting federated learning. The organization increased the accuracy of predictive maintenance, decreased equipment downtime, and improved operational efficiency by enabling local model training while protecting data privacy. This case study demonstrates the potential of federated learning in the Internet of Things contexts, where bandwidth limitations and data privacy are important factors to take into account.

References

[1] A. Nilsson and S. Smith, Evaluating the performance of federated learning. Master's Thesis, University of Gothenburg, Göteborg, Sweden, 2018.

[2] H. Kim, J. Park, M. Bennis, and S.-L. Kim, Block-chained on-device federated learning. *IEEE Commun. Lett.* 2019, 24, 1279–1283.

[3] C. Zhang, Y. Xie, H. Bai, B. Yu, W. Li, and Y. Gao, A survey on federated learning. *Knowl.-based Syst.* 2021, 216, 106775.

[4] Y. Jiang, C.J. Kone, K. Rush, and S. Kannan, Improving federated learning personalization via model agnostic meta-learning. arXiv 2019, arXiv:1909.12488.

[5] L. Li, Y. Fan, M. Tse, and K.-Y. Lin, A review of applications in federated learning. *Comput. Ind. Eng.* 2020, 149, 106854.

[6] J.S. Wiedemann, K. Müller, and W. Samek, Compact and computationally efficient representation of deep neural networks, *IEEE Trans. Neural Netw. Learn. Syst.* 2020, 31, 3, 772–785.

[7] R. Taylor, D. Baron, and D. Schmidt, The world in 2025-predictions for the next ten years, in *Proc. 10th International Microsystems, Packaging, Assembly and Circuits Technology Conference (IMPACT)*, pp. 192–195, 2015.

[8] S.K. Sharma and X. Wang, Live data analytics with collaborative edge and cloud processing in wireless IoT networks, *IEEE Access* 2017, 5, 4621–4635.

[9] A. Ghasempour, Internet of things in smart grid: Architecture, applications, services, key technologies, and challenges, *Invent. J.* 2019, 4, 1, 1–12.

[10] Cisco Visual Networking Index: Global Mobile Data Traffic Forecast Update, 2016–2021, Mar. 2017.

[11] H. Yuan and M. Zhou, Profit-maximized collaborative computation offloading and resource allocation in distributed cloud and edge computing systems, *IEEE Trans. Automat. Sci. Eng.*, 2021, 18, 3, 1277–1287, doi:10.1109/TASE.2020.3000946.

[12] H. Yuan, J. Bi, W. Tan, M. Zhou, B.H. Li, and J. Li, TTSA: An effective scheduling approach for delay bounded tasks in hybrid clouds, *IEEE Trans. Cybernetics* 2017, 47, 11, 3658–3668.

[13] H.B. McMahan, E. Moore, D. Ramage, S. Hampson, and B.A. Arcas, Communication-efficient learning of deep networks from decentralized data, in *Proceedings of the International Conference on Artificial Intelligence and Statistics*, Apr. 2017, pp. 1273–1282.

[14] J. Konečný, H.B. McMahan, F.X. Yu, P. Richtárik, A.T. Suresh, and D. Bacon, Federated learning: Strategies for improving communication efficiency, arXiv preprint arXiv:1610.05492, 2016.

[15] M. Jaggi, V. Smith, M. Takac, *et al.* Communication-efficient distributed dual coordinate ascent, in *Proceedings of the 27th International Conference on Neural Information and Processing Systems (NIPS)*, 2014, pp. 3068–3076

[16] S.U. Stich, Local SGD converges fast and communicates little, in *Proceedings of the International Conference on Learning Representations*, 2019.

[17] Y. Zhang, J.C. Duchi, and M.J. Wainwright, Communication-efficient algorithms for statistical optimization, *J. Mach. Learn. Res.* 2013, 14, 1, 3321–3363.

[18] X. Wang, C. Wang, X. Li, V.C.M. Leung, and T. Taleb, Federated deep reinforcement learning for Internet of Things with decentralized cooperative edge caching, *IEEE Internet of Things J.* 2020, 7, 10, 9441–9455.

[19] J. Kang, Z. Xiong, D. Niyato, S. Xie, and J. Zhang, Incentive mechanism for reliable federated learning: A joint optimization approach to combining reputation and contract theory, *IEEE Internet of Things J.* 2019, 6, 6, 10700–10714.

[20] X. Li, K. Huang, W. Yang, S. Wang, and Z. Zhang, On the convergence of FedAvg on non-iid data, in *Proceedings of the International Conference on Learning Representations (ICLR)*, 2020.

Chapter 13
Energy-efficient federated learning

Vijay Ramalingam[1], *A. Arul Prakash*[1], *S. Vignesh*[1], *R. Rahin Batcha*[1] *and D. Saravanan*[1]

Abstract

Federated learning (FL) is a machine learning technique which circumvents the need to centralise training data to address concerns related to security, privacy, and data amount. Addressing distributed machine learning problems entails distinct obstacles in comparison to centralised problems. Artificial intelligence algorithms enable computers to learn and make predictions or decisions without being explicitly programmed. Some of the problems include managing communication infrastructure, supervising learning processes, integrating outcomes, identifying training data sets, managing unpredictability, and operating without a verification data set. IBM federated learning offers both federation architecture and coordination. Data scientists have the ability to generate and oversee federated learning tasks by utilising centralised machine learning models, offering clear and precise guidelines for operation. The framework is compatible with both deep neural networks and conventional methods used in popular machine learning frameworks. IBM federated learning enables data scientists to shift from centralised to decentralised machine learning, therefore lowering the learning curve and facilitating deployment in different computing environments and customised merging methodologies. Energy efficiency in collective learning for Internet of Drones networks is achieved by optimising CPU frequencies to minimise total energy consumption. This is critical for protecting drone batteries during federated learning processes in dynamic situations.

Keywords: Decentralised learning; Collaborative learning; Distributed machine learning; Federated optimisation

13.1 Introduction

Federated learning (FL) is a technique employed to train machine learning algorithms on several edge devices in a dispersed manner, without the need to

[1]Department of Computer Science and Engineering, Sathyabama Institute of Science and Technology, India

share the actual training data. Thus, federated learning presents a novel approach to learning, where statistical techniques are trained on the periphery of dispersed networks [1]. The application of energy-efficient federated learning entails the utilisation of federated learning techniques to minimise energy consumption in remote machine learning systems. Federated learning enables the collaboration of several edge devices to collectively train a single machine learning model, eliminating the need for centralised data collection. This decentralised approach not only safeguards data privacy but also reduces energy consumption by reducing the frequency of data transmission to a central computer [2].

Energy-efficient federated learning is applied in the healthcare sector, particularly for personalised treatment and remote patient monitoring. Healthcare practitioners can utilise federated learning approaches to train machine learning models utilising data from various medical equipment and sensors located in different locations. This approach minimises the duration during which time-sensitive patient data needs to be sent to a central computer, resulting in energy conservation and enhanced protection of data privacy and security [3]. Energy-efficient federated learning may improve the performance of smart devices and conserve energy in the Internet of Things (IoT) domain. Energy consumption may be significantly reduced by allowing edge devices to collaborate and update machine learning models without the need for ongoing communication with a central server. These devices are especially advantageous when they have low battery life or are located in distant places with limited access (Figure 13.1).

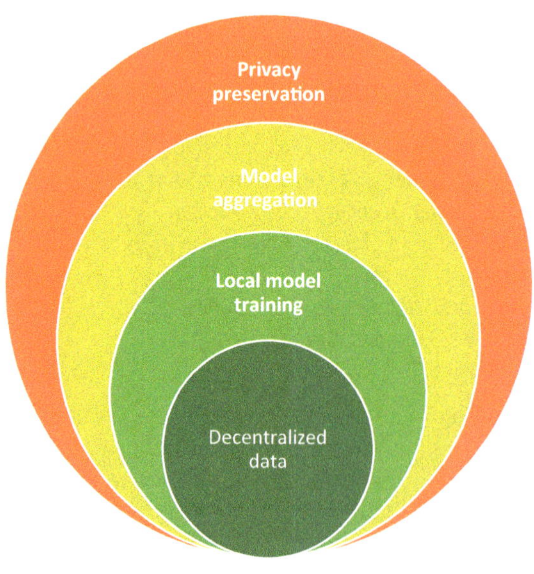

Figure 13.1 Different layer insight of federated learning

Federated learning is an energy-efficient method for doing machine learning in distributed environments, ensuring long-term privacy. By implementing collaborative learning at the edge, enterprises may achieve energy efficiency, enhance data privacy, and enhance the scalability of machine learning applications across several domains.

Decentralised data: Federated learning employs several clients or devices, every one of which autonomously saves its own data. It suggests that the data is dispersed and not centralised. The decentralised nature of data in FL serves to safeguard the privacy of local data but at the potential cost of increased communication expenses. Due to the distributed nature of the data over numerous servers, a larger volume of data needs to be transmitted between the clients and the main server throughout the training process. This results in an increase in the cost of communication [4].

Federated learning enables each client to do 'local model training' on its own data. Such localised training sessions safeguard the confidentiality of the local data, but they might also increase the cost of communication. The modifications made to the local model must be transmitted to the central computer, which consolidates it to create a global model. When there are a large number of clients or a substantial amount of data, transmitting these modifications to the central server might result in significant communication expenses.

13.1.1 Aggregating the models

After completing the training process locally, the clients transmit their updated models to the central computer for aggregation. The server aggregates the model modifications and generates a comprehensive global model which illustrates the structure of the data from all the clients. Large client numbers or significant model upgrades might result in substantial communication costs during the model aggregation process. FL, or federated learning, is employed to safeguard privacy by ensuring that local data remains confidential. However, this approach might result in increased costs associated with communication. When FL is employed for privacy protection, the data remains on the clients' devices, and only the updates to the model are transmitted to the central server. However, this implies that a greater amount of data must be sent between the clients and the computer throughout the training process, resulting in increased expenditures. The user's text is '[5]'.

Currently, there is a significant quantity of devices that are connected to each other, such as mobile devices, wearables, and autonomous cars. These devices generate a massive amount of information, which is commonly referred to as Big Data. Due to the improving computing capabilities and privacy concerns of these devices, there is a rising need to store and analyse data on the device itself rather than using cloud storage. This shift transfers computational tasks from centralised servers to the edge. Artificial Intelligence is essential for deriving valuable insights from Big Data, and deep learning is particularly effective at comprehending intricate datasets (Figure 13.2) [6].

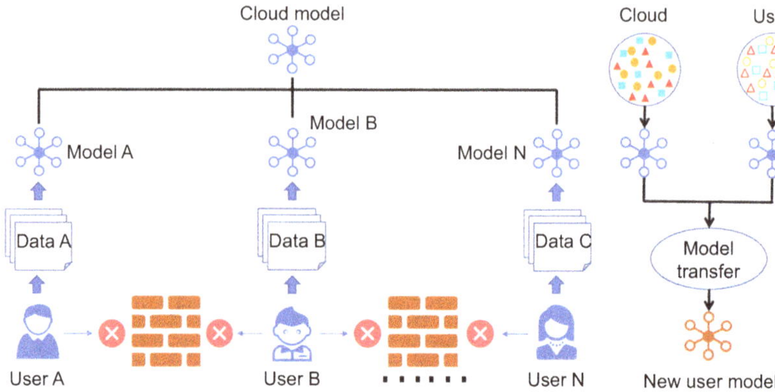

Figure 13.2 Insight model for different user function

13.2 Primary obstacles in executing energy-efficient federated learning

Token-based authentication is a security technique that uses tokens to handle user sessions once login credentials have been successfully confirmed. This approach is especially efficient in settings where confirming one's identity and safeguarding data are of utmost importance, such as in telemedical information systems.

Upon user login, the system produces a distinct encrypted token to avoid the need for continually transmitting the username and password for each transaction. Subsequently, the token is returned to the user's client, which subsequently utilises the token instead of the credentials in future interactions with the server. The token serves as a secure credential that the server may verify and authenticate to confirm the user's identity and permissions [7].

Token-based authentication offers a key benefit since it eliminates the need for the server to keep track of individual user sessions. This can lead to a substantial decrease in server workload and enhance overall performance. This may be especially advantageous in distributed systems, such as those employed in telemedicine, where ensuring high availability and performance are of utmost importance [8].

Furthermore, tokens are saved on the client side, usually in the user's browser or device, which enhances security by reducing the chance of someone intercepting the user's login information. Due to encryption, the intercepted token is rendered useless to unauthorised individuals without the decryption key [9].

Table 13.1 explains about token-based authentication facilitates scalability and seamless integration. Tokens are self-contained entities that encompass all the essential data about users, hence streamlining the procedure of sending requests to various servers or services inside the network. Effective interaction between numerous services and data sources is essential in telemedical systems to ensure complete treatment. Token-based authentication in telemedicine protects the security of sensitive medical data and restricts access to authorised individuals.

Table 13.1 Comparison setup for federated learning towards contribution and limitation

Title	Insights	Methods used	Contributions	Limitations
Energy-efficient federated learning in Internet of Drones networks	Energy efficiency in federated learning for Internet of Drones networks optimises CPU frequencies to minimise total energy consumption, crucial for preserving drone batteries during FL processes in dynamic environments	Federated learning (FL) Optimisation of CPU frequencies in drones' on-board computing units	Investigates energy-efficient federated learning in IoD networks Designs algorithm to minimise total energy consumption	Limited drone batteries affect FL performance Huge wireless network traffic and data privacy leakage
Energy-efficient federated learning in Internet of Drones networks	Energy efficiency in federated learning for Internet of Drones networks optimises CPU frequencies to minimise total energy consumption, crucial for drone mobility and FL performance in IoT applications	Federated learning (FL) Optimisation of CPU frequencies in drones' on-board computing units	Energy-efficient federated learning optimisation in Internet of Drones networks Algorithm design for minimising total energy consumption in the FL process	Limited drone batteries affect FL performance in IoD networks Aggregating all data samples leads to huge wireless network traffic
Energy-efficient federated learning in Internet of Vehicles: A game-theoretic scheme	Energy efficiency in federated learning for Internet of Vehicles is crucial to reduce energy costs during model aggregations, addressed through game-theoretic schemes improving efficiency by 68.8%	Two-stage game theories based energy-efficient federated learning scheme Multiagent reinforcement learning algorithm for coalition formation to lower energy cost	Energy-efficient federated learning scheme based on two-stage game theories Multiagent reinforcement learning algorithm for coalition formation to lower energy cost	Energy efficiency issue due to frequent model aggregations Existing research focuses on vehicular communication, neglecting true energy costs
EEFL: High-speed wireless communications inspired energy-efficient federated learning over mobile devices	Energy efficiency in federated learning is crucial for mobile devices. The proposed EEFL focuses on reducing overall energy consumption by optimising wireless communications and local training, enhancing performance	Dual decomposition technique for resource allocation Bisection search-based recursive technique for solving energy efficiency problem	Proposed a two-tier federated learning network architecture Developed an energy-efficient computation and communication resource allocation scheme	Communication and computation bottleneck at the centralised aggregator Inaccurate learning model caused by non-IID data

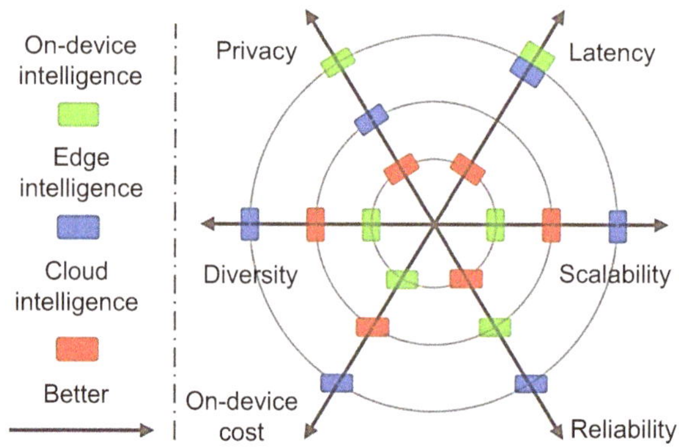

Figure 13.3 Intelligence functionality of federated learning

Ensuring patient privacy is crucial, not only to protect their confidential data but also to adhere to strict requirements such as HIPAA in the United States. HIPAA oversees the security and privacy of health information.

Token-based authentication offers a strong foundation for ensuring the security of user sessions and effectively managing permissions in intricate systems. This makes it an appropriate option for telemedical information systems that prioritise security, privacy, and performance (Figure 13.3).

Edge computing has emerged as the prevailing norm, enabling the use of applications that need substantial computational capabilities [10]. Edge Intelligence, or Edge AI, is a fusion of artificial intelligence with edge computing. This enables the use of machine learning algorithms on the edge device, where the data is generated. AIoT, short for Artificial Intelligence of Things, refers to systems that utilise machine learning and are distributed and interconnected. The predominant focus of Edge Intelligence revolves around the inference phase, whereby the AI model is executed. Additionally, they believe that the training phase, which consumes a substantial amount of resources, occurs within cloud data centres. Nevertheless, the capacity for storage and computational capabilities of interconnected edge devices is expanding, hence creating opportunities to train and utilise distributed machine learning models.

In conventional machine learning approaches, it is necessary to consolidate all the data into a single location, often a cloud-based data centre. This might potentially violate legal regulations on the protection of user information and privacy. Stringent regulations mandating the safeguarding of user privacy necessitate technology companies across many regions to exercise utmost caution while handling user data and other confidential information. The General Data Protection Regulation (GDPR) implemented by the European Union (EU) serves as an excellent illustration of this concept. Federated learning is a novel approach employed to safeguard privacy when developing the Deep Neural Network Model by including input from several customers. Federated machine learning is the solution to this challenge since it employs techniques that integrate distributed machine learning, encryption and security, and the development of incentive systems rooted in economics and game theory. Federated learning has the potential to serve as the foundation for a future iteration of machine learning that fulfils the requirements of both technology and society in the responsible development and use of artificial intelligence [11].

13.3 The applications of federated learning

FL is an innovative approach to distributed machine learning that offers enhanced data privacy and the ability to train models without relying on a central site. While FL offers several advantages, the increased level of required communication has emerged as a significant issue, particularly in terms of efficiency and scalability. The FL model involves two primary categories of communication expenses: upload costs and download charges. The first dataset contains the information that clients transmitted to the server during the training phase, whereas the second dataset contains the information that clients received from the server. The expenses are influenced by several parameters, such as the dataset's magnitude, the complexity of the model, the number of clients, and the network speed [12]. Extensive research has been conducted to examine the impact of communication costs on the efficiency of FL. Empirical research has demonstrated that communication expenses can pose significant challenges for FL systems, hence reducing their scalability and utility. Novel concepts, like as compression techniques and model quantisation, have been proposed as solutions to address these issues. Model compression techniques decrease the size of model modifications, resulting in reduced upload costs. Additionally, model quantisation enhances the precision of model parameters, further reducing upload costs.

In addition to the pursuit of communication efficiency, the objective of energy-efficient communication systems is also a highly significant concern. Employing FL to reduce connection expenses immediately results in energy conservation. Enhancing the FL process can have an impact on bandwidth and perhaps result in reduced energy expenses, as data transmission consumes energy. This is a crucial consideration for contemporary communication networks. FL's capacity to automatically minimise data transmission effectively reduces energy consumption, positioning it as a leading method for enhancing the energy efficiency of communication networks (Figure 13.4).

13.3.1 Model averaging

Many individuals in FL rely on using modelled averages as a solution to address the issue of inadequate communication. Creating an average model entails constructing multiple models on different devices and combining them into a single, highly accurate model. We will discuss the model averaging method and its potential to address FL's interpersonal issues in more detail later. Model averaging involves using the same training data on different devices to train multiple models. Each gadget independently constructs its own model using data from its respective area.

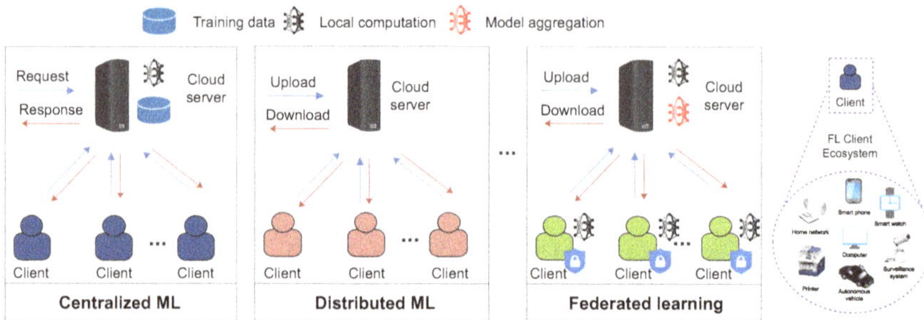

Figure 13.4 Data transmission for communication network

The models that are generated are combined to create a final model that is more accurate than any of the individual models. Combining the models involves adding up the weights of each model [13].

$$\text{Final weight } = \frac{(w_1 \times W_1 + w_2 \times W_2 + \ldots + w_N \times W_N)}{(w_1 + w_2 + \ldots + w_N)}, \tag{13.1}$$

Equation (13.1) explains the weight of different models which determines model compression. The accuracy of each model is evaluated to determine the weight it should be assigned. Less emphasis is placed on models which perform poorly on regional data, while more weight is given to instances which demonstrate better performance. During each learning session, the weights are modified repeatedly until convergence is achieved. The model's average method outperforms other methods commonly used in FL in several ways. First, it reduces the impact of a weak connection by allowing each device to create its own model in close proximity. This implies that the devices can minimise their communication with each other, which proves to be particularly advantageous in situations where the communication route is restricted. Additionally, the final model is enhanced in terms of accuracy by incorporating the knowledge acquired from various models. This is particularly beneficial when dealing with a wide range of local information and the data is dispersed across multiple devices [14].

13.3.2 Major issues in federated learning

Implementing federated learning involves addressing several significant challenges. These include ensuring optimal data transfer within the federated system, coordinating various systems in interconnected networks, and analyzing the statistical diversity of federated network datasets. Additionally, addressing privacy concerns and implementing effective safeguarding methods are critical. Strong communication skills are also essential, particularly for roles like information security analysts, as they must convey complex technical information to both technical and non-technical stakeholders. Clear and concise communication ensures that everyone understands the importance of information security and the measures needed to protect sensitive data. When developing strategies for federated networks, it is crucial to carefully consider the transmission aspect, as it can present significant challenges. One reason is that federated networks often involve a large number of devices, such as millions of mobile phones, where network connectivity can be significantly slower than local processing. Training in federated learning utilises communication-efficient algorithms to deliver concise notifications or updates to models iteratively, instead of transmitting the entire dataset over the network. There are two main ways to further reduce communication: (1) reducing the amount of messages exchanged and (2) reducing the overall number of communication sets.

Effective communication in distributed learning strategies is guided by these broad principles: One can implement a flexible approach to applying updates on multiple machines simultaneously during each communication round using local updating methods. Hence, the goal of local updating approaches is to minimise the overall number of communication rounds. By implementing model compression strategies such as quantisation, scarification, and subsampling, the volume of messages transmitted during each update round can be significantly reduced. Training that is distributed across various locations. In federated learning environments, all remote devices are connected to a central server. In situations where communication to the server is hindered, such as in networks with limited bandwidth or significant latency, a decentralised topology can serve as a viable alternative. The variability of systems: Within a federated network, nodes can vary significantly in terms of their capabilities for data storage, processing power, and data transfer. Differences often occur due to different power sources, network connectivity options (3G, 4G, 5G, Wi-Fi), and hardware components (CPU, memory). In addition, there may be instances where certain devices are not functioning consistently. Given the potential for power or connectivity issues, it is not surprising that edge devices may occasionally fail. As a result, it is important to consider the possibility that all of the devices could be unstable [15]. Given the potential for devices to unexpectedly stop during a training iteration, ensuring fault tolerance is of utmost importance. Therefore, it is crucial to develop federated learning approaches that: (1) exhibit resilience when faced with network connection drops, (2) have the ability to work with a wide range of hardware, and (3) are ready to work with minimal cooperation. Here are some key strategies for managing system heterogeneity: Iterative optimisation techniques can be parallelised by utilising asynchronous communication. An effective approach for handling stragglers in diverse environments is through the use of an asynchronous method. Sampling devices are actively used [16]. Typically, only a small subset of devices is involved in each round of training. As a result, one approach is to carefully select the devices to include in each cycle to maximise the number of updates received within a specific time frame. Ensuring resilience against mistakes: Disregarding the failure of devices with specified data characteristics is a reasonable approach to avoid bias in the device sampling strategy. Algorithmic redundancy in coded computing provides an effective measure to mitigate device failures. Understanding variability in statistics: When it comes to next-word prediction tasks, the language usage of mobile phone users can vary greatly. It is interesting to note that the data generated and collected by devices is not evenly distributed across the network. There might be a hidden pattern that connects devices and their distributions [17], and the number of data points can vary significantly across devices. This approach to data production introduces the potential for stragglers and adds complexity to the modelling process.

This involves careful analysis and assessment, which challenges the frequently employed independent and identically distributed (IID) assumptions in distributed optimisation. While training federated models with unevenly dispersed data, two significant challenges arise: accurately modelling the data and comprehending the relationship between training techniques and convergence. Addressing personal data protection concerns: In federated environments, raw data is often stored locally on each device to mitigate privacy issues. However, it is important to be cautious about sharing additional details, such as model changes, during training, as this could potentially grant access to sensitive information for the central server or a third party. Recent approaches have been exploring the use of secure multiparty computation (SMC) or differential privacy to enhance the privacy of federated learning. Regrettably, the privacy provided by those solutions can sometimes come at the cost of the models or system's efficiency or performance. Therefore, finding a solution that addresses the trade-offs and allows for private federated learning systems is a major challenge. Recently, there has been a lot of research focused on different methods to protect privacy in machine learning. For example, in the field of information security analysis, there are three main strategies that can be employed in federated setups: There are several viable options for working with encrypted data, communicating noisy data drawings, and performing secure function evaluation or multiparty computation. Differential Privacy is widely adopted as a privacy strategy due to its information-theoretic assurances, computational simplicity, and minimal systems overhead [18]. If altering a single input element does not have a substantial impact on the range of outputs, then the randomised mechanism can be considered differentially private. There is no way to determine the specific sample used in the learning process. Increasing the amount of noise can enhance differential privacy, but it can also significantly compromise the accuracy of the model. Therefore, there exists a natural trade-off between these two factors. Computing encrypted data using Homomorphic Encryption can effectively protect the learning process. Up until now, the applications have been somewhat limited, only involving a small number of entities or training linear models. Another option for performing privacy-preserving learning with sensitive datasets distributed across different data owners is SMC or secured function evaluation (SFE). Through strict adherence to these protocols, a collective of individuals can collaborate to acquire knowledge and compute a common function, ensuring that no sensitive information is disclosed beyond what is essential for comprehending the outcome. Preserving the original precision is ensured with a highly secure level of anonymity provided by SMC, which is a lossless method. When combined with differential privacy, SMC offers enhanced privacy assurances. Privacy-preserving algorithms in federated learning encounter fresh challenges when it comes to safeguarding user data. Common cryptographic techniques employed in modern privacy-preserving federated learning implementations involve SMC and differential privacy [19].

13.4 Resource management

FL relies on an interconnected system of devices to collectively train a machine learning model, making resource management crucial for its success. In addition to compute and transmission resources, the efficiency of FL systems is additionally influenced by the accessibility and quality of edge and server resources [20]. We categorise FL resources into groups depending on their location on the network edge and the server they are connected to. Furthermore, it clearly demonstrates the various approaches employed to manage client and server resources in the context of federated schooling. By effectively managing these tools, we can enhance the accuracy and utility of FL algorithms while also reducing the cost of engagement. Efficient allocation of resources is crucial for enhancing the energy efficiency of federated learning systems. It does this by optimising the utilisation of computational resources, network capacity, and storage capacity according to the system's requirements at any given moment. Dynamic resource selection aids in reducing energy consumption in federated learning through the following methods. Dynamic allocation of tasks: Dynamic resource allocation enables the distribution of computing tasks to edge devices based on the current processing load and speed. By allocating jobs to devices that possess the necessary resources instantaneously, energy consumption may be minimised and system performance can be enhanced [21].

13.4.1 Real-time resource optimisation

The ability to dynamically allocate system resources like CPU, memory, and network speed in real time to adapt to the changing requirements of federated learning tasks. Due to its flexibility, the system can rapidly adjust to variations in job and network circumstances, resulting in energy savings. Load balancing is facilitated by dynamic resource allocation, which involves transferring workloads across edge devices to guarantee an equitable distribution of labour. By distributing the computational workload over numerous devices, it is possible to decrease energy consumption and enhance the overall efficiency of the system [22].

13.4.2 Network bandwidth management

Dynamic resource allocation optimises network bandwidth utilisation by prioritising critical data transfers and dynamically modifying data transfer speeds based on the current network configuration. Reducing the energy consumption for network connectivity may be achieved by modifying the real-time data transmission methods.

13.4.3 Resource scaling

The system may dynamically adjust the allocation of resources based on the workload it is handling. The capacity to expand or contract ensures efficient use of resources, preventing devices from being either underutilised or overloaded, hence minimising energy wastage [23].

13.4.4 Energy-efficient decision-making

Dynamic resource allocation algorithms can employ energy-aware decision-making approaches to optimise resource utilisation while minimising energy consumption. Energy efficiency should be a primary consideration when allocating resources. By implementing this approach, the system may optimise its performance while minimising energy consumption.

In federated learning systems, dynamic resource sharing optimises energy consumption by equitably distributing workloads, real-time resource optimisation, load balancing, efficient network bandwidth management, resource scaling, and energy-efficient decision-making. These characteristics enhance energy efficiency, accelerate system performance, and promote environmental sustainability in dispersed machine learning settings.

13.5 Federated learning and industry data alliance

Federated education is both an economic model and a technological standard. The concept of Big Data typically elicits the immediate reaction of consolidating data, doing computations on faraway servers, and retrieving the outcomes. Utilise the outcomes: These requirements gave rise to cloud computing. With the increasing significance of data privacy and security and the strong correlation between organisations' revenues and their data, the cloud computing paradigm is facing scrutiny. All data owners, regardless of their size, will have the option to participate in the data collaboration and benefit financially. We believe that the data coalition business model and the implementation of federated learning technologies should be done together. We want to implement federated learning standards across several domains as promptly as required.

Modifying ML workflows for federated learning traditional machine learning tasks, such as data augmentation, feature engineering, neural architecture design, model selection, hyperparameter tuning, and debugging functions, face challenges when applied to distributed datasets and resource-constrained mobile devices. We will now discuss a few of these challenges:

1. Optimisation of hyperparameters.
2. Development of neural architecture.
3. Debugging and interpretability for federated learning.

Training several rounds with different hyperparameters on mobile devices with low resources may be constrained. This might result in the inefficient use of communication and computational resources for small populations of devices. Nevertheless, contemporary deep neural networks heavily depend on several hyperparameter selections for their formation, regularisation, and optimisation. Evaluating massive models and on-device datasets incurs more costs.

13.5.1 Hyperparameter optimisation

Hyperparameter optimisation (HPO) has an extensive background in Auto_ML with a primary focus on ensuring the accuracy and reliability of models, rather than prioritising communication and computational efficiency of mobility devices. Hence, it is imperative for future studies to prioritise the efficient optimisation of hyperparameters in the context of federated learning. Creating easily adjustable optimisation techniques is a significant area of research in the field of training, alongside the development of versatile ways to optimisation with large parameters. During consolidated training, it is necessary to fine-tune parameters such as learning rate, momentum, batch size, and regularisation [24].

Federated instruction may need the adjustment of many hyperparameters, including the aggregation/global model updates rule and localised client optimiser. Other factors to consider include the selection of customers per round, local steps per round, and the use of compression strategies. Hyperparameters define the trade-off between accuracy and convergence, possibly impacting the quality of the trained model. Federated learning sometimes requires longer training cycles, limited computational resources, and a search space with larger dimensions. Algorithms that can be optimised to withstand changes in hyperparameters and are adaptive or self-tuning can effectively tackle these challenges in different real-world data sets and systems.

Conducting many training sessions with different hyperparameters on mobile devices with limited resources may be restricted. This might result in the inefficient use of communication and computational resources for small groups of devices. Nevertheless, contemporary deep neural networks heavily depend on several hyperparameter selections for their formation, regularisation, and optimisation. Evaluating models with extensive and dynamic datasets of devices incurs higher costs. HPO has an extensive background in AutoML, prioritising model accuracy above the communication and computational efficiency of mobility devices. Hence, it is imperative for future studies to concentrate on effectively optimising hyperparameters in the context of federated learning.

Developing easily adjustable optimisation techniques is a significant area of research in the field of training, alongside the development of versatile ways to optimisation with large parameters. During consolidated training, it is necessary to fine-tune parameters such as learning rate, momentum, batch size, and regularisation.

Federated instruction may need the adjustment of many hyperparameters, including the aggregation/global model updates rule and localised client optimiser. Other factors to consider include the selection of customers per round, local steps per round, and the use of compression strategies. Hyperparameters define the trade-off between accuracy and generalisation, possibly impacting the quality of the trained model. Federated learning sometimes requires longer training cycles, limited computational resources, and a search space with larger dimensions. Algorithms that can be optimised to withstand hyperparameter alterations and are adaptive or self-tuning may effectively tackle these challenges in real-world scenarios and systems, regardless of the data sets involved.

13.6 Conclusions

Federated learning enables several client devices to collaboratively train a shared prediction model while preserving all training data on the device, therefore decoupling the machine learning process from the need to store the data in the cloud. This transcends the use of localised models that provide forecasts on portable devices by enabling the training of models directly on the device. Lately, there has been a substantial increase in interest in this topic, both in the corporate realm and among scholars.

Prominent technological companies have already incorporated federated learning into their practical operations, while several up-and-coming organisations have been founded with the objective of leveraging federated learning to address privacy and data collection concerns in various industries. Furthermore, the wide array of articles encompassed in this study demonstrates the growing popularity of federated learning in several academic fields such as machine learning, optimisation, information theory, statistics, cryptography, fairness, and privacy.

This paper examines the latest developments and presents a thorough collection of unresolved challenges and barriers in the field of federated learning, fuelled by the growing interest in research on this subject. To be deemed practical, the algorithms must adhere to performance requirements that are imposed by the restrictions of the system. Many of these standards are not very challenging in other settings. We argue that data privacy is a nuanced concept that cannot be reduced to a binary choice. Instead, we suggest considering a range of potential risks that might arise under various assumptions, each presenting its own unique set of concerns.

References

[1] Yao, J. and Ansari, N. Wireless power and energy harvesting control in IoD by deep reinforcement learning. *IEEE Transactions on Green Communications and Networking*, 2021;5(2):980–989.

[2] Mozaffari, M., Saad, W., Bennis, M., and Debbah, M. Drone small cells in the clouds: Design, deployment and performance analysis. *In 2015 IEEE global communications conference (GLOBECOM)* (pp. 1–6). IEEE; 2015.

[3] Tran, N. H., Bao, W., Zomaya, A., Nguyen, M. N., and Hong, C. S. Federated learning over wireless networks: Optimization model design and analysis. In *IEEE INFOCOM 2019-IEEE Conference on Computer Communications* (pp. 1387–1395). IEEE; 2019.

[4] Song, M., Wang, Z., Zhang, Z., *et al.* Analyzing user-level privacy attack against federated learning. *IEEE Journal on Selected Areas in Communications*, 2020;38(10):2430–2444.

[5] Hao, M., Li, H., Luo, X., Xu, G., Yang, H., and Liu, S. Efficient and privacy-enhanced federated learning for industrial artificial intelligence. *IEEE Transactions on Industrial Informatics*, 2019;16(10):6532–6542.

[6] Park, J., Samarakoon, S., Elgabli, A. Communication-efficient and distributed learning over wireless networks: Principles and applications. *Proceedings of the IEEE*, 2021;109(5):796–819.

[7] Zhang, C., Liu, X., Zheng, X., Li, R., and Liu, H. Fenghuolun: A federated learning based edge computing platform for cyber-physical systems. In *2020 IEEE International Conference on Pervasive Computing and Communications Workshops (PerCom Workshops)* (pp. 1–4). IEEE; 2020.

[8] Qu, Y., Gao, L., Luan, T. H., Xiang, Y., Yu, S., Li, B., and Zheng, G. Decentralized privacy using blockchain-enabled federated learning in fog computing. *IEEE Internet of Things Journal*, 2020;7(6):5171–5183.

[9] Lo, S. K., Lu, Q., Wang, C., Paik, H. Y., and Zhu, L. A systematic literature review on federated machine learning: From a software engineering perspective. *ACM Computing Surveys (CSUR)*, 2021;54(5):1–39.

[10] Zhao, B., Fan, K., Yang, K., Wang, Z., Li, H., and Yang, Y. Anonymous and privacy-preserving federated learning with industrial big data. *IEEE Transactions on Industrial Informatics*, 2021;17(9):6314–6323.

[11] Yin, B., Yin, H., Wu, Y., and Jiang, Z. FDC: A secure federated deep learning mechanism for data collaborations in the Internet of Things. *IEEE Internet of Things Journal*, 2020;7(7):6348–6359.

[12] Pokhrel, S. R. and Choi, J. Federated learning with blockchain for autonomous vehicles: Analysis and design challenges. *IEEE Transactions on Communications*, 2020;68(8):4734–4746.

[13] Nguyen, D. C., Ding, M., Pathirana, P. N., Seneviratne, A., Li, J., and Poor, H. V. Federated learning for internet of things: A comprehensive survey. *IEEE Communications Surveys and Tutorials*, 2021;23(3):1622–1658.

[14] Kong, L., Liu, X. Y., Sheng, H., Zeng, P., and Chen, G. Federated tensor mining for secure industrial internet of things. *IEEE Transactions on Industrial Informatics*, 2019;16(3):2144–2153.

[15] Lu, Y., Huang, X., Dai, Y., Maharjan, S., and Zhang, Y. Differentially private asynchronous federated learning for mobile edge computing in urban informatics. *IEEE Transactions on Industrial Informatics*, 2019;16(3):2134–2143.

[16] Duan, S., Zhang, D., Wang, Y., Li, L., and Zhang, Y. JointRec: A deep-learning-based joint cloud video recommendation framework for mobile IoT. *IEEE Internet of Things Journal*, 2019;7(3):1655–1666.

[17] Jin, S., Luo, X., and Ma, D. Determining the breakpoints of fundamental diagrams. *IEEE Intelligent Transportation Systems Magazine*, 2018;12(1): 74–90.

[18] Hoyos, W., Aguilar, J., and Toro, M. Federated learning approaches for fuzzy cognitive maps to support clinical decision-making in dengue. *Engineering Applications of Artificial Intelligence*, 2023;123:106371.

[19] Sandhu, S. S., Gorji, H. T., Tavakolian, P., Tavakolian, K., and Akhbardeh, A. Medical imaging applications of federated learning. *Diagnostics*, 2023;13(19): 3140.

[20] Feki, I., Ammar, S., Kessentini, Y., and Muhammad, K. Federated learning for COVID-19 screening from Chest X-ray images. *Applied Soft Computing*, 2021;106:107330.

[21] Yao, J. and Sun, X. Energy-efficient federated learning in internet of drones networks. *In 2023 IEEE 24th International Conference on High Performance Switching and Routing (HPSR)* (pp. 185–190). IEEE; 2023.

[22] Anand, A., Chaudhary, A., and Arvindhan, M. The need for virtualization: when and why virtualization took over physical servers. In: Hura, G. S., Singh, A. K., Siong Hoe, L. (eds), *Advances in Communication and Computational Technology* (pp. 1351–1359). Singapore: Springer; 2021.

[23] Anand, A., Arvindhan, M., Trivedi, N. K., Kumar, A., and Tiwari, R. G. Energy minimization of cloud computing data center strategies, research questions: a survey. In: Dutta, P., Chakrabarti, S., Bhattacharya, A., Dutta, S., and Piuri, V. (eds), *Emerging Technologies in Data Mining and Information Security* (pp. 523–530). Singapore: Springer; 2023.

[24] Arvindhan, M., Daniel, A., Partheeban, N., and Balusamy, B. Artificial intelligence representation model for drug–target interaction with contemporary knowledge and development. In Garg H. and Chatterjee, J. M. (eds), *Deep Learning in Personalized Healthcare and Decision Support* (pp. 81–93). London: Academic Press; 2023.

Chapter 14

Challenges future trends and research direction in FL methods

D. Saravanan[1], Vijay Ramalingam[1], A. Arul Prakash[1], S. Vignesh[1] and R. Rahin Batcha[1]

Abstract

Federated learning (FL) is a decentralized framework for training models that enables numerous clients to work together on training a global model without revealing their data in edge computing (EC) environments. Nevertheless, FL commonly encounters statistical heterogeneity, such as non-identically and independently distributed (non-IID) data, as well as system heterogeneity, including computation and communication capacity variations. These factors ultimately lead to subpar performance in model training. To address the issues above, we suggest implementing an effective FL framework called FedBR. This framework combines the concepts of block-wise periodicity and information distill (KD) with the groundbreaking FL algorithm FedAvg, specifically designed for edge computing with limited resources. More precisely, we initially partition the model into several blocks based on the hierarchical arrangement of the deep neural network (DNN) layers. The host computer transmits only specific successive model blocks to clients to optimize communication speed rather than sending the entire model. Next, the customers employ information distillation to assimilate the knowledge from global model blocks to mitigate statistical variability during localized retraining.

Keywords: Challenges; Future trends; Research directions in federated learning (FL) methods

14.1 Introduction

Federated learning (FL) faces several challenges and holds promising future trends and research directions. Here are some critical points based on current research:

[1]Department of Computer Science and Engineering, Sathyabama Institute of Science and Technology, India

FL allows multiple institutions to collaboratively develop machine learning algorithms without sharing sensitive patient data, enabling the training of high-quality models based on diverse datasets while preserving privacy. FL is a growing field with many promising uses in healthcare, but studies have yet to be published. Nearly half of the evaluated studies were judged to be at high risk of bias. Given the sensitive nature of medical data, current research focuses extensively on privacy and confidentiality aspects of training data and model sharing in FL for healthcare. Handling heterogeneous data distributions among healthcare institutions is a challenge in FL, as each client's data distribution may be a mixture of several predefined domains. Micro-FL, a fault-tolerant and scalable microservice-based platform for FL, has been proposed to address the limitations of existing FL frameworks regarding scalability and vulnerability to system faults [1–3].

14.1.1 Challenges

Communication efficiency: Addressing the communication overhead in FL systems is crucial to scaling FL to large networks.

Privacy and security: A significant challenge is to ensure robust privacy-preserving mechanisms and secure aggregation protocols to protect sensitive data during FL training.

Heterogeneity: Managing the heterogeneity of devices, data distributions, and computational resources across FL participants is a complex challenge that needs to be addressed for effective FL implementation.

Non-IID data: Dealing with nonidentically distributed (non-IID) data across devices challenges maintaining model performance and convergence in FL settings [4,5].

14.1.2 Future trends

Edge computing integration: The integration of FL with edge computing is a growing trend that aims to enhance FL's efficiency and scalability by leveraging edge devices for local model training.

14.1.3 Decentralized FL

Moving toward decentralized FL architectures can improve scalability, fault tolerance, and privacy by reducing reliance on a central server for coordination.

Adversarial robustness: Enhancing FL models' robustness against adversarial attacks is a future trend to ensure the security and reliability of FL systems in real-world scenarios [6,7].

14.1.4 Research directions

Optimization techniques: A key research direction is developing novel optimization algorithms tailored for FL settings to improve convergence speed, model performance, and communication efficiency.

Federated transfer learning: Exploring techniques for transferring knowledge across different FL tasks and domains to enhance model generalization and performance is an emerging research area in FL (Figure 14.1).

Explainability and interpretability: Research on making FL models more interpretable and explainable to enhance trust, accountability, and transparency in FL systems is gaining importance [8,9].

In conclusion, addressing challenges such as communication efficiency, privacy, and heterogeneity while focusing on future trends like edge computing integration and decentralized architectures, along with exploring research directions in optimization techniques and explainability, will shape the evolution of federated learning methods in the coming years.

The current challenges in FL methods include privacy, communication efficiency, and model performance across distributed devices. Privacy concerns arise due to the decentralized nature of FL, where data remains on local devices, necessitating secure aggregation methods. Communication efficiency is crucial in FL to minimize data exchange between devices while ensuring model accuracy and convergence. These challenges highlight the need for ongoing research and development to address privacy, communication, and performance issues in FL methods. What are the most promising applications of FL methods [10,11]?

The most promising applications of FL methods span various fields, showcasing this decentralized learning paradigm's versatility and potential impact. Some notable applications include the following (Figure 14.2).

14.1.5 Healthcare

FL in healthcare enables the collaborative training of machine learning models across multiple healthcare institutions without sharing sensitive patient data,

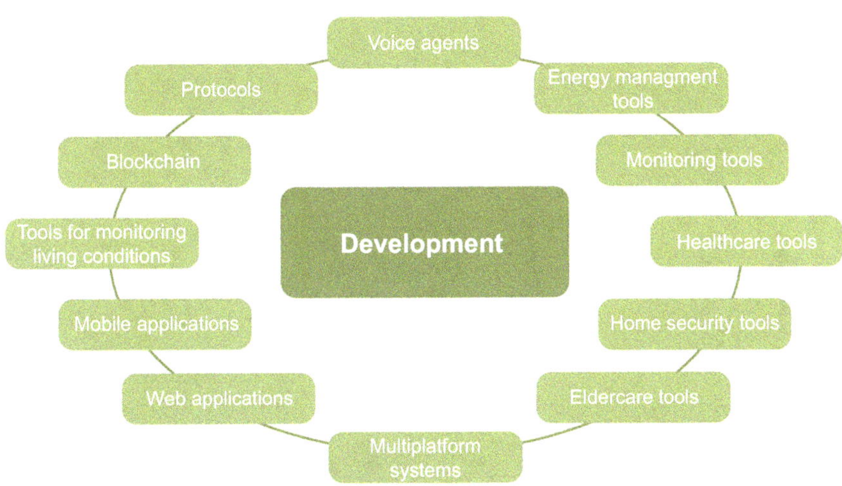

Figure 14.1 Research centric for federal learning model

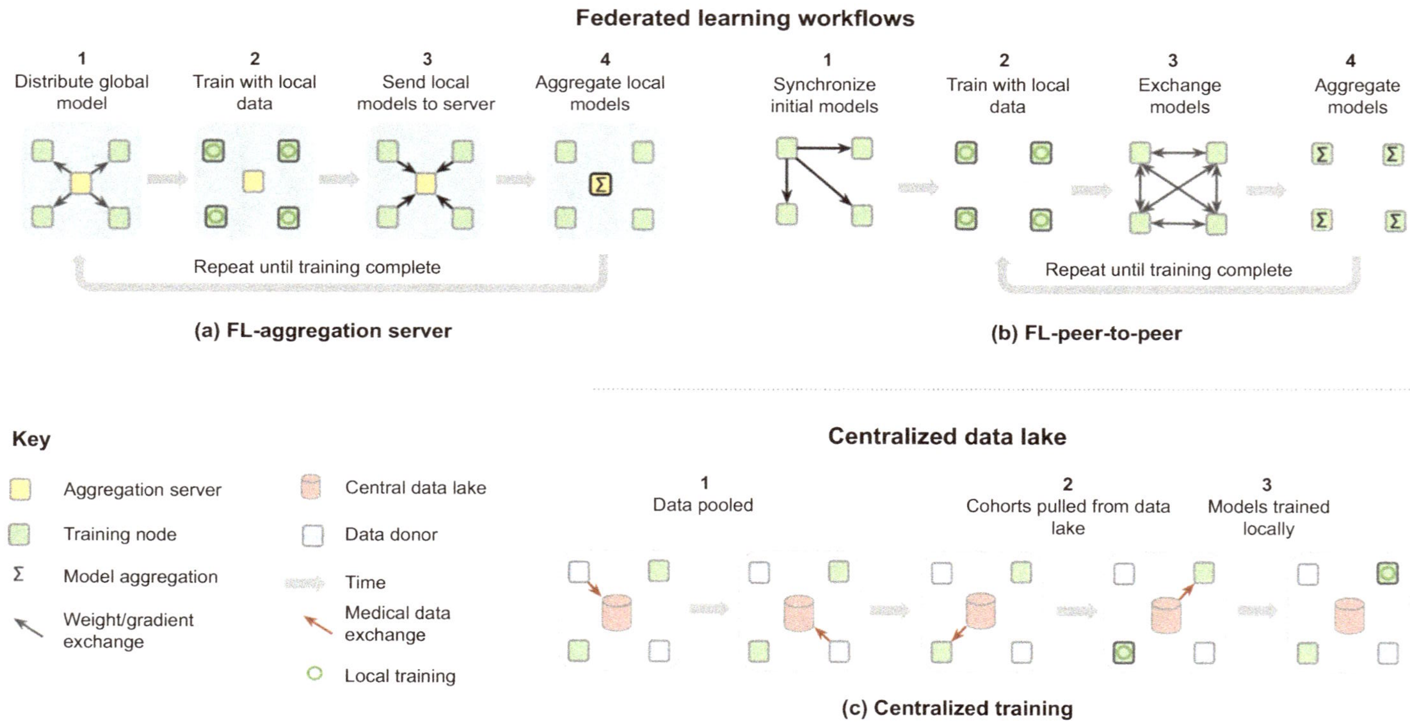

Figure 14.2 Federated learning workflow on decentralized learning

improving model accuracy and preserving data privacy. It facilitates the development of high-quality learning models based on diverse datasets from different sources, aligning with regulatory requirements and enhancing trustworthiness in healthcare decision-making processes [12].

14.2 Artificial intelligence on civil engineering

Artificial Intelligence (AI) methods, including FL, have been extensively used in civil engineering applications such as construction management, building materials, hydraulics, optimization, geotechnical, and transportation engineering. FL methods in civil engineering have been applied to estimate concrete properties, demonstrating their potential to enhance efficiency and accuracy in construction-related tasks [13].

14.2.1 Bioimaging and biomedical applications

FL methods are utilized in the development of bioimaging techniques using carbon-based nanomaterials (CNMs) for fluorescence (FL) imaging, photoacoustic imaging (PAI), and biosensing for early cancer detection. In the ever-evolving landscape of healthcare and medical research, integrating advanced bioimaging techniques and federal learning strategies has emerged as a powerful synergy, unlocking new frontiers for biomedical applications. The recent advancements in deep learning-based medical image analysis have revolutionized the field, enabling unprecedented accuracy and insights. Deep learning algorithms have demonstrated their prowess in detecting and classifying various diseases across different organ systems, from the brain to the cardiovascular system [14].

These developments have paved the way for more effective and personalized medical interventions, improving patient outcomes and reducing healthcare costs.

Federal learning, a decentralized approach to machine learning, has further amplified the impact of these bioimaging techniques (Figure 14.3).

Researchers and clinicians can collaborate seamlessly by leveraging federated learning and pooling their expertise and data resources without compromising patient privacy or data sovereignty.

One key advantage of this intersectional approach is its ability to overcome the limitations of traditional centralized data storage and processing. Federal learning enables the development of robust and generalizable models that can adapt to the unique characteristics of diverse patient populations, ensuring equitable access to advanced healthcare solutions.

Furthermore, integrating bioimaging and federal learning has facilitated the emergence of novel diagnostic and predictive tools.

Nanoengineered CNMs like graphene, carbon nanotubes (CNTs), and carbon quantum dots (QDs) offer advantages in FL sensing and imaging and show promise in multimodal biometrics and targeted therapy applications.

These applications highlight the diverse and impactful use cases of FL methods in fields such as healthcare, civil engineering, and bioimaging, demonstrating the

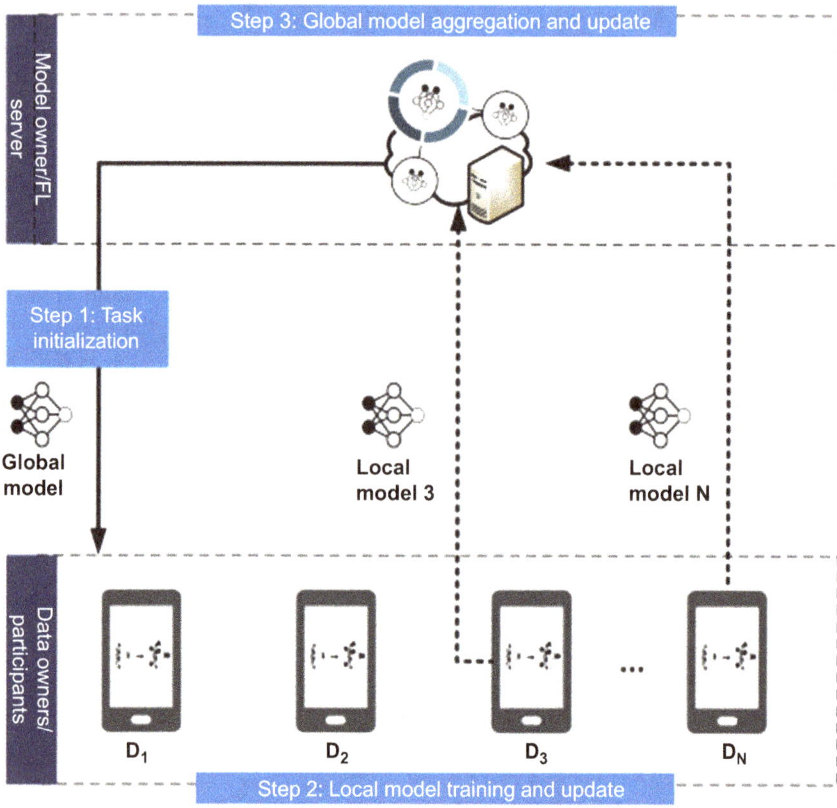

Figure 14.3 Data model training model for initialization

potential for FL to revolutionize various industries while addressing critical challenges related to data privacy and model performance [15].

The advantages of using FL methods in civil engineering are significant and encompass various aspects that enhance efficiency, accuracy, and data privacy. Some key advantages include:

14.2.2 Enhanced model training

FL allows collaborative model training across multiple institutions without sharing sensitive data, enabling the development of high-quality learning models based on diverse datasets while preserving data privacy.

In the era of rapidly evolving technology, efficient and secure data sharing has become paramount, particularly in machine learning and model training. Scenarios in which restrictions in data transfer and storage limit the possibility of composing a single dataset—also exploiting different data sources—to perform a batch-based training procedure make the development of robust models particularly challenging. Researchers have hypothesized that the recent Continuous Learning paradigm

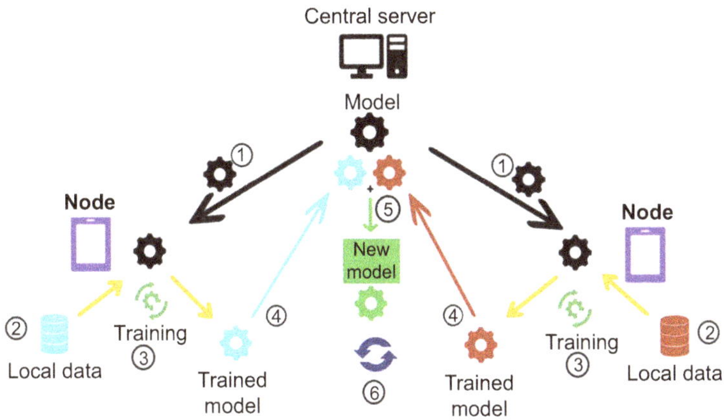

Figure 14.4 Revolution of various for addressing the model training

may represent an effective solution to enable incremental training, even through multiple sites.

Indeed, a fundamental assumption of CL is that once a model has been trained, old data can no longer be used in successive training iterations and can, in principle, be deleted.

14.2.3 Improved accuracy

By leveraging FL methods such as fuzzy logic (FL), artificial neural networks (ANNs), genetic algorithms (GAs), and fuzzy genetics (FG), civil engineering applications can benefit from improved accuracy in tasks related to construction management, building materials, hydraulic, optimization, geotechnical, and transportation engineering (Figure 14.4).

Federal learning, a novel approach to machine learning, has gained significant attention in recent years due to its potential to address various challenges traditional centralized learning models face. This research paper aims to explore the potential of enhanced ensemble models in the context of federal learning, focusing on improving the learning models' overall predictive accuracy and persistence.

Ensemble learning, as discussed in [16], combines multiple learning algorithms to enhance the model's overall prediction accuracy and persistence.

14.2.4 Data privacy preservation

FL methods enable decentralized model training, ensuring that data remains on local devices and is not shared centrally. Thus, they address privacy concerns and regulatory requirements in civil engineering applications. In the digital age, the proliferation of data has become a double-edged sword, bringing immense benefits and significant challenges.

One such challenge is preserving data privacy, particularly in federated learning, an emerging paradigm with immense promise for collaborative machine learning. Federated learning enables multiple entities, such as individuals or organizations, to jointly train a machine learning model without directly sharing their private data. This approach has the potential to unlock valuable insights while preserving the privacy and confidentiality of sensitive information. However, implementing federated learning is fraught with complexities and potential pitfalls, necessitating a deep understanding of the underlying principles and the development of robust privacy-preserving mechanisms. This chapter aims to delve into the critical aspects of data privacy preservation in federated learning, exploring the challenges, the current state-of-the-art solutions, and the future directions for protecting sensitive information [17].

14.2.5 Efficient training process

The collaborative nature of FL allows for efficient model training by leveraging data from multiple sources without the need to centralize data, reducing communication overhead and enhancing scalability in civil engineering tasks (Figure 14.5).

In the ever-evolving landscape of artificial intelligence and machine learning, federated learning has emerged as a promising approach to address the challenges of data privacy, computational resources, and model performance. Federated learning is a collaborative training paradigm where multiple clients, such as devices or organizations, work together to train a shared model while keeping their data

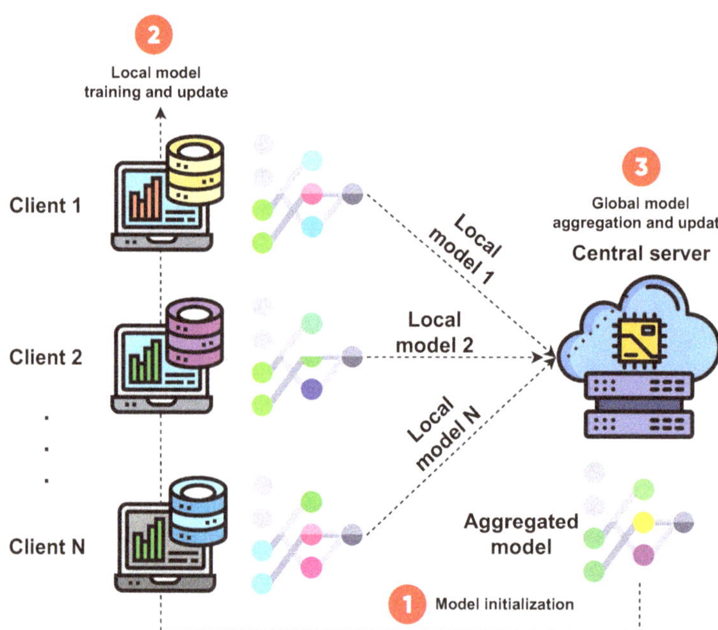

Figure 14.5 Steps involved in model initialization of data center

decentralized. The critical principle of federated learning lies in "bringing the model to the data" rather than the traditional "bringing the data to the model" approach. This paradigm shift has led to significant advancements in the field, as it allows for leveraging diverse datasets while mitigating the risks associated with data centralization. Recent research has explored various aspects of federated learning, including algorithmic improvements, system design, and privacy-preserving techniques (see Table 14.1). Federated learning systems represent a vision, hype, and reality for data privacy and protection. These studies have

Table 14.1 Practical application with AI methods used

Practical FL application	AI methods used	Data used
Detection of COVID-19 infection	Capsule network	CT images
Outcome prediction	Pre-trained ResNet-34	X-ray (CXR), vital signs, demographic, and lab values
Lung abnormalities detection	CNN-based model	Medical images
COVID-19 region segmentation	Semi-supervised learning	Chest computed tomography
Detection of COVID-19	Generative adversarial networks	COVID-19 images
Segmentation of lungs contaminated area	3D UNet	CT Image of lung
Epidemic model using mobility	Multi-task learning	Real-time mobility data sets
Automated infection detection	Chest X-ray images	Convolutional neural networks
Classification of COVID-19 and pneumonia	DenseNet-201	X-ray images
Identification of contaminated places	ResNet50	Thermal images
Prediction of COVID-19 at early stage	Multiple ML algorithms	Patient community features
Detecting COVID-19's presence	ResNet-18	X-ray and CT scan
Discovery of COVID-19	Alex net	CT images
Classification of +ve and −ve cases	Deep CNN	CXR images
Prediction of COVID-19 disease	CNN model	Chest X-rays
Medical resources' demand prediction	CETL method	Heterogeneous data
Severity assessment of COVID-19	Variants of neural networks	Chest X-ray
Prediction of COVID-19 disease	CNN models	Electronic medical records
Risk assessment system	MK-DNN model	Location maps

highlighted their potential to address challenges related to data privacy, computational resources, and model performance. These advantages underscore the potential of FL methods to revolutionize civil engineering practices by improving model accuracy, preserving data privacy, and enabling efficient and collaborative model training across diverse datasets.

14.2.6 Improving decision-making in healthcare

FL enables the distributed training of machine learning models with remotely hosted datasets, enhancing the decision-making process in healthcare by extracting knowledge from diverse and comprehensive datasets without compromising data privacy.

14.3 Enhancing regulatory compliance

FL aligns ML-based systems with regulatory requirements in healthcare, improving trustworthiness and data sovereignty by allowing organizations to collaborate on model development without sharing sensitive patient data.

14.3.1 Preserving data privacy

FL offers a solution to the challenge of handling sensitive medical data by enabling collaborative model training without centralizing data, thus ensuring data privacy and confidentiality in healthcare applications.

14.3.2 Addressing privacy concerns

FL research in healthcare focuses on the privacy and confidentiality aspects of training data and model sharing. This is crucial due to the sensitive nature of medical data, highlighting the potential of FL to address privacy concerns in healthcare settings.

These applications demonstrate the significant potential of FL methods in healthcare for improving decision-making, enhancing regulatory compliance, preserving data privacy, and addressing privacy concerns related to sensitive medical data.

Implementing FL methods in healthcare faces the following key challenges.

14.3.3 Privacy and confidentiality concerns

Addressing privacy and confidentiality aspects of training data and model sharing is crucial due to the sensitive nature of medical data.

Ensuring data privacy and confidentiality is a significant challenge in adopting FL methods in healthcare applications

14.3.4 Regulatory compliance

Aligning FL-based systems with regulatory requirements in healthcare is a challenge to improve trustworthiness and data sovereignty.

Ensuring FL methods comply with healthcare regulations is necessary for widespread adoption.

14.3.5 Heterogeneous data distributions

Handling heterogeneous data distributions among healthcare institutions is a challenge in FL, as each client's data distribution may consist of several predefined domains.

Recognizing the diversity of domains and the similarity within domains is crucial for developing robust FL models in healthcare.

14.3.6 Limited published studies

Few studies have been published on using FL in healthcare, indicating that it is still an emerging field. More research is needed to evaluate FL's limitations and promise in healthcare applications [18].

14.3.7 Bias and risk of bias

Nearly half of the studies evaluated in a systematic review were judged to be at high risk of bias using the PROBAST tool. Addressing potential biases and risks in FL models is essential for ensuring reliable and unbiased healthcare applications (Figure 14.6).

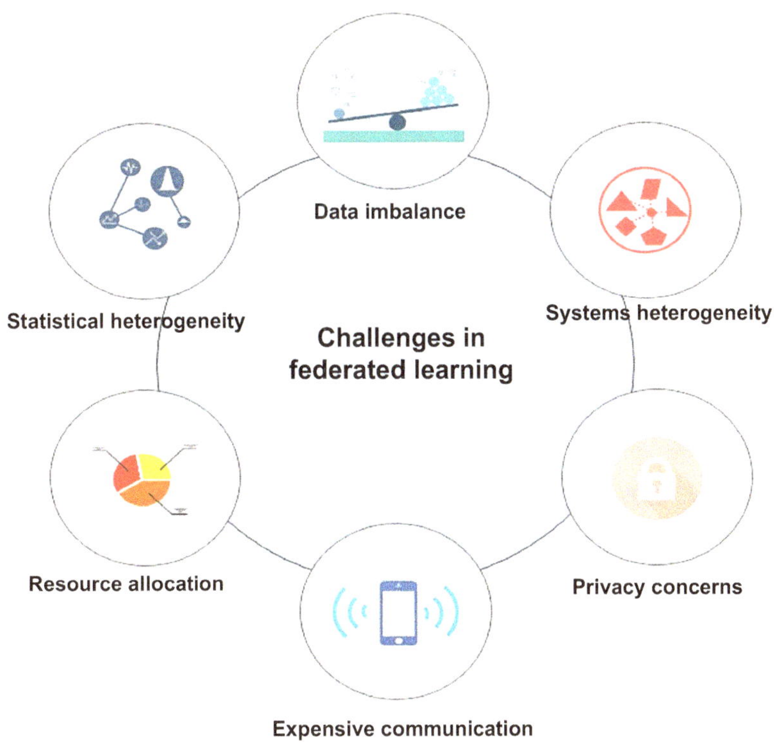

Figure 14.6 Challenges in federated learning

These challenges highlight the need for further research, development, and regulatory alignment to enable the widespread adoption of FL methods in healthcare while ensuring data privacy, regulatory compliance, and model robustness.

US federal agencies have progressively adopted machine learning models to enhance decision-making processes, aiming to improve efficiency, uniformity, and objectivity. Nevertheless, the utilization of such representations raises apprehensions over the possibility of implementing biases that might undermine the concepts of impartiality and processes.

This research article examines the potential for bias in the context of federal learning, which refers to the implementation and use of machine learning algorithms by government agencies. A critical worry is the presence of data bias, which can result from the historical and societal patterns reflected in the information used to create such models.

If the data utilized to train the algorithms does not accurately reflect the diverse population the government serves or if it reinforces existing social prejudices, the models may make judgments that routinely put particular groups at an advantage. Another possible factor that can introduce bias is the specific structure and execution of the algorithms. To avoid accidental discrimination against those in protected categories or marginalized populations, programmers and legislators need to thoroughly evaluate the characteristics and weighting included in the theories, along with selecting threshold and comprehension of results. The consequences of these prejudices can have extensive implications, as federal agencies frequently make crucial determinations that influence residents' ability to obtain essential services, benefits, and possibilities.

14.4 FL methods in healthcare and its research studies

14.4.1 Limited published studies

Few studies have been published on using FL in healthcare, indicating that it is still an emerging field with scarce research literature.

The limited availability of studies may hinder the comprehensive understanding of FL applications in healthcare and the identification of potential challenges and solutions.

14.4.2 Risk of bias

Nearly half of the studies evaluated in a systematic review were judged to be at high risk of bias using the PROBAST tool, highlighting the need for improved study quality and robustness in FL research in healthcare.

The presence of bias in FL studies can affect the reliability and validity of findings, impacting the effectiveness and trustworthiness of FL applications in healthcare settings.

14.4.3 Heterogeneous data distributions

Handling heterogeneous data distributions among healthcare institutions poses a challenge in FL, as each client's data distribution may vary, requiring strategies to address diversity and similarity within data domains.

Recognizing and managing the diversity of data domains is essential for developing robust FL models that can effectively leverage data from multiple sources in healthcare applications. These limitations underscore the need for further research, improved study quality, and enhanced strategies to address data heterogeneity and bias in FL methods to maximize their effectiveness and applicability in healthcare contexts [19].

14.5 Prospects for the future

While some progress has been made in tackling the problems mentioned in this piece, several vital areas in federated learning still need to be thoroughly investigated. Below, we provide a concise enumeration of several unresolved issues (Table 14.2).

The extent of communication required in federated learning is still being determined. By theoretical and empirical analysis, we can enhance our comprehension of one-shot/few-shot communication systems in large and diverse networks [8,20].

14.5.1 Emerging models of asynchrony

The two communication techniques most frequently examined in distributed optimization are bulk synchronous and asynchronous approaches. However, in federated networks, it is common for each device to be uncommitted to the specific task at hand, and most devices are inactive throughout any particular iteration. Is it possible to create communication models that prioritize devices and allow them to independently determine when to connect with the server, rather than being solely dedicated to the workload, going beyond the traditional synchronous and asynchronous training methods [21]?

14.5.2 Heterogeneity diagnostics

Recent studies have focused on quantifying statistical heterogeneity using several metrics, which need to be computed throughout the training process. This prompts these questions. Are there straightforward diagnostic methods available to measure the extent of systems and statistical heterogeneity before training? Can these diagnostic tools enhance the convergence of federated optimization methods? Granular privacy restrictions refer to specific and detailed limitations on privacy. Privacy is commonly defined locally, about individual devices, or globally, encompassing all devices in the network. Nevertheless, in practical terms, it could be essential to establish a more detailed definition of privacy, as privacy limitations can vary among devices or even among individual data points on a single device. Is it possible to establish more particular concepts of privacy and create strategies to manage diverse privacy limitations, whether they are related to specific devices or individual data samples?

Table 14.2 Heterogeneous data distribution in the healthcare system with limitation

Paper title	Insight	Methods used	Limitations	Merits
On knowledge editing in federated learning: perspectives, challenges, and future directions	Future trends include gradient ascent, unified framework, and knowledge disentanglement reassembly Research direction involves federated unlearning and approximate federated learning for efficiency	Federated increasing learning (FIL) federated unlearning (FU)	Scarcity of extensive literature reviews on knowledge editing in FL Federated unlearning needs to be studied in federated learning settings	Comprehensive survey of knowledge editing in federated learning (FL) Synthesizing recent research advancements and potential applications across domains
Heterogeneous federated learning: state-of-the-art and research challenges	Challenges in HFL: statistical, model, communication, device, additional heterogeneity Future trends: data-level, model-level, server-level methods for HFL	Existing methods in HFL are classified into data-level, model-level, and server-level A new taxonomy of existing HFL methods is proposed	Heterogeneous federated learning (HFL) is more challenging than traditional FL Solutions for HFL are diverse and complex	The paper systematically surveys the research challenges in heterogeneous federated learning (HFL). The paper reviews recent advances in HFL and proposes a taxonomy of existing HFL methods
A survey of federated learning from data perspective in the healthcare domain: challenges, methods, and future directions	FL faces challenges in communication, privacy, and heterogeneity Future trends focus on security, fairness, and personalized learning mechanisms	The paper introduces the basics of federated learning and its training framework The paper discusses privacy and security protection mechanisms, communication challenges, and heterogeneity problems in federated learning	FL security mechanisms can still be vulnerable to various types of attacks Attacks can threaten the reliability of the FL system and data privacy	In-depth survey and analysis of the latest papers on FL Introduction and categorization of FL, and review of latest research

(Continues)

A survey on federated learning: challenges and applications	FL faces challenges in communication, privacy, and heterogeneity Future trends focus on security, fairness, and personalized learning mechanisms	The paper introduces the basics of federated learning and its training framework The paper discusses privacy and security protection mechanisms, communication challenges, and heterogeneity problems in federated learning	FL security mechanisms can still be vulnerable to various types of attacks Attacks can threaten the reliability of the FL system and data privacy	In-depth survey and analysis of the latest papers on FL Introduction and categorization of FL, and review of latest research
Toward efficient communications in federated learning: a contemporary survey	Federated learning (FL) and discuss future research directions for communications in FL, including communication efficiency, communication environment, and communication resource allocation	Challenges: privacy risks, communication problems Future trends: efficient communication, resource allocation, environmental considerations	Privacy risks in traditional distributed machine learning Challenging communication problems in federated learning	Assessing FL communication research from three perspectives Discussing future research directions for communications in FL

Implementing federated learning in a production environment: Several practical considerations arise when implementing federated learning in a production environment. One challenge is addressing idea drift, which occurs when the data-generating model changes over time. Another issue is diurnal fluctuations.

14.6 Conclusion

The liking model is to be trained using an FL-based technique, with users' data remaining on their personal devices. What follows is the formulation of an optimization problem. Considering the restrictions of storage capacity, compute capabilities, uploading, and download bandwidth, the goal is to optimize the quantity of services needed from the edge based on user preferences. By continuously adding the service that optimizes the intended functions until resource restrictions are satisfied, a greedy method solves the optimization problem.

References

[1] W. Y. B. Lim, N. C. Luong, D. T. Hoang, *et al.*, "Federated learning in mobile edge networks: A comprehensive survey," *IEEE Commun. Surveys Tuts.*, vol. 22, no. 3, pp. 2031–2063, 2020.

[2] P. Zhang, C. Jiang, X. Pang, and Y. Qian, "STEC-IoT: A security tactic by virtualizing edge computing on IoT," *IEEE Internet Things J.*, vol. 8, no. 4, pp. 2459–2467, 2021.

[3] S. Dinesh Krishnan, D. Pelusi, A. Daniel, V. Suresh, and B. Balusamy. "Improved graph neural network-based green anaconda optimization for segmenting and classifying the lung cancer," *Math. Biosci. Eng.*, vol. 20, no. 9, pp. 17138–17157, 2023. doi:10.3934/mbe.2023764

[4] D. Yang, Z. Xu, W. Li, *et al.*, "Federated semi-supervised learning for COVID region segmentation in chest CT using multi-national data from China, Italy, Japan," *Med. Image Anal.*, vol. 70, 2021, Art. no. 101992.

[5] M. Arvindhan and H. Singh, "An innovation development of cost wise task scheduling model for complex transmission in ultra-dense cloud networks," in *2023 2nd International Conference for Innovation in Technology, INOCON 2023*, 2023.

[6] W. Zhang, T. Zhou, Q. Lu, *et al.*, "Dynamic-fusion-based federated learning for COVID-19 detection," *IEEE Internet Things J.*, vol. 8, no. 21, pp. 15884–15891, 2021.

[7] C. Shen, P. Wang, H. R. Roth, *et al.*, "Multi-task federated learning for heterogeneous pancreas segmentation," in *Clinical Image-Based Procedures, Distributed and Collaborative Learning, Artificial Intelligence for Combating COVID-19 and Secure and Privacy-Preserving Machine Learning*. Cham: Springer, 2021, pp. 101–110.

[8] A. Daniel and N. Partheeban, "An improved and efficient and dynamic load balancing approach in cloud computing environment," *Advance Innovation and Technology with Sustainability Engineering, International Journal of*

Social Ecology and Sustainable Development (IJSESD). Hershey, PA: IGI Global, 2022. DOI:10.4018/IJSESD.302469.

[9] S. Zheng, C. Shen, and X. Chen, "Design and analysis of uplink and downlink communications for federated learning," *IEEE J. Sel. Areas Commun.*, vol. 39, no. 7, pp. 2150–2167, 2021.

[10] T. Chen, S. Kornblith, M. Norouzi, and G. Hinton, "A simple framework for contrastive learning of visual representations," in *Proc. Int. Conf. Mach. Learn.*, 2020, pp. 1597–1607.

[11] A. Raj, S. Jadon, H. Kulshrestha, *et al.*, "Cloud infrastructure fault monitoring and prediction system using LSTM based predictive maintenance," in *10th International Conference on Reliability, Infocom Technologies and Optimization (Trends and Future Directions), ICRITO 2022*, 2022.

[12] S. K. Lo, Q. Lu, L. Zhu, H.-Y. Paik, X. Xu, and C. Wang, "Architectural patterns for the design of federated learning systems," *J. Syst. Softw.*, vol. 191, 2022, Art. no. 111357.

[13] P. Johri, M. Arvindhan, and A. Daniel, "Enabling technologies: A transforming action on healthcare with IoT a possible revolutionizing". *Artificial Intelligence for a Sustainable Industry 4.0*. Berlin: Springer, 2021, p. 265. https://doi.org/10.1007/978-3-030-77070-9_16

[14] T. V. Nguyen, M. A. Dakka, S. M. Diakiw, *et al.*, "A novel decentralized, federated learning approach to train on globally distributed, poor quality, and protected private medical data," *Sci. Rep.*, vol. 12, no. 1, pp. 1–12, 2022.

[15] M. Arvindhan and D. Rajesh Kumar, Analysis of load balancing detection methods using hidden Markov model for secured cloud computing environment, 2022, pp. 565–580.

[16] A. Daniel, R. Deebalakshmi, R. Thilagavathy, T. Kohilakanagalakshmi, S. Janakiraman, and B. Balusamy, Optimal feature selection for malware detection in cyber physical systems using graph convolutional network", *Comput. Electr. Eng.*, vol. 108, 2023, Art. no. 108689, https://doi.org/10.1016/j.compeleceng.2023.108689.

[17] J. S.-P. Díaz and Á. L. García, "Study of the performance and scalability of federated learning for medical imaging with intermittent clients," *Neurocomputing*, vol. 518, pp. 142–154, 2023.

[18] P. Chen, X. Du, Z. Lu, J. Wu, and P. C. Hung, "EVFL: An explainable vertical federated learning for data-oriented artificial intelligence systems," *J. Syst. Archit.*, vol. 126, 2022, Art. no. 102474.

[19] Y. Deng, F. Lyu, J. Ren, *et al.*, "Auction: Automated and quality-aware client selection framework for efficient federated learning," *IEEE Trans. Parallel Distrib. Syst.*, vol. 33, no. 8, pp. 1996–2009, 2022.

[20] T. Bernecker, A. Peters, C. L. Schlett, *et al.*, "FedNorm: Modality-based normalization in federated learning for multimodal liver segmentation," 2022, arXiv:2205.11096.

[21] P. Zhang, C. Jiang, X. Pang, and Y. Qian, "STEC-IoT: A security tactic by virtualizing edge computing on IoT," *IEEE Internet Things J.*, vol. 8, no. 4, pp. 2459–2467, 2021.

Conclusion

Balamurugan Balusamy[1], *Daniel Arockiam*[2] *and Pethuru Raj*[3]

The integration of federated learning (FL) into Internet of Things (IoT) systems represents a significant step toward building more energy-efficient, secure, and intelligent decentralized networks. This book has explored various facets of federated learning, with a particular focus on energy efficiency and security in the IoT ecosystem, presenting both theoretical insights and practical case studies. From understanding the core principles of FL to discussing cutting-edge energy-efficient algorithms and security protocols, the chapters provided a comprehensive overview of how these technologies can empower next-generation IoT networks.

Overview of federated learning and key challenges

The initial chapters offered a foundational understanding of FL, demonstrating its potential to enable decentralized intelligence by training models across distributed devices without sharing sensitive data. However, despite its benefits, FL presents significant challenges—especially in the IoT context. The need for efficient communication between devices, energy optimization, and ensuring data privacy while maintaining high model accuracy are crucial hurdles that need to be addressed. These chapters laid the groundwork for understanding how FL can be adapted to the highly constrained environment of IoT, where resources such as energy and bandwidth are limited.

Energy efficiency and federated learning

A recurring theme in this book has been the importance of optimizing energy consumption in FL-enabled IoT systems. With IoT devices often powered by batteries or energy-harvesting methods, ensuring that FL operations are energy-efficient is paramount. Various chapters examined energy-efficient FL algorithms, frameworks, and protocols designed to reduce the computational and communication overhead of FL tasks. For example, energy-efficient communication protocols and energy-harvesting

[1]Office of Dean Academics, Shiv Nadar University, Delhi-NCR, India
[2]Department of Computer Science and Engineering, Amity University Madhya Pradesh, India
[3]Edge AI Division, Reliance Jio Platforms Ltd., Bangalore, India

techniques were discussed as viable solutions to prolong the operational lifetime of IoT devices participating in FL networks. These innovations are essential for scaling FL to real-world IoT deployments, particularly in smart cities, industrial IoT, and other pervasive environments.

Security, privacy, and FL in IoT

In parallel with energy efficiency, this book also emphasized the critical need for robust security and privacy in FL-based IoT systems. As IoT devices are increasingly targeted by cyber threats, ensuring that data and model integrity are maintained throughout the FL process is a priority. Chapters on hybrid security models demonstrated how AI-enhanced security mechanisms could augment traditional methods to create more resilient systems. Likewise, discussions on secure data protection, privacy-preserving mechanisms, and adapting AI models to dynamic cyber threats provided a roadmap for safeguarding FL in highly dynamic and often vulnerable IoT environments.

Future directions and research trends

Looking ahead, there are several promising research directions in energy-efficient and secure federated learning for IoT systems. One of the key future trends is the development of lightweight FL algorithms specifically tailored for resource-constrained IoT devices. Additionally, advances in energy-harvesting technologies and communication protocols will further enhance the energy efficiency of these systems, allowing FL to become a viable solution for large-scale IoT deployments. From a security perspective, the continuous evolution of cyber threats calls for more adaptive FL models that can detect and respond to emerging threats in real time. The application of AI in security, such as AI-driven anomaly detection in FL networks, will also be a critical area of research.

Final thoughts

The convergence of federated learning, IoT, and energy efficiency offers transformative possibilities for future networks. This book not only highlighted the current state of FL in IoT environments but also pointed toward future innovations that will make these technologies more scalable, secure, and efficient. By overcoming the energy and security challenges discussed in this book, federated learning can unlock the full potential of IoT, driving advancements in everything from smart cities to healthcare and industrial automation. As we move forward, interdisciplinary research and collaboration between fields such as machine learning, cybersecurity, and IoT engineering will be crucial in realizing the full potential of FL in an energy-efficient and secure manner.

Index

www.ingramcontent.com/pod-product-compliance
Lightning Source LLC
LaVergne TN
LVHW011842200926
848484LV00002B/392